EDUCATIONAL RESEARCH

Second Edition ————————————————————

READINGS IN FOCUS

Edited by

IRVIN J. LEHMANN
Michigan State University

WILLIAM A. MEHRENS
Michigan State University

HOLT, RINEHART and WINSTON

New York   Chicago   San Francisco   Dallas   Montreal   Toronto   London   Sydney to our parents ───

Library of Congress Cataloging in Publication Data

Lehmann, Irvin J.   comp.
Educational research.

Includes bibliographies and index.
1. Educational research — Addresses, essays,
lectures. I. Mehrens, William A. II. Title.
LB1028.L38   1979   370'.78   78-27126
ISBN: 0-03-043016-X

0 1 2   090   9 8 7 6 5 4 3 2

PREFACE

This book of readings is designed primarily for students enrolled in introductory research methods courses in education and psychology. Nevertheless, the principles to be learned regarding research critique are applicable to research in all the social sciences. For the majority of students, the introductory research methods course is a terminal course, their first and last. Because of this, instructors are inclined to place major emphasis upon preparing students to become intelligent *consumers* of research, rather than attempting to prepare them as practitioners. Research consumers must have exposure to, acquaintance with, and experience in reacting to various types of research. In other words, they must be required to read and critically evaluate different kinds of research — seeing their strengths and deficiencies. The relatively naïve practitioners also need to evaluate critically studies of the general type that they are planning.

The basic purpose, structure, and organization of the first edition remain unchanged in this edition. Just as before, we would hope that by using these articles, instructors would help make students more intelligent consumers and producers of research.

The extensive updating of the second edition revolves about the research articles selected as exemplars of the different types of research. Although it is probably fair to say that there have not been any major breakthroughs in the methodology of conducting research in the behavioral sciences, where appropriate, we have incorporated new knowledge.

The first chapter of this book and the individual introductions for the remaining chapters written by the editors may serve as a main text for some instructors. If so, they should be supplemented with selected outside readings and fairly complete lecture notes. This book is more likely to serve as a supplement to one of the standard introductory research texts. It is not intended to obviate the need for the student's being exposed to the library. It is designed to permit both student and instructor to focus attention on specific articles. This focus should assist both students and instructor — the former by acquainting them with the different kinds of research and by demonstrating that even good studies can be made better; the latter by providing a common set of materials to facilitate evaluation of students' progress and knowledge.

We have chosen to organize this book via the common procedure of using a methodological classification of educational research. Of course, any such classification is somewhat arbitrary. Different authors have used slightly different schemes. Below are listed the schemes used in some of the existing textbooks of educational research.

Ary et al. (1972)	Best (1977)
Historical	Historical
Descriptive	Descriptive
Ex-Post-Facto	Experimental
Experimental	

Borg (1971)	Mouly (1978)
Historical	Historical
Descriptive	Survey: Descriptive
Causal-Comparative	Survey: Analytical
Correlational	Experimental
Experimental	Predictive

Wiersma (1975)	
Nonexperimental	
Historical	
Survey	
Ex-Post-Facto	
Experimental	

The editors chose the particular scheme in this book because it made sense to them and because it seemed to follow the general patterns used in other basic books on educational research.

Following an introductory chapter written by the editors, the book is divided into five areas: historical, descriptive, correlational, ex-post-facto, and experimental research. The introductory chapter covers the nature and purposes of educational research and offers some guidelines for evaluating research.

At the beginning of each of the other five chapters an introduction explains the major educational purposes of that type of research, its basic features, and some of the cautions and limitations of which the critical reader and producer of research should be cognizant. Following each chapter introduction are several research articles. At the end of each article the editors have presented a series of comments and questions designed to make the reader think through some of the methodology and findings of the study. We have tried to write questions that require critical thinking and evaluation on the part of the reader.

Readers may occasionally feel that some of the articles have been misclassified. That is, some may prefer to classify an article we have called descriptive as ex-post-facto or vice versa. This is acceptable to us. The colleagues whose opinions we have sought have agreed, in general, with our placement of articles within categories. However, many articles have different aspects of several of the methodological classifications we have chosen and so a classification is always somewhat arbitrary. We did not choose articles just because they fit neatly into our classification scheme.

How does this edition differ from the first edition? First, about 70 percent of the articles used as exemplars of the various types of research are new. Second, most of the errors of omission and commission in the first edition have been detected and corrected. Third, we have tried to select articles that had rebuttals or counterarguments. Fourth, we have tried to write questions at the end of each article that went beyond requiring a simple yes or no response.

The general criteria for selecting articles for this book were as follows:

1. Interest: The articles had to deal with topics that would be intrinsically interesting — articles students would want to read.

2. Publication date: In general, the articles are all quite recent. Their median publication date is 1975.

3. Understandability: While we are quite enthusiastic about many of the recent methodological advances in educational research, we have tried to avoid choosing articles where the sophistication in design and statistical procedures would leave the beginning student of research confused. Some of the articles are probably at a level of sophistication that will make them difficult for the beginning researcher to comprehend fully. But careful study of these articles should prove very rewarding.

4. Quality of research: All the articles in this book are, in our opinion, better than the average quality of published research. Like *all* research, these studies have faults (and we hope the readers can detect them), but their redeeming qualities are prevalent.

5. Diversity: As well as being interesting, recent, and well done, we chose articles that would represent a variety of areas: administration, child development, counseling, curriculum, learning, and measurement are all represented. We hope that the selections are diverse enough to serve the learning and teaching needs of most students and instructors in introductory research methods courses.

6. Controversy: We have in this edition chosen more articles that have been evaluated by other scholars in print. These critiques, and in some cases their rebuttals, have also been included. This should add interest to the reading but, more importantly, should help the reader understand that even scholars do not always agree as to research methodology or how to interpret results.

We would like to thank all the publishers and authors who have so graciously granted us permission to use their materials. Any merits of this book must be due, in large part, to the merits of the individual research articles it contains. We are also grateful to several anonymous colleagues for their helpful suggestions.

East Lansing, Mich.   *I. J. L.*
November 1978   *W. A. M.*

CONTENTS

Contents

Contents

INTRODUCTION

chapter one ————————————————————————

All individuals make decisions daily. Hopefully, those decisions are based on *sound information*. But this is not so. Sometimes we do not have any information (knowledge), in which case our decisions are like lotteries. Other times we base our decisions on incorrect information. This happens frequently enough to suggest that "it ain't the things we don't know that get us in trouble. It's the things we know that ain't so."

The purpose of research is to gain or verify knowledge. Sound research should provide us with sound information, not tell us things that "ain't so." It is very important for the individual who wishes to engage actively in research to have considerable research competency. The *producer* of research must acquire many skills including the ability to formulate meaningful problems, design studies, use appropriate statistics, and write clearly and concisely. Unfortunately, educators have evidently found it less obvious that professional educators at all levels must be *consumers* of research and that these consumers also need some research competency.

Why are we concerned with the research competence of both producers and consumers of research? Because currently much research is wrong, or at least has many shortcomings. The literature is probably much worse than you realize. In the Ward et al. study reproduced in this book expert researchers reviewed published research articles. Acting as if they were editors they rated only 9 percent of the articles as being worthy of publication as written. Hopefully, more research knowledge among educators would reduce the percent of poor articles published and increase the detection of unsound articles by the readers of the research.

But do all practicing educators need to read or understand research? Is it worth all the "hard work" for an educator to study research methodology and keep up with published research? The answer depends upon many considerations. Is the field of education static or dynamic? We say dynamic. Should an educator be a trained technician or a professional? We say professional. Unlike the technician the professional must have the knowledge to make correct decisions. That knowledge must come, in part, from research.

All educators should have a grasp of what research is so that they can be cogently aware of the ways in which psychological laws governing educational practice are obtained. They need to understand terminology and methodology to enable them to understand and critically evaluate the professional literature. Research can provide the means of obtaining the knowledge needed to make wise educational decisions. The critical reading of educational research keeps teachers abreast of educational developments and will reduce the lag that typically exists between research findings and their applications. The reading of research should increase teachers' enthusiasm for the improvement of instructional procedures and education in general.

Educators also need to be knowledgeable enough about research to communicate to pupils the role scientific investigations play in advancing our society. Certainly, any teacher of social, biological, or physical science has a responsibility to teach the scientific methods of problem solving. In addition, as Van Dalen points out:

> Society holds you [the teacher] responsible for helping exceptionally able youths to become interested in a career in research, and for guiding them in the selection of academic experiences needed to realize their aspirations. You cannot perform these services satisfactorily unless you become well acquainted with research.[1]

By discussing the nature and purposes of educational research as well as presenting some guides in evaluating research this opening chapter will hopefully impress upon the reader that educational research is beneficial, that *all* educators need to be knowledgeable consumers of research, and that most should be competent to engage in research of an applied or evaluative nature. By paying attention to particular aspects of the research process, educators can, with some practice, become proficient consumers and producers.

I. Nature and Purposes of Educational Research

We indeed live in a world of fantastic scientific accomplishments. Men have walked on the Moon. Organ transplants are becoming more and more common. We can destroy most of Earth's inhabitants (without destroying

[1]Deobold B. Van Dalen, *Understanding Educational Research* (Rev. Ed.). New York: McGraw-Hill, 1966, pp. 13–14.

buildings) by pushing a few buttons. Some people even believe cloning of humans to be possible—which positively makes some scientists beside themselves! These and many other scientific accomplishments (most beneficial, some potentially very harmful) have been obtained through the processes of research. While research is not the only way of acquiring new knowledge, it appears to be one of the most productive. In fact, we live in a research-oriented world.

A. WHAT IS EDUCATIONAL RESEARCH?

The goal of science is to be able to understand, predict, and/or control the events of the world. Research is simply controlled inquiry concerning a certain event or events with the purpose of furthering and/or verifying knowledge that will help scientists achieve their goal. There are several steps in the scientific method. These involve selecting (and careful delineation of) the problem, developing the hypotheses, planning the research procedures, collecting and analyzing the data, drawing appropriate conclusions, and writing the report.

Educational research has the same general goals as other research and follows the same scientific method of investigation. It is, of course, restricted in scope to educational issues. Travers states that, "The scientific goal of educational research is to discover laws or generalizations about behavior which can be used to make predictions and control events within educational situations."[2]

B. THE EXTENT OF EDUCATIONAL RESEARCH

The amount of time, effort, and money being expended on educational research has increased considerably over the past decade. The total federal appropriation for educational research and related activities was $1 million in 1957. The total requested for 1970 exceeded $135 million. Based on the Interagency Research Information System there were more than 4400 projects funded in 1976 by the federal government devoted just to research on children and youth. More than half a billion dollars were spent on these projects.[3] This expansion of educational research has come about, in part, because of the increased responsibilities society has placed on the educational enterprise. As Bloom points out, "Education is looked to for solutions to problems of poverty, racial discord, crime and delinquency, urban living, peace, and even for problems arising from affluence."[4] It seems that for every existing social ill there

[2]Robert M. W. Travers, *An Introduction to Educational Research* (2d Ed.). New York: Macmillan, 1964, p. 5.
[3]Maure Hurt and Pamela Mintz, Federally funded educational research by the local education agency: How much and for what? Mimeograph, AERA, Toronto, Canada, 1978.
[4]Benjamin S. Bloom, Twenty-five years of educational research. *American Educational Research Journal*, 3 (1966), 212.

exists someone who strongly advocates that the responsibility for the solution lies with education. (It is even quite popular to blame education for the original causes of many social ills.)

Since educators do not have the repertoire of skills necessary for these solutions and, in many instances, don't even know what caused the problems or what skills are needed to alleviate them, much more research is necessary. To help find solutions to education's new tasks, an increasing range of disciplines have become involved in educational research. Anthropologists, biologists, communication experts, economists, geneticists, political scientists, psychologists, and sociologists are all doing educational research.

Not only has there been an expansion in quantity, there has also been some improvement in the quality of educational research. (See the Ward et. al. article in Chapter Three.) There have been many methodological advances in educational research (e.g. meta-analysis), and educators are increasingly better trained to make use of these advances.

C. CLASSIFICATION OF RESEARCH BY PURPOSE

In the preface we classified research by method. Other ways to classify research would be by area of interest (philosophical, psychological, sociological, among others) or by the type of data collection procedure (for example, interview, questionnaire, observation, standardized tests). Still another way to classify research is by purpose. Is the research designed to be of immediate use, or is it designed to add knowledge to the field which may or may not be of any practical value? There has been considerable debate among educators as to which type of research is of more value.

The terms basic and applied refer to the extent to which research is directed toward the solution of currently existing problems.

> Basic research is designed to add to an organized body of scientific knowledge and does not necessarily produce results of immediate practical use. Applied research is undertaken to solve an immediate practical problem and the goal of adding to scientific knowledge is secondary.[5]

As Hilgard[6] pointed out, the distinction is really a continuum more than a dichotomy. Educators occasionally write as if the distinction is dichotomous, but that is only for convenience. People who argue for more (or less) basic

---

[5]Robert M. W. Travers, *An Introduction to Educational Research* (2d Ed.). New York: Macmillan, 1964, p. 4.
[6]Ernest R. Hilgard, A perspective on the relationship between learning theory and educational practices. In *Theories of Learning and Instruction,* E. R. Hilgard (Ed.), Part I of the 63d Yearbook of the National Society of the Study of Education. Chicago: University of Chicago Press, 1954, pp. 402–415.

research are talking about the *degree* of purpose rather than a dichotomy of purpose.

Educational research seems to be primarily of the applied variety. Most writers feel that a greater proportion of it should be more basic. Cronbach in arguing for more basic research states that:

> Educational improvements that really make an impact on the ignorance rate will not grow out of minor variations of teaching content and process. Effective educational designs, worth careful development and field trial, can emerge only from a deep understanding of learning and motivation.[7]

Sax believes that:

> Basic research has too often been neglected and overlooked by those intent upon improving educational practice. . . . Unless there is a background of theory and empirical research to back up some proposed educational innovation, it may be necessary to evaluate every whim and fad in the public shools to see if they will work.
>
> Unfortunately, this is exactly what has happened in education.[8]

Wittrock agrees with the previous two authors and states that:

> Educational psychology should invest most of its resources into its most important activity—basic research aimed at control and understanding of the problems and phenomena of instruction in schools.[9]

Carroll[10] takes a similar position and feels that somewhere between 15 and 25 percent of research funds should be applied toward basic research. (This is a far greater proportion than is currently being expended under most definitions of basic research.) Kerlinger[11] and Travers[12] have both recently indicated that basic research is of more importance than applied research in its impact on education.

Ebel in a cogently written article argues what among researchers is the minority position.

> Let us also push, and rather more strongly, the kind of survey research that

[7]Lee J. Cronbach, The role of the university in improving education. *Phil Delta Kappan,* 47 (1966), 540.

[8]Gilbert Sax, *Empirical Foundations of Educational Research.* Englewood Cliffs, New Jersey: Prentice-Hall, 1968, p. 33.

[9]Merlin C. Wittrock, Focus on educational psychology. *Educational Psychologist,* 4 (1967), 17.

[10]John B. Carroll, Basic and applied research in education: Definitions, distinctions, and implications. *Harvard Educational Review,* 38 (1968), 263–276.

[11]Fred N. Kerlinger, The influence of research on education practice. *Educational Researcher,* 6:8 (1977), 5–11.

[12]Robert N.W. Travers, *An Introduction to Educational Research* (4th Ed.). New York: Macmillan, 1978, p. 25.

provides data crucial to the decisions we must make. Let us not worship pure science and basic research unrealistically and irrationally.[13]

In addition to basic and applied research, we should mention four other terms: conclusion-oriented, decision-oriented, action, and evaluative research. Cronbach and Suppes[14] use the terms conclusion-oriented and decision-oriented inquiry so that they closely correspond with what Travers calls basic and applied research. The conclusion-decision terminology seems to be preferred by many present educational writers. This is in part true because of a subtle change in the connotation of "basic" research in education. Educators no longer feel it necessary to reduce all educational activities to psychological phenomena in order to "add to scientific knowledge." Education itself is now more apt to be considered a science, and "basic" educational research can be carried out in such areas as instruction, curriculum, and classrooms interaction. Since this "basic" research can have some immediate practical use, the distinctions between basic and applied have become more blurred.

Some writers use the term "decision-oriented" as being synonymous with evaluative research. Certainly the terms applied, decision-oriented, and evaluative research are similar in meaning although they are probably listed in decreasing order of breadth. That is, there may be some applied research that is not decision-oriented, and some decision-oriented research that is not evaluative. The term "evaluative research" is used most often to refer to the systematic procedures used to collect and analyze data regarding the effectiveness of a particular program. One may, and should, evaluate a program at several stages. If one evaluates at intermediate stages while changes can still be made in the program, it is called *process* or *formative* evaluation. Evaluation at the completion of the program is referred to as *summative* evaluation. For example, if one has initiated a curriculum or instructional innovation in a school, a systematic attempt should be made to evaluate each stage of the project, improve it as it proceeds on the basis of this evaluation, and then, at the completion of the project, summative evaluation should be conducted. Strong advocates of basic research may not want to label evaluation as research at all.[15] However, there is no doubt that such evaluation studies are very important. All social action programs (such as project Headstart) and curriculum innovations should be systematically evaluated both during the program to incorporate improvements, and at the end to obtain summative (or decision-oriented) evaluation.

Action research, according to the originator of the term, is research undertaken by practitioners so that they may improve their practices.[16] Thus,

[13]Robert L. Ebel, Some limitations of basic research in education. *Phi Delta Kappan*, 49 (1967), 84.

[14]Lee J. Cronbach and Patrick Suppes (Eds.), *Research for Tomorrow's Schools: Disciplined Inquiry for Education.* New York: Macmillan, 1969, 281 pp.

[15]See Egon G. Guga, Significant differences. *Educational Researcher*, 20, 3 (1969), 4, 5.

[16]Stephen M. Corey, *Action Research To Improve School Practices.* New York: Teachers College, Columbia University, 1953, 145 pp.

action research is a type of applied or decision-oriented research, but with the stipulation that the researcher is the same person as the practitioner who will make and live with the decision. As Helmstadter points out:

> The basic idea represents an attempt to make use of the sound learning princi-
> ple that behavioral changes occur only when the learner himself becomes
> actively involved. The advocates of action research would contend that the only
> way to change the behavior of practitioners is to get them involved in carrying
> out research studies on problems which are of concern to themselves.[17]

The term "action research" was used more widely 25 years ago than it is today. Evaluative research where the evaluation is done by the staff of the project rather than by an external agent would be an example of action re-search.

Whatever an individual's persuasion regarding the relative importance of basic and applied (or conclusion vs. decision-oriented) types of research, both will continue to be done. Most educators will likely engage in applied or at least evaluative research. Consumers of research should read both types. Applied research is obviously of value to the consumer. Almost by definition, the pro-ducer of basic research is not going to concern himself with its practical value. Therefore the practical values to be gleaned from basic research must be ac-quired by the sophisticated consumers.

D.   PROBLEMS IN EDUCATIONAL RESEARCH

As mentioned earlier, the purposes and goals of educational research are broad, and expanding. Both the quality and quantity of research have increased. Research has made many contributions to education. In fact, most of our knowledge in such areas as learning, motivation, development, assessment methods, and classroom dynamics has been obtained through research. The tendency to "bad-mouth" educational research may occasionally be overdone. Page,[18] for example, argues that the decade from 1965 to 1975 has been the decade of greatest accomplishment "for concept after concept has been shar-pened and tested, and myth after myth has been exposed." Nevertheless, educational research has fallen short of its goals. It has not given educators all the answers they need. Why has educational research fallen short?

Many of the problems confronting educational researchers are of the same type as those confronting other researchers. Obtaining knowledge through research is an arduous task, and one shouldn't expect too much. But it should be obvious that the giant advances made in the biological and physical sciences have not been equaled in the social sciences. This is partly because education is a more complex field to research. The behavioral scientists must

---

[17]G. C. Helmstadter, *Research Concepts in Human Behavior*. New York: Appleton-Century-Crofts, 1970, p. 406.
[18]Ellis B. Page, Accentuate the negative. *Educational Researcher*, 4:4 (1975), 5.

deal with many variables simultaneously. Rigid control of these variables is hard to achieve, and quantification of these variables is often very difficult. Because of the difficulty of controlling and quantifying these variables, many feel it is indeed amazing that we have learned as much as we have about the educational process.

Also, there are ethical issues which need to be considered in research with humans. Humans have the right of nonparticipation in research, the right to remain anonymous, and the right of confidentiality. They have the right to insist that any research in which they participate will not be of any harm to them. We urge researchers to remember the importance of these ethical considerations and follow all ethical guidelines. But doing so does make social science research more difficult.

In addition to social science being more complex, society seems to have a much different attitude toward research in the social sciences than in the natural sciences. As Remmers[19] pointed out in the late 1940s, our thinking is quite different in the areas of natural and social sciences. In natural science the public has an experimental attitude. Old ideas are considered invalid and the past is viewed with amusement. Change is welcomed as progress. In social science there is more of a "stand pat" attitude. Cherished traditions, beliefs, and loyalties are hard to give up. New ideas are viewed as unsound and the future viewed with alarm. Change, having been identified with cultural decay, is opposed. With public attitudes such as these it is no wonder that so little time and money have been expended in research, that so little has been accomplished, and that the public has resisted new findings. It does appear that this attitude has changed somewhat in recent years. One indication of this change is the increased funding of educational research that was mentioned earlier.

Unfortunately, *teachers'* attitudes are still not all that favorable toward research. However, Moore and Carriker[20] report a study which shows that "outstanding teachers" (as judged by Jaycees) scored significantly higher on a Scale of Attitude toward Research than did a group of teachers in general. (Of course we do not know whether or not having more favorable attitudes toward research helped make them better teachers. We only know the relationship existed.)

There has been another affective problem associated with educational research that is just the opposite of the one mentioned above. While many people resist research findings, far too often there is an unwarranted and uncritical acceptance of research findings. All scientists realize that the general public can't evaluate their research procedures. But it seems that the public, having more and stronger biases about social science, are more gullible in

[19]Hermann H. Remmers, The expanding role of research. *North Central Association Quarterly*, 23 (1949), 369–376.
[20]Arnold J. Moore and M. Don Carriker, The futility of educational research in curriculum development. *Phi Delta Kappan*, 55:7 (1974), 492.

accepting "findings" that agree with their biases (and, as mentioned, more likely to reject those that don't). This is natural, and a problem educational researchers will have to live with. A problem that does seem solvable is the gullibility of professional educators. Professional physicists can critique physical research. Professional biologists can critique biological research. Why can't professional educators be critical of educational research? Glass suggests that educators' gullibility stems from two causes:

> 1. an insensitivity—which is a venial sin in the layman, but a mortal one in the professional—to the nature of empirical evidence; and
> 2. a commitment by professionals to "help" the child rather than understand him or his circumstances, a commitment which engenders an uncritical wish to believe that the latest educational nostrum . . . is miraculously effective.[21]

Glass reports several examples of this will to believe and how the desire to help children renders people irrational and gullible. Sipay[22] wrote a report of a fictitious research project entitled "The Effect of Prenatal Instruction on Reading Achievement." It was a satire on the attempts to teach reading to younger and younger children. In this imaginary study lessons were broadcast to unborn children in an experimental group by means of a fetoscope. At the end of the first grade these children could read better than control groups. Sipay, as reported by Glass, has had people writing him in all seriousness asking for more information about his fetoscope and his techniques!

Another example of this will to believe is the reaction to *Pygmalion in the Classroom* by Rosenthal and Jacobson.[23] In their book they present findings that suggest students will become brighter if their teachers are lied to about their abilities. (That is, if teachers are told the children score higher on aptitude tests than they really do.) Now this finding has some intrinsic appeal. If we really could increase the abilities of children by systematically duping their teachers, it would be a simple solution to many educational problems. However, some researchers have pointed out methodological deficiencies in the study (see, for example, Thorndike[24]). What seems unfortunate to us is the fact that many educators accepted the Rosenthal and Jacobson results without looking critically at the *research*. Also, some educators have overgeneralized the findings and have drawn unwarranted inferences. Hopefully, teachers (and certainly professors of education), in the near future, will have enough research sophistication so that they can accept or reject research findings on their merit rather than on their emotional appeal.

[21]Gene V. Glass, Educational piltdown men. *Phi Delta Kappan*, 50 (1968), 148.
[22]Edward R. Sipay, The effect of prenatal instruction on reading achievement. *Elementary English* (April 1965), 431–432.
[23]Robert Rosenthal and Lenore Jacobson, *Pygmalion in the Classroom*. New York: Holt, Rinehart and Winston, 1968.
[24]Robert L. Thorndike. Review of Rosenthal and Jacobson, Pygmalion in the Classroom. *American Educational Research Journal*, 5 (1968), 708–711.

The commitment by professionals to help children is good rather than bad. But when this commitment blinds us to the fallacies of poor research (or causes us to reject good research) then the commitment itself can impede the realization of the desired outcomes. This problem is made more serious by the fact that so much poor and/or insignificant research is published. Bloom[25] regarded only about 70 of the 70,000 studies listed in the *Review of Educational Research* over 25 years as being crucial and significant. This is approximately three studies per year! The Ward et al. article, reproduced in Chapter Three, makes the same general point. Their research suggests that 27 percent of the articles published in educational journals were unworthy of publication and should have been rejected. While the Bloom and Ward et al. standards may be a little too rigid, it is obvious that a professional educator—one who is a competent consumer of research—must sort considerable chaff from the wheat. (One, however, must not be hypercritical. A single article, for example, may have some chaff and yet have considerable wheat.)

Another already suggested hypothesis as to why educational practice has advanced less than other areas (such as, say, medical practice) is that the wrong type of research has been overemphasized. A great amount of research has been applied rather than basic. Many feel this has left us knowing too little about the theoretical aspects of education.

Whether or not there has been too little emphasis on basic research, most educators agree that there is a gap between findings and practical applications. Some have suggested that the lag between the publication of research findings and the implementation of those findings is as long as 50 years. This lag is partly due to distrust of research, partly due to the inability of educators to read and understand research reports, and partly due to insufficient funds for implementing change. Unfortunately, we suspect the lag in educational practice is partly due to the human tendency toward laziness. We are reminded of the farmer who, when the government agent offered him free pamphlets that would explain better farming practices, replied, "Why bother, I ain't farming half as good as I know how to now."

In summary, it is apparent that educational research has not advanced the practice of education to the degree hoped for, or indeed even to the degree necessary in this complex society. There have been many reasons posited for this: lack of public support, distrust of social science research, poorly trained researchers, and even more poorly trained practitioners of education. It would seem that one of the more promising solutions to the problems of educational research is to improve our training of both producers and consumers of research. The goal of this book is to make more educators more competent in both these areas. The book is oriented, however, toward the consumer.

[25]Benjamin S. Bloom, Twenty-five years of educational research. *American Educational Research Journal*, 3 (1966), 211–221.

II. (Evaluating Educational Research)

Communication of research findings requires both an articulate writer *and* an intelligent, critical reader. In order to be a critical reader and hence interpreter and evaluator of research findings (articles), the reader should ask himself a series of questions as he reads a research report. In a sense, the questions may be considered somewhat analogous to a checklist used by commercial airline pilots, who would never attempt to take off before completing their checklist. Similarly, one who reads research—regardless of his motive (whether he is a consumer, practitioner, student)—should ask a series of questions during or at least after he has read a research report. One must question (maybe challenge) the assumptions made (or question those not made), the significance of the problem, the appropriateness of the hypotheses tested, the method of gathering the data, the reliability and the validity of the instruments used, the appropriateness of the analytical tools, the representativeness and adequacy of the sample, the conclusions drawn, and the implications made.

As was mentioned earlier, educational research can be defined in a variety of ways. Research, regardless of type or discipline follows no universal pattern. All research reports, however, are characterized by some general format such as (1) a statement of the problem, (2) well-generated hypotheses that hopefully have a theoretical rationale and that are operational (amenable to testing and/or scientific inquiry), (3) a thorough description of the procedure employed in studying the problem, (4) a presentation of, and discussion of the findings, and (5) a section discussing the conclusions, implications, and limita-

**CHECKLIST FOR EVALUATING
RESEARCH ARTICLES**

table 1 ─────────────────────────────────────

1. Is the problem clearly stated?
2. Does the problem have a theoretical rationale?
3. How significant is the problem?
4. Is there a review of the literature? If so, is it relevant?
5. How clearly are the hypotheses stated?
6. Are operational definitions provided?
7. Is the procedure (or method) used to attack and answer the problem fully and completely described? Was a sample used? If so, how was it selected?
8. Are there any probable sources of error that might influence the results of the study? If so, have they been controlled?
9. Were statistical techniques used to analyze the data? If so, were they appropriate?
10. How clearly are the results presented?
11. Are the conclusions presented clearly? Do the data support the conclusions? Does the researcher overgeneralize his findings?
12. What are the limitations of the study? Are they stated?

tions on the generalizability of the findings. Recognizing that there is no universal recipe for conducting (and hence evaluating) research, we have set forth, in Table 1, a *general* guide to the kinds of questions that *must* be asked by the reader of research reports. Follow Francis Bacon's advice: "Read not to contradict and refute, nor to believe and take for granted . . . but to weigh and consider." Be critical but not hypercritical; emphasize the important facts not the trivia, and remember, there is no perfect piece of research as long as researchers are humans. (See the article by Goldiamond on page 25 for a humorous, yet serious, parable concerning the danger of being overly picayune in critiquing research articles).

A. POINTS TO PONDER WHEN READING RESEARCH

In the past, much educational research has been severely criticized because (1) the problem of the study was of little value or significance, (2) the hypotheses did not have an adequate theoretical rationale, and/or (3) the researchers often overgeneralized their findings (for example, they studied second-graders in School A but generalized their results to all second-graders in the country).

In this section, we shall discuss in somewhat greater detail the questions that a reader of research reports should ask himself. These questions are designed to make you a critical reader (not hypercritical, mind you) of research reports. The questions that follow are by no means mutually exclusive nor are they totally inclusive. They are, however, the ones that the writers feel are most significant. The textual material is designed to help shed some light on the questions. For example, rather than just ask about the adequacy of the review of literature, we have discussed, albeit briefly, *why* the review of literature is important and how to determine its adequacy. In addition to the questions that follow, there is a series of questions in the introduction to each of the major types of research—historical, descriptive, correlational, ex-post-facto, and experimental. These questions are of particular importance to the specific type of study. Finally, at the end of each article, we have presented some comments and questions on the strengths and weaknesses of the article. Many, but not all of these comments will be related to the general questions presented in Table 1 (and discussed in more detail below) and/or the more specific questions raised in the chapter introductions. The questions and comments following each article are intended to help you focus on some specific characteristic(s) of the research. For this reason, it should be recognized that these questions and comments are *supplementary*. They are *not* a replacement for the general questions (or a subset of them that is applicable for a particular type of research) that the reader should ask himself either as he reads through the article or after he completes his reading of the research.

Problem

1. How clearly and succinctly is the problem stated?
2. Is it sufficiently delimited so as to be amenable to investigation? And, at the same time, does it have sufficient practical value (to educators, students, parents) to warrant study?
3. Possibly with the exception of some historical and/or descriptive research, is it stated in such a way that it expresses the relationship of the two or more variables?
4. Does it have a theoretical rationale?
5. Has the problem been studied before? If so, should this problem be studied again? If so, is the study likely to provide further answers?
6. Is the problem decision-oriented or conclusion-oriented?
7. Will the findings give rise to further hypotheses thereby increasing the probability of adding to existing knowledge?

All educational research should begin with a carefully formulated problem. This is harder than it appears. There are many persons who think that an idea automatically generates itself into a carefully formulated problem. There is a difference, however, between an idea or a topic or an area of investigation and the eventual formulation of a problem that is amenable to scientific inquiry. No one in his right mind would say that his problem is to study, for example, achievement, age, and the training of elementary school teachers. These are topics about which problems *might* be formulated but as stated they are *not* scientific problems.

If we think for a moment, we shall recognize that any kind of research should emanate from a felt need. That is, the individual must feel that it is important that he achieve some solution to his problem. Let us suppose, for example, that an individual is interested in studying achievement. What is it that one might want to know about achievement? In some instances problems can be clarified by formulating a series of specific questions. What kind of achievement are we interested in studying? Will we expect achievement to differ between boys and girls, between persons from different socio-economic strata, or between persons of different ages? What criteria are to be used to judge achievement? These are just some of the questions that one might formulate about achievement, depending upon one's interest and the situation. Lamke succinctly summarizes the problem stage when he states " . . . the trick is to so state, define, and delimit a problem that the subsequent action which must be taken to solve it is clearly specified."[26] Your critical evaluation of the problem then is "Did the researcher do what Lamke suggested?"

[26]Tom A. Lamke, A primer in research . . . lesson I: Defining the problem. *Phi Delta Kappan*, 38 (1957), 129.

Review of Literature

1. How adequately has the literature been surveyed?
2. Does the review present pertinent material or is it just "filler"?
3. Were primary or secondary sources used? Were secondary sources relied on too heavily?
4. Does the review critically evaluate previous findings and studies or is it only a summary of *what* is known without pointing out any possible deficiencies or alternative explanations?
5. Does the review support the need for studying the problem?
6. Does the review establish a theoretical framework for the problem?

The review of literature is a very significant aspect of the research process. It helps the researcher by giving him some information about the status quo of knowledge in the area he intends to study. It should provide the researcher with ideas of the type of study and/or type of design that he may eventually use in conducting his research.

It should be evident to both the consumer and producer of research that in any research study a review of literature *must* be included, whether it be as a separate, discrete topic, or whether it be incorporated in, say, the problem or introductory statement. A question that is frequently raised by both the researcher and the reader is "How thorough should the review of literature be?" There is no clear-cut answer to the question of thoroughness or adequacy of the literature survey. The review must be selective, in the sense that it is relevant to the problem, as well as able to demonstrate the relationship of the study at hand to previous studies. It should not be done in haste lest valuable information be neglected or overlooked.

The review of literature may be of value in a variety of ways. It may assist the researcher by pointing out deficiencies in existing research. It may help the researcher avoid errors that plagued other researchers studying the same or a similar problem. It should help the researcher develop a theoretical framework. The researcher using questionnaires, checklists, observation schedules, or interviews often is uncertain of what should be asked, observed, and/or recorded, and the review of literature may help him.

Educational research, in order to be sound, must make use of carefully formulated hypotheses. There is no denying the fact that "No scientific undertaking can proceed effectively without well-conceived hypotheses. . . Without hypotheses, research is unfocused, haphazard, and accidental."[27]

An hypothesis is a tentative answer to the problem stated in the study. An hypothesis is the guide to the researcher in that it delineates and describes

---

[27]Deobold B. Van Dalen, The role of hypotheses in educational research. *Educational Administration and Supervision*, 42 (1956), 457.

Hypotheses

1. Are any assumptions advanced with respect to the hypotheses? If so, are they explicit—they should be—or are they implicit?
2. Are the hypotheses consistent with theory and known facts?
3. Are they testable?
4. Do they provide a suggested answer to the problem?
5. Are all terms adequately defined in operational fashion?

(either explicitly or implicitly) the procedure to be followed in studying the problem. Although these hypotheses may be either stated formally or implied, it is suggested that they be stated formally. Hypotheses are important because they tell the researcher *what* to do and *how* to do it. Unless one has some idea of where he is going, he will have much difficulty in reaching his goal. As Cohen succinctly states: "Without some guiding idea, we do not know what facts to gather. Without something to prove, we cannot determine what is relevant and what is irrelevant."[28] We should not use the Baconian approach that is characterized by gathering a plethora of data and then wondering what to do with the data once they have been obtained. In Bacon's time, it might have been expected that from this cornucopia of information something would surely emanate. Maybe that is true, but we would be in a much better position if we had an hypothesis to guide us in the kinds of data to collect.

Another reason for establishing carefully formulated hypotheses is that they frequently are the working tools of theory and, as such, can be tested. We often study the relationships (between the variables) stated by the hypothesis and hence we "test" these relationships. Statistical tools test the probability of an event occurring or not occurring. Although we *never* prove or disprove hypotheses, we can test them and state that they are probably true or probably false. Kerlinger says, "The scientist cannot tell positive from negative evidence unless he uses hypotheses."[29]

Hypotheses are of two types: *research* (sometimes referred to as *substantive*) and *statistical*. Regardless of the type, they should be formulated as early as possible and much thought should be given to their formulation. Very early in the researcher's thinking, there is a stage where he begins to make some tentative formulations about the causes, relationships, or possible solutions to the problem. (Note: There are some historical and descriptive studies which are amenable to a research hypothesis but not a statistical hypothesis.) For example, a researcher might be interested in studying the effect of reading comprehension on academic performance as measured by the grade-point aver-

---

[28]Morris A. Cohen, *A Preface to Logic.* New York: Meridian, 1956, 148.
[29]Fred N. Kerlinger, *Foundations of Behavioral Research,* 2d Ed. New York: Holt, Rinehart and Winston, 1973, p. 26.

age. This researcher might conjecture *a priori* that those students who are good readers will have higher GPA's than those students who are poor readers. He might further conjecture that this relationship is due to the verbal nature of the final examinations. These formulations or conjectures are commonly referred to as *research* hypotheses.

Strictly speaking, the research hypothesis is not testable; it must be translated into operational and experimental terms. *Operational* definitions assign meanings to constructs or variables (such as intelligence or reading comprehension) studied by specifying the procedures to be followed in measuring the variables. Operational definitions are a *must* in educational (or for that matter, any kind of) research. Unless one can translate his variable into something observable he cannot measure it and hence he would not be able to research his problem. For example, achievement is a construct (a concept deliberately created by the researcher for a specific purpose). But, before we are able to manipulate or even measure achievement, we must define it very carefully. Is it verbal or nonverbal? If verbal, is it reading, writing, or mathematics? If reading, what tests or instruments or procedures will be used to measure it? Constructs, in order to be operational and hence amenable to scientific inquiry, must be delimited and specific. All terms should be carefully defined so that another researcher (if he wishes) can replicate the study using the same procedures, the same design, and the same measurement device(s). A major purpose of operationalization is to make the transition from theory to data (and back again later).

The statistical or *null* hypothesis (the null hypothesis was invented by Sir Ronald Fisher, a man who made a monumental contribution to modern statistics and research design) states essentially that there is no relationship between the variables being studied, and that any observed differences can be attributed to sampling errors, that is, chance fluctuations. If the difference observed is greater than one would expect by chance, the null hypothesis is rejected. Remember, prior to testing the null hypothesis, descriptive hypotheses have been formulated. It is the descriptive hypothesis that tells us what to conclude if the null hypothesis is rejected. For example, the researcher's null hypothesis is that mean A equals mean B. He then advances an alternative hypothesis that (1) mean A is less than mean B, *or* (2) mean A is greater than mean B, *or* (3) mean A does not equal mean B. Which *one* of these three alternative hypotheses he chooses is determined by his descriptive hypothesis.

It should be readily evident that the researcher begins with some ideas as to the relationship, tests these relationships, and, depending on the outcome of the statistical test, may reformulate new ideas or possible explanations. In conclusion, the statistical hypothesis is a "guesstimate" of how the statistics used to analyze the data will turn out, that is, the mean of the class taught by Method A will be higher than (or greater than) mean B; or the relationship between reading comprehension and GPA is 0.75, or the relationship between reading comprehension and GPA is smaller than 0.75.[30]

In your reading of research, you will frequently encounter the terms "one- and two-tailed tests of significance." If the researcher posits a directional difference (such as mean A is less than mean B or mean A is greater than mean B), he should use a one-tailed test of significance. If, however, he has no reason to hypothesize which group would be superior, his alternative hypothesis would be "mean A does not equal mean B" and he would use a two-tailed test of significance.

The level of probability that leads one to reject the null hypothesis is somewhat arbitrary. Some researchers leave this decision to the consumer and simply report a probability value for the statistical test made. A statement "$p < 0.01$" in a research report means that the probability is less than 1 in 100 that the difference observed could have occurred by chance. More often, a significance level is set in advance by the researcher. Conventionally, the significance level is set at either 0.01 or 0.05. Occasionally, it is set at 0.10, 0.15, or some other value. The decision depends upon what kinds of risks the investigator is willing to make, which in turn is related to the purpose of the study. For example, in an exploratory study of the carcinogenic effect of certain foods, the significance level may be set at .10 or .15 (high) so as not to miss any promising leads, whereas in an experimental study comparing a new expensive teaching method with an older, less expensive one you would want to be very certain that the new method is really better before adopting it.

There are two types of errors that one can make in drawing inferential conclusions. A *Type I error* occurs when one rejects the null hypothesis when it is in fact true. In other words, one labels a difference as real, when in actuality it occurred by chance. The level of significance gives us the probability of making a Type I error. If we set the level of significance at 0.01 and reject the null hypothesis, this means that the chances are 99 in 100 that the differences are real. If we reject the null hypothesis at this level, we shall be wrong one percent of the time. A *Type II error* occurs when one does not reject the null hypothesis when, in fact, it is false and should be rejected. The lower we set our level of significance the less chance we have of making a Type I error, but the greater our chance of making a Type II error. In education we generally seem to be more concerned with Type I errors so we set our level of significance small (say 0.05 or 0.01). This is because Type I errors are often more costly.

A final point should be made in this section. Not all results that are of statistical significance are of practical significance. And, tests of hypotheses are tests of statistical significance. If a researcher uses a very large sample, quite

---

[30]The coefficient of correlation is one way to measure the degree of relationship between two variables. It is expressed by r and will be discussed in greater detail in Chapter Four.

small observed differences can be statistically significant. This does not necessarily mean that they are great enough to be of importance to the practitioner. This is a value judgment. For example, a researcher finds that there is a statistically significant relationship between a very expensive diet (the food in this diet costs $35.00 per day per child) and academic performance. However, because of the size of the sample (it was very large), only a slight relationship had to be obtained to be statistically significant. Do you think that this researcher should advocate this special, expensive diet? On the other hand, there may be only a slight relationship between drug X and remission of certain tumor growths. Should the researcher advocate the use of this drug even though it also is expensive? This is what we mean by saying that the *practical* significance of a statistical test is a value judgment.

Data and Procedures
1. Are the procedures, design, and instruments employed to gather the data described with sufficient clarity so as to permit another researcher to replicate the study?
2. Is the population described fully? Did the researcher use the total population or did he sample from it? If a sample is used, is it representative of the population from which it was selected? Note: The manner and the size of sampling are very important.
3. If locally prepared instruments were used, is evidence presented to attest to their validity and reliability?
4. Were the "best" (most economical, most feasible, most valid and reliable) instruments or techniques used?
5. Was a pretest used? Was there a pilot study? If so, why? What were the results? Was the problem or original hypothesis or procedure changed as a result of the pretest or pilot study, and if so, was this modification justifiable and/or desirable?
6. Are there any obvious weaknesses in the over-all "design" of the study?

Good research is characterized by careful attention to the manner in which the data are collected. We are not concerned at this time with whether the data are collected by means of tests, observation schedules, interviews, etc. However, regardless of the procedure that is used to collect the data the researcher must be certain that his method is valid and reliable.

If interviews were used, how were the responses recorded and quantified? For example, if interviewers are employed, we must consider the individuals who are gathering the data. Are they qualified? Do special and/or particular methods of training need to be employed to prepare the interviewers to gather valid data? How were the interviewers trained? How much agreement and/or consistency is there among the interviewers? Were there changes in interviewers and/or procedures during the study?

Careful attention must be paid to the method in which the data are expressed. Are they quantitative or qualitative, and how meaningful are they? Are the data presented clearly? Are the results complete? If tables, diagrams, or charts are used, are they well organized and are they communicative in and of themselves?

Other questions you should ask yourself are the following: Would I be able to replicate the study from the information given? Would I be able to evaluate the validity of the data collected in reference to the problem and hypotheses? If you were to answer "no" or "I don't know" or "I am not sure," then the methods of data collection would be inadequately defined.

Good research is characterized by the thoroughness with which the population of subjects or objects is chosen for study. Normally, we select a sample of this population of subjects or objects rather than use the total population. Naturally, one must begin with a well-defined population. One might think that if we announced our intention of studying the characteristics of successful doctors who graduated from eastern colleges, we would *ipso facto* have a well-defined population of subjects. But let us raise the following questions: By "doctor" do we mean an M.D., a D.O., or a D.C.? If it is an M.D., are we referring to general practitioners or specialists, and if specialists, which ones? Assuming that we have been able to define the term "doctor," what is a successful doctor? Is our study limited to doctors who have been in practice for a certain period of time? Is it to include those who are retired? Is it to refer to those who have been in practice at least 10 years, but not more than 15 years? Are we interested in studying doctors regardless of where they are practicing? What is an eastern college? Are we to restrict ourselves to private schools, public institutions, large institutions, small institutions? These are just some of the questions that we could raise to show that our seemingly well-defined population really and truly is not so well defined. Poorly defined populations will make interpretation(s) using samples very difficult, if not impossible.

As stated earlier, because of pressures of time, money, and energy it is sometimes necessary to select and study a sample from the total population. But sampling is a very difficult and sometimes complex task.

Evaluation of the sample, if one has been used, is a very important step. What is a population? What is a sample? What is sampling? A population refers to *all* of a specified group of objects (usually persons). A sample is a smaller number of elements selected from a population and hopefully representative of that population. Sampling is a procedure whereby a small number of observational units, people or test scores, are selected for study with the aim of generalizing the findings to the larger population, called the *universe*, from which the sample was selected. The sample is always smaller than the population; however, a sample in one study might be the population in another and vice versa. Possibly the following example will help clarify the latter point:

	POPULATION		SAMPLE
(a)	All high-school students in Michigan	(a)	All high-school students from three randomly chosen Michigan counties—Ingham, Wayne, and Clinton
(b)	All high-school students in Ingham, Wayne, and Clinton Counties, Michigan	(b)	Random sample of 5 percent of the high-school students from the three counties

---

In nearly all types of educational research, we use and study samples rather than populations. Sampling can be achieved in a variety of ways. If at all feasible, the researcher should employ a random sample. In a random sample, every object in the population has a specified probability of being selected.

A random sample does not necessarily represent the characteristics of the total population, but when the choice of subjects is left to chance the possibility of bias entering the selection of the sample is reduced. By chance, of course, one could select a sample that did not accurately represent the total population. The more heterogeneous the units are and the smaller the sample, the greater is the chance of drawing a "poor" sample.[31]

There are a variety of ways in which one might choose a random sample. We shall not discuss these approaches (they are described in most introductory research texts). What is important, however, is for the reader to ascertain (1) whether a sample has been used, and if so, whether the method of selecting that sample was fully described, and (2) whether or not the sample is representative of the population from which it was chosen. Are Kinsey's females representative of American women? Are the individuals used in the Johnson-Masters sex study representative of Americans in general?

Random sampling should be a control for sampling bias. However, if random sampling is not used, we are more likely to have sampling bias. This is especially true if volunteers are used. If a study were longitudinal, you would

---

[31]Deobold B. Van Dalen, *Understanding Educational Research* (Rev. Ed.). New York: McGraw-Hill, 1966, p. 299.

have to ask whether there was any subject mortality, that is, were any subjects lost during the study?

You must ask yourself a variety of questions about the sample. How well defined was the population and hence the sample? What sampling method was used? Have subjects been randomly selected? If an experimental study, have subjects been randomly assigned to the experimental and control groups? (This is a hallmark for experimental research — it allows for internal validity.) Was the sample sufficiently large? Is a large sample better than a small sample? Not always. A large sample in itself is no assurance of reducing sampling bias. But, other things being equal, a large random sample will result in less sampling error than a smaller sample. However, large samples may be misleading in that the infinitesimally small difference may be "statistically significant" but of no practical importance. How big, then, should the sample be? We must collect a sample size (there are procedures to determine optimal sample size) that will allow us to detect a relationship or difference that is large enough to be of *practical* importance and at the same time with an optimal sample size we should not detect trivial differences.

There are times when a researcher is unable to use commercially available instruments either because such instruments are not available or because the instruments that are available may not be suitable for his purpose. When this is the case, it is necessary for the researcher to construct his own tests, scales, instruments, etc. We do not quarrel with the researcher who develops his own tools. We do, however, insist that he demonstrate the validity and reliability of his instrument(s) and describe fully the manner in which the psychometric qualities (validity and reliability) of his instrument(s) were studied.

There are many instances, especially where research is being conducted that involves the measurement of achievement and aptitude, where the researcher can choose between two or more standardized tests. The reader, however, should not assume that the researcher selected the "best" test. It is incumbent upon the researcher to explain why he used, say, the Stanford Achievement Tests rather than the Iowa Tests of Basic Skills. We are not arguing that the researcher did not know the difference between these two achievement batteries. But the reader does not always know (and should be told) the reason(s) for Test A being selected over Test B. The choice of one standardized test over another is often related to content validity considerations. However, it can be related to differences between the tests with respect to such factors as test reliability, training needed to administer and/or interpret the tests, amount of time needed, cost, and the like.

Good research is characterized by the care taken in the analysis of the data. The major purpose of any statistical analysis is to compare the obtained results with what we would expect to get by chance. If the obtained differences are greater than chance, we say that they are statistically significant. If the

Analysis and Results

1. Are statistical techniques needed to analyze the data?
2. Was the most appropriate and meaningful statistical technique(s) employed?
3. Were any assumptions related to using a particular statistic violated? And, if so, how would this affect the findings?
4. Have the results been adequately presented?

obtained differences are smaller than what would be expected by chance, we say that the findings are not statistically significant. Kerlinger, talking about the future of educational research, states that one can see in the literature today "increased sophistication in the use of theory, hypothesis and alternative hypothesis, research design, operational thinking and definitions, and analytical tools."[32]

However, before considering the analysis of the data as such, one must ask himself, "What data are to be analyzed? What part of the data are important and why are they important? How are these data to be categorized? If the data are such that they have to be categorized, are there previously established categories, and are there guides for the individual who will eventually be faced with categorizing the data? Would other individuals, following these same guides, come out with the same categorization?" After these preliminary questions have been considered and handled, it is necessary to choose the most meaningful and appropriate tool to analyze these data. One of the major deficiencies in educational research is the lack of sophistication on the part of researchers in choosing the most meaningful statistical tool to analyze their data. This does *not* mean that the tool chosen will necessarily be either inappropriate or incorrect. It does mean, however, that another procedure might provide the researcher with more meaningful information.

There are a multitude of statistical procedures that one can use to analyze his data. The kind of statistic one uses is determined by the nature of his hypothesis. It is essential that both the consumer of and the producer of research be familiar with these statistical procedures. We are unable to deal with them in this text, but we strongly recommend that the reader consult any introductory statistics text for a discussion of these topics.

Good research is characterized by carefully formulated inferences, generalizations, and conclusions. Every reported study should include a final summary and conclusions section. In this section, the investigator summarizes his findings. Many things should be considered by the reader: Are the generalizations, inferences drawn, and/or conclusions made supported by the data? Are there any evident conclusions that have not been commented upon by the

[32]Fred N. Kerlinger, Research in education. In *Encyclopedia of Educational Research* (4th Ed.), Robert L. Ebel. New York: Macmillan, 1969, p. 1140.

Conclusions, Implications, and Generalizations

1. Are the conclusions and generalizations consistent with the findings? What are the implications of the findings? Has the researcher overgeneralized his findings?
2. Does the researcher discuss the limitations of his study?
3. Are there any extraneous factors that might have affected the findings? Have they been considered by the researchers?
4. Are the conclusions presented consistent with theory and/or known facts?
5. Have the conclusions (both those relevant to the original hypothesis and any serendipitous findings) been adequately presented and discussed?

investigator? Has the researcher gone beyond his data for the conclusions he has drawn?

If in reading the conclusions the reader notes findings that are contradictory with those of previous research, he should be suspicious and carefully review the report to see whether or not there are any deficiencies in the design and execution of the study.

B. A CONCLUDING STATEMENT

The above-mentioned criteria (although neither mutually exclusive nor exhaustive) are suggestions that should be carefully considered by anyone engaged in, involved in, and responsible for conducting research. They are also guides and criteria that should be used by the consumer of research. There is no denying the fact that one of the more effective methods of gaining knowledge is by reading. One cannot overemphasize the importance of clear, concise, complete descriptions — be they of the problem, hypotheses, review of literature, methodology, or conclusions. Unless a report of research is described in sufficient detail so as to permit another completely independent (and, yes, sometimes untrained) investigator to replicate the study, it is *inadequately* described. A good axiom to remember is "There is no such thing as overdescription." The problem must be clear, concise, delimited, brief, and have a sound theoretical rationale. The hypotheses must be operationally defined, the method of collecting the data fully described, and the selection (and if in an experimental study, the assignment of subjects to treatments) of subjects explained fully.

Quite often, research reports do not use specific headings such as (1) the problem, (2) hypotheses, (3) procedure, (4) analysis of data or findings, (5) discussion, and (6) conclusions. Frequently, the problem and hypotheses are to be found in the introduction, procedures are included with the findings, and conclusions and inferences with the discussion. What is important is *not* whether distinct, discrete headings are used — only that these aspects are treated in the research report.

The consumer of research — be he a classroom teacher interested in finding a more effective manner in which to teach his subject matter; be he an administrator who is interested in trying to find the most efficient method of scheduling; be he a counselor who is concerned with ascertaining the best predictor for an aspect of an individual's behavior; be he a parent who is interested in trying to understand his children better — should consider all the factors we have discussed.

It should be recognized that even the best designed and conducted research seldom results in earth-shattering, volcanic conclusions that markedly affect American educational practices. There are, however, many studies, which, when considered collectively, could and have altered our classroom teaching methods. The research conducted in "transfer of training" is one such example.

Not every researcher will follow these guides in a cookbook fashion. In fact, one of the characteristics of researchers is the degree of flexibility in which they approach the solution of problems. However, it is indeed important that these general guides be considered very seriously when one is involved either in conducting research or in evaluating research findings.

A CRUCIAL EXPERIMENT RESUBMITTED *

ISRAEL GOLDIAMOND

The experiment below settled an issue for its period; unfortunately, even as today, later generations chose to address the same issues so decisively settled by previous research. On the supposition that present investigators might be just as ignorant of the report, despite its appearance in a well-known and authoritative source, and because of the continued social relevance of the report, I submitted it for publication to see how it might fare. Since the reviewers' comments raise methodological and ethical issues that are relevant today, I am attaching the report and reviewer comments just as they were received from the editors.

The Crucial Experiment

17 As soon as Ahab saw Elijah, he said to him, "Is it you, you troubler of Israel?" "It is
18 not I who have troubled Israel," he replied, "but you and your father's family, by
19 forsaking the commandments of the Lord and following Baal. But now, send and
summon all Israel to meet me on Mount Carmel, and the four hundred and fifty
prophets of Baal with them and the four hundred prophets of the goddess Asherah,
20 who are Jezebel's pensioners." So Ahab sent out to all the Israelites and assembled
21 the prophets on Mount Carmel. Elijah stepped forward and said to the people, "How
long will you sit on the fence? If the Lord is God, follow him; but if Baal, then follow
22 him." Not a word did they answer. Then Elijah said to the people, "I am the only
prophet of the Lord still left, but there are four hundred and fifty prophets of Baal.
23 Bring two bulls; let them choose one for themselves, cut it up and lay it on the wood
without setting fire to it, and I will prepare the other and lay it on the wood without
24 setting fire to it. You shall invoke your god by name and I will invoke the Lord by
name; and the god who answers by fire, he is God." And all the people shouted their
approval.
25   Then Elijah said to the prophets of Baal, "Choose one of the bulls and offer it first,
for there are more of you; invoke your god by name, but do not set fire to the wood."
26 So they took the bull provided for them and offered it, and they invoked Baal by
name from morning until noon, crying, "Baal, Baal, answer us"; but there was no

*Reprinted from *American Psychologist*, 32:8 (1977), pp. 669–671. Copyright 1977 by
the American Psychological Association. Reprinted by permission.

27 sound, no answer. They danced wildly beside the altar they had set up. At midday
Elijah mocked them: "Call louder, for he is a god; it may be he is deep in thought, or
28 engaged, or on a journey; or he may have gone to sleep and must be woken up." They
29 cried still louder and, as was their custom, gashed themselves with swords and spears
until the blood ran. All afternoon they raved and ranted till the hour of the regular
sacrifice, but still there was no sound, no answer, no sign of attention.
30 Then Elijah said to all the people, "Come here to me." They all came, and he
repaired the altar of the Lord which had been torn down. He took twelve stones, one
31 for each tribe of the sons of Jacob, the man named Israel by the word of the Lord.
32 With these stones he built an altar in the name of the Lord; he dug a trench round it
33 big enough to hold two measures of seed; he arranged the wood, cut up the bull and
34 laid it on the wood. Then he said, "Fill four jars with water and pour it on the
whole-offering and on the wood." They did so, and he said, "Do it again." They did it
35 again, and he said, "Do it a third time." They did it a third time, and the water ran all
around the altar and even filled the trench. At the hour of the regular sacrifice the
36 prophet Elijah came forward and said, "Lord God of Abraham, of Isaac, and of Israel,
let it be known today that thou art God in Israel and that I am thy servant and have
37 done all these things at thy command. Answer me, O Lord, answer me and let this
people know that thou, Lord, art God and it is thou that (dost bring them back to
38 their allegiance). Then the fire of the Lord fell. It consumed the whole-offering, the
wood, the stones, and the earth, and licked up the water in the trench. When all the
39 people saw it, they fell prostrate and cried, "The Lord is God, the Lord is God."
40 Then Elijah said to them, "Seize the prophets of Baal; let not one of them escape."
— I Kings 18, xvii–xl[1]

Comments of Reviewer A

This is a poorly designed experiment. There is no guarantee that there was no difference between the two bulls. What should properly have been done was to split one bull in half and by flipping a coin assign one side of beef to one treatment and the other side of beef to the other treatment; this should then have been repeated on the second bull. Better still, 24 bulls should have been randomly assigned to each treatment.

Another problem arises, namely, the timing of the day. The Baal treatment was done first and the Lord treatment second. Systematic differences may have ensued. More bulls should have been run in an order that was counterbalanced for time of day. Also, the Lord treatment was initiated at what the experimenter himself says was "the hour of the regular sacrifice." If this regular hour was the optimal one, this biases the outcome in favor of the Lord treatment. The obvious experimental balance is necessary. If the regular hour was merely a conventional one, this should be indicated in the text.

The question raises itself of personal effects upon experimental outcomes. Elijah was the sole adherent of his position; the others were clearly more popular. Scientific isolates who work against the mainstream have a repu-

[1]From *The New English Bible* © The Delegates of the Oxford University Press and The Syndics of the Cambridge University Press, 1961, 1970. Reprinted by permission.

tation for persistence, single-mindedness, intensity, and unswerving dedication to their positions bordering on the fanatical. Could this kind of intensity have produced the results, as an artifact, rather than the variables manipulated? It is a presumption that the Baal experts were equally dedicated. Being the accepted majority, they may have been more casual. Would 450 followers of the Lord have produced a total zero? The author might consider various controls which have been proposed for such artifacts and sources of bias, for example, having the same people use *both* treatments, double-blind, etc.

Even a single experiment incorporating all these corrections would be capable of interpretation as a chance outcome. I would suggest that the author first attempt to replicate the results.

Also, he talks of two measures of seed. What are their metric equivalents? What are volumes of the jars, dimensions of trenches, and appropriate descriptions of the bulls? What time was the regular sacrifice? What were the solar azimuth and solar radiation readings? I find the absence of such numeration and of graphs distressing. The two treatments can be compared graphically, with each hour on the abscissa, and the magnitude of the effects on the ordinate.

As it stands, the report has no scientific merit. It should not be published. It will probably create more support for Baal than for the Lord.

Comments of Reviewer B

(Methodological comments like those of Reviewer A.)

Writing too hurried and without regard to audience. Triteness or cuteness. For example, in Line 29, couldn't the author think of something less trite than "they raved and ranted"—does he think he originated the term? Also, the fire "licked up the water"! And the "fire of the Lord fell"—is this supposed to be science fiction? At least, given this penchant for triteness, the author spared us and didn't say the "fire struck like a bolt from the blue, making the people feel their hearts were in their throats." And if Asherah is the Phoenician Asherat (Jezebel's father was King of Sidon), then Asherah is the mother of Baal (and of his sister, Astarte = Aphrodite, Venus). Why is this elevant information withheld?

Article should be rewritten to conform to standard format for scientific writing. Present order makes comparison with related work difficult.

Comments of Reviewer C

The author displays a remarkable lack of sensitivity to ethical and other social issues of importance which are serious enough to question his suitability for professional employment. On this basis alone, the article should be rejected and administrative steps be immediately taken to ensure nonrepetition. Any volume in which an article of this dubious nature appears will be suspect, as to the morality, ethics, and sensitivity to social issues of the entire volume. Consider the following five points:

1.   Was it necessary to sacrifice two bulls and were the sacrifices performed according to standards set up for humane treatment of animals? Granted, it is at times necessary to sacrifice animals to study their brain, etc. This occurs when it is necessary to ensure that differences in outcome were not due to experimentally induced organic change. But in such cases, such sacrifice, though regrettable, is possibly justified since it is essential to interpretation of the results. *This is not the case here.* The purpose of this experiment was to differentiate the efficacy of two treatments. Certainly the efficacy of Baal or the Lord could have been tested by means other than the gratuitous sacrifice of two bulls. Simply lighting or not lighting the wood which surrounded the bulls would have sufficed to demonstrate a difference—and, as a matter of fact, did. Why was the life of the bulls then taken so unnecessarily? Next thing we know, Elijah will be slaughtering the prophets of Baal as well—all 450 of them.

2.   Were the prophets of Baal and Asherah informed in advance that they were to be put on trial in an experiment? Was informed consent obtained under conditions whereby they could decline to participate in the experimental trial? We are not told who (or what) this Ahab is. Apparently, he commands sufficient authority not only to summon the audience but the prophets as well. As the article is written it looks like the prophets of Baal and Asherah were simply ordered by the Dean (or is AHAB a division of NIH?) to compare their procedures in front of an audience without the prophets being forewarned or given time for advance preparation. Not only were the timing and audience sprung on them by Elijah, but the test was done under conditions and at times Elijah had set up. We can presume these would not have been chosen by Elijah to prejudice his case. For the other prophets to have backed out in front of the audience, under what seemed to be fair conditions (although upon reflection they might not have thought so—I leave this to my scientific colleagues to ascertain) would have been damaging. It is quite clear that whatever consent was then obtained was under coercion, in addition to not having been presented in advance under conditions when withdrawal was possible at no jeopardy to them. At that point, alternatives should have been made available, to meet ethical guidelines.

3.   The prophets of Baal and Asherah having been coerced into the experiment, both were found wanting. But as far as Asherah is concerned, this is guilt by association. The audience was not asked to choose between the Lord, Baal, *and* Asherah—only the Lord and Baal. It is the 450 prophets of Baal who invoke *his* name; there is no evidence that the 400 prophets of Asherah invoked *her* name. If they were not given an altar for their bull (or cow?), why is their position considered as disproven along with that of Baal? The attempted equa-

tion of groups by size (450 and 400) seems an almost deliberate effort to have us overlook the inequality of experimental treatments. This impression of deliberate bias is supported by the order at the end to "seize the prophets of Baal." There is no similar seizure ordered for the followers of Asherah. Possibly this might have been too raw and the inequalities might then have come to light. As it stands, the prophets of Asherah might have been so affected by the fate accorded the Baalians, that they were thereby coerced into silent acquiescence. Is there a sexist bias here?

4.   Was the audience coerced into attendance? And into staying throughout a day so hot that the heavens could ignite wet kindling? Could people leave if they desired? And what would have been the consequences? Were they told that this was to be an all-day affair? Were there adequate medical provisions for heat prostration and collapse? Were toilet facilities provided? And so on.

5.   Stones were taken from the neighborhood, trenches dug, trees chopped down for firewood, and other changes were made to provide enough room for a whole multitude to assemble to applaud the preordained conclusion. What happened to the grass and other flora in a clearing made large enough to assemble a horde this large? Was an environmental impact statement filed?

HISTORICAL RESEARCH

chapter two _____

Historical research is concerned with determining, evaluating, and understanding past events primarily for the purpose of gaining a clearer understanding of the present and a better prediction of the future.

Although historical studies are difficult to do well, they can be very important. Understandings of some current educational problems cannot be obtained by any other method. Integration, federal aid to education, accountability, state aid to parochial schools, and school bond elections are examples of issues that can only be understood in the light of history. Historical research also can enable the educator to recognize the fads and frills for what they are, and may diminish the uncritical acceptance of new innovations (such as the fetoscope mentioned in the Introduction). As Travers states:

> The *amateur* reformers in the field of education would probably drop most of their plans for the remodeling of public education if they had a better understanding of the failures of the past. (italics added)[1]

The processes in historical research are basically the same as in other types of research. The researcher should:

1. define the problem and formulate hypotheses,
2. collect the data,
3. critically analyze the data,
4. interpret and report the findings.

[1]Robert M. W. Travers, *An Introduction to Educational Research* (4th Ed.). New York: Macmillan, 1978, p. 390.

Some of these steps, however, are slightly different for the historical researcher.

Formulating the Problem

Where many authors of historical research fail is in adequately defining the problem and thinking through the purposes of their study. The problem must be clearly defined and hopefully at least tentative hypotheses should be formulated prior to the data gathering. While the researcher should not become unduly attached to a hypothesis, nevertheless, as Borg points out, without specific testable hypotheses "historical research often becomes little more than an aimless gathering of facts."[2] It is, of course, possible that the researcher had specific hypotheses in mind prior to starting the study but failed to elucidate these clearly in the written report. Much historical writing is not meant to be a *report* of research even though the writing may be based on information obtained by using historical research methods. It is not always easy to tell whether the author intended to write a research report, do a review of literature, or write an essay. If his intent was the latter, we need not expect to find hypotheses.

Sources of Data

A second point the producer and critical consumer must be alert to is the adequacy of the source data. The historical researcher does not create data; he must use what is available. The reader must attempt to decide whether adequate data are available and if the researcher used them.

Sources of data can be either *primary* or *secondary*, and either records or remains. In a primary source, data have been recorded by an actual witness (this may be a personal document or a record) or the historical object itself (remain) is available for examination. In a secondary source the recording has been done by a person who obtained his data indirectly. Primary data are harder (or impossible) to obtain, and many historical reports are overloaded with secondary sources. One must be cautious of data from secondary sources. As an example, the newspaper account of decisions reached at a school board meeting may differ considerably from a reading of the secretary's minutes.

Records (sometimes called "documents") are differentiated from remains (relics) according to whether there was a conscious effort to preserve information. Fox[3] refers to records as deliberate sources and remains as inad-

---

[2] Walter R. Borg, *Educational Research: An Introduction* (2nd Ed.). New York: McKay, 1971, p. 261.

[3] David J. Fox, *The Research Process in Education*. New York: Holt, Rinehart and Winston, 1969, p. 412.

vertent sources. As Fox points out, each type of source has its advantages and disadvantages. The deliberate source is concerned directly with the event at hand but is, for that very reason, somewhat subjective. The inadvertent source is objective, but is being used for something other than was intended.

Sampling of Data

The critical consumer and producer of historical research must be alert to the adequacy of the sampling of the data. As mentioned, researchers often use an overabundance of secondary sources and too few primary sources. In addition, occasionally the sample will be biased. This can occur for two reasons. First, only a portion of the data relevant to any particular study is available. One has to try and determine whether the data that have survived are biased. They probably would be, for example, if a researcher were attempting to determine what proportion of the studies conducted in educational research produced statistically significant results since research with nonsignificant results tends not to get published. Second, there is also usually a sampling of the available data, and the sample could be biased. An historical researcher, consciously or unconsciously, may sample data that are more in agreement with his hypotheses. Most historical researchers try very hard to adequately sample the available data and usually, within their report, discuss how good the available data are and whether a significant portion of the original relevant data has been lost.

Evaluating Data

The historical researcher should be cognizant of two aspects related to evaluating data: external criticism and internal criticism. The purpose of external criticism is to determine whether the record or remain is authentic. Is the evidence really what it appears, or has a forgery or fraud been perpetrated? Most historical documents used in educational research can withstand external criticism quite well—forgeries are unlikely and the authenticity of the records is usually established. Internal criticism is concerned with establishing the meaning and worth of the data contained in the document. This is a much harder task. Such aspects as the competence, integrity, and the motivation of the original author must be considered. A good historical study should report the internal criticism conducted by the researcher, and his views as to the adequacy of the data in this respect.

Examples of Historical Research

The following four articles are reports of historical research. They vary considerably in length, style, and topic. For each article you should be observant of all the points raised in the introduction on evaluating research. You should also consider the following questions.

---

1. Did the author allow personal bias to influence his sampling and/or interpretation of the data?
2. Was the source material mostly primary or secondary?
3. Did the author evaluate his data adequately with respect to internal and external criticism?
4. How well did the author synthesize and analyze his information?

THE CHILD IN PEDAGOGY AND CULTURE:
Concepts of American Preadolescence as Revealed in Teaching Theories and as Related to the Culture, 1900–1914*

ANNABEL LEE

Recipients of the Pi Lambda Theta fellowships are required to make a report for publication on the dissertation for which the award was made. Following is an abstract of a doctoral dissertation submitted by Annabel Lee, to the University of Washington in Seattle. This report fulfills requirements in effect when the fellowship was granted.

The Problem

The problem for the study was the establishment of interrelationships among (a) selected concepts of the nature of the preadolescent child, (b) teaching theories, and (c) the culture in which they both appear. The setting selected was America in the Progressive Era, between 1900 and 1914. The method has been that of historical research. The concepts of child nature used for comparing methodologies and relating them to prevalent ideas of the culture were creativity, free moral choice, and the individual in his society. These particular concepts were also viewed as extensions of the great philosophical dialectic between individual freedom and determinism.

Resources

Materials in education written between 1900 and World War I provided the primary resources for the research. If the relationship of educational thought to the thought trends of the times were to be established, it was essential to view the beliefs, theories, conditions, and problems—the whole ideological world of education—as nearly as possible through the eyes of the people who were there. Materials employed were:

*From "The Child in Pedagogy and Culture: Concepts of American Preadolescence as Revealed in Teaching Theories and Related to the Culture," 1900–1914, by Annabel Lee; *Educational Horizons*, 46:3 (1968), pp. 134–140. Reprinted with permission.

1. The yearbooks of the National Society for the Scientific Study of Education, appearing twice a year, from 1901 to 1914.[1]

2. The *Cyclopedia of Education*, edited by Paul Monroe.[2]

3. Histories of education published between 1900 and 1914.[3,4]

4. Books presenting general educational principles.[5,6]

5. Books on specific methods.[7,8,9]

6. Books written by persons who between 1900 and 1914 were in various combinations analyzing the American philosophic and educational scene, studying the child, and formulating innovative teaching theories.[10,11,12,13,14,15,16]

In order to determine what the major intellectual and cultural trends were for the nation as a whole during these same years, reference was also made to secondary sources—general, intellectual, cultural, and philosophic histories, written throughout the twentieth century until the present.[17,18,19,20,21,22,23,24]

[1]*Yearbooks of the National Society for the Scientific Study of Education,* I–XIII (Chicago: University of Chicago Press, 1901–13).

[2]Paul Monroe, editor, *A Cyclopedia of Education* 5 vols. (New York: Macmillan, 1911).

[3]Samuel Chester Parker, *A Textbook in the History of Modern Elementary Education* (Boston: Ginn, 1912).

[4]Frank Pierrepont Graves, *A History of Education* (New York: Macmillan, 1913).

[5]William Estabrook Chancellor, *A Theory of Motives, Ideals and Values* (Boston: Houghton Mifflin, 1907).

[6]Ernest Norton Henderson, *A Textbook in the Principles of Education* (New York: Macmillan, 1910).

[7]Edmund Burke Huey, *The History and Pedagogy of Reading* (New York: Macmillan, 1915).

[8]Colin A. Scott, *Social Education* (Boston: Ginn, 1908).

[9]Walter Sargent, *Fine and Industrial Arts in Elementary Schools* (Boston: Ginn, 1912).

[10]John Dewey, *School and Society* (Chicago: University of Chicago Press, 1899).

[11]William James, *Talks to Teachers* (New York: W. W. Norton, 1899).

[12]Edward L. Thorndike, *Principles of Teaching Based on Psychology* (New York: A. G. Seiler, 1906).

[13]Charles E. Strickland and Charles Burgess, editors, *Health, Growth and Heredity, G. Stanley Hall on Natural Education* (New York: Teachers College, Columbia University, 1965).

[14]Amy Eliza Tanner, *The Child* (Chicago: Rand McNally, 1904).

[15]Ellwood P. Cubberley, *Changing Conceptions of Education* (Boston: Houghton Mifflin, 1920).

[16]Willystine Goodsell, *The Conflict of Naturalism and Humanism* (New York: Teachers College, Columbia University, 1910).

[17]Harry Elmer Barnes, *An Intellectual and Cultural History of the Western World* (Rayway, New Jersey: Cordon, 1937).

[18]Theodore Brameld, *Philosophies of Education in Cultural Perspective* (New York: Dryden Press, 1955).

[19]John S. Brubacher, *A History of the Problems of Education* (New York: McGraw-Hill, 1947).

[20]Freeman R. Butts and Lawrence A. Cremin, *A History of American Education in American Culture* (New York: Holt, Rinehart and Winston, 1953).

[21]Henry Steele Commager, *The American Mind* (New Haven: Yale University Press, 1950).

[22]Merle Curti, *Social Ideas of American Educators* (Paterson, New Jersey: Littlefield, Adams & Co., 1963).

[23]Richard Hofstadter, *Social Darwinism in American Thought* (New York: George Braziller, 1959).

[24]John Herman Randall, *The Making of the Modern Mind* (Boston: Houghton Mifflin, 1926).

Procedure

The procedure for the study has been essentially the following:

1. Materials in elementary education which were being written and presumably read by educators and teachers between about 1900 and 1914 were gathered, surveyed, and examined.

2. After a period of reading and analysis, the principal lines of educational thought bearing on educational theory and practice during the time were identified.

3. The aspects of the historical and cultural background were sought that made each theory seem logical and right to its adherents.

4. In each theory the beliefs implicitly or explicitly expressed as to creativity, free moral choice, and the individual in his society were searched out.

5. After the general rationale and the related selected concepts of the child's nature had been formulated for each educational theory, the question was asked: "How did these concepts parallel broader ideologies of 1900–14, or those of the times in which the ideas first arose?" To attempt to find answers to this question, educational, cultural, social, and philosophic histories were perused.

6. The central problem regarding school theory and child nature as functions of the culture was kept in mind for each principal division of the study. Within the limits of time, space, and the capacities of the student, answers to this problem have been synthesized for each theory in turn.

7. The conclusion was a reassessment of the material brought together in the study (a) in terms of the original research problem, (b) as highlights of the findings, and (c) as possible significance of the findings.

Findings

Eight teaching theories were discovered to exist in educational writings between 1900 and 1914. Four originated before Darwin's *The Origin of Species*[25] appeared in 1859. These were Mental Discipline, the Hegelianism of William T. Harris, Herbartianism, and Froebelianism. Four theories appearing after Darwinism had entered American thought, and built on assumptions derived from evolution, were those of G. Stanley Hall, Edward Thorndike, William James, and John Dewey.

It was confirmed that each of the eight teaching methodologies stated or assumed different characteristics for the child. In general terms, the formal disciplinarians believed that the child gained mental and moral power by exer-

[25]Charles Darwin, *The Origin of Species* (London: J. Murray, 1859).

cising his inborn faculties; the Hegelians held that the child was spiritually evolving by a dialectic process in a universe also evolving upward; Herbartians theorized that the child developed by incorporating idea fragments, or reals, into his apperceptive mass; Froebelian kindergartners held that the child was a self-active being, growing toward the self-conscious "Absolute Unity" whence came both man and nature; followers of G. Stanley Hall were sure that the child was recapitulating the evolutionary history of the human race, and that his learning must conform to the genetic sequence of his development; adherents of Thorndike saw a child with a mind comparable to that of an animal in that he learned in near mechanical fashion by connecting responses to stimuli; the child perceived by James learned through motor activity, and judged ideas and acts by results; and disciples of Dewey were convinced that the child became a human being only by interacting in a social community, and judged the worth of his acts by their social results. With such different children to teach, it is not surprising that educators disagreed on methodology.

The backgrounds against which the theories and the associated concepts of child nature appeared also differed. The stern and duty-bound mental discipline had been carried along in Western culture since medieval times. Hegelianism, Herbartianism, and Froebelianism had originated in a Germany permeated by Newtonian science, philosophic idealism, and the belief that cultures were in various stages of spiritual evolution. All four of these theories had been changed somewhat through interaction with the American culture and adaptations by disciples, but, as they were used in the schools, they still were based on the willing submissiveness of the child to authority and his place in life—with little or no admission of free choice or creativity until the child could be depended upon to obey the laws and make "right" choices. These seemed to accord with Calvinist and fundamentalist religious values and, thus, found response with a large proportion of the nation's people.

Nevertheless, at the time under study, American culture was in a state of change and resistance to change. The Industrial Revolution was underway. Darwinism interpreted into human evolution had divided, and had developed into two schools of social theory. Herbert Spencer and William Graham Sumner, building on concepts of Newtonian science as well as Darwinism, held that natural laws of competition and survival of the fittest were advancing man's welfare, his "evolution." Man's part was to learn and observe the laws, but not to interfere with their operation; this became known as social or conservative Darwinism. Though conservative Darwinism was still widely held by 1900, Lester Ward, followed by scientists, social scientists, and intellectuals, had proposed a second interpretation of Darwinism: that man's mind was a unique evolutionary tool which permitted him to control and direct his own evolution. The method was that of the new experimental sciences, replacing Newtonian science; Ward's theory, with its applications, became known as reform or progressive Darwinism.

The second group of four educational theories was based on premises of

Darwinism. Hall's child recapitulated early stages of the race; Thorndike's child had a mind related to his animal forebears. These two are identified mainly in the conservative Darwinism classification. The children of James and Dewey learned through motor activity, because motor activity had preceded mental activity in the racial development. In the reform Darwinism pattern, James also saw pragmatism as a device for man's continuing evolutionary development, a sort of survival of the fittest ideas. Dewey agreed with James, and he had the genius to apply Jamesean insights to man's condition in the industrial revolution, which Dewey recognized as a new and continuing condition.

The six theories which were largely conservative were found to be widely used in the schools and well represented in the writings of professional educators of the times. The two that represented the new philosophy of change allied with reform Darwinism, social planning, and political progressivism were of great interest to intellectuals, both in school and out, but they found limited support among the considerable majority of the people and their teachers.

Summary and Conclusions

Seven of the eight educational theories studied were invented by individual men, to take specific account of what they considered true and significant advances in science and philosophy. One theory, mental discipline, was in accord with long established religious and scholastic tenets. The culture, the men, the theories, and the concepts of child nature, thus, appear inseparable. Certain analytic constructions are however possible:

1. *Although the theories reflect individual insights, they were culturally centered.* Undoubtedly the theories reflected differing temperaments, backgrounds, and idea-sets of the men who devised them. For example, Froebel's introspection of his own mystical nature meant quite as much as the search for broad scientific principles which he had accepted from his age. The preoccupation of Hall with Darwinian paleontology is another personal view which became educational theory; Dewey's over-riding concern with the social disruptions of the industrial revolution is another.

What prevents these personal interpretations from being seen as merely idiosyncratic is the proposition, confirmed by the anthropologist, that all inventions, of ideas as well as of things, are culturally rooted. An invention appears when the culture has produced the elements that make it possible, and when the time is ripe for it. This is not to imply determinism, but only that "there is a definable relation between a specific condition of a given culture and the making of a particular invention."[26] How much credit goes to the personal genius of the inventor, and how much to the cultural elements with which he has to work is difficult to establish. But the anthropologist affirms that the more

[26]A. L. Koreber, *Anthropology* (New York: Harcourt, 1948), p. 364.

any invention is analyzed, "the larger do the antecedents loom, and by comparison the less outstanding does the new step or increment appear. This is contrary to the popular view, which condenses a complex and gradual process into a single dramatic act by one individual, with whom we can identify ourselves emotionally."[27]

This being true, beliefs about the child and methods for teaching him were confined closely to the scientific, social, and philosophic ideas which had developed as integral parts of subcultural units of the total American environment. The fact that the theories of mental discipline were not identifiable inventions, but accretions with beginnings in the Middle Ages only confirms the interrelationship of school, culture, and the child belonging to both.

2. *The older accepted ideas were tenacious.* As an instance, although scientists and intellectuals were certain that Darwinian evolution and experimental science were confirmed by evidence and experience, and that the great principles of the "Newtonian World Machine" must be challenged and altered by new knowledge, the "people" clung to value systems of which Newtonian science was firmly a part. Darwinism challenged literal interpretations of the Bible; fundamentalists ignored or rejected Darwinism. In the schools, the theory systems that were long established and well understood were mental discipline, Hegelianism, and Froebelianism. These stressed the child's moral responsibility and his acceptance of his place in his society—all in accord with Newtonian laws, with religious subservience, and with Spencer's social Darwinism. Herbartianism and the theories of G. Stanley Hall had both reached their peaks of influence in the 1890's. Their "scientific" approach to education plus their areas of agreement with the older accepted theories, and their support of the basic conformity of the people had allowed educational thought quickly to absorb elements from their teachings; these elements persisted, even after their "scientific" foundations were discounted by other discoveries. Again, the anthropologist places this persistence phenomenon in broader perspective.

> A large part of mankind just is fundamentally conservative—which means that they like their culture and their personal stake in it. This personal stake and its rewards might well be bigger for the average man, and he is likely to be trying to make it a bit bigger, but mostly he does so without any notion of changing the rules, except perhaps at a spot or two. This is not a statement of what should be, but an attempt to summarize the attitude of most people, primitive, barbarous, and highly advanced, throughout history and all over the earth.[28]

The general adherence to the accustomed and accepted produced two noteworthy results: new ideas, even if they were to gain eventual ascendancy, did not replace old receding ones in the culture; rather the new and old existed

[27]*Ibid.*, p. 360.
[28]*Ibid.*, p. 346.

side by side, or in conflict. In such a situation, it would have been unfair to tag the school as peculiarly guilty of "cultural lag." The schools could not move far ahead of the cultural sophistication of the people who hired the teachers, or of the teachers themselves, who in the years under study were little set apart from the "people." The lag was a phenomenon of society itself.

3. *The prevalent physical and biological sciences of the time set the directions for the social sciences and the philosophies.* The receding (yet persisting) sciences were based on Newtonian principles and conservative social Darwinism. The advancing ones were reform Darwinism and experimental science. Reasoning from first principles to establish what course nature would follow differed sharply from experimenting and measuring to see how nature operated, in order to control it. The inherent philosophic split was an important theme of the study: determinism, conformity to what was, versus freedom of the individual to make a difference and, in some degree, to turn the environment to his own purposes. Each of the two scientific positions had its cluster of accompanying ideologies. For the deductive sciences, there were Spencer's social Darwinism, economic laissez-faire, and the religious beliefs that stressed humble acceptance of one's lot on earth in order to merit reward in afterlife. In agreement with the inductive sciences were reform Darwinism, pragmatism or the problem-solving method, and the social gospels which stressed improving the lot of men on earth rather than waiting till after death. As to school theories, by the measures of creativity, free moral choice, and the individual in his society employed in the study, the weighting was strongly toward the conservative or deterministic end of the scale. No theory was completely at one end of the range. They fell between in various combinations.

Permitting almost no freedom or unpredictability to the child were Hegelianism, Herbartianism with its laws of apperceptive learning, and Thorndike's stimulus-response learning. Permitting almost full freedom were the pragmatism of James and the social instrumentalism of Dewey. In an inverted way, the child of the disciplinarians, through rigorous "disciplining" of his will, was granted full freedom, in which he was expected to choose, through the use of his reasoning faculty, moral virtue and duty. Hall's child lost his racial freedom in his youth period, and learned to conform to society; limited freedom through law was granted the Froebelian child. Thus, the reverberations of the scientific thought of each age can be identified.

4. *The law-centered world was giving way to a man-centered world.* As long as man's first purpose in life was the following of moral, social, or universal laws far above and outside himself, he did not need to ask direction, because it seemed to be established for him. Within narrow limits, he must accept his legalistic world as it was. When, however, man found himself in on the creative act of controlling his own destiny, he began seeking his own welfare, though it was not easy to determine what his best interests were. Veblen, the economist; Holmes, the jurist; Robinson, the historian; Dewey, the philosopher; and the other rebels against formalism listed by social historians were proposing that no

longer was man merely subservient to the laws of his society. Rather, the laws should serve man and his purposes. The Progressive Movement in its varied forms was a first gathering of momentum toward a man-centered world.[29,30]

In this setting, the often criticized freedoms and child-centered schools of G. Stanley Hall, Colonel Francis Parker, and John Dewey seemed to find a natural habitat. Lawrence A. Cremin describes as "truly Copernican" the effects of the changes in emphasis from "the school with its well-defined content and purposes" to "children with their particular backgrounds and needs."[31] Cremin's term could equally well apply to the change of emphasis from the "Great Universal" of the gradually evolving society of Hegel and Spencer, to men, with their particular backgrounds and needs. Again, a common trend is seen drawing together the school, society, and changed concepts of the human individual.

5. *The fragmentation of the American culture involved the schools in burdens and tensions.* A number of overlapping subdivisions of American society figured in various relationships to the schools throughout the study. Among these were the rural farmers, the scientists, the intellectuals, the reformers, the educators who wrote books, the factory owners, the genteel middle class, the slum dwellers, the immigrants, the "masses," the religious fundamentalists, the social Darwinists, the reform Darwinists, and of course the teachers and children. Altogether, American society was well delineated by Theodore Brameld's description of a cultural totality carrying many smaller totalities within it, "smaller clusters of institutional and behavioral experience, which, while capable of differentiation, are also interwoven within larger clusters at innumerable points."[32]

To the degree that subgroups are integrated, they have certain recognized characteristics. They tend to consider outsiders in error because they differ from themselves, in a manner comparable to primitive tribes who consider themselves "men," and outsiders as "less-than-human."[33] Such groups want not only to maintain themselves and their ways of thinking and doing, but to increase their numbers and power. In the years under study, the school was the accepted means for perpetuating cultural values, hence each group wanted its special interests to be represented in the curriculum. Not only was this true, for example, of the Herbartians who wanted moral character taught by joining "reals" to the apperceptive mass, and the industrialists who pressed for indus-

[29]Morton White, *Social Thought in America* (New York: Viking Press, 1949).

[30]Christopher Lasch, *The New Radicalism in America, 1889–1963* (New York: Alfred A. Knopf, 1965).

[31]Lawrence A. Cremin, *The Transformation of the School* (New York: Alfred A. Knopf, 1961), p. 104.

[32]Theodore B. H. Brameld, *Philosophies of Education in Cultural Perspective* (New York: Dryden Press, 1955), p. 43.

[33]Margaret Mead, "Our Educational Emphases in Primitive Perspective," *Education and Culture,* ed. George D. Spindler (New York: Holt, Rinehart and Winston, 1963), p. 312.

trial training, but it also included the segment of the intellectuals known as the social reformers or instrumentalists. These last were so highly literate that the historian seeing their shelves of books, is apt to forget the less articulate, but more populous, groups who were also concerned with the schools. Whether or not theirs was the way of salvation for society, the reformers were in this period one of many pressure groups who wanted children to learn their particular points of view in the schools. The teacher, often intellectually naive, frequently found himself at the focal point of differences between groups and was pulled at by whatever subgroups were dominant in his community.

In summation, between 1900 and 1914, the factors that changed cultural patterns affected what men believed about themselves and their children. Scholarly men in university research centers, upon finding new "scientific truths," and cultural assumptions about children, sought educational theory and practice that would conform to their discoveries. During these years, the nation's elementary classrooms were slow about absorbing the new theories, but this was understandable, considering the essential conservatism of most subgroups of the public. If classroom teachers were also mainly conservative, it is to be remembered that they were selected and hired by conservative local communities.

There are numerous parallels between the conservative-progressive tensions in the changing first decade of the century, and the conservative-progressive tensions of the present; most are too obvious to repeat. In the Progressive Era, argument over the schools could not abate as long as there were shifting circumstances and values among the numerous segments of society itself. It seems apparent that until there is unanimity about the nature of the child, there can hardly be agreement about method. In a changing multi-culture, such unanimity appears impossible.

Complexities abound for the teacher. Educational research which is carried out for one cultural subgroup or during one decade may produce results which are inappropriate for another group or time. If the teacher is to avoid drifting at the mercy of random social pressures, he must be sure of his own identity and beliefs, as he balances his relationships with the cultural subgroups whose children he teaches. If he is to avoid professional stagnation, he must engage in perpetual search for the nature of this year's children in this year's segmented society. How else can he judge the suitability of materials and methods to use in his daily lessons?

In a cumbersome, fascinating, pedagogical merry-go-round, the teacher does his work in the faith that his performance in the classroom makes a difference to the child, and thus affects society. But a changing society produces ever new children to send to the schools, and teachers are often caught off guard by the altered concepts of who the new children are. Perhaps if society and educators understood this circular dilemma more profoundly, there would be fewer mutual recriminations, and greater willingness to work together.

comments and questions _____

    1. Would it not be nice if all authors of historical research stated their problem and described their procedure as clearly as Lee?

    2. Do you feel that Lee has adequately answered her problem? Why? Why not?

    3. In the section entitled "Findings," should Lee have presented more documentation?

    4. Should the "Procedure" section have been described more fully? (Perhaps we are being too critical of Lee and a little unfair to her inasmuch as this report was only an abstract of her dissertation.)

SOCIOECONOMIC INFLUENCES ON SCHOOL ATTENDANCE:
A Study of a Canadian County in 1871[*]

FRANK T. DENTON and PETER J. GEORGE

I. Introduction

A recent special issue of the *Quarterly*[1] was devoted to "Education and Social Change in English-Speaking Canada." In his interesting and impressive contribution to this issue, Michael B. Katz suggested that many hypotheses[2] concerning the determinants of school attendance may be tested by employing data relating to "the status and structure of the family and household" contained in the manuscript census. "By starting with the census one may study the gross patterns of attendance among the children of any group, religious, ethnic, occupational, or any other into which the census material can be arranged."[3]

This paper reports on the use of a methodological approach different from that of Katz and summarizes some results that we have obtained recently from an analysis of historical census records.[4] More specifically, the paper reports on an application of modern cross-section regression techniques to records of individuals drawn from the manuscript of the 1871 population census, with the object of assessing, in a systematic fashion, the influence on school

[*]Reprinted from *History of Education Quarterly*, 14:2 (Summer 1974), pp. 223–234 by permission of author and publisher.

[1]*History of Education Quarterly*, 12, 3 (Fall 1972).

[2]For example, "school attendance varied inversely with the proportion of Irish immigrants in a community . . . (and) . . . directly with the proportion of the workforce employed in professional and commercial occupations." Michael B. Katz, "Who Went to School?", *History of Education Quarterly* 12, 3 (Fall 1972), 435.

[3]*Ibid.*, p. 437

[4]This project has been supported by the McMaster University Urban Research Unit, and has focussed on variations in family size and school attendance. Various aspects of this research project are discussed in Frank T. Denton and Peter J. George, "An Exploratory Statistical Analysis of Some Socioeconomic Characteristics of Families in Hamilton, Ontario, 1871," in *Social History*, 5 (April 1970), 16–44, and "The Influence of Socioeconomic Variables on Family Size in Wentworth County, Ontario, 1871: A Statistical Analysis of Historical Micro-Data," forthcoming in the *Canadian Review of Sociology and Anthropology*, (November 1973).

45

attendance of parental birthplace, age, religion, ethnic origin, occupation, and other variables for which some influence might reasonably be hypothesized.

The area chosen for the study is Wentworth County, a county in Ontario which includes the City of Hamilton and neighbouring municipalities. Wentworth County was selected for two reasons. First, it was a region of old settlement dating from the 1780s yet, at the same time, of recent immigration, especially into the urban industrial and service sectors. Secondly, it represented the juxtaposition of a rural, agricultural area with an area of urban, industrial character. Thus, if afforded the opportunity of studying a population with a wide range of social and economic characteristics. To anticipate the results it appears that the effects of many of these characteristics on school attendance may, in fact, have been considerably less than Katz's findings would suggest.

II.   The Sample of Census Returns

Wentworth County consisted of three enumeration districts for the purposes of the 1871 Census: Wentworth South (District 22), Wentworth North (District 23), and the City of Hamilton (District 24). Wentworth South was rural. So was Wentworth North, except for the town of Dundas which, together with Hamilton, comprised the urban area. The total population of the county in 1871 was reported as 57,599. The urban population was reported as 29,851 and the rural population as 27,748.[5]

The returns for individuals in the 1871 Census were made available recently on microfilm by the Public Archives of Canada.[6] The microfilm records are in a form which is convenient for sampling, since households are numbered in order of their visitation by the enumerator and individuals within each household are listed in sequence. For each individual, the enumerator recorded demographic and socioeconomic information,[7] and occasionally made notes on characteristics which he regarded as unusual and worthy of comment.

A sample of enumerated dwellings was drawn for purposes of this study, the sampling ratio being ten percent in Hamilton and twenty percent in the rest of the county.[8] In order to minimize the influence of unusual family

---

[5]Government of Canada, *Census of Canada 1870–71*, Volume I (Ottawa 1873), pp. 8–9.

[6]The individual returns for Wentworth County are contained in Ontario Census 1871, Public Archives Microfilm Reel Nos. C-615 and C-616.

[7]Surname and given names, sex, age, month of birth for children born within the previous twelve months, country or province of birth, religion, ethnic origin, profession, occupation or trade, marital status, whether or not married in the last twelve months, whether or not going to school, literacy, and infirmities.

[8]The sampling was what is known as "random systematic." That is to say, a random starting point from 1 to 10 was chosen in the case of Hamilton and from 1 to 5 in the case of the rest of the county. This defined the initial household in each case. Thereafter, every 10th or every 5th household was selected.

circumstances on the results, only "normal" families were included in the sample. (A "normal" family is defined for our purposes as one in which the husband and wife were both present, and the husband was in the range 20 to 59 years of age, inclusive.)[9]

The sampling yielded 1,100 "normal" families in Wentworth County. Of this total, 429 families were located in the urban areas of Hamilton and Dundas, and the remaining 671 in the rural areas of Wentworth South and North. The 1,100 "normal" families contained 1,016 children from ten to sixteen years of age, and these constitute the observations on which the analysis of school attendance is based.

III. Construction of an Occupational Classification System

The development of a satisfactory system for classifying fathers according to occupation presented difficulties. Information on fathers' incomes and levels of education would have been highly desirable but was not available from the 1871 Census. In the absence of such information, we have attempted to use the reported occupational data in such a way as to represent income-education effects, at least crudely. A socioeconomic index of 320 occupations in the 1961 Census of Canada has been developed by Bernard R. Blishen,[10] the ordering of occupations being represented as a function of income and education. In the absence of anything comparable for the latter part of the nineteenth century, this index was adapted for use with the 1871 Census to produce a rough classification of reported 1871 occupations into five categories, ranging from high-income-education occupations, at one end, to low-income, unskilled occupations, at the other.[11]

[9]By far the largest proportion of dwellings remaining in the sample were single-family dwellings. However, dwellings containing two or more families were occasionally encountered and it was decided to include two or more "normal" families living in the same dwelling only if they were enumerated separately. Once the decision rule to include only "normal" families enumerated separately had been invoked, there still remained some difficulties, with a few observations — problems of partial illegibility of surnames and given names, incomplete returns for the characteristics of a husband or wife in a family, apparent transcription errors in the recording of answers by enumerators, children of different surnames from the husband and wife, etc. Families were discarded from the sample when illegibility precluded the interpretation of data pertinent to the study, when the returns were incomplete for either the husband or wife, or when the returns were apparently incorrect in some respects. Families with children of different surnames were retained in the sample, and any children not over sixteen years were placed in a separate category referred to as "other dependents sixteen years and under."

[10]Bernard R. Blishen, "A Socioeconomic Index for Occupations in Canada", *Canadian Review of Sociology and Anthropology*, 4 (1967), 41–53. Also see Blishen, "The Construction and Use of an Occupational Class Scale," *Canadian Journal of Economics and Political Science*, 24 (November 1958), 519–531.

[11]Whereas Blishen calculated an index of the socioeconomic rank of occupations to two decimal points, we are mainly concerned with defining broad groups and have employed summary

IV.   Regression Analysis of School Attendance

The 1,016 observations on children from ten to sixteen years of age were analysed by means of regression techniques. These techniques were employed to study the extent to which attendance or nonattendance at school in 1871 was related to "demographic" variables (age and sex of child, total number of children in the family, age of father), to differences in father's occupation, to differences in the religion, birthplace, and ethnic origin of both father and mother, and to basic urban-rural and farm-nonfarm differences. Results are presented in Tables 1 and 2. The regression equation estimated with all variables included, and the results of t-tests for individual variables are presented in Table 1. Table 2 provides the results of F-tests for groups of variables. The definitions of the variables and the symbols used are listed at the end of the paper.

The analysis makes use of "dummy variables"—variables that have value one if particular conditions are satisfied and value zero if they are not. The extensive use of such variables is now common in modern survey analysis but equally applicable to analyses of historical data.[12] For example, we define a variable BFI and specify it to have value one if the father was born in England, value zero otherwise; we define a variable RM3 and specify it to have value one if the mother's religion is Presbyterian, value zero otherwise. Except for those that pertain to age of child or of father and to number of children in the family, all variables used in the analysis are of this type. The dependent variable itself, GTS, is a dummy variable, having value one if a child is attending school and value zero otherwise.

The regression analysis employs sets of such variables—a set for father's occupation, a set for mother's religion, and so on. A difficulty which arises immediately has to do with the fact that the dummy variables for each set always add to one. This makes necessary the imposition of certain restrictions on the regression equations in order to avoid a well-known problem in regres-

---

categories with arbitrary bounds. We certainly do not regard the 1961 occupational categorization as strictly appropriate for 1871; rather, it represents merely a rough initial guide for classifying 1871 occupations, the application of which has been tempered in many cases by our "judgment."

It may be noted that Katz used a different approach in devising a scale of occupations which he believed to be representative of mid-nineteenth century conditions. See Michael B. Katz, "Social Structure in Hamilton, Ontario," in Stephan Thernstrom and Richard Sennett, eds. *Nineteenth Century Cities: Essays in the New Urban History* (New Haven, 1969), p. 25, and "Occupational Classification in History," in *The Journal of Interdisciplinary History*, 3 (Summer 1972), 63–88.

[12]A general discussion of the use of dummy variables in regression analysis can be found in a number of places. A treatment that is particularly relevant to the present analysis is given in Emanuel Melichar, "Least-Squares Analysis of Economic Survey Data," *Proceedings of the Business and Economic Statistics Section of the American Statistical Association,* (1965), 373–385.

DEFINITIONS OF VARIABLES USED IN ANALYSIS OF SCHOOL ATTENDANCE

GTS   — dummy variable = 1 if child goes to school; 0 otherwise
AGEC   — age of child expressed as difference in years from sample mean
AGEC2   — square of AGEC
SEX   — dummy variable = 1 if child is male; 0 otherwise
CHILD   — number of children in family with family surname
AGEF   — age of father in years (actual age, not difference from mean)
OCCF   — occupation of father: dummy variables based on index scale
                 OCCF3 = 1 if index 50.00–59.99; 0 otherwise
                 OCCF4 = 1 if index 40.00–49.99; 0 otherwise
                 OCCF5 = 1 if index 30.00–39.99; 0 otherwise
                 OCCF6 = 1 if index less than 30.00; 0 otherwise
                 OCCF7 = 1 if index 60.00 or greater; 0 otherwise
RF   — religion of father: dummy variables
                 RF1 = 1 if Church of England; 0 otherwise
                 RF2 = 1 if Roman Catholic; 0 otherwise
                 RF3 = 1 if Presbyterian; 0 otherwise
                 RF4 = 1 if Baptist; 0 otherwise
                 RF5 = 1 if Methodist; 0 otherwise
                 RF6 = 1 if any other religious denomination;0 otherwise
RM   — religion of mother: dummy variables defined in the same way as corresponding variables for father — RM1, RM2, RM3, RM4, RM5, RM6
BF   — birthplace of father: dummy variables
                 BF1 = 1 if England; 0 otherwise
                 BF2 = 1 if Ireland; 0 otherwise
                 BF3 = 1 if Scotland; 0 otherwise
                 BF4 = 1 if U.S.A.; 0 otherwise
                 BF5 = 1 if Canada; 0 otherwise
                 BF8 = 1 if any other birthplace; 0 otherwise
BM   — birthplace of mother: dummy variables defined in the same way as corresponding variables for father — BM1, BM2, BM3, BM4, BM5, BM8
OF   — ethnic origin of father: dummy variables
                 OF1 = 1 if English; 0 otherwise
                 OF2 = 1 if Irish; 0 otherwise
                 OF3 = 1 if Scottish; 0 otherwise
                 OF4 = 1 if German; 0 otherwise
                 OF9 = 1 if any other ethnic origin; 0 otherwise
OM   — ethnic origin of mother: dummy variables defined in the same way as corresponding variables for father — OM1, OM2, OM3, OM4, OM9
URBAN — dummy variable = 1 if family lives in an urban area; 0 otherwise
FARM   — dummy variable = 1 if family head is a farmer; 0 otherwise

sion analysis and to permit the equations to be estimated. This requirement we have satisfied by following a common practice and omitting one dummy variable from each set in the specification of the regression equations. The category represented by the variable excluded from a particular set is then to be re-

**REGRESSION EQUATION FOR SCHOOL ATTENDANCE AND RESULTS
OF SIGNIFICANCE TESTS (TWO-TAIL T-TESTS) ON COEFFICIENTS OF
INDIVIDUAL VARIABLES (DEPENDENT VARIABLE GTS;
39 INDEPENDENT VARIABLES; 1016 OBSERVATIONS)**

table 1

Independent variable	Regression coefficient	t-ratio	IS COEFFICIENT SIGNIFICANTLY DIFFERENT FROM ZERO AT THE –		
			1% level?	*5% level?*	*10% level?*
1. Constant term	.7946	—	—	—	—
2. AGEC	−.0864	13.18	YES	YES	YES
3. AGEC2	−.0202	5.57	YES	YES	YES
4. SEX	.0099	.40	NO	NO	NO
5. CHILD	.0045	.69	NO	NO	NO
6. AGEF	.0005	.26	NO	NO	NO
7. OCCF3	.2152	3.00	YES	YES	YES
8. OCCF4	.1352	2.71	YES	YES	YES
9. OCCF5	.0525	1.32	NO	NO	NO
10. OCCF7	.1466	1.68	NO	NO	YES
11. RF6	.2371	.94	NO	NO	NO
12. RF2	−.0017	.02	NO	NO	NO
13. RF3	−.1745	1.50	NO	NO	NO
14. RF4	−.0972	.79	NO	NO	NO
15. RF5	−.0952	.92	NO	NO	NO
16. RM6	−.2701	1.07	NO	NO	NO
17. RM2	.0014	.01	NO	NO	NO
18. RM3	.0945	.81	NO	NO	NO
19. RM4	.0960	.79	NO	NO	NO
20. RM5	.0185	.18	NO	NO	NO
21. BF1	.0337	.64	NO	NO	NO
22. BF2	.0713	1.08	NO	NO	NO
23. BF3	.0316	.42	NO	NO	NO
24. BF4	.1874	3.01	YES	YES	YES
25. BF8	−.1004	.80	NO	NO	NO
26. BM1	−.1131	2.25	NO	YES	YES
27. BM2	−.0378	.71	NO	NO	NO
28. BM3	−.1270	1.88	NO	NO	YES
29. BM4	−.1172	1.64	NO	NO	NO
30. BM8	.1186	.94	NO	NO	NO
31. OF9	−.1857	1.96	NO	NO	YES
32. OF2	−.0852	1.11	NO	NO	NO

Independent variable	Regression coefficient	t-ratio	IS COEFFICIENT SIGNIFICANTLY DIFFERENT FROM ZERO AT THE –		
			1% level?	5% level?	10% level?
33. OF3	.0536	.71	NO	NO	NO
34. OF4	−.0172	.26	NO	NO	NO
35. OM9	.0154	.16	NO	NO	NO
36. OM2	.0017	.03	NO	NO	NO
37. OM3	.0695	1.00	NO	NO	NO
38. OM4	−.0200	.30	NO	NO	NO
39. URBAN	−.0722	2.15	NO	YES	YES
40. FARM	.0636	1.36	NO	NO	NO

Note: t-ratio is ratio of regression coefficient to its estimated standard error; coefficient of determination for the regression equation is .2484 before correction for degrees of freedom (R^2) and .2183 after correction ($\bar{R}^2$); omitted dummy variables are OCCF5, RF1, RM1, BF5, BM5, OF1, and OM1.

garded as a reference category, and the coefficient of any other variable in the same set is to be interpreted as the difference between the original coefficient of that variable and the original coefficient of the variable that has been excluded. Thus, for example, the variable BF5 has been omitted from the set of birthplace variables; if β_5 is thought of as the original coefficient of this variable and β_1 as the original coefficient of the variable BF1, then .0337, the regression coefficient of BFI reported in row 21 of Table 1, is to be interpreted as an estimate of $\beta_1 - \beta_5$.

The standard t-test can be applied to individual variables in a regression equation such as the one in Table 1 in order to determine whether their influences are statistically significant (i.e., whether their estimated coefficients differ significantly from zero). However, in the type of regression analysis with which we are concerned here, it is often of greater interest to consider the variables in groups rather than individually, and to test for significance the total contribution of each group, as a whole. There exists a form of the F-test for this purpose [13] and the results reported in Table 2 are based on this test.

Among the "demographic" variables (DEM), age of child is seen to be

[13]See Melichar, "Least Squares Analysis of Economic Survey Data," for a discussion of this test. When the dependent variable is a dummy variable the assumption of normality of errors in the regression equation is violated and the F and t-tests, which are based on this assumption, must be regarded as approximate only. For a discussion of the problem, see the note by Orley Ashenfelter in Appendix A of William G. Bowen and T. Aldrich Finegan, *The Economics of Labor Force Participation* (Princeton, 1969), pp. 644–648.

**RESULTS OF SIGNIFICANCE TESTS (F-TESTS) FOR SELECTED GROUPS
OF INDEPENDENT VARIABLES IN REGRESSION ANALYSIS OF SCHOOL
ATTENDANCE (DEPENDENT VARIABLE GTS; 1016 OBSERVATIONS)**

table 2 ──

GROUP	NUMBER VARIABLES IN GROUP	F-RATIO	IN CONTRIBUTION OF GROUP SIGNIFICANT AT THE - 1% level?	5% level?	10% level?
1. All variables	39	8.27	YES	YES	YES
2. DEM	5	48.84	YES	YES	YES
3. URBAN	1	4.59	NO	YES	YES
4. FARM	1	1.85	NO	NO	NO
5. URBAN+FARM	2	6.30	YES	YES	YES
6. DEM+URBAN+FARM	7	36.27	YES	YES	YES
7. OCCF	4	3.68	YES	YES	YES
8. RF	5	.74	NO	NO	NO
9. RM	5	.51	NO	NO	NO
10. RF+RM	10	.95	NO	NO	NO
11. BF	5	2.15	NO	NO	YES
12. BM	5	2.21	NO	NO	YES
13. BF+BM	10	2.01	NO	YES	YES
14. OF	4	1.54	NO	NO	NO
15. OM	4	.37	NO	NO	NO
16. OF+OM	8	1.43	NO	NO	NO
17. RF+BF+OF	14	1.64	NO	NO	YES
18. RM+BM+OM	14	1.08	NO	NO	NO
19. RF+BF+OF+ RM+BM+OM	28	1.44	NO	NO	YES
20. OCCF+RF+BF+OF+ RM+BM+OM	32	2.06	YES	YES	YES

Note: For purposes of this table, the group DEM ("demographic" variables) includes AGEC, AGEC2, SEX, CHILD, and AGEF; F-ratios are computed from $F = (R_A^2 - R_B^2)(1 - R_A^2)^{-1}(n - k_1 - k_2 - 1)(k_1)^{-1}$, where R_A^2 and R_B^2 are the coefficients of determination in regressions which include and exclude, respectively, the group of independent variables being tested, n is the number of observations, k_1 the number of independent variables in the group, and k_2 the number of independent variables not in the group.

highly significant, as one would certainly expect: the probability[14] that a child will be attending school is obviously much less for a sixteen-year-old than for a ten-year-old. The implication of the negative coefficients for both AGEC and

[14]The true value of GTS must be zero or one. However, the value of GTS calculated from a regression equation will probably not be one of these values. Following common practice, we may interpret the calculated value as the *probability* that a person with given characteristics will be going to school, on the assumption that the value lies between zero and one. Although there is no guarantee that the calculated value will lie between these bounds in every case, in practice the assumption is a reasonable one for most cases.

AGEC2 is that this probability falls more rapidly toward the upper end of the age range. This finding generally accords with those of Katz for 1851 and 1861; he concluded that attendance dropped rapidly after 13 in 1851 and after 14 to 15 in 1861.[15] Surprisingly enough, the sex of the child does not turn out to be significant at even the relatively weak 10 percent level of significance. Age of father also is not statistically significant. Contrary to Katz's conclusion that "a large family size . . . frequently promoted school attendance,"[16] our results suggest that the number of children in the family was not an important determinant, once other factors have been taken into account and controlled for.

With respect to the influence of birthplace and ethnic origin (Katz seems to use these terms interchangeably), Katz states that, in 1851, Irishborn were least likely and Scottish- and Canadian-born most likely to send their children to school. With reference to religion, he observes that Roman Catholics were least likely and members of the Church of Scotland, Wesleyan Methodists, and especially Free Church Presbyterians most likely to send their children to school. He writes: "The obvious conclusion is that Irish Catholicism and Free Church Presbyterianism, respectively, retarded and promoted school attendance."[17] He arrives at a similar conclusion for 1861.

Based on our data for 1871, only one of the origin variables for the father tests as significant at even the 10 percent level; aside from this, religion and origin of either father or mother give no evidence of influencing school attendance. Birthplace performs a little better: when the ten variables representing birthplace for mother and father are considered together, the F-test indicates significance at the 5 percent level and three of the variables, taken separately, display evidence of significance at levels ranging from 10 percent to 1 percent. On the basis of the complete set of variables for religion, birthplace, and origin, the father's characteristics test as significant at only the 10 percent level, the mother's characteristics not at all (lines 17 and 18 of Table 2).

Katz's conclusion that wealth and occupation influenced school attendance is borne out by our study. Although wealth data have not been used in this study, occupation data, as a proxy for socioeconomic status, were available. Occupation of father appears to have a strong influence on school attendance. As a group, the four occupation variables are significant at the 1 percent level. Two of the individual variables are significant at the 1 percent level and a third at the 10 percent level. The general pattern of the regression coefficients indicates that the probability of school attendance is greater the higher the father's occupation on the index scale. (The one departure from this pattern occurs at the upper end, the coefficient being lower for the group at the top than for the one immediately preceding it. This may well be a consequence of deficiencies in the ranking of occupations.)

---

[15]Katz, "Who Went to School?", pp. 438, 443.
[16]Ibid., p. 441
[17]Ibid., p. 439.

Urban-rural differences appear to be important, as one would have expected. The variable *Urban* itself tests as significant at the 5 percent level, and when it is paired with the variable *Farm*, the two together test as significant at the 1 percent level.

The general picture that emerges with respect to the determinants of school attendance is as follows: Except for the obvious influence of the child's own age, "demographic" variables have no discernible effect. Religion and ethnic origin appear also to have little or no effect. Birthplace does give indications of being significant in some degree and father's occupation appears highly significant. Urban-rural differences also appear significant, especially when combined with a farm-nonfarm categorization of households.

V.   *Summary and Conclusions*

This paper has been concerned with the application of cross-section regression techniques to historical Census micro-data. A sample of "normal" families in Wentworth County, Ontario, was drawn from microfilm records of the 1871 Census. An attempt was made to determine the influence on school attendance of age and other "demographic" variables, of urban-rural and farm-nonfarm variables, and of variables representing occupation, religion, birthplace and ethnic origin. Extensive use was made of dummy variables in the regression analysis.

Aside from age of child, "demographic" characteristics were not found to be significant in the determination of school attendance; even sex of child was not found to be significant. Urban-rural combined with farm-nonfarm differences were found to be important. Occupation was also found to be important, with the probability of a child attending school generally greater the higher on the index scale the father's occupation. There was some moderately strong evidence to indicate that parents' birthplace may be important, but none to suggest any significant influence on the part of religion or ethnic origin.

Historical literature has often assigned an important role to the influence of socioeconomic factors on human behaviour without much in the way of rigorous statistical analysis. While Katz has done an impressive job of compiling and classifying data and has provided an interesting descriptive analysis, there remains a basic methodological problem in his handling of the data, as he himself appears to realize.[18] Two-way tables depicting percentage distributions of characteristics do not hold other factors constant, and con-

---

[18]Katz's methodological dilemma is summarized in the following, "The obvious conclusion is that Irish Catholicism and Free Church Presbyterianism, respectively, retarded and promoted school attendance. However, this explanation takes no account of other factors; it could be that Irish Catholics were poor and Scottish Presbyterians prosperous, and therein lay the difference. The point is of some importance, for it raises the question to what extent school attendance was a product of religion and to what extent a result of economic factors." Ibid., p. 439.

sequently the unique and separable effects of the many social and economic factors cannot be disentangled one from the other. Only techniques such as the regression analysis which we have employed permit this.

3a   **REPLY***

MICHAEL B. KATZ

Denton and George have attempted to test my findings about school attendance with multiple regression analysis. The comparison of results obtained through different statistical means is an interesting and instructive undertaking. It is a pity, therefore, that their paper does not permit such a comparison.

In large part the problems with their paper stem from their lack of historical sensitivity. Thus, they imply that because their findings in 1871 partly differ from mine for 1851 and 1861 that mine are probably, in part, not valid. The problem they overlook is that the 1860's in urban Wentworth County, that is, mainly Hamilton, were years of rapid and significant industrialization. This, it is my suspicion, had a marked effect on school attendance. Indeed, my preliminary inspection of some 1871 data shows marked differences from what existed a decade or two earlier. Briefly, I expect that the expansion of employment opportunities for young people actually lowered school attendance among adolescents. At the same time the system of education introduced in the 1850's had become increasingly universal for younger children. Indeed, the early 1870's was the time when school attendance became compulsory.

However, even if we could expect the situation to be comparable across the decades, Denton and George would still not provide an adequate comparison. For they lump together rural and urban in most of their analysis. That is, they tell us that living in urban areas increased school attendance. But they do not differentiate between the effects of various factors in rural and urban areas. For instance, they do not find, as I did, that large families in certain circumstances sent more of their children to school. Now my expectation is that this was the case in urban areas where schools were used as baby-sitters, especially by poor families. I would not expect it to be the case in the country. Indeed, the only other study that I know that has tested the influence of family *size* has arrived at the same conclusion. Daniel Calhoun found that a

*Reprinted from *History of Education Quarterly*, 14:2 (Summer 1974), pp. 233–234 by permission of author and publisher.

large family size promoted school attendance in the urban areas of mid-nineteenth century Dutchess County, New York, but not in the rural ones.[1] Until Denton and George provide this kind of discrimination their results cannot have very much meaning.

Their sample, moreover, has a serious deficiency. The decision to restrict their study to "normal" families prejudged the nature of family structure. On what basis did they decide that a particular family structure was "normal" in the nineteenth century and that only "normal" families were relevant for the study of school attendance? They do not say. I suspect there is no very good defense.

Despite their regression analysis, Denton and George do not answer the most obvious and important descriptive questions. What proportion of children went to school? How many boys and how many girls attended at different ages? (Is it really necessary to do a regression analysis to determine the influence of sex when all one has to do is to inspect the relative proportion of each sex attending at each age?) At the end of it all they do not tell us in any straightforward terms what kinds of families were more or less likely to send their children to school. As far as I can see, the paper, thus, is of very little help in historical interpretation.

It is not the case, moreover, that my paper relies solely on two-way cross-tabulation. The introduction of three-way tabulation, in fact, provided some of the most discriminating analysis, for instance, the relation between wealth, family size and school attendance. Nor is it fair to argue, as Denton and George do, that one must choose between two-way cross-tabulation and regression analysis. This point must be stressed, or their argument could leave the wrong impression with readers. Cross-tabulation can be a powerful tool. It is possible, first, especially with computer programs such as SPSS, to do three- or four-way cross-tabulations. More than that, it is possible to do cross-tabulation with very complex variables. One might, for instance, create variables which are a combination of family size, birthplace of father and occupation. That is, one could compare, for instance, the propensity of Irish Catholic labourers with large and small families to send their children to school. And so on. It is quite straightforward, but it does take time, experimentation and a great deal of thought to create meaningful categories. This is what multiple regression avoids. Despite its complexity, it is an easy way out: a formula for everything. The problem is that the results are not very instructive: not very instructive, that is, if one wants to know quite exactly and concretely who it was that did and did not go to school.

[1]Daniel Calhoun, *The Intelligence of a People* (Princeton 1973), p. 99.

SOCIOECONOMIC INFLUENCES ON SCHOOL ATTENDANCE:
A Response to Professor Katz*

3b

FRANK T. DENTON
PETER J. GEORGE

The comments by Katz on our paper reflect a misinterpretation of our aims and considerable confusion regarding the methodological issues involved. Let us take up some of the points that he raises.

1. The paper was not intended as a criticism of Katz's work and it is unfortunate and misleading to have it interpreted as such. Various approaches are possible in historical analysis. What we have attempted to do is to highlight the differences between our methodology and his and to compare our general conclusions about socioeconomic influences in 1871 with his general conclusions for earlier periods.

2. We are accused by Katz of lacking "historical sensitivity" (whatever that is!) and of implying "that because (our) findings in 1871 partly differ from (his) for 1851 and 1861 that (his) are probably, in part, not valid." Historical sensitivity or no, it is as evident to us as to anyone else that 1871 is not 1861 or 1851 and that real changes in the nature of socioeconomic influences may have taken place in the 1860's. But that hardly makes the case for avoiding all comparisons between two studies concerned with the same subject matter in roughly the same area in roughly the same part of the nineteenth century, which is what his comments seem to imply.

3. The suggestion that our sample has a serious deficiency and that "the decision to restrict (our) study to "normal" families prejudged the nature of family structure" is naive. The term "normal" was given a precise definition in the paper. If one does not like that term, another would do as well: it is the definition that matters, not the label. Surely it is obvious from a reading of the paper, and from the use of the quotation marks, that the word is being used in a particular sense for the particular purposes of the analysis. Families with school-age children in which one parent is absent,

*This note is a response to the comments of Michael B. Katz on our paper "Socioeconomic Influences on School Attendance: A Study of a Canadian County in 1871." Reprinted from *History of Education Quarterly*, 14:3 (Fall 1974), pp. 367–369 by permission of authors and publishers.

or in which the father is very young or old, may be taken to be families in which there are special circumstances which may bear on the school attendance of the children in those families but which have nothing to do with the broad patterns of socioeconomic influence with which we are concerned. In order to avoid the distortion which such special circumstances would introduce into the analysis, we have excluded families of this kind. Put differently, we have divided the total population of families into two classes and have confined our attention to the class in which the effects of broad socioeconomic influences on school attendance are most likely to be discernible. This procedure is entirely consistent with the objectives of the study.

4. Katz says, "Despite their regression analysis, Denton and George do not answer the most obvious and important descriptive questions." The statement reveals, once again, a misinterpretation of the purposes of the paper. (As a matter of interest, some basic descriptive material is contained in an earlier paper.[1]) What is most distressing though, from a methodological point of view, is his suggestion that to determine the influence of sex "all one has to do is inspect the relative proportion of each sex attending at each age." The whole purpose of multiple regression analysis, both in our paper and in thousands of others, is to disentangle the separate influences of different variables which are operating at the same time and to provide a framework for the carrying out of statistical tests of significance of these influences. This requires that the variables be analysed simultaneously. To say that one can evaluate the influence of a particular variable by simple inspection of it, in isolation from other variables, is to miss the point entirely. It ignores both the useful properties of regression analysis and the limitations of the simple descriptive techniques employed by Katz for dealing with situations in which the influences of many variables are mingled.

5. We are accused of not indicating "in any straightforward terms what kinds of families were more or less likely to send their children to school." What is the meaning of "straightforward" here? The increments or decrements to the probability of attending school associated with particular variables are indicated in Table 1 of our paper. A positive regression coefficient indicates an increase in probability, a negative one indicates a decrease, and the degree of confidence to be attached to each coefficient is indicated by the yes/no answers in the last three columns of the table. What could be more straightforward?

6. Katz argues the virtues of cross-tabulation. "It is quite straightforward," he says, "but it does take time, experimentation, and a great deal of thought to create meaningful categories. This is what multiple regression avoids. Despite its complexity, it is an easy way out: a formula for everything." Nonsense! Multiple regression is, and has been for decades, a standard tool in many branches of physical and social sciences. It can be used wisely

[1]See Denton and George, "An Exploratory Statistical Analysis of Some Socioeconomic Characteristics of Families in Hamilton, Ontario, 1871," *Social History*, 5 (April 1970), 16–44.

or unwisely and its results can be interpreted properly or improperly. Criticize the craftsman for misusing the tool, if you will, but it makes no sense to criticize the tool itself. To damn it by saying that "despite its complexity, it is an easy way out" is somewhat like damning the airplane because it is easier to fly from Boston to New York than to go by bicycle. The disentangling of the various influences on school attendance is precisely the sort of problem for which multiple regression analysis is designed. This type of analysis has been found to be immensely useful in many other fields of study. It would be quite remarkable if it could not be of help in quantitative studies in the history of education.

7. We would certainly not wish to suggest that the results presented in our paper are anything like the last word on the subject of historical socioeconomic influences on school attendance. Far from it. But we would like to think that they do represent a contribution. To have the methodology and the results rejected out of hand, as suggested by Katz's comments, does not advance the cause of research into the history of education.

comments and questions

1. Do you think that Denton and George criticized the Katz methodology or were they only illustrating another approach? Explain.
2. Have Denton and George been clear and thorough enough in their explanations of solving regression equations with dummy variables so that the typical historiographer would understand them? Would the typical historian understand them? Do *you* understand them? Since references are provided, have they fulfilled their obligations with respect to this point?
3. Do the preceding article and responses contain any information which would allow one to make inferences about the relative appropriateness of the regression and cross tabulation approaches? If so, what is that information?
4. What was Denton and George's purpose? Was it primarily to report on a methodological technique for historical analysis or to report some significant findings? If the latter, how does the geographic sample limit any generalizations?
5. To what extent have Denton and George extended historiographers' knowledge of the relationship between socioeconomic status and school attendance?

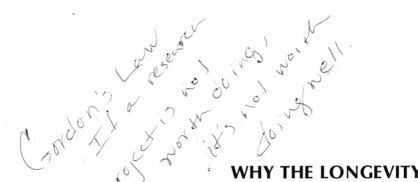

WHY THE LONGEVITY
OF THE McGUFFEY *READERS?*[*][1]

JOHN A. NIETZ

No series of American textbooks enjoyed so long and popular circulation as the McGuffey *Readers*. Most of the many biographies and articles written about the McGuffeys[2] and their *Readers* give most credit for this to the original authors.[3] It is not the purpose of the writer to belittle the great contribution made by the McGuffeys, but an analysis of the facts needs to be made to obtain a true picture of the matter.

William H. McGuffey wrote the original editions of the *Primer*, the *First, Second, Third*, and *Fourth Readers*, and his younger brother Alexander wrote the *Fifth* and most of the *Sixth Readers*. The various revisions of these books were not made by the McGuffeys, The *First* and *Second Readers* were first published in 1836, the *Primer, Third*, and *Fourth* in 1837, the *Fifth* in 1844, and *Sixth* in 1857.[4]

These were revised a number of times. The *First Reader* was revised in 1841, 1844, and 1848; the *Second* in 1838, 1841, and 1844; the *Third* in 1838, 1843, and 1848; the *Fourth* in 1844 and 1848. Then in 1853 all five readers

---

[*]Reprinted from the *History of Education Quarterly*, 4:2 (June 1964), pp. 119–125, with the permission of the publisher and author.

[1]Much has been written about the McGuffeys and their *Readers*. Minnich's book includes a bibliography of six pages prepared by George C. Crout. (See Note 5, 95ff.) Some has been written since. However, for the purposes of this article the writer largely depended upon books that were mainly based upon primary sources. Furthermore, the writers Old Textbook Collection contains sixty-eight McGuffey *Readers* of various titles, dates, imprints, and editions, including four first editions. These were amply used.

[2]Alice McGuffey Ruggles, *The Story of the McGuffeys* (Cincinnati, 1950). She is the granddaughter of Alexander McGuffey and thus had access to intimate human interest information about the McGuffeys.

[3]Benjamin Franklin Crawford, *William Holmes McGuffey: The Schoolmaster of the Nation* (Delaware, Ohio, 1963). This is a small but interesting book about William McGuffey and about the McGuffey Societies.

[4]Henry H. Vail, *A History of the McGuffey Readers* (Cleveland, 1911), 4, 5. Mr. Vail became an employee of the Wilson, Hinkle & Company in 1871, and in 1890 became one of the four active partners of the newly formed American Book Company. Thus he had direct access to all preserved materials and iinformation pertaining to the publishing of the McGuffey *Readers*.

reappeared as "Newly Revised." In 1857 certain changes in the gradation and redistribution of some lessons were made, and the *Sixth* first appeared. In 1879 all six readers were rather radically revised and appeared in uniform brown binding. Finally, in 1901 and in 1920 they were recopyrighted with only minor changes.[5]

Apparently it is not now certain exactly how many copies were sold during each of the earliest years, but Mr. Louis Dillman, president of the American Book Company in 1920, estimated the total sales to have been as follows to 1920:[6]

DATES	YEARS	MILLIONS
1836 to 1850	14	7
1850 to 1870	20	40
1870 to 1890	20	60
1890 to 1920	30	15
Totals	84	122

Granting the population and the schools were constantly increasing in number, yet it must be recognized that the greatest number of sales occurred after the major revisions of the readers. But what brought about the revisions? Great credit must be given to the alertness of the publishers to sense the need for keeping the books up-to-date with the changing times and growing competition. Who were the publishers? The following firms have been the parent publishers of the McGuffey *Readers:*

Truman and Smith	1834–1841
W. B. Smith	1841–1852
W. B. Smith & Company	1852–1863
Sargent, Wilson & Hinkle	1863–1868
Wilson, Hinkle & Company	1868–1877
Van Antwerp, Bragg & Company	1877–1890
American Book Company	1890–

[5] Harvey C. Minnich, *William Holmes McGuffey and His Readers* (Cincinnati, 1936), 39–40. This is a book of about 200 pages written nearly entirely from primary sources, containing reproductions of many pictures of the *Readers* and of some selections. It also lists the *Readers* found in four leading McGuffey Collections: (1) Miami List, (2) Henry Ford List, (3) Maud Blair List, and (4) the Ohio State List.

[6] Harvey C. Minnich, "William Holmes McGuffey and the Peerless Readers," *Miami University Bulletin* (Oxford, Ohio, 1928), 92. He was for years the Dean of the School of Education at Miami University, and was largely responsible for developing The McGuffey Museum there and later became its Curator. This pamphlet contains a list of The Collection of McGuffey Readers in the Museum.

From this list it may appear that there were marked changes in the publishing firms from time to time, yet this was not true. As the senior members grew older and the business larger, younger men were added and trained to assume leadership. Thus new names appeared as heads of the firm. but there always was an overlapping continuity of personnel.[7]

When the need for a revision was sensed, the publishers employed very competent help to do it. The needs for changes from time to time were stimulated by criticisms sent in by the agents who represented the company. These agents called on school boards and at schools. Then, too, representatives of competing book companies often tended to criticize the McGuffey *Readers*. Such competition was strongest in the East, where the McGuffey *Readers* made little headway. Their largest circulation was in the Mid-west and in the South. In fact, for more than fifty years they had nearly exclusive adoption in a large fraction of the schools in these two areas. The readers providing the strongest competition were written by Lyman Cobb, S. G. Goodrich, Charles W. Sanders, Ebenezer Porter, Lucius Osgood, and the *Appleton Readers* by William T. Harris, Andrew J. Rickoff, and Mark Bailey.

The revisions were largely made by professional help carefully selected by the publishers. One of the first engaged by Mr. Smith, the first publisher, was Dr. Timothy S. Pinneo, who later on his own became the author of rather popular grammars of English, Latin, and Greek. Pinneo helped revise the *Third* and *Fourth Readers* in 1843, and the entire series in 1853. Daniel G. Mason, a Cincinnati teacher, helped revise the *First* and *Second* in 1843. In the 1850's Mr. Obed J. Wilson, a very literary man, joined the publishing firm. He did considerable editorial work in connection with the readers.[8]

In 1874 the firm decided to provide its own McGuffey competition by employing Mr. Thomas W. Harvey to prepare a new series to be known as the Harvey *Readers*. These proved to be unequal to compete, particularly with the *Appleton Readers*. So in 1878 the publishers decided to abandon the Harvey *Readers* and to have the McGuffey *Readers* drastically revised. The revision was to involve both matters of method and content. To do this work the firm invited Miss Amanda Funnelle and Robert W. Stevenson to revise the lower three readers, and Thomas W. Harvey and Dr. Edwin C. Hewett to work on the upper three. These were all experienced educators. The three lower books became drastically new, the *Fourth* was largely new matter, and the *Fifth* and *Sixth* considerably revised and included brief biographies of the authors of the selections, as well as many explanatory textual notes. New pictures were also introduced. Thus the 1879 edition became the best and most popular of the McGuffey *Readers*. Likewise its sale was greatest.

Next consideration should be given to the changes made in these revisions. One was the nature of the pictures. Except the *Primer* and *First Reader*

[7]Vail, *op cit.*, 39 ff.
[8]*Ibid.*, 48 ff.

the earliest editions contained few or no pictures, and those were not original. They were mostly copied from British books. In successive revisions more and original pictures were gradually added. In 1863 the firm employed a Mr. E. J. Whitney, an artist in wood engraving, to improve the pictures in the McGuffey *Readers*. For the famous 1879 edition new improved procedures for preparing illustrations were used, and many more pictures were introduced, even in the upper readers. For the 1901 edition photo-engraving largely supplanted wood engraving.[9]

The greatest changes involved in the revisions were either the shifting or the changing of the selections. Hughes found that 607 of the 1067 titles in all the editions of the *Fourth, Fifth,* and *Sixth Readers* appeared in only one edition, showing a lack of consensus among the compilers concerning what the child should read. Five of the fifteen most repeated titles occurred in all three upper readers. Hughes further found that 247 titles appeared in readers of more than one level. The fame of these readers likely rested upon the 247 titles that were repeated.[10]

Another change in the three upper readers was in the use of selections by English versus American authors. While the total number of lessons written by English authors was the same as by American, each contributing 741, these were written by 178 English authors and 218 different Americans. Of these writers, 143 Americans contributed one title, and 99 appeared only once; while 109 English authors contributed one title, and 72 were used only once. Of the British authors, the writings of Shakespeare, Scott, and Byron were used most often, while the writings of Irving, Longfellow, Whittier, and Bryant among the Americans were used most.[11]

Other changes involved matters that may be termed as teaching aids. The presentation of key words, drills, explanatory notes, pictures, biographies of authors, and review questions were changed from time to time, usually to make the reading more meaningful and more interesting.

What were the outstanding qualities of the McGuffey *Readers*? From the beginning the series was to be known as the *Eclectic Readers*. The word "eclectic" is not commonly used today, but it meant that the content was *choice* or *chosen* material from various sources and of different types. Apparently this word, when properly explained, helped sell the series for many years.

The fundamental aims of the McGuffey *Readers* were about the same as of most other readers during the nineteenth century; namely, to teach morals and effective oral reading. However, the authors and publishers believed that the McGuffey *Readers* taught these aims more emphatically and effectively. Both W. B. Smith and William McGuffey believed that teaching to fulfill these

[9]*Ibid.,* 67–70.
[10]Raymond Grove Hughes, "An Analysis of the Fourth, Fifth, and Sixth McGuffey Readers," (unpublished doctor's dissertation, University of Pittsburgh, 1943). This includes an analysis of the selections and lessons contained in all the editions of these readers.
[11]*Ibid.,* 145.

aims was sorely needed among the rough and ready frontiersmen of the New West. Cincinnati, where these readers were published, was then the cultural and commercial center of the West.

Religious content was presented both in prose and verse. For example, both the ten commandments and the Lord's Prayer appeared in verse in several editions. Nearly 30 per cent of the selections of the 1844 *Fourth Reader* was religious in nature. However, this percentage gradually decreased in the later editions until it was only 3 per cent in the 1901 edition. On the other hand, the emphasis on morals increased until it reached 40 per cent in the 1879 edition.[12] The aim was to set high social and moral standards for those western pioneering people. It was to be "enough Puritan to fit into the religious mental mode of the descendants of the Ohio Land Company; enough Cavalier to fit into the moral and mental mode of the blue blood of Kentucky, Virginia, and North Carolina; enough economic to fit into the thrifty mental mode of the Germans and Scots."[13] Many of the truths and poetic expressions memorized from these *Readers* were quoted by parents, preachers, and others to counteract acts of intemperence, vulgarity, laziness, brutality, dishonesty, and lawlessness, which were altogether too common among frontier people.[14]

The fields of politics, religion, and culture demanded that the pioneers should learn to speak effectively. Thus the emphasis on oral reading was strong. The *Third Readers* early mentioned "Plain Rules for Reading." The 1843 edition even included lessons on enunciation. The 1844 edition of the *Fourth* began with twenty-six pages dealing with such matters as articulation, tones, inflections, and emphasis. The first edition of the *Fifth* (1844) devoted sixty pages to an "Analysis of the Principles of Elocution."[15]

The selections were generally concrete and practically understandable rather than abstract and often theological and philosophical, as was true of many Eastern published readers. The authors were aware that the pioneers of the rural West were not as literary as those in the East, particularly in New England. Nevertheless, the *Readers* from the beginning evidenced literary merit. Both William and Alexander McGuffey were very literary minded. This was likewise true of those who revised the *Readers*. It was in the upper readers particularly that the fine literary pieces were presented, both in prose and verse. In the 1879 *Sixth* "111 great authors were quoted: Shakespeare, 9 times; Longfellow and Scott, each four times; Bryant, Irving, Webster, and the Bible, each three times; Addison, Beecher, Dickens, Holmes, Johnson (Samuel), Thompson, Whittier, and Wilson, each two times."[16]

Except possibly the earliest editions, the books were well printed; the

---

[12]*Ibid.*, 66.

[13]Minnich, *op. cit.*, 69.

[14]John A. Nietz, *Old Textbooks* (Pittsburgh, 1961), 78. Ten pages of this book deal with the McGuffey *Readers*.

[15]*Ibid.*, 77 ff.

[16]Minnich, *op. cit.*, 72.

approaches explained; word lists, drills, and review questions generally included; and the selections and pictures well arranged.

In summary, then what is the answer to the question asked in the title
of the article — why did the McGuffey *Readers* remain popular so long?

First, much credit should go to the McGuffeys as the original authors,
but certainly not *all* the credit. It is true that they set the pattern for the books
in the original editions, yet the many revisions in the successive editions indicate that the readers would not have remained popular very long without
changes. Hughes found that of all the titles in all the editions of the upper three
readers only one third of them were contributed by the McGuffeys; however,
he found that these titles were responsible for 52 per cent of the lessons.

Much credit should go to the publishers for seeing the need for Western written readers for a frontier market. Special credit should go to W. B.
Smith for this vision. He sought the authors to write such readers. Too, he soon
saw the need to appoint agents to go out to meet with school boards and visit
schools to secure the adoption of these books. It has been recognized as a fact
that in later years these agents or book representatives began to constitute a
pressure group to see that their publisher rather than others got the book
adoptions. Thus not always were textbooks adopted on their pure merit.

Much credit should go to the various educators employed by the publishers to make the various revisions of the *Readers*. These persons apparently
used their pedagogical sense and experience in making wise changes so that the
books would hold their mass appeal. Of course, these changes would be made
in consultation with the editorial staff of the publishers.

Lastly, the interest aroused by the McGuffey Societies since 1918 has
no doubt helped keep up at least a limited sale of the McGuffey *Readers* to the
present time. Likewise, the agitation of these societies has done much to
stimulate the writing of abundant numbers of articles and books about the
McGuffeys and the *Readers*.

comments and questions _____

1. The problem and hypothesis are essentially similar in this study, that is, the purpose
    is an attempt to ascertain the popularity of the McGuffey *Readers*. Neither the
    problem nor the hypothesis is explicitly stated. Should they be? Why? Why not?
    Has Nietz presented a thorough analysis of the probable factors accounting for the
    popularity of the McGuffey *Readers*? Are there any instances of contradiction?
2. Of what educational relevance is this research? If you were a journal editor, would
    you accept the article? Why? Why not?
3. There are several instances where Nietz appears to make statements that he fails to
    document—for example, "the readers providing the strongest competition were
    written by . . ." or "Cincinnati . . . was then the cultural and commercial center of

the West." Is this a limitation of this study? Do you feel that there was too much subjectivity in interpreting the data? Why? Why not?

4. Was there any evidence that the source data (which was largely from secondary sources) were evaluated? Where is this evidence?

5. If, in your opinion, there are inadequacies in this study, what are they and how would you have conducted the study?

PATTERNS OF DEPENDENCY AND CHILD DEVELOPMENT IN THE MID-NINETEENTH CENTURY CITY:
A Sample from Boston 1860*

HARVEY J. GRAFF

The nature and state of the family has long been a major concern in the United States. It has been apparent in the literature and criticism since the Puritan arrival in the seventeenth century and may be followed thereafter. However, the family has not been a major concern of American historians. As Edward Saveth reminds us, in the 1962 Presidential Address of the American Historical Association, Carl Bridenbaugh spoke of the need for research in the neglected field of American family history and suggested that the profession assign a priority to this general area. Saveth, in 1969, concluded that "apart from some impressive work in historical demography, the situation has not altered."[1]

In 1971, we are witness to a rise in family studies, as viewed in the work of Joseph F. Kett, John Demos, Philip Greven, Jr., and the recent issue of the *Journal of Interdisciplinary History* (Autumn 1971). Various methodological approaches are apparent in this research. Some of it rests on the quantitative basis of family reconstitution, some on the adaptation of Eriksonian stages of the life cycle, while others have examined the child-rearing literature, memoirs, and medical-psychological literature of their period.

Of special interest is the mid-nineteenth century. This essay will examine the state of child and adolescent dependence among families in Boston in 1860.[2] Dependence here is viewed broadly to take into account the relationships between the family, the school, and work. The conceptual framework is derived from the recent studies by William E. Bridges, Joseph Kett, and John

*Reprinted from *History of Education Quarterly*, 13:2 (Summer 1973), pp. 129–133 by permission of author and publisher.

[1] Edward A. Saveth, "The Problem of American Family History," *American Quarterly*, 21 (Summer 1969), 311.

[2] This research was conducted as a "feasibility study," thus the small and probably biased sample. However, it is hoped that the method is recognized as workable. For another recent attempt to study family history from a developmental perspective, using an age-structuring methodology, see Lutz K. Berkner, "The Stem Family and the Developmental Cycle of the Peasant Household: An Eighteenth-Century Austrian Example," *American Historical Review*, 77 (April 1972), 298–318.

67

and Virginia Demos;[3] this will be developed below. But first let us consider the empirical evidence.

Methodology

In order to advance our understanding of the family and its dynamics, this study attempts to frame some tentative generalizations from empirical evidence. The source is the United States Federal Census of 1860 and the sample was drawn from the twelfth ward of Boston, Massachusetts, South Boston. The ward, a large and relatively homogeneous area in 1860, was selected at random.

A sample population of five hundred families was drawn and coded. These were chosen by selecting the first five hundred fathers forty years of age or older who had children residing at home as indicated on the Census. For each family the following information was noted: occupation of father, value of real estate, value of personal estate, number of children at home, number attending school, age of eldest son at home, his occupation, whether or not he was attending school, value of any personal or real estate, age of eldest daughter, her occupation, and her school attendance. No married children who remained at home were considered.

While all of this information was not utilized in this analysis, it appears that one may learn a great deal about family dependence from such an approach. In the analysis which follows, the variables principally employed were the ages, occupations, and school attendance of the eldest sons and daughters, and the occupations of the fathers. Some use of the ethnicity and wealth of the fathers has been made as well.

Analysis of oldest children at home by age provides a viable and useful way of studying the family in terms of child dependency, especially as it relates to school attendance and work patterns. Indeed, it may be suggestive of the way in which a child grew up in mid-century Boston or mid-century urban America.

Analysis of the Data: A Five Stage Interpretation

First, consider the eldest sons at home of these families. There were 381 sons in the sample of five hundred families, however only 353 or those five

---

[3]William E. Bridges, "Family Patterns and Social Values in America," *American Quarterly*, 17 (Spring 1965), 3–11; Joseph F. Kett, "Growing Up in Rural New England," *Anonymous Americans*, ed. *Tamara Hareven (Englewood Cliffs, N.J., 1971), pp.* 3–16; and "Adolescence and Youth in Nineteenth-Century America," *Journal of Interdisciplinary History*, 11 (Autumn 1971), 282–298; and John and Virginia Demos, "Adolescence in Historical Perspective," *Journal of Marriage and the Family*, 31 (November 1969), 632–638.

| | | | | | | SAME OCCU- | |
AGE	NUMBER	IN SCHOOL	PERCEN-TAGE	WORKING	PERCEN-TAGE	PATION AS FATHER	APPREN-TICED
5	11	6	54.54	—	—	—	—
6	11	10	90.90	—	—	—	—
7	10	9	90.00	—	—	—	—
8	9	9	100.00	—	—	—	—
9	6	6	100.00	—	—	—	—
10	20	19	95.00	—	—	—	—
11	16	15	93.75	—	—	—	—
12	17	16	94.11	—	—	—	—
13	11	11	100.00	—	—	—	—
14	20	18	90.00	1	5.00	—	—
15	25	23	92.00	1	4.00	—	—
16	21	9	42.85	11	52.38	3	5
17	25	6	24.00	15	60.00	2	1
18	17	2	11.76	14	82.35	5	1
19	24	3	12.50	20	83.33	5	6
20	16	—	—	13	81.25	4	3
21	24	2	8.33	20	83.33	6	—
22	15	—	—	14	93.33	5	—
23	14	—	—	13	92.85	5	—
24	12	—	—	10	83.33	4	—
25	11	—	—	11	100.00	5	—
26	5	—	—	5	100.00	2	—
27	2	—	—	2	100.00	—	—
28	2	—	—	2	100.00	—	—
30	2	—	—	2	100.00	1	—
31	1	—	—	1	100.00	—	—
33	1	—	—	1	100.00	—	—
34	3	—	—	3	100.00	—	—
36	1	—	—	1	100.00	—	—
39	1	—	—	1	100.00	—	—

table 1 — **THE SONS**

years of age or older will be taken into account directly. The age distribution of these sons is given in Table 1, which includes summary detail on the characteristics of sons of each age.

From this distribution it is possible to postulate stages of development in the life cycle of this child in the family. Five stages are apparent;[4] the first would include children aged one to four years, not yet in school and completely dependent on the mother. The second stage would include sons aged five to fifteen (for the stages for sons, see Table 2). This was for the urban children of mid-century Boston, the period of schooling. Of 156 oldest sons in this group,

[4]No attempt will be made here to relate these stages to psychological development and life cycle theory. However, no immediate contradictions are apparent; and, indeed, this is a major concern for further research.

table 2   **SONS — STAGES OF DEPENDENCY**

AGES	NUMBER	IN SCHOOL	PERCENTAGE	WORKING	PERCENTAGE
1– 4	28	2	7.14	—	—
5–15	156	142	91.02	2	1.28
16–21	127	22	17.32	93	73.22
22–25	52	—	—	48	92.30
26–39	18	—	—	18	100.00

142 or 91.02 percent were indicated as attending school. This would of course relate to the compulsory education laws of Massachusetts passed in 1852, but surprisingly, well over one-half of the fifteen-year-olds were still in school, whereas the law required attendance only to age fourteen. The fifth year was the transition point as only one half of the sons attended, but to age fifteen the percentage of the children attending school never dipped below ninety percent. A minor caveat is in order here, before this stage is adopted for wider application. It would seem that this is a very high percentage of boys in school for the period. Figures for other urban areas (such as Hamilton, Ontario) would suggest that these children are somewhat extraordinary. Undoubtedly, when a larger sample from Boston and from other cities is drawn, this stage would contract, and perhaps overlap more with the next.

The third stage, from ages sixteen to twenty-one, would seem to be a very important one in the dependency relationships of sons. Sixteen was a transition age at which slightly over one-half of the sons were at work. This represents an increase from four percent to 52 percent. The percentage of sons working gradually increased to age twenty-one, with a few sons remaining in school. The sons of poorer fathers in lower rank occupations would seem to be the first to leave school and enter the workforce. Ethnically, the sons of Irish fathers were least likely to continue in school, while the sons of native-born fathers of a variety of occupations continued on.[5]

Ages sixteen to twenty-one are also the period of apprenticeship. It would seem logical to suggest that sons who were apprentices and living at home were more dependent on their families than other sons who were employed. Sixteen of the 103 sons, or 15.53 percent of those aged sixteen to twenty, were listed as being apprenticed, with the oldest apprenticeship at twenty years of age. Another facet of dependency is revealed by the number of sons who held the same occupation as their fathers. Of all sons at home over

[5]To move beyond a simplistic discussion of occupational variation, it is necessary to link these census records to city assessment rolls. One should be extremely wary of making conclusions about class, status, wealth, or mobility from occupational titles. For a fine discussion of this and related problems, see Michael B. Katz, "Occupational Classification in History," *Journal of Interdisciplinary History*, III (Summer 1972), 63–88. For record-linkage, see Ian Winchester, "The Linkage of Historical Records by Man and Computer: Techniques and Problems," *Journal of Interdisciplinary History*, 1 (Autumn 1970), 107–124.

fifteen 23.35 percent had the same occupation; of those sixteen to twenty-one, 19.68 percent did.

The relatively constant and high number of sons in this stage suggests that stage three is a period of semidependency for most sons. Three-fourths in this age group, 73.22 percent, may be regarded as semidependent; they held remunerative positions but still resided with their families. However, it seems likely that those sons who were apprenticed were more dependent than other working sons, dependent on their family with whom they resided and dependent upon their master. Moreover, the 17.32 percent who were still in school must be regarded as more dependent than those who were employed. Sons who held the same occupation as their fathers did may have been more dependent, but this conclusion remains uncertain. Thus, stage three may be seen as an important and complex period for these eldest sons. It marked their introduction into the workforce, in various ways, but found them remaining under the parental household. This was the commencement of semidependency for many sons.

Stage four spans four years, from ages twenty-two to twenty-five. For the sons who remained at home and for whom we have information, this was a continuation of the semidependent relationship established in stage three. Twenty percent more of the sons, or 92.30 percent in all, were recorded as being employed and none were apprenticed, nor were any in school. Interestingly more of the sons in this stage held the same occupation as their fathers. It may well have been this connection, of occupational security and a resulting psychological dependence, which kept these sons at home. Nineteen of the 52 or 36.53 percent were recorded as holding the same kind of employment, predominantly skilled, semiskilled, and unskilled forms of labor. What this means is as yet unclear, but the possibility of a psychological component related to dependency arising from this relationship is suggestive. However, it may reveal little more than the working out of the age-old adage of son following the father's line of work.

Stage four thus represents the continuation and maturation of the semidependent status of working sons continuing to reside at home. However, there is a second importance to this stage. There would seem to be a definite drop in numbers of sons at home in the ages twenty-two to twenty-five. In stage three, the number of sons in each age bracket was consistently in the twenties and high teens. But at age twenty-two, the number falls to fifteen and never rises above it again (see Table 1). What is suggested here is that stage four for many, although perhaps not a majority of sons, was a period of leaving home. Ages twenty-two to twenty-five for them would mark the beginning of a new independence, freedom from the parental household. This is not to claim that all vertiges of psychological or economic dependence had disappeared. This state was attained slightly earlier than in the colonial period, as Greven and Demos have shown that most sons remained at home until their midtwenties or longer. In addition, it is possible that this earlier state of independence would correlate positively with the decreasing age of first marriage. Further research on age of marriage for males is necessary here, although it remains possible that some sons were leaving home upon marriage, whereas for others marriage need not have brought about the onset of independence from the parental household.

Before proceeding to the fifth stage, one must note the presence of sixteen sons, aged sixteen to twenty-four, who were neither employed nor attending school. These sons, about whom nothing else is known (although there is no uniformity among their fathers) comprise slightly less than ten percent of all sons in these groups, a figure of some significance. It must be concluded that they, for reasons unknown, existed in a state of complete dependence.

Stage five, ages twenty-six to thirty-nine for the Boston sons, tends to confirm the picture. Only eighteen sons are left at home after age twenty-five. Fully one hundred percent are employed, with no apprentices or scholars. Only two sons share their fathers' occupations. For the vast majority of sons then stage five was the culmination of independence. Some few would remain at home, perhaps never to depart, continuing in a state of semidependency until parental death.

Five stages of development seem to surround the dependency relationships of sons in these South Boston families, and it seems that they revolve on the interworkings of the family, school, and work.[6] The male child's development thus may be viewed in light of the model of changing dependency; from complete dependence to varying degrees of semidependence to independence. It must be noted that the guidelines of each stage by age would only be an approximation of reality, at best, as they would vary to some degree for each son; as well, some sons may not achieve independence until the death of the father or even mother. The dynamics of these dependency relationships are as yet unclear, but some of the lines may emerge from studies of census data. Above all, the psychological correlates of such dependency patterns must be sought out and understood.

The eldest daughters of the five hundred South Boston families must also be examined. There were 383 eldest daughters residing at home in 1860. Five stages of development of dependency relationships are apparent here, too, but the stages differ in two ways: chronological divisions and dependency characteristics. These, as will be shown, are important differences in male-female development. (For these stages, see Table 4; for the age breakdown of daughters, see Table 3).

The first stage, as for the sons, is infancy and early childhood—a state of complete dependency. There were twelve daughters in this stage in the sample, aged one to three years. The second stage comprises the years four to

---

[6]An alternative possibility would be a four-stage interpretation, with the third stage comprising ages sixteen to twenty-one for about one-half of the sons and ages sixteen to twenty-five for the rest.

table 3 ━━━━━━━━━━━━━━━━━━━━━━━━━━━━━━━━━━━━━

AGE	NUMBER	IN SCHOOL	PERCENTAGE	WORKING	PERCENTAGE
4	2	2	100.00	—	—
5	11	10	90.90	—	—
6	10	10	100.00	—	—
7	10	10	100.00	—	—
8	16	15	93.75	—	—
9	11	10	90.90	—	—
10	15	15	100.00	—	—
11	18	18	100.00	—	—
12	17	16	94.11	—	—
13	29	27	93.10	—	—
14	26	25	96.15	—	—
15	25	18	72.00	—	—
16	15	8	53.33	1	6.66
17	15	5	33.33	1	6.66
18	26	4	15.38	8	30.76
19	18	1	5.55	7	38.88
20	22	1	4.54	12	54.54
21	11	—	—	7	63.63
22	20	1	5.00	3	15.00
23	14	—	—	5	35.71
24	6	—	—	2	33.33
25	9	—	—	3	33.33
26	7	—	—	3	42.85
27	1	—	—	—	—
28	6	—	—	3	50.00
29	1	—	—	—	—
30	3	—	—	2	66.67
32	3	—	—	1	33.33
33	1	—	—	—	—
35	2	—	—	2	100.00
38	1	—	—	—	—

sixteen. This is the age of schooling, as 184 of 205 or 89.75 percent of the eldest daughters were recorded as attending school. This is only slightly less than the percentage of sons in school, revealing no great discrepancy in educational opportunity for these daughters. Also the stage of schooling appears to be slightly longer for daughters than for the sons; this points to a prolonged state of dependency for the female which would perhaps correspond to either the lack of employment opportunities for young girls at this time or to a desire to protect the female for a slightly longer period; this is seen too in high school attendance rates. Examining the eldest daughters by ages, we discover a substantial decrease in rates of school attendance of ages fifteen and sixteen, falling from 96 percent at fourteen to 76 percent at age fifteen and to 53 percent at sixteen. However, employment did not rise in a corresponding manner as it did for sons. Only one daughter was employed at age sixteen. This leads to a conclusion that these daughters remained in a state of dependency throughout stage two. The options available to them were school or a continued place in the home. A majority attended school through age sixteen, but the gradual falling off in attendance was not replaced by semidependency.

Stage three indicates a limited commencement of semidependency, as this status was never attained by a majority of eldest daughters aged seventeen to twenty. Only 34.56 percent secured employment, 28 of 81 in this group. More daughters continued in school to ages seventeen and eighteen than did sons. However, it was not until age twenty that a majority of daughters, 54.54 percent, were able to secure employment and attain the point we consider as semidependent status. Predominantly, the daughters of native-born fathers with skilled laborer or higher status occupations, with a variety of values of wealth, continued in school. Daughters of a great variety of fathers, ethnically and occupationally, joined the workforce—no great differences are readily apparent in the status of fathers. Nor were any of the daughters' occupations exceptional; dressmakers, tailoresses, and teachers predominated, with the daughters of native-born or Scottish fathers more often as teachers. What is most important here is that most daughters continued to be dependent at the point when sons became semidependent. An absolute majority of these females, forty-three, held no position outside the home, and fifty-four were either in school or at home, both states of continued dependency on their families.

Stage four is a most interesting period in the development of these eldest daughters. This stage has been defined as comprising ages twenty-one to twenty-three, and perhaps it is questionable whether this is really a distinct stage in the cycle of dependency relationships; however, for our purposes it is assumed to be so. This is the transition period between the mixture of dependency and semidependency found in stage three and the leaving of the parental household. Whether this departure marks the commencement of complete independence or a new form of dependency as a wife, servant, nurse, governess, etc., would vary from daughter to daughter.

Age twenty-one, while revealing a smaller number of daughters at home, marks the greatest advancement of semidependency as 63 percent were employed. Again one finds great variance in the ethnic and occupational status of the fathers. Age twenty-two represents something of a paradox, as there is a substantial increase in the numbers at home (although undoubtedly related to the limits of the sample population), but very few are employed—85 percent are completely dependent. Remarkably, the one daughter who is recorded as attending school is the daughter of an Irish laborer. The number of girls twenty-three falls again, but a rise in the percentage employed occurs. Thus, it would seem likely that stage four indicates the beginnings of the transition to a new status outside the parental home, but notably, the majority of females, two-thirds, never attain semidependent status.

			DAUGHTERS — STAGES OF DEPENDENCY		
table 4					
AGES	*NUMBER*	*IN SCHOOL*	*PERCENTAGE*	*WORKING*	*PERCENTAGE*
1– 3	13	1	7.62	—	—
4–16	205	184	89.75	1	0.01
17–20	81	11	13.58	28	34.56
21–23	45	1	2.22	15	33.33
24–38	40	—	—	16	40.00

Finally, stage five represents the point at which most daughters have left or will soon be leaving home. The number at home remains rather low consistently. This is indicative of the falling age of marriage which one would expect to have reached ages twenty-two to twenty-four by 1860, as Robert V. Wells reports it at 21.6 by 1880–1889.[7] As mentioned above, it is impossible to discern if these daughters advanced from semidependence to independence, dependence to independence, remained dependent but in a new way, or returned to a state of dependence. For those who remained at home, aged twenty-four or older, we discover that more than in any other group are employed, 40 percent. For those daughters this is the stage of semidependency, for some to last a life-time, while a majority continue to remain dependent—for both a time of spinsterhood.

The Census data from Boston thus allow us to examine the development patterns and dependency relations for sons and daughters as they relate to family, work, and school. Sons, it would seem, advance through stages of dependency and semidependency to achieve independence some time after the age of twenty-two. Daughters, on the other hand, remain to a large degree dependent until leaving the family at approximately twenty-two to twenty-four.

While it is hoped that some new insight on the dependency relationships of children to their families may be gained from this study, its central limitations must be made clear. First, using such census data from one year requires an effort to abstract dynamics from a static source. This is problematic, but perhaps, I would urge, not a complete disability, to a first step in this research. More may be learned from this, possibly, than from an examination of selected memoirs which reveal the development of some exceptional persons. The second difficulty may be more severe. This arises from the nature of the sample itself and begs the question, how much can we isolate from such uncertain age distributions? Larger samples would control for this somewhat, but we will never be able to assume a perfect equality of numbers in each age group. Some variance must be expected and has been taken into account. Abnormal age distributions would skew the results, unless the age-sex structure of the

[7]Robert V. Wells, "Demographic Change and the Life Cycle of American Families," *Journal of Interdisciplinary History*, II (Autumn 1971), 281.

population is taken into account. In addition, the size of the sample is small and does not allow for firm control of ethnic, occupational, and wealth variables or for family size.

The importance of the study at this point does not lie specifically in the model of five stages presented. The stages are uncertain and vague. But it is the progression of the son or daughter through the construct of these stages that is important for what it reveals about the nature of dependency in the family with relation to school and work.

But what does this pattern of growing up mean? Recent studies have considered the nineteenth-century family and the problem of adolescence. By reexamining the empirical evidence in light of this work, we shall be able to put it into context as well as to test some ideas.

The question of adolescence and opinions concerning childhood and youth in the nineteenth century have central bearing on the problem of dependency and the family. John and Virginia Demos, while arguing that adolescence as a concept we now understand and employ did not exist before the last two decades of the century, discovered that it did incorporate older attitudes that were prevalent during the period of this study. Common ideas about childhood and youth from 1800-1875 were revealed in a rapidly developing literature of child-rearing advice and a large body of books aimed at the young people of the country. This development related to a deepening interest in the recognition of childhood as a distinct period of life, not comparable to the later years of maturity, and grew from a previously felt indifference or even ignorance of the problem.

Significantly, the Demoses conclude that the predominant concern evident in these books related to the problem of authority.[8] This of course reflects upon the dependency of children. The basic message in one form or another was that the authority of parents must be established early in a child's youth and firmly maintained throughout the years of growth. Even small infants were "willful" as a result of a "depraved nature."[9] This danger was to be suppressed by training in obedience before it could develop beyond control and result in grave implications for the adult personality. As Catherine Beecher phrased it in *A Treatise on Domestic Economy*, "But children can be very early taught, that their happiness, both now and hereafter, depends on habits of submission, self-denial, and benevolence."[10] This was the intellectual aura in which the dependency of Boston's youth must be understood. Many scholars, in the face of observations by Toqueville, Martineau, and others, have con-

[8]Demos and Demos, "Adolescence," 633.

[9]*Ibid.*

[10]Catherine Beecher, *A Treatise on Domestic Economy for the Use of Young Ladies at Home, and at School* (Boston, 1842), p. 224; see also *Young Bride at Home* (Boston, 1836); Mrs. Child, *The Mother's Book* (Boston, 1831); W. A. Alcott, *The Young Mother* (Boston, 1836); *The Mother's Assistant* (Boston, 1840–1850); and Bernard Wishy, *The Child and the Republic* (Philadelphia, 1967), Part 1.

cluded that such injunctions seemed of pronounced importance because of fears that parental authority was diminishing. Spirits of independence, disorder, disobedience, licentiousness, and indulgence were seen as prevalent in children and had to be confronted by the family, especially the mother.[11] Beecher stated that in the training of children, all temptations to which they were liable must be taken into account, particularly deceit, dishonesty, and debt, which were "common" in the United States.[12]

Another category of books developed in addition to the child-rearing literature — books written specifically for the "youth" or adolescents of the time. In these works, the Demoses and Kett find the emergence of an awareness of "youth" as a critical transition period. While the word "adolescence" appeared rarely outside of scientific writing before G. Stanley Hall's monumental work was published, ideas about adolescence were prevalent in the nineteenth century, constituting a distinct development from the seventeenth and eighteenth centuries.[13] This new awareness of childhood involved an effort to protect juvenile innocence and related to the fears sketched above. Kett relates this desire to the "immense importance which common school reformers attached to the location of school houses away from the busy scenes of secular life and to the gradual conversion of the school 'into an asylum for the preservation and culture of childhood.' "[14] As well, such sentiments were echoed by the founders of boarding schools, as James McLachlan shows superbly.[15] Much of this was to protect the youth from the onset of sexual passions which accompanied puberty. This adds some insight to the lengthy dependency and semidependency found in South Boston.

Kett points to the inclusion of age-grading in education which occurred at roughly the same time as the heightened awareness of adolescence. The fact that a majority of sons and daughters left school in the same year lends some support to the success of age-grading in urban Boston. But direct causal relationship between views on adolescence and the introduction of grading in common schools is uncertain; it does merit further attention.

On the basis of the evidence from Boston, we may offer some urban contrasts to Kett's age-delineations of "growing up" which are rural-oriented.[16] These contrasts have an importance in the urbanization processes which were then accelerating. The pattern suggested by the census data is that teenage experiences in urban areas by 1860 were beginning to be graded by numerical age. It would appear that there was a common age for leaving school, and, at least for the sons, a common age for starting work. Apprenticeship began at age

---

[11]Demos and Demos, "Adolescence," 633; Wishy, *The Child and the Republic*, Part 1; and Bridges, "Family Patterns," *passim*.

[12]Beecher, *op cit.*, *passim*.

[13]Kett, "Adolescence and Youth," pp. 285 and 286.

[14]*Ibid.*, 287.

[15]James McLachlan, *American Boarding Schools: A History* (New York, 1971).

[16]Kett, "Growing Up," passim, and "Adolescence and Youth," 294.

sixteen and did not continue beyond nineteen or twenty. Only three sons, aged fifteen, sixteen, and nineteen (son of an Irish laborer), were recorded as both working and attending school, a possible discontinuity of experience. The nature of relationships in these urban families makes it possible to suggest whether a son or daughter were dependent or semidependent, a process which would be more difficult in rural New England. For sons, semidependency or a partial removal from the parental household generally followed leaving school. The length of semidependency had shortened from the seventeenth century, but perhaps not as much as Kett would have us believe on the basis of his rural evidence. He maintains that the critical period of permanent separation came between ages seventeen and twenty-one.[17] The Boston sons, I would argue, generally did not leave home before age twenty. Finally, the regularity of the pattern of dependency in Boston suggests that the initiative attributed to the nurture of a rural boyhood was restrained somewhat by the urban environment, for there was a greater continuity of experience and the social institutions were probably tighter, if we accept Kett's terms.[18]

This too would add some insight to the working out of the tensions pointed to by Bridges, as a restraint on the environment of striving for success. This, however, is not made clear by the evidence, and is only one possible hypothesis.

The desirability of prolonging youth or adolescence was, in some respects, a nineteenth-century discovery, Kett reveals. But the corollary of encouraging a postponement of career or vocational choice which G. Stanley Hall and twentieth-century opinions have emphasized was not yet prevalent before 1860.[19] Thus the sons in South Boston remained at home for a pronounced period of time, but they generally began working early, at sixteen or seventeen. How rigid their choices were, how many positions they would hold, how much they were influenced by the economic or class status of their family, we cannot tell. This too merits further research.

Kett follows the Demoses in their interpretation of the nature of urban life on the process of growing up.[20] They postulate that before the nineteenth century, most families, farm families, were characterized by a high degree of internal unity. Children and adults shared the same tasks, entertainments, friends, and expectations: there was a continuum between the generations. But this began to change. Kett has shown the effects of growing up in New England from 1800 to 1840. City children, they argue, did not often have a significant economic role within the family as a whole. This was certainly the case in the Boston sample. So, the Demoses maintain, the children are placed into closer proximity with other families and have a new opportunity to develop numerous contacts among their own peers. "Thus there develops in the urban setting an

[17]Kett, "Growing Up," 10.
[18]*Ibid.*, 13, 14.
[19]Kett, "Adolescence and Youth," 296 and 297.
[20]*Ibid.*, 288; Demos and Demos, "Adolescence," 636–637.

important 'discontinuity of age groups.' "[21] Children and adults become more obviously separated from one another and peer group activity could be seen as a weakening of parental authority. This is important to grasp, but one must be wary of drawing firm lines between rural and urban, for as Kett notes, there is abundant evidence of peer groups in small towns. This may well have been the case for the Boston children, with so many in school together. The key question is, however, what effect did the prolongation of semidependency past adolescence have on this process, as adolescence was not yet institutionalized to any significance. Research on youth groups in the mid-nineteenth century, such as Natalie Davis has done for early modern France, is strongly needed.[22]

Finally, Kett reveals that one reason for the emphasis on later adolescence was that the perils of the late teen years were of a more absorbing interest than those of the earlier years. The perils of leaving home, which would not be found until the immediate post-adolescent years in Boston, were critical. "As the image of home became more sentimentalized in the nineteenth century, one's entry into the world of affairs appeared more threatening. Or, we can argue, the more menacing the world became, the greater the disposition to drench home and family with sentiment."[23]

In this way, we may view William Bridges' conclusion that between 1825 and 1875 "the home and the market place became the foci of opposite sets of values, one stultifyingly static and the other recklessly dynamic. Each was the more extreme for the presence of the other, while each acted as a brake on the other."[24] The experience of South Boston's youth, dependence and semidependence to the early twenties, makes sense in this framework of "advance-with-safety, progress-with-restraint, exploit-with-control." The counterweight of the family to the forces of a rapidly changing society and economy perhaps under the guidance of the mother as urged by the authors of child-rearing manuals, may be seen in the length of child residence at home. This points to the partial failure of training in detachment Bridges found. This may well have been the way children, at least in South Boston, grew up and how acculturation within the family took place.[25]

comments and questions _____

    1. Does this article address a clearly stated problem?
    2. Do you agree with the author that "analyses of oldest children at home by age

[21]Demos and Demos, "Adolescence," 637.

[22]Natalie Z. Davis, "The Reasons of Misrule: Youth Groups and Charivaris in Sixteenth-Century France," *Past and Present,* 50 (February 1971), 41–75.

[23]Kett, "Adolescence and Youth," 295.

[24]Bridges, "Family Patterns," 10.

[25]For a fascinating study of "growing up," comparing data over time, see Michael B. Katz, "Growing Up in the Nineteenth Century," Working Paper 31, Canadian Social History Project, *Interim Report,* 4 (Toronto 1972), 50–101.

provides a viable and useful way of studying the family in terms of child dependency?"

3. Both the location of the population studied and the process of sampling that population have implications for the generalizability of the findings. Discuss the population/sample and its effect on any generalizability. Does Graff address this point?

4. Does Graff draw different conclusions about patterns of dependency between sons and daughters?

5. If this study were replicated this year, do you think similar findings about patterns of dependency would be obtained?

DESCRIPTIVE RESEARCH

chapter three _____

Descriptive research, as we are using the term, is concerned with determining the nature and degree of existing conditions. Some authors use the term in a broader sense and include what we have labeled as correlational and ex-post-facto under descriptive research. Others lump correlational and ex-post-facto under measures of relationship. Many studies cannot easily be classified under only one of these headings because they contain descriptions as well as measures of relationship. Our differentiation is based on both the methodology and primary purposes of the studies. Descriptive research may contain data on either one or more groups. Correlational studies are likely to involve only one group but must contain measures on more than one variable for each person in the group. Ex-post-facto studies must involve at least two groups. The purpose of the study also helps determine the classification. If a study is primarily intended to describe existing conditions and not make predictions or causal inferences we have classified it as descriptive. If the study is primarily designed to predict or study the degree of relationship of two or more variables, we have classified it as correlational. If the study is primarily intended to help answer causal questions (but is nonexperimental in design) we have classified it as ex-post-facto.

There are diverse approaches that might be employed in descriptive research. One might employ a *case study* approach where an extensive study is made of a few individuals or a *survey* approach where many individuals are sampled. Some descriptive research is *cross-sectional,* other research is *longitudinal* in nature. In cross-sectional research, data are gathered at one point in time, but different subgroups are sampled. In longitudinal research, data are gathered on the same subjects at different points in time. Since cross-sectional research can be completed much quicker it is often the favored approach.

However, one must be careful not to draw longitudinal conclusions from cross-sectional research. For example, Wechsler,[1] when norming the Wechsler Adult Intelligence Scale (WAIS), found that older people did not perform as well on the verbal aspects of intelligence as did people in their late twenties. Some people interpreted these data as indicating that intelligence *declines* with age. However, in Wechsler's sample the younger groups had a higher educational level than the older groups, and this could have accounted for the differences he found. Bayley,[2] using longitudinal evidence, did not obtain the same results and concluded that there is continued intellectual growth until age 50.

As with other types of research, there are particular problems in descriptive research for which both users and consumers need to be watchful. For the most part these involve the data-gathering procedures or instruments.

Sampling of Data

Too often a researcher chooses a sample that is convenient rather than one that is representative. This is true in all types of research. One type of descriptive research, however, has an additional sampling problem. In *survey* research the response rate is often so low that the results are questionable even when the original sample was adequate. A low response rate is most prevalent in research where data are collected by mail questionnaires, but a low response rate can also occur in interview situations through a refusal to be interviewed. (This has recently become more of a problem in interviewing inner-city residents. Fear and hostility combined often make for a very low response rate in urban areas. Many residents do not even answer a knock on their door.)

A low response rate can certainly result in misleading data. Suppose we were to ask the following question in a survey: "Do you think survey research is valuable?" Suppose 70 percent of the questionnaires are returned and that 70 percent of these have been marked affirmatively to the question. Ignoring the nonrespondents, it appears that a substantial majority think favorably of survey research. But what about the 30 percent that did not respond? It may be that they did not respond precisely because they *do* think survey research is worthless. If one added these to the 21 percent of the original sample (30 percent of the respondents) who responded "no" there is a majority (51 percent) who have negative feelings about survey research.

When reading survey research literature, you should always look to see if the response rate is reported. Warwick and Lininger[3] have suggested that 40

---

[1]David Wechsler, *Wechsler Adult Intelligence Scale Manual.* New York: The Psychological Corporation, 1955.

[2]Nancy Bayley, On the growth of intelligence. *American Psychologist,* **10** (1955), 805–818.

[3]Donald P. Warwick and Charles A. Lininger, *The Sample Survey: Theory and Practice.* New York: McGraw-Hill, 1975, p. 129.

or 50 percent is considered a good return on mail questionnaires whereas 75 percent is often a minimum acceptable level in surveys using telephone interviews. Unfortunately, many studies do not even report the percentage of returns—probably because they are embarrassingly low. You should tend to discount results if response rate is not reported.

If the response rate is too low, the researcher should attempt to adjust the results to compensate for the nonresponses. Any such adjustment should be fully described by the researcher.

One might, for example, obtain information that allows comparisons of the respondents and nonrespondents on some set of independent variables. If it is found that there are some significant differences, appropriate weighting procedures can be employed to approximate the data that one would have obtained had the total original sample responded. If it is found that the two groups are not different on this set of independent variables, it might be assumed that there would also be no differences on the dependent variables and that no adjustment is necessary. This is, of course, a risky assumption. There may still be differences on the dependent variables. Thus, rather than resorting to this type of statistical manipulation, it is more desirable that the researcher extend special efforts to obtain dependent variable information on a sample of the original nonrespondents to see whether they do differ on the dependent variables. The final results can be adjusted on the basis of this information. In general, any adjustment of results is a very poor substitute for an original high response rate, but it is usually better than a low response rate with no attempt to adjust.

In longitudinal research one must be concerned with subject mortality. Say one started with an unbiased sample of 200 six-year-olds and wished to obtain longitudinal data on these individuals for the next ten years. But, due to subjects moving too far away, refusing to cooperate at later points in time, or dying, longitudinal data can only be obtained on 100 of the original 200. A bias similar to a response rate bias may result, and the investigator should handle this mortality problem similarly to the response rate problem. Just as the response rate on questionnaires should be reported, so also should subject mortality data be reported.

Data-Gathering Procedures

Descriptive research, in general, makes more use of observational techniques, interviews, and questionnaires than do other types of research. Each of these methods has certain problems related to it, and a report on research that used one of these methods should contain a sufficiently complete description of the procedure so that a reader can ascertain whether the problems were alleviated—or at least minimized.

OBSERVATIONAL TECHNIQUES

An observational technique is a procedure whereby the researcher gathers his data by noting certain behaviors of his subjects in specific situations. The major problem in observation is in assuring that the behavior is recorded objectively and reliably. To observe and record is a difficult task. Observers have to be well trained on what to observe and what to ignore in order to do their job correctly.

In addition to using well-trained observers, this procedure requires that the recording forms be well thought out. The time sampling of the behavior and the effect of the observer on the person being observed also need to be considered by the researcher. The research report must describe how the researcher handled all these aspects, and should actually include some coefficient of observer reliability.

A common fault in using observation schedules or checklists is that too often the checklist contains too many aspects of human behavior. A general rule is to have no more traits than can be noted and recorded by the observer. Another problem is attempting to evaluate behavior that occurs so infrequently that reliable observations cannot be made.

QUESTIONNAIRES

The major problem with questionnaires is that the results are often quite misleading. This is due to incorrect wording of the questions. Occasionally, questionnaires will contain leading questions and a consumer must be careful to note whether the wording of the questions influenced the respondent in a certain direction. Suppose, for example, we wished to poll the public to determine their attitudes toward the busing of elementary school children for the purpose of achieving racial balance.

The question:

> What do you think of busing elementary school children to achieve racial balance in the schools?_____For_____Against_____Undecided.

would not be considered leading. The following questions would probably lead to different results.

> Do you think young children should be forced to ride a bus for an hour to attend school when they could attend one within walking distance?
> _____Yes_____ No_____Undecided.

A leading question in the opposite direction might be worded as follows.

> All children should have the opportunity to attend school with others from all walks of life._____Agree_____Disagree_____Undecided.

To interpret the responses to each of these questions as providing us with the proportion who are in favor of busing would obviously be incorrect.

Another example of different wordings of a question that would lead to different responses is as follows:

1. No one in this country should have to go to bed hungry.
2. The government has an obligation to care for the poor.
3. Parents of undernourished children have a right to expect governmental aid.
4. Parents of undernourished children should demand aid from the government.

In interpreting results of questionnaires, one must carefully look at the wording of the questions. At times the respondents may be answering something quite different from what the researcher intended.

As mentioned earlier, one of the major problems encountered when using questionnaires is a low response rate. Some suggestions for minimizing low response rate are:

1. Have a questionnaire that is not complicated to answer.
2. Write a cover letter describing the purpose of the study. Where possible have this letter signed by an "authoritative" person.
3. Enclose a stamped, self-addressed envelope.
4. Send a follow-up post card about two weeks after the questionnaire is mailed.
5. After a lapse of about four weeks send another questionnaire in the event the first was lost or misplaced.
6. Try to make personal or telephone contact if no reply is obtained after a lapse of about six weeks.

A limitation with some of the preceding suggestions (especially no. 6) is that they cannot be done and still maintain anonymity. Another suggestion is to enclose along with a stamped, self-addressed envelope, a stamped, self-addressed postcard which the respondents sign and return simultaneously with their questionnaires. Thus, anonymity of response is maintained but the researcher can get an idea of who responded and who did not.

The reader of research should ask himself these questions as he progresses through a research study that employed questionnaires:

---

1. Are the directions to the respondent clear and concise?
2. Are there any questions where the respondent may not possess the information? An example would be asking a third-grader whether Nationalist China should be excluded from the U.N.
3. Are all the questions asked relevant to the problem? For example, asking

whether we should have a graduated or a flat rate income tax would be inappropriate for a questionnaire dealing with school integration.

4. Does the questionnaire permit the responder to accurately depict his feelings?
5. Are some questions asked where the information could be gathered more easily from other existing sources?
6. How are the responses recorded? Could another method have been employed to make tabulation easier?
7. Has the questionnaire been pretested to obtain answers to the questions listed above?

INTERVIEWS

Interviews are even harder to do correctly than observations. Training of the interviewers is extremely important and their qualifications and training should be explicitly presented in the research report. More training is necessary to conduct unstructured than structured interviews,[4] but in both cases the potential for inadequate results due to poorly trained interviewers is prevalent. The interaction between the interviewer and interviewee can lead to undesirable results. If questions are at all of a personal nature, considerable hostility can result.

Inasmuch as interviews are really nothing more than vocal questionnaires, the cautions previously described and the questions to be raised are equally applicable for both questionnaires and interviews. However, there are some additional questions that must be raised by the reader when he reads studies that have employed the interview as the method of gathering data. These questions are:

1. For both the structured and the unstructured type of interview, but more so for the latter, it is very difficult to quantify (or classify) and analyze the data. How did the researcher handle this?
2. Were probes used appropriately? Did the interviewer probe when he should have? Did he probe when he should not have?
3. If an unstructured interview was used, how were the responses recorded? Verbatim, by tape, and so on? Might the procedure used have introduced any error in the data?
4. How were the subjects motivated? Could this be an uncontrolled source of error in the study?
5. Were there any traits or characteristics of the interviewer that may have influenced the reliability of the data gathered?
6. Was the interviewer(s) trained?
7. What is the reliability of the data?

[4]In a structured interview all the specific questions to be asked, and the extent to which one will probe for the answers, is determined in advance. An unstructured interview is more analogous to a counseling interview. The specific questions asked may well vary from interview to interview. An unstructured interview is most apt to be used in exploratory studies.

All these factors must be carefully considered by the researcher, and his attempts to control them should be clearly presented in the written report.

Examples of Descriptive Research

The examples of descriptive research included in this section cover many different areas. As you read them keep in mind the points raised in the first chapter as well as those points raised in the previous paragraphs.

EVALUATION OF PUBLISHED EDUCATIONAL RESEARCH:
A National Survey*[1]

ANNIE W. WARD
BRUCE W. HALL and
CHARLES F. SCHRAMM

This study is an evaulation of educational research articles published during 1971. It repli-cates a study conducted in 1962 by a committee of AERA. As in the earlier study, it was found that most published research is of mediocre quality. Articles published in journals of "re-lated professions" were rated higher than those published in education journals. However, the discrepancy between the classes of journals was not as great as in 1962. The most frequently cited shortcomings of research articles were in the areas of "procedures," "data analysis," and "summary and conclusions."

This study was designed to determine the quality of educational re-search articles published in educational journals and in journals of related professions. Published educational research is the delivery system by which professional educators acquire much of their understanding of today's educa-tional problems. In this critical communicative process, the need for sound research yielding meaningful, interpretable information is imperative. Yet, considerable doubt has been raised as to the quality of published educational research and, therefore, as to the validity and significance of the data being provided educators via the research reported (Bloom, 1966; Michael, 1963; Scriven, 1960). The only recent comprehensive study of the quality of pub-lished educational research was carried out on a representative sample of 1962 research articles by an *ad hoc* Committee on Evaluation of Research (1967) established by the AERA. That study found that a majority of research articles published in 1962 contained serious flaws. More disturbing, less than 7 percent of the research articles published in education journals were rated as being worthy of publication, and the quality of research published in education jour-

*Reprinted from *American Educational Research Journal*, 12:2 (1975), pp. 109–128. Copyright 1975, American Educational Research Association, Washington, D.C.
[1]The authors gratefully acknowledge the assistance of Larry Schwartz, Jeffrey Moore, George Ross, Mary Brueggeman and Liz Royston in the conduct of this study.

nals was found to be markedly inferior to that published in journals of related professions, primarily psychology.

Numerous guidelines for evaluating educational research have appeared in the last 20 years, attesting to the need for informed, critical evaluation of the material appearing as research (e.g., Best, 1970; Borg, 1963; Dvorak, 1956; Farquhar & Krumboltz, 1959; Johnson, 1957; Kohr & Suydam, 1970; Strauss, 1969; Symond, 1956; Van Dalen, 1958; Wiersma, 1969). However, empirical studies on the question of the quality of actual research have been almost nonexistent. No follow-up of the 1962 work of the AERA Committee on Evaluation of Research has heretofore been undertaken.

The years since 1962 have brought many ostensible advances in educational research (Gallagher, 1970). Membership in the AERA has grown tremendously since 1962; new journals have been established to publish educational research. Educational research is now recognized as a specialty in its own right, not simply a subspecialty of psychology. The years since 1962 have also been the years of federally funded projects in educational research and for programs with a mandate for "evaluation." A consideration of these changes led to the decision to replicate the earlier study.

The purpose of the present study was to determine the quality of the current body of educational research published in journals. In examining the general question of quality of published educational research, the investigators focused on the following specific questions:

1. What percent of the educational research articles published in journals are considered by experts in educational research to (1) merit publication without change, (2) need minor revision to make them acceptable for publication, (3) need major revision to make them acceptable for publication, (4) be so low in quality they should not have been published?

2. How do the experts rate representative educational research articles on specific characteristics related to the quality of research and of research reporting?

3. Is there a difference in quality, both overall and on the specific characteristics, between educational research articles published in (1) research-oriented education journals, (2) nonresearch-oriented education journals, and (3) related professional journals?

4. What specific shortcomings are most frequently cited by experts to substantiate a judgment to reject or require major revisions in an article?

In order to compare the findings with those of a decade ago, the study was, insofar as feasible, a replication of the work of the AERA Committee on Evaluation of Research (1967). Procedural departures from the earlier work were taken where necessary in an attempt to strengthen the research design. Some changes were also required because of changes over the decade in the population of journals and reviewers. Many of the procedural changes were based on recommendations of the earlier investigators (Committee on Evaluation of Research, 1967), or inspired by difficulties that they encountered.

Method

The sampling and data gathering procedures of the study were identical to those of the earlier study of the AERA Committee on Evaluation of Research (1967), except where specifically noted.

SELECTION OF JOURNALS AND ARTICLES

The first task was the identification of the population of educational research articles and selection of a representative sample of the articles. An article was operationally classified as a research article if it contained (1) a statement of the problem, (2) the presentation of data (although not necessarily quantitative data), (3) an analysis of these data, and (4) a statement of conclusions. The following criteria were established for identifying journals publishing educational research: (1) The journals must have been indexed in the *Education Index*, and (2) they must have been cited 10 or more times in chapter bibliographies of the *Review of Educational Research* during the full three year cycle immediately preceding the year selected for study.

Journals were classified as "Related Profession" (RP) if they were indexed in *Ulrich's Periodicals Directory* under the headings of psychology, sociology, and medical science. The remaining journals were classified as either "Educational, publishing primarily research" (ER) or "Educational, publishing primarily non-research" (NR), depending upon the percentage of articles (exclusive of reviews and comments) that were research. The criterion for classification as "primarily research" was 51 percent or more of the articles devoted to research.[2] The 1971 population of journals is reported in Table 1.

In comparing the population of journals with that of the earlier study, the following changes were found:

1. Fifty-seven journals met the selection criteria in 1962, but only 46 met them for 1971. Eight journals in 1962 and two in 1971 had no research articles, leaving a population of 49 for 1962 and 44 for 1971.
2. In 1962, only 5 journals were classified as "Educational, publishing primarily research." In 1971 there were 13, a dramatic change. The number of NR journals decreased from 27 in 1962 to 22. There was no change in the number of RP journals.
3. Several journals selected in 1971 were classified differently than in 1962.

[2]The 1963 study used "percentage of total journal pages devoted to research."

**POPULATION AND SAMPLE OF
EDUCATIONAL RESEARCH ARTICLES PUBLISHED IN 1971**

table 1

		NUMBER OF ARTICLES	
	Journal	Population	Sample
Education Journals with Primarily Research Articles			
1.	AV Communications Review	15	1
2.	American Educational Research Journal	35	3
3.	British Journal of Educational Psychology	37	3
4.	Counselor Education and Supervision	23	2
5.	Educational and Psychological Measurement	40	3
6.	Exceptional Children	58	5
7.	Journal of College Student Personnel	59	5
8.	Journal of Educational Measurement	30	2
9.	Journal of Educational Research	81	6
10.	Journal of Experimental Education	56	5
11.	Journal of Negro Education	27	2
12.	Journal of Research in Science Teaching	49	4
13.	Psychology in the Schools	49	4
	(Total)	(559)	(45)
Educational Journals with Primarily Non-Research Articles			
1.	American Vocational Journal*	6	—
2.	Arithmetic Teacher*	2	—
3.	Audiovisual Instruction*	4	—
4.	Comparative Educational Review	9	1
5.	Educational Leadership	14	1
6.	Elementary School Journal	11	1
7.	Journal of Creative Behavior*	2	—
8.	Journal of School Health	26	2
9.	Journal of School Psychology	31	2
10.	Journal of Special Education	8	1
11.	Journal of Teacher Education	19	2
12.	Mathematics Teacher*	6	1
13.	Personnel and Guidance Journal	7	1
14.	Phi Delta Kappan*	4	—
15.	School Counselor	15	1
16.	School Review*	5	—
17.	School Science and Mathematics	30	2
18.	Science Education	30	2
19.	Science Teacher*	4	1
20.	Teachers College Record*	1	—
21.	Vocational Guidance Quarterly	22	2
22.	Volta Review*	4	1
	(Total)	(260)	(21)
Related Professions			
1.	American Journal of Mental Deficiency	109	9
2.	American Journal of Orthopsychiatry	19	2
3.	Child Development	120	10

		NUMBER OF ARTICLES	
	Journal	Population	Sample
4.	Journal of Applied Psychology	94	8
5.	Journal of Counseling Psychology	97	8
6.	Journal of Educational Psychology	77	6
7.	Journal of Speech and Hearing Disorder	38	3
8.	Journal of Speech and Hearing Research	96	8
9.	Sociology of Education	17	1
	(Total)	(667)	(55)
	Grand Total	1486	121

*Ten journals published less than 7 research articles in 1971. The 38 articles from these journals were treated as a single group for purposes of sampling. A total of 3 articles were chosen from this group with the restriction that no more than one article could come from any given journal. As a result, 7 journals were excluded from the sample.

Three 1962 NR's were ER's in 1971; two 1962 ER's were 1971 NR's, and one 1962 RP became ER in 1971.

4. Of journals added to the list, 6 were ER's, 11 NR's, and 4 RP's; of those deleted, 1 was ER, 15 NR's, and 3 RP's.

One unanticipated difficulty from this objective process of selecting articles was that five articles from three "Related Profession" journals (*American Journal of Mental Deficiency, Journal of Speech and Hearing Research, Journal of Speech and Hearing Disorders*) were so technical in a noneducational specialty that the reviewers were unable to review them. For each such article, a replacement was randomly selected from the same journal. In future studies of this type, perhaps a criterion of "relevance to education" should be added to the selection criteria for the population of articles.

The sample was formed by stratifying the population of articles ($N = 1486$) by journal, and drawing an 8 percent sample of articles at random within each stratum (journal), thereby creating a proportionate stratified random sample of 121 articles (see Table 1). The earlier study sampled from a population of 827 research articles. The 1486 research articles in the 1971 population represents a marked increase in number from a decade earlier, although the 1971 population is contained within fewer journals (44 as compared to 49).[3]

SELECTION OF JUDGES

Judges for the 1962 study were selected from the AERA directory on the basis of their "professional reputation in educational research methodol-

[3] A complete list of the articles used in the study is available from the authors.

ogy." The investigators in the present study decided to begin with a random sample of the members in Division D (Measurement and Research Methodology) of the 1971–72 AERA Directory. The first step was the selection of a 10 percent sample of the approximately 5000 regular members of Division D, selecting the first person randomly, then proceeding to select every 10th person in the directory. The approximately 500 Division D members selected were then sent reply cards inviting them to serve as judges. Of the 489 members who responded, 353 indicated a willingness to participate and supplied information about their background.

Of the 1962 judges 98 percent held a doctorate, 63 percent had taught research courses, 75 percent had supervised a dissertation, and 78 percent had supervised a thesis. The median number of published articles was 16 and the median number of years of full-time research experience was 7. The volunteers for the present study departed somewhat from the original group of judges as to these characteristics, so an attempt was made to select from the pool of volunteers a group which was as similar as possible to the original group of judges. After first being selected in regard to "earned doctor's degree," the volunteers were rank ordered as to "number of publications." An attempt was then made to select those with the greatest number of publications. The final criterion was supervision of theses and dissertations. Even with this deliberate selection, the present sample of judges had fewer publications and a little less research experience than judges for the earlier study, perhaps indicating that they were generally a younger group than those in the 1962 study. The final group of judges selected numbered 171; 121 to serve for the main rating study and 50 to serve in a reliability study of the ratings. The characteristics of the judges are reported in Table 2.

The great majority of judges in the earlier study (84 percent) were members also of the American Psychological Association. A post hoc check of judges in the present study found only 44 percent to be members of APA.[4]

ASSIGNMENT OF ARTICLES TO JUDGES

One of the 121 articles to be evaluated was assigned at random and mailed to each of the 121 judges drawn randomly from the total group of 171 judges. Following a recommendation in the earlier study, the investigators attempted to reduce possible bias on the part of the judges by having all articles reproduced with the name of the journal and the names and addresses of the authors omitted. The remaining 50 judges were each randomly assigned and mailed one of the 121 articles being evaluated by the larger group of judges. The paired ratings thereby derived on 50 of the 121 articles was the basis for a reliability study of the evaluative ratings. A check on the assignment process

[4]A complete list of judges is available from the authors.

table 2

CHARACTERISTICS	PERCENTAGE	MEDIAN	P_{10}	P_{90}
Has earned doctor's degree	100			
Has taught course in methods of educational research	83			
Has supervised doctoral dissertation	73			
Has supervised master's thesis	80			
Has served as a review editor of a journal	56			
Member of APA	44			
Years of "full time equivalent" research experience		6.00	2.13	19.00
Number of educational research articles published		10.05	3.81	48.10

revealed that in no case did a judge receive an article of which he was an author.

Rating data were not received on seven of the 121 articles. Any resulting bias is assumed to be minimal because the missing ratings are distributed across six different journals and all three journal categories. However, for the analysis reported below, the missing ratings reduced the N of the study to 114 and the reliability N to 43.

EVALUATION INSTRUMENT

The evaluation instrument was a modification of that devised by the AERA Committee on Evaluation of Research (1967). It required three types of reactions to the article: (1) ratings on specific characteristics, (2) overall rating, and (3) justification of overall rating.

Each judge was asked to rate his assigned article in terms of 33 characteristics deemed desirable as aspects of quality in conducting and reporting research. For each characteristic, a five-point scale was used, representing five levels of quality:

LEVEL OF QUALITY	DESCRIPTION
5 — Excellent	A model of good practice
4 — Good	A few minor defects
3 — Mediocre	Not good, not bad
2 — Poor	Some serious defects
1 — Completely incompetent	A horrible example

If a characteristic was not appropriate to the research article, the judge was asked to place an "X" by the characteristic.

The 33-item rating scale was an expansion of a 25-item scale used in the earlier study. The investigators added 8 items to the original scale, 2 that were suggested by the earlier study and 6 that arose from the investigators' personal experience in research consumption. The 33-item scale was composed of the following seven subscales: (A) Title (1 item), (B) Problem (6 items), (C) Review of Literature (5 items), (D) Procedures (9 items), (E) Data Analysis (4 items), (F) Summary and Conclusions (5 items), and (G) Form and Style (3 items).

Each judge was next asked to assume the role of editor of a journal that published educational research and to make one of four choices in regard to his assigned article: (1) accept as is for publication, (2) accept for publication after minor revisions, (3) accept only after major revisions, or (4) reject it. This four-choice rating is hereafter referred to as the ARRR rating. Finally, those judges who assigned their article an ARRR rating of 3 or 4 were asked to indicate which of the 33 specific shortcomings they would cite to substantiate their judgment.

In the original study the judge had only three choices in his role as editor: accept as is, accept after minor revisions, or reject. The earlier investigators found that many judges stretched the second category to include major as well as minor revisions. Therefore, "accept after major revision" was added as an explicit category in the present study.

INTERNAL VALIDATION OF THE INSTRUMENT

Since there was no external criterion against which to validate the rating scale, an attempt was made to gauge the consistency of the ratings within the instrument. A total score was computed for each article, by adding the numerical values of the 33 ratings and dividing by the number of items rated.[5] Similarly, a mean rating was computed for each of the seven subscales of the rating scale. The internal consistency of the instrument was checked in two ways:

1. Computation of intercorrelations of all the subscales. These ranged from .20 to .67 with a median value of .48. All intercorrelations were significant ($df = 112$) beyond the .025 alpha level.

2. Computation of the tetrachoric correlation between the total scale score and the ARRR rating on which raters judged the articles on a four-point scale. The ARRR ratings were split so that categories 1 and 2 formed one group and categories 3 and 4 formed the other group. The r_t was .87 ($df = 112$) which is significant beyond the .005 alpha level.

[5]The total scale score from some articles was based on somewhat less than 33 items because one or more items were marked "not applicable" by the judge.

INTERJUDGE RELIABILITY OF THE INSTRUMENT

For 43 articles ratings were received from two judges. Interjudge correlations were computed for all subscales, for the total scale, and for the ARRR ratings. The subscale interjudge correlations ranged from .11 for "Title" to .68 for "Review of the Literature." The median value of these r's was .22. For the total scale, the interjudge r was .44. The interjudge r for the ARRR ratings was .21. In addition, a check was made of the extent of agreement between pairs of judges on the ARRR scale. There were no cases in which an article rated "Reject" by one judge was rated "Accept as is" by the other and vice versa. Of the judgments, 20 percent differed by two categories, 50 percent differed by only one category, and 30 percent were identical.

Findings

Before the data were analyzed, a check was made to see whether the characteristics of the judges were related to their ratings. It was found that the ratings were significantly lower $(p<.01)$ for (a) judges who were members of APA, (b) judges who had taught courses in educational research, and (c) judges who had supervised doctoral and masters' theses. On the other hand, judges who were above the median for "years of research experience" and those who were above the median for "number of articles published" had higher ratings $(p<.01)$ than those below the median. The ratings for judges who had served as journal reviewers did not differ from those of judges who had not been reviewers.

Since it was found that the judges with varying characteristics were quite well distributed among the three types of journals, it was decided to ignore the characteristics of judges in further analyses.

OVERALL QUALITY

The findings on the ARRR ratings of the 114 educational research articles for all journals and across the three journal categories are summarized in Table 3.

A chi-square analysis was made on the distribution of ARRR ratings across the three journal categories, ER, NR, and RP. A chi-square value of 2.50 was obtained $(df = 6)$, which was nonsignificant. The distribution of ratings on overall quality was, therefore, interpreted to be comparable, regardless of the type of journal.

For all journals, only 8 percent of the research articles were rated "acceptable as is for publication," 31 percent were rated "acceptable after

table 3

	NUMBER OF ARTICLES IN SAMPLE	RATED AS *			
SOURCE		ACCEPT AS IS	MINOR RE- VISIONS	MAJOR RE- VISIONS	REJECT
		N %	N %	N %	N %
Education Journals, Primarily Research	42	3 (7)	14 (33)	14 (33)	11 (26)
Education Journals, Primarily Non-research	21	1 (5)	4 (19)	10 (48)	6 (29)
Related Professional Journals	51	5 (10)	17 (33)	15 (29)	14 (28)
All journals	114	9 (8)	35 (31)	39 (34)	31 (27)

* X^2 for distribution of ratings by journal categories, 2.50; *df*, 6; *ns*

minor revisions, 34 percent were rated "acceptable only after major revisions," and 27 percent were rated "reject."

RATINGS ON THE 33 CHARACTERISTICS

The mean ratings on the 33 specific characteristics of the 114 educational research articles for all journals, for all education journals, and across the three journal categories are presented in Table 4.

For all journals the highest mean rating was assigned to "title is well related to content" (3.80) and the lowest was assigned to "limitations of the study are stated" (2.37), followed closely by "validity and reliability of data gathering procedures are established" (2.43). Median rating was 3.26. For all education journals the mean ratings ranged from 2.21 to 3.55, with a median of 3.00.

The mean ratings of the 33 characteristics for the articles in ER journals ranged from 2.19 to 3.60, with a median of 3.04. For the articles in NR journals, the mean ratings ranged from 2.16 to 3.76, with a median of 2.90. For the articles in the RP journals, the mean ratings ranged from 2.54 to 4.13, with a median of 3.45.

On the following characteristics, the assigned ratings were considerably below the median for all three journal categories: (1) limitations of the study are stated, (2) validity and reliability of data gathering procedures are established, (3) studies are examined critically, (4) assumptions are clearly stated, (5) research design is free of specific weaknesses, and (6) method of sampling is appropriate.

The following characteristics received ratings considerably above the median for all three journal categories: (1) title is well related to article, (2) problem is significant, (3) sources of important findings are noted, (4) data gathering methods are described, (5) conclusions are relevant to the problem, (6) report is logically organized, and (7) tone of the report displays an unbiased attitude.

RATINGS ON THE SUBSCALES

The mean and standard deviations across the rating subscales are presented for the three journal categories and for all journals in Table 5.

A MANOVA was performed using journal category as an independent variable composed of three levels (ER, NR, RP) and using the 7 subscale ratings as correlated dependent variables. The MANOVA yielded a multivariate F value of $2.17 = 14; 210$, with alpha less than .01, indicating the existence of differences across journal categories on the rating subscales. The differences were in favor of the RP journals.

Univariate F's were generated for each of the 7 subscales separately. With an effective significance level set at .005 to control for alpha over the 7 analyses, the table shows differences across journal categories for dependent variable A (Title) and dependent variable C (Review of the Literature). The differences favored the RP journals.

In an attempt to gain further insight into the behavior of the rating values, a Type 1 ANOVA for subscales by journal categories was performed and the results summarized in Table 6. The ANOVA revealed a main effect on journal category significant beyond the .001 alpha level and a main effect on subscales also significant beyond the .001 alpha level. There was no significant interaction between the two variables.

The post hoc analysis for the subscale means indicated that the difference between A (Title) and G (Form and Style) was not significant, while the means for both of these scales differed from those for the other five subscales. The means of the other five subscales did not differ significantly from each other. For the journal categories, the post hoc analysis indicated that the mean for RP journals was significantly higher than that for both ER and NR journals, but the difference between the means of the ER and NR journals was not significant. However, the difference between RP journals and the education journals was not as great as in the 1962 study.

SPECIFIC SHORTCOMINGS CITED BY JUDGES

Each judge who, in the role of editor, chose to "reject" his article or to "accept only after major revisions" was asked to indicate the specific shortcomings he would cite to substantiate his judgment.

table 4

MEAN RATINGS OF 33 CHARACTERISTICS OF 114 RESEARCH ARTICLES PUBLISHED IN 1971

CHARACTERISTICS	EDUCATION JOURNALS, RESEARCH	EDUCATION JOURNALS, NON-RESEARCH	ALL EDUCATION JOURNALS	RELATED PROFESSION JOURNALS	ALL JOURNALS
A. Title					
(1) Title is well related to content of article	3.60	3.45	3.55	4.13	3.80
B. Problem					
(2) Problem is clearly stated	3.49	2.95	3.31	3.80	3.54
(3) Hypotheses are clearly stated	2.90	2.75	2.84	2.93	2.88
(4) Problem is significant	3.28	3.38	3.31	3.78	3.52
(5) Assumptions are clearly stated	2.45	2.32	2.41	2.76	2.56
(6) Limitations of the study are stated	2.19	2.33	2.24	2.54	2.37
(7) Important terms are defined	2.94	2.70	2.86	2.86	2.86
C. Review of literature					
(8) Coverage of the literature is adequate*	3.05	2.80	2.97	3.62	3.27
(9) Review of the literature is well organized*	3.05	2.85	2.98	3.55	3.24
(10) Studies are examined critically*	2.24	2.16	2.21	2.94	2.55
(11) Source of important findings is noted*	3.18	3.16	3.18	3.84	3.48
(12) Relationship of the problem to previous research is made clear	3.03	3.00	3.02	3.82	3.39
D. Procedures					
(13) Research design is described fully	3.07	3.19	3.11	3.68	3.36
(14) Research design is appropriate to solution of the problem	2.98	2.71	2.89	3.44	3.14
(15) Research design is free of specific weaknesses	2.49	2.48	2.48	2.90	2.67
(16) Population and sample are described	3.02	3.24	3.10	3.67	3.35
(17) Method of sampling is appropriate	2.61	2.75	2.66	2.77	2.71
(18) Data gathering methods or procedures are described	3.10	3.24	3.15	3.84	3.46

(19)	Data gathering methods or procedures are appropriate to the solution of the problem	2.95	2.95	2.95	3.15
(20)	Data gathering methods or procedures are used correctly	3.14	3.30	3.19	3.37
(21)	Validity & reliability of data gathering procedures are established	2.19	2.52	2.31	2.43
E.	Data Analysis				
(22)	Appropriate methods are selected to analyze data	3.20	2.95	3.12	3.27
(23)	Methods utilized in analyzing the data are applied correctly	3.24	2.80	3.09	3.41
(24)	Results of the analysis are presented clearly	2.91	3.05	2.95	3.17
(25)	Tables and figures are effectively used*	3.23	2.70	3.05	3.08
F.	Summary & Conclusions				
(26)	Conclusions are clearly stated	3.38	3.20	3.32	3.43
(27)	Conclusions are substantiated by the evidence presented	3.02	2.80	2.95	3.01
(28)	Conclusions are relevant to the problem*	3.50	3.21	3.41	3.55
(29)	Conclusions are significant*	2.90	2.88	2.89	2.94
(30)	Generalizations are confined to the population from which the sample was drawn	2.49	2.80	2.59	2.80
G.	Form & Style				
(31)	Report is clearly written	3.14	3.76	3.35	3.49
(32)	Report is logically organized	3.32	3.43	3.36	3.56
(33)	Tone of the report displays an unbiased, impartial, scientific attitude	3.29	3.43	3.33	3.55
	Median	3.04	2.90	3.00	3.26

* Variables not in 1962 survey.

**MEANS AND STANDARD DEVIATIONS
OF 7 SUBSCALES FOR 3 CATEGORIES OF JOURNALS**

table 5

				TYPE OF JOURNAL					
		Education, Research		*Education, Nonresearch*		*Related Profession*		*All Journals*	
	Subscale	*M*	*SD*	*M*	*SD*	*M*	*SD*	*M*	*SD*
A.	Title	3.60	1.01	3.45	.92	4.13	.97	3.80	.97
B.	Problem Statement	2.84	.76	2.77	.94	3.14	.75	2.96	.79
C.	Review of Literature	2.88	1.01	2.72	1.10	3.53	.87	3.14	.97
D.	Procedures	2.86	.92	2.94	.90	3.34	.81	3.09	.87
E.	Data Analysis	3.09	1.07	2.87	1.07	3.44	.90	3.21	1.00
F.	Summary and Conclusions	3.08	.94	2.97	.72	3.31	.76	3.16	.83
G.	Form and Style	3.25	.96	3.54	.93	3.78	.77	3.54	.88
	Total	2.99	.73	2.94	.78	3.41	.62	3.17	.72

**ANALYSIS OF VARIANCE FOR 7 SUBSCORES
AND 3 CATEGORIES OF JOURNALS**

table 6

Source of Variation	*MS*	*df*	*F*	*p*
Between Journal Categories (J)	19.11	2	6.10	<.001
Error	3.13	111		
Between Subscales	7.96	6	13.95	<.001
(J) ×(S)	.73	12	1.27	ns
Error	.57	666		

The 10 most frequently cited shortcomings of articles in all journals in order of frequency and with percent of articles affected were:

1. Research design is free of specific weakness (27 percent).

2. Research design is appropriate to solution of the problem (23 percent).

3. Validity and reliability of data gathering procedures are established (22 percent).

4. Conclusions are substantiated by the evidence presented (22 percent).

5. Methods of sampling are appropriate (21 percent).

6. Appropriate methods are selected to analyze data (21 percent).

7. Conclusions are significant (20 percent).

8. Limitations of the study are stated (19 percent).
9. Tables and figures are used correctly (18 percent).
10. Results of the analysis are presented clearly (16 percent).

The pattern of shortcomings in the total sample of articles was generally common across all three journal categories. A Kendall coefficient of concordance (W) computed on the three sets of rankings was found to be .71, indicating a significant $(p<.001)$ relationship among the rankings across the three journal categories. Virtually all of the most frequently cited characteristics were contained within the following three subscales: (1) Procedures, (2) Data Analysis, and (3) Summary and Conclusions. Those characteristics relevant to Title, Problem, Review of Literature, and Form and Style were relatively free of frequent citations.

DISCUSSION

The findings and conclusions of this study should be interpreted in light of the following limitations:

1. As in the original study, the articles were evaluated by judges who were considered expert in educational research but not necessarily in the specific area of the study which they evaluated. Matching specialty of the article to specialty of the judge might have produced somewhat different results.

2. The population of articles in the study was created using an arbitrary, though objective, operational definition of "educational research." Undoubtedly, a change in this definition would alter the population makeup and possibly result in a population with characteristics different from the one in this study.

3. Generalizations from this study should be limited to articles published in the year 1971. Although it is reasonable to suggest that similar patterns may exist for articles published during other years, no evidence bearing on this point is at hand.

CONCLUSIONS

The present study was a replication of a study conducted in 1962 by an *ad hoc* committee of the AERA. Interpretation of the findings necessarily requires some comparisons with those of the earlier study. These comparisons must consider three variables: (1) The quality of the articles, (2) biases of the judges for or against a class of journals, and (3) the reference point or rating standard of the judges.

The primary concern of the investigators was with the first variable, i.e., the quality of the research. However, all conclusions and comparisons regarding the quality of the research must be tentative because effects due to the other two variables are unknown at the present time.

If the possible problems of judge bias and judge standards are ignored, the following conclusions may be drawn:

1. The percentage of published articles rated "reject" was lower for 1971 (27 percent) than for 1962 (40 percent), but the percentage rated "accept as is" was also lower (9 percent in 1971, 19 percent in 1962). These data are confounded by the change in the rating scale from a three-point scale in 1962 to a four-point scale in 1971. If the "minor revisions" category for the 1971 study is collapsed with "accept as is," then the percentage of acceptable articles is still only 39 percent.

2. The superiority of the "Related Profession" journals over "Education" journals is not as apparent in this study as it was in the 1962 study. Unlike the results of the earlier study which found a significant difference in favor of the RP journals on the ARRR rating, there was no difference in the percentage of each of the ARRR ratings assigned to each category of journals in the present study. For the means of the ratings on the 33 specific characteristics, the difference between education and RP journals, although significant, was less pronounced than in 1962. The median of the item ratings for all education journals in 1971 (3.00) was very close to the median in 1962 (3.03) while that for RP journals was lower than for 1962 (3.45 for 1971, 3.93 for 1962).

3. As in the 1962 study, the present study found the quality of published educational research to be generally mediocre. For example, the median of the item ratings for all journals in the present study was 3.26, barely above 3.0, defined in the study as "mediocre—not good, not bad." The comparable median in the 1962 study was 3.27. In the present study, only 12 percent of the articles were rated 4.00 or better and only 4 percent were rated below 2.00.

4. In the present study, the greatest deficiencies of articles were in characteristics related to "Procedures," "Data Analysis," and "Summary and Conclusions." The specific characteristics with the lowest ratings generally came from these three sections, as did the most frequently cited shortcomings. In the 1962 study, four characteristics were cited with great frequency by the judges in regard to being shortcomings of 1962 research articles. All four were among the 10 most frequently cited shortcomings of articles in the present study. These characteristics were concerned with (1) the validity and reliability of the evidence, (2) the appropriateness of methods used to analyze data, (3) the substantiation of the conclusions by the evidence presented, and (4) the clarity of the presentation of results. All four of these characteristics are critically important to consumers of research to assure proper interpretation of research findings.

DISCUSSION

The preceding conclusions are based on two assumptions: (1) that no biases for or against the various journal categories existed in either study, and (2) that the judges in the present study used essentially the same standards of excellence as were used by the judges in 1962.

The first assumption is clearly open to question. In the 1962 study the judges knew the author of the article and the journal in which it was published. It is quite possible that the judges in that study were biased in favor of journals of "Related Professions," since 84 percent of them were members of a related profession (APA). In the present study an attempt was made to remove this source of bias by using "blind" reviewers. Furthermore, only 44 percent of the judges were APA members. A more reasoned assumption, therefore, is that the role of human bias differed across the two studies, being more suspect in the earlier study.

The second assumption is supported by the similarity of judge characteristics in the two studies and by the fact that virtually identical procedures were used for both studies in defining the population, sampling articles, and gathering the rating data. However, there is a possibility that the judges' expectations are higher now than ten years ago. There are now more educational journals devoted primarily to research (13 compared to 5 in 1962). Furthermore. 89 percent of the 1971 sample of educational journals list a board of "reviewers" and the statement of their editorial process indicates that articles are reviewed by someone other than the editor. In 1962 only 52 percent of the editors of educational journals indicated that they used such a referee process. In both studies all RP journals were refereed.

The preceding discussion suggests that a "masking" effect may have occurred; i.e., that the quality of published research may have improved but that the judges' expectations may have been revised concomitantly. If indeed judges' standards have been raised and if selective bias favoring RP journals operated in the 1962 study but not in the present study, then one could conclude that research published in educational journals (if not in RP journals) has improved in quality since 1962.

There is still cause for concern that journals are publishing articles which judges generally found less than acceptable. This situation is especially puzzling since the judges were drawn out of essentially the same universe as the referees of the journals. In fact 56 percent of the judges has served as journal reviewers and there was no difference between the ratings of judges who had served as reviewers and those of judges who had not. This situation suggests that journal reviewers, in reviewing articles for actual publication, use criteria different from those that were used in this study.

The generally mediocre rating data and other data of the study also suggest a relative lack of consensus on research standards in the field. For example, of nine articles rated "reject" by the first reliability judges, only 3 were rated "reject" by the second reliability judges while 3 were rated "accept after major revisions" and 3 were rated "accept after minor revisions." The interjudge reliability estimates of .44 for the total scale and .21 for the ARRR ratings are indicative of a diversity in standards.

On the other hand, it is possible that the relative lack of consensus on research standards in the study is an artifact of the random assignment of articles to judges; no attempt was made to match specialty of the article to specialty of the judge, as a journal editor might do. Two reviewers from a common specialty could be expected to agree more than judges from dissimilar specialties, provided that the criteria for excellence were made explicit as they were in the present study.

references _____

American Educational Research Association, Committee on Evaluation of Research (E. Wandt, chairman). An evaluation of educational research published in journals. Unpublished (1967).

Best, J. W. *Research in education.* Englewood Cliffs, N.J.: Prentice-Hall, 1970.

Bloom, B.S. Twenty-five years of educational research. Presidential address presented to the American Educational Research Association, Chicago, 1966.

Borg, W. R. *Education research: An introduction.* N.Y.: McKay, 1963.

Dvorak, E. A. General guide to a study of research reports. *Peabody Journal of Education,* 1956, *34,* 141–144.

Farquhar, W. W., & Krumboltz, J. D. A checklist for evaluating experimental research in psychology and education. *Journal of Educational Research,* 1959, *52,* 353–354.

Gallagher, J. J. The changing face of educational research and development. An address at the American Educational Research Association convention, Minneapolis, 1970.

Johnson, G. B. A method for evaluating research articles in education. *Journal of Educational Research,* 1957, *51,* 149–151.

Kohr, R. K., & Suydam, M. N. An instrument for evaluating survey research. *Journal of Educational Research,* 1970, *64,* 78–85.

Michael, W. B. Teacher personnel: A brief evaluation of the research reviewed. *Review of Educational Research,* 1963, *33,* 443.

Scriven, M. The philosophy of science in educational research. *Review of Educational Research,* 1960, *30,* 426.

Strauss, S. Guidelines for analysis of research reports. *Journal of Educational Research,* 1969, *63,* 165–169.

Symond, P. M. A research checklist in educational psychology. *Journal of Educational Psychology,* 1956, *47,* 100–109.

Van Dalen, D. B. A research checklist in education. *Educational Administration and Supervision,* 1958, *44,* 174–178.

Wiersma, W. *Research methods in education: An introduction.* N.Y.: Lippincott, 1969.

comments and questions _____

1. Quality of educational research articles was determined by "expert" opinion. Do you think that, in addition, the researchers might have looked at frequency of citations in other journals as an index of quality? What is a possible disadvantage of judging quality by frequency of citations?

2. The authors drew a proportionate stratified random sample of 8 percent of the total number of articles. Will this result in a sufficiently stable sample? What is the basis for your answer?

3. The interjudge reliability for the ratings was .21. This indicates considerable discrepancy between judges. If editor reliability is similarly low does this make acceptance for journal publication somewhat of a lottery?

4. To the extent that articles are submitted to appropriate journals, the editors should be familiar with the subject matter involved. However, to eliminate bias, the 121 articles were randomly assigned to 121 judges who were randomly selected from a group of 171. As the authors point out, this means that some judges may not have been reviewing an article within their substantivefields. Would this be a liability in their abilities to rate the items pertaining to the "problem" and "Review of Literature" sections? Why?

5. Given that over one-half (61 percent, see Table 3) of the published articles reviewed were rated as either needing major revision or unsuitable for publication, why do you suppose they were published originally? Why were these judges more critical than the original journal editors? Is this question related to the preceding one?

6. We commend the authors for their clarity and thoroughness.

7. As pointed out in the Introduction, educators need to be better qualified to conduct research as well as being critical in reading research. This study lends support to our contention.

LEG POSITION AND PSYCHOLOGICAL CHARACTERISTICS IN WOMEN*

7

JOHN A. BLAZER

Numerous studies have been conducted on the various aspects of behavior. Studies have included investigations of both physical and psychological characteristics.

Yet, to date, there has been no scientific study on leg-crossing or position reported in the literature.

The present study was designed to test a theory of "leg position analysis" or "observational psychology," using standardized psychometric tests and methods to gather and analyze the data.

Experimental Design

doesn't expand — no fit Ref.

PROBLEM

The problems encountered in this study included determining the commonly used methods of leg-crossing or position; evaluating level of intelligence and educational attainment; and determining specific need strengths and interests in a specified sample.

(1) The first hypothesis tested was: The preferred method of leg-crossing or position generally used by a woman is indicative of her need strengths and basic values or interests.

not null for so won't be a statistical

2) The second hypothesis was: Intelligence and education have no effect upon preference of leg-crossing or position in women.

SUBJECTS

One thousand American women of the Caucasian race were used as the sample. The sample was chosen at random (from 1379 responses) through newspaper advertisements, personal appeals to women's clubs, notices on college bulletin boards, clients appealing to a state psychological agency for assistance, etc. There was no attempt to establish any other kind of minimum

*Reprinted from *Psychology—A Journal of Human Behavior*, 3:3 (August 1966), pp. 5–12, with the permission of the publisher and author.

criterion. Therefore, the sample was not homogeneous. It is considered appropriate to generalize the results to the general population because the study was designed to investigate a fundamental aspect of behavior that is assumed not to be affected by any of the uncontrolled variables.

METHOD

The most common method of leg-crossing or position of each subject was determined by visual observation.

The Edwards Personal Preference Schedule (Edwards, 1959) was used to determine the relative strength of 15 manifest needs in each subject.

A Study of Values (Allport, Vernon, & Lindzey, 1951) was used to determine basic interests or values of each subject.

The Wechsler Adult Intelligence Scale (Wechsler, 1955) was administered to each subject to obtain a level of intellectual functioning.

Educational attainment was obtained verbally from each subject.

PROCEDURE

The tests were administered and scored by the investigator and two university professors of psychology, in the order previously noted.

To determine the most common method of leg-crossing or position used by each subject, the subjects were instructed to appear before this investigator in two modes of dress: "dressy" (high heel shoes, hose, etc.) and casual or sport. The subject did not know the reason for the interview, and a wide variety of subjects were discussed. The subjects were unaware that leg-crossing or position was noted. The interview in each mode of dress was continued until the subject had crossed her legs five consecutive times in the same manner, or used the same position of legs throughout the interview. The leg-crossing or position observed was assumed to be the one generally preferred by the subject. After the interview each subject was asked her general preference of leg position. Inconsistency in leg-crossing or position in the interview or with her stated preference resulted in 58 subjects being removed from the sample.

ANALYSIS OF DATA

In the first hypothesis, the relationship between leg-crossing or position and each of the variables was determined by comparing the subjects who preferred each type of leg position with each other on each variable. The "very high" or "outstandingly high" score on each variable was determined by reference to the standardization data of the tests—on the EPPS, a T score of 70 and above; on the Study of Values, scores above 55.

The relationships within the second hypothesis were determined by comparing the variables to the subjects within each type of leg position.

RESULTS

The final formulation of types of leg-crossings or positions are presented in Table 1. Slight variations in positions were considered to be of no great importance. After all completed data were in, the sample was limited to the first 100 subjects to fall within each type of leg position.

Eighty-eight of the 100 subjects who preferred type 1 leg position were characterized by a "very high" (average T of 75) need strength in Order, and "outstandingly high" (average score of 55) Aesthetic interest.

Eighty-seven subjects using type 2 leg position were characterized by "very high" (average T of 78) strength in need Endurance, and "outstandingly high" (average score of 56) Theoretical interest.

Of the 100 subjects preferring type 3 leg position, 83 were characterized by "very high" (average T of 74 and 87, respectively) need strengths in Abasement and Deference, and "outstandingly high" (average score of 56) Social interests.

Eighty-seven of the subjects preferring type 4 leg position were characterized by "very high" (average T of 83) Achievement need strength, and "outstandingly high" (average score of 54) Political interests.

Eighty-seven subjects of the type 5 leg position were characterized by "very high" (average T of 89) need strength in Deference, and "outstandingly high" (average score of 67) Social interests.

Eighty-seven of the type 6 leg position subjects were characterized by "very high" (average T of 74 and 74, respectively) need strengths in Affiliation and Nurturance, and "outstandingly high" (average score of 53) Social interests.

Eighty subjects preferring the type 7 leg position were characterized by "very high" (average T of 74) Nurturance need strength, and "outstandingly high" (average score of 52) Social interests.

Eighty-eight subjects using a type 8 leg position were characterized by "very high" (average T of 82 and 72, respectively) need strengths on Autonomy and Change, and "outstandingly high" (average score of 57) Political interests.

Eighty-four of the subjects preferring type 9 leg position were characterized by "very high" (average T of 82) Exhibition need strength, and "outstandingly high" (average score of 51) Political interests.

Eighty-seven of the type of 10 leg position subjects were characterized by "very high" (average T of 74) need strength in Heterosexuality, and "outstandingly high" (average score of 59) Economic interests.

Of the 88 subjects with a high need strength for Order, 63 had a high (more than one SD above the mean) Picture Completion (WAIS subtest) score, suggesting a superior ability to utilize details (Rapaport, 1945, p. 230; Wechsler, 1944, p. 91); 61 had a high Picture Arrangement score, suggesting superior (1) ability to integrate and predict, (2) non-verbal organization, and (3) planning ability (Rapaport, 1945, p. 214; Wechsler, 1944, p. 88); and 73 had a

**TEN TYPES OF LEG POSITION—REPRESENTATIVE
DRAWINGS AND VERBAL DESCRIPTIONS**

table 1

TYPE	DRAWING (FRONT VIEW)	DESCRIPTION
1	‖	Knees together; feet together; legs extended.
2	═	Knees together; feet together; legs under body.
3	✕	Knees together; ankles crossed; legs extended.
4	⋀	Knees together; legs crossed.
5	╈	Knees together; one leg under body.
6	✕	Knees together; legs crossed, one twisted around the other.
7	✕	Knees apart; ankles crossed; legs extended.
8	✕	Knees apart; legs crossed; legs under body.
9	⊤	Knees apart; legs crossed.
10	\/	Knees apart; legs extended.

high Block Design score, suggesting superior (1) ability to break down into component parts, integrate, and look ahead, and (2) abstract conceptualization (Rapaport, 1945, p. 271; Wechsler, 1944, p. 92). Forty subjects had two of these subtests, and 27 had three.

From the 87 subjects with a high Endurance need strength, 57 had a high (more than one SD above the mean) Arithmetic (WAIS) subtest score, suggesting superior mental effort and active concentration in dealing with the environment (Rapaport, 1945, p. 194; Wechsler, 1944, p. 82); and 63 had a high Digit Span score, suggesting superior passive concentration and attention (Rapaport, 1945, p. 176; Wechsler, 1944, p. 84). Forty-nine subjects had both of these subtests.

Sixty-three of the 83 subjects who had high need strengths for Abasement and Deference had a low (more than 1 SD below the mean) Picture Arrangement (WAIS subtest) score, suggesting inferior (1) ability to integrate and predict, (2) non-verbal organization, and (3) planning ability (Rapaport, 1945, p. 214; Wechsler, 1944, p. 88).

Of the 87 subjects with a high need strength for Achievement, 71 had a high (120 or above) IQ and 68 a high (college degree) education. Fifty-six subjects had both.

From the 87 subjects with a high Affiliation need strength, 66 had a high (more than 1 SD above the mean) Picture Arrangement (WAIS subtest) score, suggesting superior (1) ability to integrate and predict, (2) non-verbal organization, and (3) planning ability (Rapaport, 1945, p. 214; Wechsler, 1944, p. 88); and 56 had a high Object Assembly score, suggesting superior insight (Wechsler, 1944, p. 98). Forty-seven subjects had both of these subtests.

Sixty-one of the 88 subjects who had a high need strength for Autonomy had a low (more than 1 SD below the mean) Comprehension (WAIS) subtest score, suggesting inferior (1) capacity to delay first impulses, and (2) social judgment and moral codes (Rapaport, 1945, p. 112; Wechsler, 1944, p. 81); and 59 had a low Picture Arrangement score, suggesting inferior (1) ability to integrate and predict, (2) non-verbal organization, and (3) planning ability (Rapaport, 1945, p. 214; Wechsler, 1944, p. 88). Fifty-six subjects had both of these subtests.

Of the 84 subjects with a high need strength for Exhibition, 63 had a low (more than 1 SD below the mean) Comprehension (WAIS subtest) score, suggesting inferior (1) capacity to delay first impulses, and (2) social judgment and moral codes (Rapaport, 1945, p. 112; Wechsler, 1944, p. 81).

Each of the variables above, comparing need scores to WAIS subtest scores, indicates a positive relationship between them, and supports the general conclusions of this study.

In the second hypothesis, intelligence scores ranged from 87 to 143, with a mean of 108. Within the individual types of leg position, there was a wide range of scores and no consistent pattern could be established (r of .02 was not significant at the .05 level of confidence). There were few duplications of scores, and 504 of the subjects scored over 100 on the intelligence scale.

Education of the subjects within each type of leg position was not consistent (r of .05 was not significant at the .05 level of confidence). The overall scale ranged from high school graduation through seven years of college, with a mean of .5 years of college.

Discussion

Due to the manner of limiting the number of subjects within each leg position category, no attempt was made to estimate the prevalence of each type of leg position within the general population.

The findings of this study support the acceptance of both hypotheses.

Generally speaking, the following behavioral characteristics can be assumed to occur together:

Type 1 leg position, desire for neatness and orderliness in work, likes to make plans, doesn't like change and uncertainty, organizes life according to a rigid schedule, appreciates the orderliness of each experience.

Type 2 leg position, likes to stick to one task until it is finished, able to concentrate for great periods of time, enjoys approaching a task with critical and intellectual attitudes.

Type 3 leg position, blames self easily, expects punishment often, enjoys blaming self, generally feels inferior, enjoys following direction of others, identifies with those felt to be superior, dislikes unconventional behavior, puts interests of other people ahead of self interest.

Type 4 leg position, eager to get ahead, likes to surpass other people, seeks personal fame, likes to influence and direct other people.

Type 5 leg position, enjoys following direction of other people, identifies with those felt to be superior, dislikes unconventional behavior, puts interests of other people ahead of self interest.

Type 6 leg position, enjoys other people, dislikes being alone, enjoys helping other people, sympathetic, affectionate, generous, puts interests of other people ahead of self interest.

Type 7 leg position, enjoys helping other people, sympathetic, affectionate, generous, puts interests of other people ahead of self interest.

Type 8 leg position, independent, unconventional, selfish, critical of authority, avoids responsibilities, likes change, enjoys travel and new experiences, follows new fads and fashions, likes to influence and direct other people.

Type 9 leg position, humorous, enjoys telling of personal experiences, seeks attention, likes to influence and direct other people.

Type 10 leg position, seeks numerous love affairs, talks and reads about sex, seeks attention of men, seeks constant sexual excitement, enjoys that which is useful and practical to self.

Summary

This study tested a theory of leg-crossing or position as related to certain personality and behavioral characteristics.

One thousand female subjects were administered the Edwards Personal Preference Schedule. A Study of Values, and the Wechsler Adult Intelligence Scale. The preferred method of leg-crossing or position and the educational attainment were determined for each subject. The relationship between preferred method of leg-crossing or position and needs, interests, intelligence, and education was determined.

The findings offer evidence in support of a theory of observational psychology as related to leg-crossing or position and psychological characteristics.

references _____

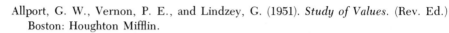

Allport, G. W., Vernon, P. E., and Lindzey, G. (1951). *Study of Values.* (Rev. Ed.) Boston: Houghton Mifflin.

Edwards, A. L. (1959). *Edwards Personal Preference Schedule.* (Rev. Ed.) New York: Psychol. Corp.

Rapaport, D. (1945). *Diagnostic Psychological Testing.* Vol. 1. Chicago: Year Book.

Wechsler, D. (1944). *The Measurement of Adult Intelligence.* (3rd Ed.) Baltimore: Williams and Wilkins.

Wechsler, D. (1955). *Wechsler Adult Intelligence Scale.* New York: Psychol. Corp.

comments and questions _____

1. Would you believe this study was illustrated in *Playboy* magazine?
2. The researcher states that this study was designed to test a theory. Does his formulation of the two hypotheses specify the theory?
3. Considering the method by which the researcher selected his sample, is he justified in stating "it is considered appropriate to generalize the results to the general population . . ."?
4. The researcher states that after the first interview, the subject was asked for her general preference of leg position. Would this not influence the observations during the second interview?
5. In discussing observational techniques we stated that: "To observe and record is a difficult task. Observers have to be well trained on what to observe and what to ignore in order to do their job correctly." Do you think we should be concerned about whether the observers in this study attended to their task?
6. Did the analysis of data as stated test the hypotheses stated?
7. Do the behavioral characteristics presented in the "Discussion" follow from the findings?
8. Was this study really conducted or is Blazer "pulling our leg"?

PARENTAL UNDERSTANDING OF THEIR CHILD'S TEST RESULTS AS INTERPRETED BY ELEMENTARY SCHOOL TEACHERS*

GORDON HOPPER

The objective of this study was to determine how well parents of fourth- and fifth-grade students remembered the norm groups and standardized test results reported to them in parent–teacher conferences. Interviews were conducted with parents during a two-week period following the conferences. Parents were asked to indicate the stanine in which their child had scored on the subtests of the Stanford Achievement Test and to indicate the norm group or groups with whom the child had been compared. The findings indicated considerable misunderstanding and erroneous perceptions held by parents about test results from the test interpretations made by elementary school teachers.

During the course of a school year, most students are given some type of standardized achievement test. The results of the test are usually communicated to the student and his parents. Ricks (1959), Durost (1961), and Ebel (1963) feel that parents are entitled to information gained about their child through standardized testing. They caution, however, that test information must be explained in terms that the parents can easily understand.

In the 1960s there was a good deal of concern about the training of people who interpret standardized test results. Noll (1961) and Rosner (1961) expressed the need for increased teacher competency in the use and interpretation of standardized tests; they felt that undergraduate preparation was not adequate.

The objective of this investigation was to determine how well parents remembered their child's test results on the Stanford Achievement Test after attending a parent-teacher conference in which results of the test were reported using stanines. Teachers used a visual profile accompanied by verbal interpretation to communicate the test results to parents. Two criteria were used to determine whether or not the test interpretations were well understood. First, the parents were asked to recall the stanine at which the child scored on each of the ten subtest areas. Second, the parents were asked to recall the group or groups with whom the child's performance was compared.

*Reprinted from Measurement and Evaluation in Guidance, 10:2 (1977), pp. 84–89. Copyright 1977 American Personnel and Guidance Association, with permission.

Procedure

Several steps were taken in order to make the sample of parents selected for the investigation as representative as possible of the total elementary school population. The population was a small city in Iowa with a rather high socioeconomic standing. There were at least two elementary schools in each of the five geographical areas of the school system. All fourth- and fifth-grade class lists from one school in each of the five geographical areas were supplied through the central school office. These class lists were then numbered. Using a table of random numbers, a sample of one hundred parents was selected. The sample was approximately ten percent of the population.

Once the selection of the sample had been accomplished, contact letters were sent to the parents. Interview appointments were made by telephone. All interviews were scheduled to take place within two weeks following the parent-teacher conferences. In this way, it was felt that the effect of loss of recall over time might be held to a minimum.

In an attempt to maintain some degree of control over communication, the same interviewer, who was considered knowledgeable in interviewing techniques and assessment terminology, conducted all the interviews. Each interview was structured according to an established pattern and was recorded on an interview form. The interview form asked the parent for two types of information: norm group description and individual subtest performance. Eighty-eight of the one hundred parents contacted responded favorably and were interviewed.

Subtest Performance Results

The Stanford Achievement Test yielded ten subtest scores for each child. The interview format obtained data reporting how the parent perceived his child had performed on each of the ten subtests. These parent-reported scores were then checked against the actual scores that the child had earned in relation to the national norm. The amount of deviation for each subtest score was noted. If there was no deviation between a reported subtest score and the actual score, a "0" was recorded. If the reported score was one stanine above the actual stanine score, a "1" was recorded. If the reported score was one stanine below the actual stanine score, a "-1" was recorded. In this manner, it was possible to record each subtest item in terms of deviation scores. There was a possible yield of 880 deviation scores in this investigation. These data are presented in Table 1.

In Table 1, only 34.8 percent of the parents' responses were accurate in

FREQUENCY AND PERCENTAGE OF SUBTEST RESPONSES IN
DEVIATION SCORES WITHOUT REFERENCE TO STUDENT,
SUBTEST, TEACHER, OR SCHOOL

table 1

DEVIATION SCORE	FREQUENCY	%
+5	2	0.23
+4	3	0.34
+3	24	2.73
+2	102	11.60
+1	179	20.30
0 (correct)	306	34.80
−1	176	20.00
−2	65	7.40
−3	15	1.70
−4	5	0.57
−5	0	0.00
No response	3	0.34
N = 880		

placing the pupil's subtest achievement at the proper stanine level. However, it should be noted that 40.3 percent of the responses were only off by one stanine.

In order to investigate any possible trends in overrating and underrating, the data were treated in regard to the varying achievement levels of the 880 responses. If an actual score was in stanines 7, 8, or 9, it was considered representative of high achievement level. Scores in stanines 4, 5, and 6 represented average achievement level; scores in stanines 1, 2, and 3 represented low achievement level performance.

If an actual score occurred in stanine 7 and the parent reported a stanine level of 9, the score would have a deviation of +2 which would indicate that overrating was taking place. Table 2 presents the frequency of overrating, accurate rating, and underrating in terms of high, medium, and low achievement performance levels. Parents of high achievement students tended to be the most accurate in rating their children, with a slight tendency to underrate them. Parents of students with average achievement were next most accurate in their ratings. They tended to both overrate and underrate their students' achievement. Parents of low achievement students were the least accurate in their ratings. They exhibited a strong tendency to overrate their child's performance. The tendency to overrate, therefore, increases while the accuracy of rating and tendency to underrate both decrease.

These results indicate that parents tend to recall test information like the students studied by Froehlich and Moser (1954), Lane (1952), and Collins (1968) did. Students who had high achievement scores tended to underrate themselves in recall and in estimation. They also tended to be more accurate in

table 2

FREQUENCY OF OVERRATING, ACCURATE RATING, AND
UNDERRATING IN REGARD TO HIGH, MEDIUM AND LOW ACHIEVEMENT

table 2

DEVIATION SCORE	HIGH STANINES 9, 8, 7	MEDIUM STANINES 6, 5, 4	LOW STANINES 3, 2, 1
+5			2
+4			3
+3		14	10
+2	15	57	30
+1	44	102	33
0 (correct)	149	139	18
−1	81	90	5
−2	51	14	
−3	12	3	
−4	5		
−5			
No response		4	2

rating themselves than did average or low achievement students. It was also found in this study that parents of children who had high achievement scores tended to display the same recall characteristics.

These other studies also found that low achievement students over-rated themselves and were less accurate in rating than were average or high achievement students. The parents of low-achieving students interviewed for this study displayed the same tendencies with 76.3 per cent overrated re-sponses and 17.6 per cent accurately rated responses being given by them. Parents of students with average achievement scores overrated more often (41.1 per cent) than they underrated (25.4 per cent).

Norm Group Identification Results

The norm group section of the interview form yielded one description that was selected by the parents as being representative of the group or groups with whom the pupil had been compared on the Stanford Achievement Test. There was a total of five sentences for selection purposes. The parent could select any one of the first four statements that described national, state, local and classroom norms, or any combination of the four. If the parent didn't know, he could select the fifth choice, "I do not know with whom my child was compared." The correct response was national and classroom norms. These data were recorded by the frequency of totally correct responses, partially correct responses, totally incorrect responses and "I don't know" responses. Table 3 reports the percentage of norm group descriptions that fell into each of the six categories.

PERCENTAGE OF THE 95 NORM GROUP RESPONSES
WITH REFERENCE TO THE SCORING CATEGORIES

table 3

CATEGORIES	%
Correct: national and classroom	20.0
Partially correct: national	30.5
Partially correct: classroom	28.5
Partially correct: national, classroom, and another	5.3
Incorrect	12.6
Did not know	3.1

It can be seen from the data presented in Table 3 that only twenty percent of the parents interviewed knew the correct norm group description. Many of the parents knew either the national norm or the classroom norm, but not both.

Discussion

Based on the findings of this investigation, parents do not seem to be very accurate in their recall of their child's test performance or of the norm group with which their child's performance was compared. If the assumption is valid that the accuracy of recall of performance and of the norm group is indicative of parental understanding of test results, then parents do not appear to understand test results very well. It should be noted, however, that a large percentage of parental responses did indicate at least partial understanding of these test data.

The fact that many of the parents were only partially accurate in their recall of test data probably means that their understanding of test results could be improved. The problem appears to be one of defining what may have caused parental misunderstanding and to decide what can be done to improve test interpretation. It would seem reasonable to consider some possible problem areas such as the type of information reported, the method used to report scores, interpretation techniques, parent motivation, and parent interest.

During the investigation interviews, parents often expressed concern over being asked to recall so many subtest areas, they usually felt unsure about how the child had performed in each of the areas. One might question whether asking parents to recall ten subtest areas, even within a two-week period after exposure, would prove anything about the parents' understanding of the test results. It should, however, be remembered that parents were told about the ten subtest areas during the teacher conferences. If the parents were not ex- pected to remember and use the results to better understand their child and his relation to the areas of education and work, it might be asked why they were even told the test results. A possible improvement might be to tell the parents only the composite scores, such as language, arithmetic, social studies, and science. If more specific information were desired, it could be given to those parents requesting it.

The norm group description seemed to be highly prone to incomplete understanding. Since a simple comparison of the child's performance with one norm group should not be too difficult to remember, the problem may be one of complexity caused by multiple norm group comparisons. A possible solution might be to train the teacher to emphasize only one norm group and only make comparisons with that norm group.

Whether or not the stanine used to report the test scores in this investigation is better than another possible measure is difficult to determine without a companion study using other reporting means. The fact that the stanine is a rather broad category method of reporting measured achievement might result in a more accurate recall by parents.

There appeared to be considerable parental misunderstanding and distorted perceptions as a result of these test interpretations made by elementary school teachers. The number of teachers involved in this study is small ($N = 18$), the sample was drawn from only one school district, and the makeup of the city is largely middle socioeconomic. The study needs to be replicated using different ways of interpreting test results (grade equivalent, percentile band, percentile rank), different teacher populations, and different pupil populations. Perhaps a series of such studies would point a way to our being better able to translate some of the specialized measurement language into terms laypersons can understand rather than getting trapped in the prisons of specialized language that tend to lead to misunderstandings and misconceptions by those we are trying to help through testing.

references

Bowman, H. In-service training for teachers in measurement. *National Council on Measurement in Education Yearbook*. 1961, *18*, 43–49.

Collins, T. A study of the comparative effectiveness of media treatment in test scores reporting to college freshmen. *Dissertation Abstracts*, 1968, *38*, 3992A–3993A.

Durost, W. How to tell parents about standardized test results. *Test Service Bulletin 23*, New York: Harcourt, Brace and World, 1961.

Ebel, R. The social consequences of educational testing. *Invitational Conference on Testing Problems: Proceedings*, 1963, 130–143.

Froehlich, C. P. and Moser, W. E. Do counselees remember test scores? *Journal of Counseling Psychology*, 1954, *1*, 149–152.

Goldman, L. Tests and counseling: The marriage that failed, *Measurement and Evaluation in Guidance*, 1972, *4*, 213–220.

Lane, D. *A comparison of two techniques of interpreting test results to clients in voca-*

tional counseling. Unpublished doctoral dissertation, Columbia University, New York, 1952.

Noll, V. Problems in the preservice preparation of teachers in measurement. *National Council on Measurement in Education Yearbook*, 1961, *18*, 35–42.

Ohlsen, M. M., Pearsen, R., Wurm, P. Research implications for test interpretation. *National Association of Secondary School Principals Bulletin*, 1965, *49*, 11–22.

Ricks, J. On telling parents about test results. *Test Service Bulletin No. 54*, New York: Harcourt, Brace and World, 1959.

Rosner, B. Substance of training in measurement and evaluation in preservice preparation of teachers. *National Council on Measurement in Education Yearbook*, 1961, *18*, 51–54.

Symposium: Tests and counseling—the marriage that failed, *Measurement and Evaluation in Guidance*, 1972, *5*, 394–429.

comments and questions

1. Hopper's sample adequately represents the population being studied. To what extent can his findings be generalized? Would a more heterogeneous population have produced different results? Are his data suggestive of what these differences might have been? Explain.

2. Does this study lend support to the hypothesis that interpretation of low test scores results in students or their parents having inaccurately low estimates of student achievement? Why or why not?

3. Could you outline a study that would help answer the following question: How can teachers most effectively communicate test scores to parents?

4. What, if any, are some psychological explanations of the findings of this study?

5. Do you think general knowledge of the results of this study would increase or decrease the concerns of testing and test score interpretation? Support your answer.

ATTITUDES AND CHARACTERISTICS
OF BLACK GRADUATE STUDENTS*

CHRISTINE H. CARRINGTON and WILLIAM E. SEDLACEK

One hundred and twenty Black graduate students reported that the things they liked most about their university were the location and quality of education; the things they liked least were the racism and red tape. Changes they most wanted to see were better teaching, more Black faculty, and less racism. Implications for educators are discussed.

During the past 10 years an increasing number of predominantly white colleges and universities in the United States have made efforts to increase the enrollment of Black students on their campuses (Astin et al. 1975; Sedlacek & Pelham 1976). These efforts have stemmed from a general pressure to extend equal opportunity to all educational levels through affirmative action and other equal opportunity programs. Although there has been some reporting about Black undergraduate students on white campuses (e.g., Miller & Dreger 1973; Sedlacek & Brooks 1976), little information is available on Black graduate students. What data are available appear to concern admissions and numbers of degrees awarded. There is almost nothing available on how Black graduate students feel about their education or student services and what changes they would suggest.

Blackwell (1975) reports that approximately 48,000 PhDs are produced each year, yet there is still a critical shortage of Black PhDs. Blacks constitute about four percent of all PhD sociologists, five percent of PhD psychologists, two percent of the economists, and one percent of the historians, physicists, biologists, and chemists. This extreme underrepresentation of Blacks among holders of the doctorate degree exists despite increasing efforts to produce more Black PhDs. The 976 Blacks who received doctorates in 1973, out of a total of 33,727 awarded that year, included 760 Black American citizens, 56 non-U.S.-citizen immigrant visa holders, and 160 non-U.S. citizens.

The Graduate Record Examination Board, in conjunction with the

*Reprinted from *Journal of College Student Personnel*, 18:6 (1977), pp. 467–471. Copyright 1977 American Personnel and Guidance Association, with permission.

Council of Graduate Schools in the United States, conducted a survey of graduate school programs for minority/disadvantaged students (Hamilton 1973). The main findings of the study were the following:

1.   Of the 110 schools surveyed, 80 indicated that they had specifically designed policies or procedures aimed at meeting the needs of minority disadvantaged students at the graduate level.

2.   The number of enrolled minority students at the graduate level has tended to increase since the initial survey was conducted in 1969.

3.   Continuous evaluation of an institution's efforts for minority students has generally been lacking or, for the most part, based only on limited criteria. Little attention has been given to the student's life outside the classroom or to his or her postdegree requirements.

4.   The size of an institution's graduate program and its location on a rural to urban continuum are powerful determinants of its ability to respond to pressures for increases in minority enrollment. Size has the function of increasing an institution's ability to finance such students; location tends to determine what kinds of activities are undertaken.

A related and important finding of this national survey was that although a number of institutions have made demonstrable efforts to recruit and enroll minority students, only half of them have developed academic programs specifically designed for the interests of these students (Hamilton 1973).

Studies concerning Blacks in professional schools have also tended to focus on institutional head count data (Baird 1974; Smith 1972), although Johnson and Sedlacek (1975) report that

> Medical students are often thrown into a rigid academic environment. Faculty members or others who have established this environment may not be prepared to provide more flexible programs for students, from different backgrounds, with different learning styles and different understandings of what medical school is all about. (p. 932)

The purpose of the current study is to assess the feelings and reactions of Black graduate students toward their academic and nonacademic environment.

Procedure

A random sample of 770 Black graduate students enrolled at the University of Maryland was sent an anonymous questionnaire and a cover letter explaining the study. Thirty questionnaires were returned because of incorrect addresses. Mail and telephone follow-ups resulted in 120 completed questionnaires. Follow-ups were possible because the students returned a postcard indicating their name separately from the anonymous questionnaire.

Results

The sample was 56 percent female and 44 percent male. Most of the students were married (62 percent) and had been attending graduate school for at least two years (63 percent). Of the 77 percent who were working, 44 percent worked full time. Fifty-two percent were pursuing a PhD degree, 21 percent an MA, 12 percent an MS, 6 percent an EdD, 3 percent an A.G.S., and 6 percent another degree. The most common majors were education (44 percent), business (13 percent), psychology (9 percent), agriculture (7 percent), English (5 percent), and economics (4 percent). Fifty-three percent were receiving some kind of financial aid; 16 percent had graduate assistantships. Their primary reasons for attending the University were location (36 percent), a program of study of interest (36 percent), and quality of education offered (12 percent). Eight percent indicated that Maryland was not their first choice of school.

The variables that had contributed most to their educational development during the past year were coursework in major field (40 percent), independent study (33 percent), and work experience outside the University (19 percent). Forty-seven percent reported there were no Black faculty in their department, 19 percent reported one, 17 percent reported two, and 17 percent reported three or more Black faculty in their department.

Table 1 shows the means and standard deviations of the students' responses to 16 Likert-type attitude items. They tended to agree most strongly that they were certain of their vocational goal, that there was at least one person in their department they could talk to regularly, that Black students usually take longer to get their degrees than white students, that Black faculty seem interested in Black students, and that the racial climate on campus is generally tense.

They tended to disagree most strongly with statements indicating that students have ample opportunity to participate in policymaking, that channels for expressing student complaints are readily available, that social life for Black students on campus is good, that most administrators act as if they really care about students, and that there is good communication between Black students and the administration.

There were only two significant differences ($t = .05$) between male and female responses to the attitude items. Females, compared to males, tended to feel that Black faculty were more interested in Black students and that campus social life was better for Black students.

In one open-ended item, students reported that what they liked most about the University was the location (29 percent) and the quality of education (27 percent). They liked least the racism they encountered (23 percent), the bureaucracy and red tape (23 percent), and the lack of an intellectual atmo-

MEANS AND STANDARD DEVIATIONS OF BLACK GRADUATE
STUDENT RESPONSES TO ATTITUDE ITEMS

table 1 ───

ITEMS	M	SD
University students have ample opportunity to participate in University policymaking.	3.57	.85
Channels for expressing student complaints are readily available.	3.45	.97
Social life for Black students on campus is good.	3.41	.80
Most administrators here act like they really care about students.	3.37	.92
There is good communication between Black students and the administration.	3.35	.95
Most of my courses are stimulating and exciting.	3.19	1.09
Most faculty advisers here act like they really care about students.	3.17	1.02
Most instructors here act like they really care about students.	3.13	1.06
I would recommend the University of Maryland to a Black friend.	2.97	1.16
White faculty in my department seem interested in Black students.	2.96	1.09
White faculty seem to have lower expectations for Black students than for white students.	2.91	1.14
The racial climate at Maryland is generally tense.	2.88	.96
Black faculty in my department seem interested in Black students.	2.68	.90
Black students usually take longer to get their degrees than do white students.	2.58	1.07
There is at least one person in my department who is available for me to talk with on a regular basis.	2.43	1.21
I am certain of my vocational goal.	1.75	.95

Note: 1 = strongly agree; 5 = strongly disagree.

sphere (14 percent). When the students were asked what they would like to see changed at the University, they most often indicated better teaching (23 percent), more Black faculty (19 percent), changing the racist attitudes and practices of faculty, staff, and students (12 percent), and more Black students (9 percent).

Discussion

On many of the items, the Black graduate students responded similarly to students in general, regardless of race or year in school. For instance,

Schmidt and Sedlacek (1972) reported that attitudes of faculty and administration and availability of channels for expressing student complaints are among the key variables related to the satisfaction of undergraduates in general. Also programs offered and geographical location have been the primary positive features of the University to undergraduate students in general (Handley & Sedlacek 1975), Black undergraduates (Sedlacek, Brooks & Herman 1971; Van Arsdale, Sedlacek & Brooks 1971), and no-shows who were accepted but did not matriculate (Carrington & Sedlacek 1975). Although the percentage (44 percent) of Black graduate students majoring in education may seem high, it is similar to the percentage for whites in education (Blackwell 1975).

It appears that there is support for the contention that graduate students could benefit from some student services traditionally aimed at or limited to undergraduates. Services focusing on counseling and adjusting to and dealing with the educational system appear to be particularly called for. Future research on the possible nature of these services and comparisons of Black and white graduate student needs should be fruitful. The reader is cautioned against concluding that Blacks must always be compared to whites in order for them to achieve some sort of identity or before services can be offered. This study provides some preliminary information on Black graduate students that can have some usefulness of its own, regardless of future findings or comparisons.

A program for minority "pregraduate" students, which has resulted in 40 percent going on to graduate school with increased confidence and experience, was begun in Florida ("Opening doors . . ." 1976). The program involves cooperation between Florida's predominantly Black colleges and the University of Florida. Undergraduates work on independent research projects with graduate professors. The student explores a field and learns to cope with the expectations of graduate school. This appears to be a likely approach for student personnel services to use for such students and it could be applied in other states or locations.

The unique findings of the current study seem to relate to racial variables. Although undergraduate Blacks have also shown concern for racial variables (Brooks, Sedlacek & Mindus 1973), in this study the focus on Black faculty and the relationships of the graduate students to them is more pronounced. Graduate students are more limited to contacts with faculty within their major departments than are undergraduates and Black graduate students are closer to the faculty in training and career orientation. This increases their need for role models they can look to for advice and counsel.

That Black graduate students see racism as a problem in their education has the greatest implication for what needs to be done in graduate education. Racism should not be dismissed as the rhetoric of the unreasonable or the malcontent, i.e., the obligatory verbiage that comes with being Black. In fact, much evidence indicates that the best Black students are most likely to detect and understand racism (Sedlacek & Brooks 1976). According to Sedlacek and Brooks (1976):

> Individual racism is action taken by one individual toward another which results in negative outcomes because the other person is identified with a certain group. The group may be racial, cultural, sexual, ideological, etc. Institutional racism is the action taken by a social system or institution which results in negative outcomes for members of a certain group or groups. (p. 5)

One procedure designed to eliminate or reduce racism that has been employed in a variety of educational settings has been proposed by Sedlacek (1974) and Sedlacek and Brooks (1976). Their model has been demonstrated to be useful in changing racist attitudes among undergraduate students (Chapman 1974); increasing the knowledge about racism of incoming freshmen (Sedlacek, Troy & Chapman 1976); altering admissions practices at the undergraduate level (Sedlacek & Brooks 1973) and in medical school (D'Costa et al. 1974; Johnson & Sedlacek 1975). Use of the model has also resulted in the development of a course entitled "Education and Racism," which is available to graduate and undergraduate students at the University of Maryland (Sedlacek & Brooks 1973). The model has also been employed in graduate, undergraduate, and professional school settings and unpublished evaluations support its success. The specific techniques and design of the model have been detailed elsewhere (Sedlacek 1974, 1977; Sedlacek & Brooks 1976).

references _____

Astin, A. W.; King, M. R.; Light, J. M.; & Richardson, G. I. *The American freshman: National norms for 1975.* Los Angeles: American Council on Education and University of California at Los Angeles, 1975.

Baird, L. L. A portrait of blacks in graduate studies. In *Findings, Vol. 2.* Princeton, N.J.: Educational Testing Service, 1974.

Blackwell, J. E. *Access of black students to graduate and professional schools.* Atlanta, Ga.: Southern Education Foundation, 1975.

Brooks, G. C., Jr.; Sedlacek, W. E.; & Mindus, L. A. Interracial contact and attitudes among university students. *Journal of Non-White Concerns in Personnel and Guidance*, 1973, *1*, 102–110.

Carrington, C. H., & Sedlacek, W. E. Characteristics of "no-shows" accepted for admission at a large university, *Journal of College Student Personnel*, 1975, *16*, 504–507.

Chapman, T. H. *Simulation game effects on attitudes regarding racism and sexism.* Unpublished doctoral dissertation, University of Maryland, 1974.

D'Costa, A. et al. *Simulated minority admissions exercises workbook.* Washington, D.C.: Association of American Medical Colleges, 1974.

Hamilton, I. B. *Graduate school programs for minority/disadvantaged students.* Princeton, N.J.: Educational Testing Service, 1973.

Handley, A. A., & Sedlacek, W.E. *A profile of University of Maryland, College Park freshmen, 1975–76* (Counseling Center Research Report #9-75). College Park: University of Maryland, 1975.

Johnson, D.G., & Sedlacek, W.E. Retention by sex and race of 1968–72 U.S. medical school entrants. *Journal of Medical Education*, 1975, *50*, 925–933.

Miller, K. S., & Dreger, R. M. (Eds.) *Comparative studies of blacks and whites in the United States.* New York: Seminar Press, 1973.

Opening doors to graduate school; Florida's program for minority students. *Carnegie Quarterly*, 1976, *24*, 6–7.

Schmidt, D.K., & Sedlacek, W. E. Variables related to university student satisfaction, *Journal of College Student Personnel*, 1972, *13*, 233–238.

Sedlacek, W. E. *Racism in society: A behavioral model for change.* (Behavioral Sciences Tape Library #82220) Teaneck, N.J.: Sigma Information, 1974.

Sedlacek, W. E. Test bias and the elimination of racism. *Journal of College Student Personnel*, 1977, *18*, 16–20.

Sedlacek, W. E., & Brooks, G. C., Jr., Racism and research: Using data to initiate change. *Personnel and Guidance Journal*, 1973, *52*, 184–188.

Sedlacek, W. E., & Brooks, G. C., Jr. *Racism in American education: A model for change,* Chicago: Nelson-Hall, 1976.

Sedlacek, W. E.; Brooks, G. D., Jr.; & Herman, M. H. *Black student attitudes toward a predominantly white university* (Cultural Study Center Research Report #8-71). College Park: University of Maryland, 1971.

Sedlacek, W. E., & Pelham, J. C. *Minority admissions to large universities: A seven-year national survey* (Cultural Study Center Research Report #1-76). College Park: University of Maryland, 1976.

Sedlacek, W. E.; Troy, W. G.; & Chapman, T. H. An evaluation of three methods of racism-sexism training. *Personnel and Guidance Journal*, 1976, *55*, 196–199.

Smith, M.A. (Ed.) *Minorities and the health professions: An annotated bibliography.* Washington, D.C.; Association of American Medical Colleges, 1972.

Van Arsdale, P. W.; Sedlacek, W. E.; & Brooks, G. C., Jr. Trends in black student attitudes at a predominantly white university. *Negro Educational Review*, 1971, *22*, 133–145.

comments and questions _____

1. Does the statement "A random sample of 770 Black graduate students" connote that 770 was the population or the sample? If the latter, what was the population?
2. What limitation(s) do you see in the results due to the fact that only 120 out of 770 questionnaires were returned? Do the authors discuss the limitations of the low response rate?
3. Although the authors described the sample's characteristics quite well, they still can be faulted for: (a) not indicating when the study was conducted; and (b) not describing how the sample characteristics (e.g., percent male) compare with the total population characteristics.

4. Do you feel it would have been valuable for the researchers to have presented and discussed the data separately for different college majors? Why?

5. The authors state that "on many of the items, the Black graduate students responded similarly to students in general, regardless of race or year in school." They cite a reference but give no empirical data here to support their statement. Should they have?

6. The authors state that "Racism should not be dismissed as the rhetoric of the unreasonable or the malcontent. . ." Is this statement sufficiently documented?

NINTH ANNUAL GALLUP POLL OF THE PUBLIC'S ATTITUDES TOWARD THE PUBLIC SCHOOLS*

10

GEORGE H. GALLUP

Purpose of the Study

Problem

This survey, ninth in the annual series, has sought to measure the attitudes of American citizens toward their public schools. Funding this year was provided by /I/D/E/A/, the Institute for Development of Educational Activities, Inc., an affiliate of the Charles F. Kettering Foundation.

Each year an effort is made to deal with new issues—as well as with certain perennials from earlier studies—that are of greatest concern to both educators and the public. To accomplish this, letters were sent to educators nationwide, asking for their ideas. In addition, a selected panel of citizens met with staff members of Gallup and /I/D/E/A/ to pinpoint issues for inclusion in this year's survey.

The group of panel members included: Terrel H. Bell, commissioner, Utah System of Higher Education, Salt Lake City, Utah (and former U.S. commissioner of education); Edward Brainard, chairman, Colorado State Committee, North Central Association of Colleges and Schools, University of Northern Colorado, Greeley, Colorado; B. Frank Brown, director, /I/D/E/A/ Information and Services Program, Melbourne, Florida; Alonzo A. Crim, superintendent, Atlanta Public Schools, Atlanta, Georgia; Joseph M. Cronin, superintendent of public instruction, State Department of Public Instruction, Springfield, Illinois; Stanley Elam, director of publications, Phi Delta Kappa, Bloomington, Indiana; Nolan Estes, general superintendent, Dallas Independent School District, Dallas, Texas; Jack D. Gordon, senator, Thirty-fifth District, Florida, Miami Beach, Florida; Samuel Halperin, director, Institute for Educational Leadership, Washington, D.C.; James E. Kunde, director of urban affairs, Charles F. Kettering Foundation, Dayton, Ohio; Sidney P. Marland, Jr., president, College Entrance Examination Board, New York, New

*A project jointly conducted by the Gallup poll and the Charles F. Kettering Foundation. From *Phi Delta Kappan*, September 1977, pp. 33–47, © 1977, by Phi Delta Kappa, Inc.

York; Helen Moore, teacher, Detroit, Michigan; Samuel G. Sava, executive director, /I/D/E/A/, Dayton, Ohio.

We wish to thank these individuals for their valuable help.

Research Procedure

THE SAMPLE

The sample used in this and every survey in this series is described as a modified probability sample. A total of 1,506 adults (18 years and older) comprised the national cross section. Personal, in-home interviews were conducted in all areas of the nation and in all types of communities. A complete analysis of the sample appears at the end of this report.

TIME OF INTERVIEWING

The fieldwork for this study was conducted from April 28 through May 2, 1977.

THE INTERVIEWING FORM

All questions included in the survey were pretested by the staff of interviewers maintained by the Gallup organizations.

Findings from this report apply only to the country as a whole and not to specific local areas. Local surveys, using the same questions, can be conducted in order to compare local communities with the national norm.[1]

Major Problems Confronting the Public Schools in 1977

Discipline continues to top the list of major problems facing the public schools of the nation, as it has during eight of the last nine years. In fact, the percentage who cite discipline as the major problem is the highest found during the period in which these annual surveys have been conducted.

Parents of children now attending public school, perhaps the group best suited to judge the schools, cite discipline as the number one problem and by the highest percentage yet recorded.

[1] Suggestions for such a local survey are outlined in *The Gallup Polls of Attitudes Toward Education, 1969–1973*, Ch. 7: "A Look into Your School District." Available from Phi Delta Kappa, Eighth & Union, P.O. Box 789, Bloomington, IN 47401, $2.25.

The problem that seems near solution is the problem of adequate facilities. Nine years ago "lack of proper facilities" drew enough votes to place it second on the list of major problems facing the schools. In this year's survey, for the second straight year, only 2 percent of the sample cite this as the major problem.

The list of problems remains substantially the same as in previous years, with integration/segregation/busing being in second place, and lack of proper financial support in third.

The problem of drug usage is mentioned by fewer persons than last year, going from 11 percent in 1976 to 4 percent this year.

Below, in order of mentions, is the list of top problems:

1. Lack of discipline
2. Integration/segregation/busing
3. Lack of proper financial support
4. Difficulty of getting "good" teachers
5. Poor curriculum
6. Use of drugs
7. Parents' lack of interest
8. Size of school/classes
9. Teachers' lack of interest
10. Mismanagement of funds/programs

1977 Ratings of the Public Schools

The quality of education, as perceived by U.S. adults, has declined during the last year. The 1977 ratings show a significant drop since 1974, when the present rating method was first employed.

The five-point scale used to measure the public's perceptions of the quality of public school education in their own communities is one that is widely used by the schools themselves. It reads as follows:

> Students are often given the grades A,B,C,D, and FAIL to denote the quality of their work. Suppose the *public* schools themselves, in this community, were graded in the same way. What grade would you give the public schools here—A,B,C,D, or FAIL?

Here are the national ratings given the public schools by residents for the last four years:

Ratings Given the	NATIONAL TOTALS			
	1977	1976	1975	1974
Public Schools	%	%	%	%
A rating	11	13	13	18
B rating	26	29	30	30
C rating	28	28	28	21
D rating	11	10	9	6
FAIL	5	6	7	5
Don't know/ no answer	19	14	13	20

It may bring some comfort to public school educators to know that the ratings given by parents who have children now enrolled in public schools have shown no decline since last year. In fact, if the top two ratings—A and B—are combined, the rating is 54 percent, which compares with a score of 50 percent in 1976.

The lowest ratings come from persons who have no children attending school and from those parents whose children are enrolled in parochial and private schools. These two groups are responsible for the decline in the national scores.

	National Totals	No Children in Schools	Public School Parents	Parochial School Parents
	%	%	%	%
A rating	11	9	18	6
B rating	26	22	36	29
C rating	28	28	26	31
D rating	11	11	9	16
FAIL	5	5	4	10
Don't know/no answer	19	25	7	8

The number of U.S. families with children of school age has declined. Consequently, the drop in the national ratings of the schools can be explained in part by this fact.

Analysis of the findings by socioeconomic groups reveals that the following groups give the lowest ratings to their local schools:

1. young adults (18 to 29 age group);

2. residents of cities over one million;

3. persons living in the Western states;

4. blacks, particularly those living in the Northern states.

	A %	B %	C %	D %	FAIL %	Don't Know/ No Answer %
NATIONAL TOTALS	11	26	28	11	5	19
Sex						
Men	11	25	30	11	5	18
Women	11	28	26	12	4	19
Race						
White	12	27	28	11	5	17
Nonwhite	8	23	25	14	5	25
Age						
18 to 29 years	5	25	38	16	4	12
30 to 49 years	15	28	28	10	6	13
50 years and over	13	26	20	9	4	28
Community size						
1 million and over	10	20	28	13	10	19
500,000–999,999	11	26	30	11	4	18
50,000–499,999	12	27	25	11	4	21
2,500–49,999	11	32	26	9	4	18
Under 2,500	12	27	31	11	3	16
Education						
Grade school	17	17	20	5	8	33
High school	10	27	31	12	4	16
College	10	30	26	14	5	15
Region						
East	15	25	31	8	5	16
Midwest	10	29	28	11	3	19
South	13	28	25	10	3	21
West	6	21	28	17	9	19

What's Particularly Good about the Local Schools?

To provide an opportunity for the respondents in the present survey to tell what they thought was particularly good about the local schools, the following question, asked in some of the earlier surveys in this series, was repeated:

In your own opinion, in what ways are your local *public* schools particularly good?

The two responses offered most frequently were "the curriculum" and "the teachers." These have been the two most frequently mentioned in earlier surveys. Here are the top 10 responses, in order of mention:

1. The curriculum
2. The teachers
3. Extracurricular activities

4. School facilities
5. Equal opportunity for all students
6. Good administration
7. Parental interest/participation
8. Good student/teacher relationships
9. Good discipline
10. Small school or small classes

The Back-to-Basics Movement

The decline in national test scores and frequent media reports of illiteracy among high school graduates have given impetus to what is now widely referred to as the back-to-basics movement.

To discover how widely known this movement is and to obtain evidence of its popularity, three questions were included in the survey. The first asked simply:

Have you heard or read about the back-to-basics movement in education?

Understandably, the better educated and those with children now attending school are more familiar with the movement.

	National Totals %	No Children in Schools %	Public School Parents %	Parochial School Parents %
Yes, have heard of the term	41	38	47	62
No, have not	57	60	52	36
Don't know/no answer	2	2	1	2

Many laymen interested in education, as well as educators, think of other subjects as "basic" besides the traditional three Rs. But does the general public?

This question was asked, therefore, of those who said that they were aware of this movement:

When this term is used, do you think of anything besides reading, writing, and arithmetic?

The responses to this question, on the whole, indicate that the public regards the basics largely in terms of the traditional three subject areas.

Other subjects are mentioned—history, geography, spelling, citizenship, science, music, art, physical education—but not frequently.

However, many respondents think of the term, not in relation to subjects or courses, but in relation to the educational process itself. Thus, "back to basics" is interpreted as meaning a return to schooling of earlier years. To many respondents it means "respect for teachers," "good manners," "politeness," "obedience," "respect for elders," "structured classrooms," "back to the old ways of teaching."

A third question asked of those familiar with the term was this:

Do you favor or oppose this back-to-basics movement?

All groups in the population express overwhelming approval of the movement.

	Favor %	Oppose %	Don't Know/ No Answer %
		RESULTS BASED ON THOSE AWARE OF TERM	
NATIONAL TOTALS	83	11	6
Sex			
Men	83	10	7
Women	83	11	6
Race			
White	84	10	6
Nonwhite	75	20	5
Age			
18 to 29 years	79	14	7
30 to 49 years	82	12	6
50 years and over	87	7	6
Community size			
1 million and over	78	12	10
500,000–999,999	77	13	10
50,000–499,999	85	12	3
2,500–49,999	88	5	7
Under 2,500	85	9	6
Education			
Grade school	93	6	1
High school	84	9	7
College	81	13	6
Region			
East	77	15	8
Midwest	89	6	5
South	85	11	4
West	81	11	8

Early Graduation from High School

Although the traditional in education always exerts a strong influence in shaping the public's views, wide support is shown for a proposal to permit some high school students to graduate early.

This question was asked:

If high school students can meet academic requirements in three years instead of four, should they, or should they not, be permitted to graduate early?

Nationally, 74 percent of those sampled said that students should be permitted to graduate early; 22 percent said they should not. All groups in the population widely favor this proposal—especially those under 30 years of age.

	National Totals %	No Children in Schools %	Public School Parents %	Parochial School Parents %
Should be permitted to graduate early	74	77	68	67
Should not	22	18	31	27
Don't know/no answer	4	5	1	6

The results by major groups:

	Yes, They Should %	No, They Should Not %	Don't Know/ No Answer %
NATIONAL TOTALS	74	22	4
Sex			
Men	73	22	5
Women	74	22	4
Race			
White	73	23	4
Nonwhite	81	13	6
Age			
18 to 29 years	82	16	2
30 to 49 years	68	29	3
50 years and over	73	20	7
Community size			
1 million and over	76	18	6
500,000–999,999	78	18	4
50,000–499,999	73	22	5
2,500–49,999	75	21	4
Under 2,500	69	29	2
Education			
Grade school	75	14	11
High school	72	25	3
College	76	21	3
Region			
East	74	23	3
Midwest	74	21	5
South	73	22	5
West	75	21	4

College Courses in Fourth Year of High School

A related proposal also wins favorable support among respondents. The following question was asked:

> Should high school courses be arranged to make it possible for some students to finish one year of college work while they are still in high school, so that these students can graduate from college in three years instead of four?

The findings show that 63 percent of the total sample say that courses should be arranged to allow college work; 31 percent say no. Young people in particular favor this proposal. The greatest opposition is found in the small communities—those which would have the greatest difficulty in providing staff or facilities to add college courses for high school seniors.

	National Totals %	No Children in Schools %	Public School Parents %	Parochial School Parents %
Yes, courses should be arranged to allow college work	63	62	66	63
No, they should not	31	30	31	36
Don't know/no answer	6	8	3	1

By socioeconomic groups:

	Yes, Courses Should Be Arranged to Allow College Work %	No, They Should Not %	Don't Know/ No Answer %
NATIONAL TOTALS	63	31	6
Sex			
Men	60	34	6
Women	65	29	6
Race			
White	62	33	5
Nonwhite	68	19	13
Age			
18 to 29 years	68	29	3
30 to 49 years	61	35	4
50 years and over	61	29	10
Community size			
1 million and over	69	24	7
500,000–999,999	65	27	8
50,000–499,999	67	28	5

	Yes, Courses Should Be Arranged to Allow College Work	No, They Should Not	Don't Know/ No Answer
2,500–49,999	55	37	8
Under 2,500	59	37	4
Education			
Grade school	68	16	16
High school	60	35	5
College	65	31	4
Region			
East	66	29	5
Midwest	59	34	7
South	63	29	8
West	66	30	4

Absenteeism

Few school systems have found adequate ways to cope with the thorny problem of absenteeism. In one city (New York), only 71 percent of enrolled high school students are in school on a given day.

To see what suggestions parents of schoolchildren and others might have, this "open" question was asked:

> In your opinion, what can·be done by the schools to reduce student absenteeism (truancy)?

The suggestions offered tend to fall in about equal numbers into three broad categories.

Category 1 — Persons who, in general, believe that the schools and the teachers are chiefly to blame for absenteeism.

These typical direct quotations indicate how persons in this category would deal with the problem: "The courses should be made more interesting. Few teachers ever bother to make what they are teaching exciting or important to the students." "Teachers should spend more time with students, be more dedicated, and avoid being clock watchers." "Courses should be more practical, more 'today'-related." "Get the students who stay away from school most often to sit down and talk over their school problems and make their own suggestions about solving the problem." "Incentives should be devised. . . . Have each class compete with other classes. The one with the highest attendance gets a half-day off."

Category 2 — Persons who, in general, start with the conviction that parents are chiefly to blame for absenteeism.

Some of their suggestions follow: "Parents, whether they are at home or work, should be immediately notified if their child fails to show up at school." "Parents in many cases do not realize how important attendance is. They should be brought together and told exactly why attendance is so important." "When a child stays away from school the parents should be made to confer with the teachers, with the child present, to find out why." "The schools and the local authorities should get after the parents. Put them on the block and make them see that they are responsible."

Category 3 — Persons who, in general, regard truancy as a matter for the police and local authorities.

Some typical suggestions: "More truant officers should be hired and local laws should be strictly enforced." "The police should be ordered to stop any child of school age who is on the streets during school hours. If the child doesn't have a written excuse, he or she should be taken into custody."

Other suggestions: "Children who are frequently absent should have to obey earlier curfew laws." "They should have to make up their schoolwork on Saturdays or during summer vacation." "They should be put to work cleaning up the parks and playgrounds."

Punishing Parents for Student Absenteeism

Since many people hold the view that parents are responsible for their children's absenteeism from school, the proposal has been made that parents be brought into court and fined if their children continually fail to attend. To learn how much support this proposal might have throughout the nation, the following question was included in the survey:

> In your opinion, should, or should not, parents be brought into court and given a small fine when a child of theirs is frequently absent without excuse (truant) from school?

A slight majority of all respondents vote for such a penalty. Parents of children who are now attending school, and who would be affected by such a ruling, are more evenly divided, but still more favor the proposal than oppose it.

	National Totals %	No Children in Schools %	Public School Parents %	Parochial School Parents %
Yes, should fine	51	52	48	46
No, should not	40	39	44	48
Don't know/no answer	9	9	8	6

Analysis of the vote by groups brings to light these facts: Older citizens favor the proposal; young adults oppose. The only region of the nation where a majority opposes the plan is the West. Both blacks and whites favor the proposal, as do those in the lowest educational level.

By socioeconomic groups:

	Yes, Should Fine %	No, Should Not %	Don't Know/ No Answer %
NATIONAL TOTALS	51	40	9
Sex			
Men	52	40	8
Women	50	41	9
Race			
White	52	40	8
Nonwhite	46	40	14
Age			
18 to 29 years	39	56	5
30 to 49 years	51	40	9
50 years and over	60	29	11
Community size			
1 million and over	56	33	11
500,000–999,999	39	50	11
50,000–499,999	50	45	5
2,500–49,999	51	42	7
Under 2,500	53	37	10
Education			
Grade school	65	25	10
High school	48	43	9
College	48	44	8
Region			
East	55	38	7
Midwest	48	41	11
South	53	37	10
West	44	50	6

Rearranging School Hours for Working Fathers and Mothers

With an increasing number of mothers having jobs outside the home, the question arises as to whether school hours should be changed so that children will not be left unsupervised in the afternoons while they await the return of their parents.

The question:

Most people who have jobs today do not get home from work until 5:00 p.m. or later. In your opinion, should the schools arrange the afternoon school schedule so that children would get home at about the same time as their parents, or not?

Taking all respondents into account, this proposal fails to win majority approval. Nationally, the vote is nearly 2-1 opposed. The proposal wins a higher favorable response among those persons who do not have children in school than it does from those who do. Persons in the lowest education group also favor the plan.

	National Totals %	No Children in Schools %	Public School Parents %	Parochial School Parents %
Yes, should change schedule	33	38	22	17
No, should not	59	52	73	76
Don't know/no answer	8	10	5	7

By socioeconomic groups:

	Yes, Should Change Schedule %	No, Should Not %	Don't Know/ No Answer %
NATIONAL TOTALS	33	59	8
Sex			
Men	32	58	10
Women	33	61	6
Race			
White	32	60	8
Nonwhite	38	54	8
Age			
18 to 29 years	29	65	6
30 to 49 years	24	69	7
50 years and over	43	46	11
Community size			
1 million and over	32	59	9
500,000–999,999	30	64	6
50,000–499,999	37	55	8
2,500–49,999	31	59	10
Under 2,500	31	62	7
Education			
Grade school	50	38	12
High School	30	64	6
College	29	62	9
Region			
East	33	58	9
Midwest	30	62	8
South	34	58	8
West	35	60	5

Advantages of Schools in Small Communities

Two to three decades ago it was widely believed that big-city schools, with their large enrollments, were better suited to provide quality education than the schools in small communities. In fact, it was this belief that to a great extend powered the movement for regionalization and for consolidating schools into still larger units.

Today bigness in almost every field is out of vogue. Decentralization is popular in government, business, and (judging from results of this survey) in education as well. The vast majority of persons throughout the nation believe that students get a better education in schools located in small communities than they do in the big cities.

Size alone, obviously, cannot account fully for the disfavor in which many big-city schools are held. The racial mix has changed greatly in the last two decades, with the migration of upper- and middle-class white families to the suburbs.

Apart from the question of quality of education, the fact that most people today believe that education in the small communities is better will almost certainly induce more families with children of school age to leave the city for the suburbs or other small communities.

In general, do you think that students today get a better education in schools that are located in small communities or in schools located in big cities?

	Small Communities %	Big Cities %	Makes No Difference %	Don't Know/ No Answer %
NATIONAL TOTALS	68	11	12	9
Sex				
Men	67	12	12	9
Women	68	10	13	9
Race				
White	68	11	13	8
Nonwhite	61	12	10	17
Age				
18 to 29 years	70	15	10	5
30 to 49 years	67	11	12	10
50 years and over	67	7	15	11
Community size				
1 million and over	71	10	12	7
500,000–999,999	52	16	19	13
50,000–499,999	67	12	12	9
2,500–49,999	70	10	11	9
Under 2,500	73	8	11	8
Education				
Grade school	61	8	17	14
High school	71	10	12	7
College	66	13	12	9
Region				
East	73	7	13	7
Midwest	69	10	12	9
South	61	16	12	11
West	68	9	14	9

Meeting Energy Shortages

The very cold winter of 1976–77 closed many schools for varying periods of time. With the prospect of energy shortages in the future, the question arises as to whether schools should close during the coldest weeks of winter.

To get the public's reaction, and especially the reaction of those parents with children now of school age, this question was asked:

> In order to save energy (fuel oil, gas), it has been suggested that the schools be closed in the middle of the winter. Children would make up lost school time by starting the school year in late August and ending the school year around the first of July. Would you favor or oppose adopting this plan here?

The results, nationally, show that the public is opposed to this proposal by the ratio of 56 percent to 36 percent, with 8 percent having no opinion. Parents of children now attending public schools are even more generally opposed. They vote against the plan 64 percent to 32 percent.

	National Totals %	No Children in Schools %	Public School Parents %	Parochial School Parents %
Favor closing	36	38	32	26
Oppose closing	56	51	64	67
Don't know/no answer	8	11	4	7

Although no group or section of the nation votes in favor of the plan, many observers of the public scene, knowing the reluctance of the public to accept changes in the educational system, may be surprised at the size of the minority who favor the proposal.

	Favor %	Oppose %	Don't Know/ No Answer %
NATIONAL TOTALS	36	56	8
Sex			
Men	37	56	7
Women	35	55	10
Race			
White	36	57	7
Nonwhite	34	50	16
Age			
18 to 29 years	39	55	6
30 to 49 years	33	60	7
50 years and over	37	51	12
Community size			
1 million and over	35	54	11

	Favor	*Oppose*	*Don't Know/ No Answer*
Community size			
500,000–999,999	36	56	8
50,000–499,999	36	56	8
2,500–49,999	41	46	13
Under 2,500	33	62	5
Education			
Grade school	37	50	13
High school	34	58	8
College	39	55	6
Region			
East	37	55	8
Midwest	37	55	8
South	39	53	8
West	29	61	10

Media Coverage of Education

Many educators complain that the news media give too much play of a negative character to happenings in the public schools. At the same time, they say the media pay too little attention to what the schools are achieving or trying to achieve.

To determine how the public stands on this issue, the following question was asked:

> Do you think the news media (newspapers, TV, and radio) give a fair and accurate picture of the public schools in this community, or not?

While many persons agree with the educators who hold this view, a greater number disagree.

	National Totals %	*No Children in Schools* %	*Public School Parents* %	*Parochial School Parents* %
Yes, give fair and accurate picture	42	39	48	41
No, do not	36	34	39	42
Don't know/no answer	22	27	13	17

Significantly, more parents of children now attending the public schools say that the media are fair and accurate than hold the opposite view. Only in the Western states do more respondents say that the media are unfair.

Nationally, the results show that 42 percent say the media are fair and accurate; 36 percent say they are not; and 22 percent have no opinion on this issue.

The results by major groups in the population follow:

	Yes, Give Fair and Accurate Picture %	No, Do Not %	Don't Know/ No Answer %
NATIONAL TOTALS	42	36	22
Sex			
Men	43	35	22
Women	41	37	22
Race			
White	42	36	22
Nonwhite	40	35	25
Age			
18 to 29 years	45	37	18
30 to 49 years	46	37	17
50 years and over	37	32	31
Community size			
1 million and over	36	36	28
500,000–999,999	46	32	22
50,000–499,999	44	38	18
2,500–49,999	42	34	24
Under 2,500	43	36	21
Education			
Grade school	32	27	41
High school	42	40	18
College	47	33	20
Region			
East	45	33	22
Midwest	45	35	20
South	40	35	25
West	36	42	22

Improving Media Coverage

To find out what the news media could do to better report on local education, all respondents included in the survey were asked:

> In your opinion, how could the media (newspapers, TV, and radio) improve their reporting of education in the local schools?

The answers elicited by this question often referred to the paucity of news about the schools reported in many communities. But the most frequent response dwelt on the need for more positive news—interesting things the schools are doing to achieve their educational goals.

Many specific suggestions were offered which the media might well consider. Among these were:

"Reporters should be sent into the school rooms to see what goes on there. They should put themselves in the teacher's place, and in the student's place."

"It would be interesting to find out about all the different courses that are offered."

"Why don't they [the media] tell us about the standing of the local schools—how well they do in comparison with the private schools, and with other schools in nearby cities."

"I should like to know more about the changes that are being introduced and why. There should be more background information about education and about new programs."

"Outstanding students should be written up and praised the way top athletes are."

"An interesting series could be built around the idea of a typical day at school with a typical seventh-grader, ninth-grader, etc. I can remember what went on in my day. I wonder if it is the same now."

"I hear a lot about the gadgets now used in the schools and in the classrooms to teach different subjects such as foreign language and I would like to know more about them."

"The media report on the school budget, but they never tell, in detail, just where the tax dollars are spent."

"In the magazines I read about 'open' classrooms, 'team teaching,' and such things, and I wonder if our local schools go in for these new ideas."

Decision-Making Authority of Advisory Committees

One of the most useful and popular means of increasing citizen participation in school and civic affairs and of taking advantage of the training and expertise of these citizens is to create citizen advisory groups.

The question arises as to how much authority these citizen advisory groups should have. Should final decision-making authority be left with the advisory groups, or should it remain with the school board?

Three questions, probing views in respect to advisory group authority concerning curriculum, staff selection, and the budget, were included in the survey instrument to obtain the views of the public.

The results show that people want the final decision-making authority to remain where it is: with the school board.

Although there is slightly more sentiment for giving advisory groups authority over the budget than over curriculum or staff selection, the overwhelming majority believe that the school board should retain its present authority.

These findings should not be taken to mean that school boards should not listen to advisory groups on all three matters. However, if the public believes that school boards are making wrong decisions, it has the right to elect new board members.

The first question asked:

Many school systems have committees made up of citizens who serve in an advisory capacity. Do you think these advisory groups should have the final decision-making authority over the *curriculum*, or should the final authority remain with the school board?

	National Totals %	No Children in Schools %	Public School Parents %	Parochial School Parents %
Authority with citizen groups	17	18	15	23
Authority with school board	71	68	78	71
Don't know/no answer	12	14	7	6

The second question:

How about decisions regarding *staff selection*—should the final authority be given to these citizen committees or should the final authority remain with the school board?

	National Totals %	No Children in Schools %	Public School Parents %	Parochial School Parents %
Authority with citizen groups	15	15	13	18
Authority with school board	75	73	80	76
Don't know/no answer	10	12	7	6

The third question:

And decisions about the *budget* — should the final authority be given to these citizen committees or should the final authority remain with the school board?

	National Totals %	No Children in Schools %	Public School Parents %	Parochial School Parents %
Authority with citizen groups	19	20	19	32
Authority with school board	70	68	72	65
Don't know/no answer	11	12	9	3

Courses for Parents on How To Deal with Their Children's Problems

Throughout the nation there is wide acceptance of the view that parents must work closely with the schools if students are to reach their full educational potential.

Problems of discipline, motivation, poor work and study habits, drug and alcohol addiction, and many others normally have their origin in the home. Unless something is done to correct the home situation, the best efforts of teachers will fail.

It is probably no exaggeration to say that the next great advance in education will come when parents and teachers work as a team, with parents taking full responsibility for problems that arise in the home.

The 1976 survey revealed that more than three in every four U.S. adults approve of the idea of offering courses to parents as a regular part of the public school educational system. And parents of schoolchildren in the public schools voted nearly 4-1 for this plan. As further evidence of their approval, they said they were willing to pay additional taxes to support such a program.

In fact, in every survey in which this proposal to help parents, through a course of instruction, to help their children in school has been asked, sizable majorities have voted in favor of such courses.

In the present survey an effort was made to discover the specific subjects that might be included in such a course for parents. Presumably, if the plan were to be carried out by a school, then the parents of children in a given grade would meet together to discuss the problems of children of that age.

From a total of 16 suggested topics, parents of children now attending school were asked to choose those that interested them most.

The question was worded in this manner:

The subjects listed on this card are some that could be covered in a special course for parents offered by the local schools. Which of these subjects would interest you the *most*?

(A card was then given to each respondent, with 16 suggested topics.)

Listed below in order of mention are the 16 suggested topics for parents whose eldest child is 13 to 20 years of age.

1. What to do about drugs, smoking, use of alcohol
2. How to help the child choose a career
3. How to help the child set high achievement goals
4. How to develop good work habits

149

5. How to encourage reading
6. How to increase interest in school and school subjects
7. How to help the child organize his/her homework
8. How to improve parent/child relationships
9. How to improve the child's thinking and observation abilities
10. How to deal with the child's emotional problems
11. How to use family activities to help the child do better in school
12. How to improve the child's school behavior
13. How to reduce television viewing
14. How to help the child get along with other children
15. How to improve health habits
16. How to deal with dating problems

Ranked below in order of mention are the 16 suggested topics for parents whose eldest child is 12 years or younger.

1. What to do about drugs, smoking, use of alcohol
2. How to help the child set high achievement goals
3. How to develop good work habits
4. How to improve the child's school behavior
5. How to improve the child's thinking and observation abilities
6. How to deal with the child's emotional problems
7. How to increase interest in school and school subjects
8. How to help the child organize his/her homework
9. How to improve parent/child relationships
10. How to help the child choose a career
11. How to use family activities to help the child do better in school
12. How to encourage reading
13. How to help the child get along with other children
14. How to reduce television viewing
15. How to deal with dating problems
16. How to improve health habits

Experience in carrying out such a program of instruction would undoubtedly uncover other areas to include in future courses.

Significantly, the topics selected as most interesting by parents who have attended college are not markedly different from the topics regarded as most interesting by those who have had little schooling. This would indicate that home problems are very much the same in the best-educated, highest-income families and those farther down on the socioeconomic scale.

In short, virtually all parents freely admit that they need help, and they would like to have the local schools offer this help and guidance by regular courses and by discussion.

Government-Mandated Programs

Public school and college administrators are becoming more and more vexed by rules and regulations promulgated by Washington that require certain actions to be taken without regard to the additional time and cost entailed.

Making provision for physically and mentally handicapped students is one of these. Local schools are required to bear the added costs of special programs without help, in most instances, from the federal government.

To measure the public's views on this issue, the following question was included in the survey:

> Services for the physically and mentally handicapped student cost more than regular school services. When the local schools are required to provide these special services by the federal government, should the federal government pay the extra cost, or not?

The overwhelming majority of those interviewed say the federal government should pay the extra cost of such programs. In fact, every important group in the population and every region of the nation supports the idea that the federal government should pay the extra costs.

	Yes, Government Should Pay Extra Cost %	No, Should Not %	Don't Know/ No Answer %
NATIONAL TOTALS	82	11	7
Sex			
Men	80	13	7
Women	83	9	8
Race			
White	82	11	7
Nonwhite	81	10	9
Age			
18 to 29 years	83	11	6
30 to 49 years	81	11	8
50 years and over	81	11	8
Community size			
1 million and over	83	11	6
500,000–999,999	77	16	7
50,000–499,999	81	13	6
2,500–49,999	78	10	12
Under 2,500	86	8	6

	Yes, Govern-ment Should Pay Extra Cost %	No, Should Not %	Don't Know/ No Answer %
Education			
Grade school	81	8	11
High school	83	10	7
College	79	15	6
Region			
East	85	11	4
Midwest	80	13	7
South	81	9	10
West	79	14	7

Local Control of Federal Programs

Another source of concern is the federal government's insistence that local school authorities follow strict regulations when funds are awarded. Often-times, local authorities have different ideas about how best to spend these funds.

Respondents again reveal their anti-Washington, anti-red tape at-titudes in their answers to the following question:

> When federal agencies appropriate money for educational programs, they usu-ally require the schools that receive this money to spend it as these agencies direct. Should, or should not, this be changed to permit local school authorities to decide how the money is to be spent?

The nation's adults vote 2-1 for giving local school authorities jurisdic-tion over how the money is to be spent to carry out the program locally. Every major group in the population is in agreement on this issue, as the findings show.

By socioeconomic groups:

	Yes, Change to Allow Local People to Decide %	No, Should Not Change %	Don't Know/ No Answer %
NATIONAL TOTALS	62	29	9
Sex			
Men	64	28	8
Women	60	30	10
Race			
White	63	28	9
Nonwhite	53	32	15
Age			
18 to 29 years	61	33	6
30 to 49 years	64	28	8
50 years and over	61	26	13

	Yes, Change to Allow Local People to Decide %	No, Should Not Change %	Don't Know/ No Answer %
Community size			
1 million and over	63	27	10
500,000–999,999	55	34	11
50,000–499,999	66	27	7
2,500–49,999	59	29	12
Under 2,500	62	29	9
Education			
Grade school	53	29	18
High school	62	30	8
College	65	27	8
Region			
East	60	31	9
Midwest	62	28	10
South	62	29	9
West	64	26	10

Take Education Out of HEW?

Frequent complaints are made that the present Department of Health, Education, and Welfare is so huge that education is not given the attention that it merits. Some believe that funding of education by the federal government would be increased if it did not have to compete with health and welfare in the same department. Still others believe that public education is so important that it deserves cabinet status in its own right.

For these reasons, the issue was taken to a representative sample of the people of the nation to get their views. The question asked was this:

> In your opinion, should *Education* be taken out of the present Department of Health, Education, and Welfare and made a separate department of the federal government, nor not?

Sentiment on this issue is fairly evenly divided, with slightly more respondents voting to keep it in the present department rather than make it a separate department.

The results:

	National Totals %	No Children in Schools %	Public School Parents %	Parochial School Parents %
Favor making education a separate department	40	40	40	42
Oppose	45	42	49	47
Don't know/no answer	15	18	11	11

A plurality of voters in cities of one million and over in population, as well as those living in the East and those who are college-educated, favor making education a separate department in the federal government.

	Yes, Should Be Separate Department %	No, Should Not %	Don't Know/ No Answer %
NATIONAL TOTALS	40	45	15
Sex			
Men	41	45	14
Women	40	44	16
Race			
White	42	43	15
Nonwhite	30	51	19
Age			
18 to 29 years	44	46	10
30 to 49 years	39	48	13
50 years and over	39	40	21
Community size			
1 million and over	46	37	17
500,000–999,999	37	48	15
50,000–499,999	39	47	14
2,500–49,999	37	50	13
Under 2,500	41	42	17
Education			
Grade school	31	43	26
High school	39	47	14
College	48	41	11
Region			
East	43	41	16
Midwest	36	48	16
South	42	45	13
West	41	43	16

Tenure

A recurring issue of recent years has to do with tenure for teachers. During the nine years that these studies dealing with the public's attitudes toward the public schools have been conducted, views on tenure have been probed on three occasions by questions that contained an explanation of the issue.

The point often arises, however, as to how many persons in the general public are familiar with the term "tenure" and how persons who are better informed in this respect view the problem.

In this connection, a question was first asked of all persons included in the survey:

Do you happen to know what the word "tenure" means as it applies to teachers' jobs?

A second question asked of those who replied "yes":

Just as you understand it, what does tenure mean?

A third question, limited to those who gave a correct answer, asked:

Do you favor or oppose tenure for teachers?

A total of 28 percent of the adults interviewed nationally could give a correct definition of tenure as it applies to teachers' jobs.

When persons who know what the term means are asked whether they favor or oppose tenure, a majority say they oppose tenure. The same conclusion was reached in the three earlier surveys in which tenure questions were asked.

Persons who have no children in the schools are more likely to favor tenure than those who have children in school. Among the former, 44 percent favor tenure and 45 percent oppose it; in the case of parents with children in the public schools, 54 percent oppose and 37 percent favor it. In the case of parents with children in parochial or private schools, 84 percent oppose and 16 percent favor tenure.

(Based on Those Who Know What the Term Means)	*National Totals* %	*No Children in Schools* %	*Public School Parents* %	*Parochial School Parents* %
Favor tenure	40	44	37	16
Oppose	50	45	54	84
Don't know/no answer	10	11	9	--

Parent/Teacher Conferences

At least in theory, parents should follow the educational progress of their children by holding frequent conferences with their children's teachers. But do they? Obviously, the situation changes from school to school and state to state.

To shed light on the frequency of parent/teacher conferences, this question was asked of those parents who now have children attending school:

Thinking about your eldest child, have you at any time since the beginning of the school year discussed your child's progress, or problems, with any of your child's teachers?

Fieldwork for the present survey was conducted during the period April 28 through May 2, 1977. The figures must, therefore, be interpreted accordingly.

The findings show that 79 percent of all parents whose children are 12 years of age and under had talked to one or more of their child's teachers about his/her progress since the beginning of the school year. But only 55 percent of parents whose children are 13 years old and over had talked to any teacher.

A second question, asked of those who had talked to one of their child's teachers, sought to discover how many conferences had been held:

> About how often (have you talked to your child's teachers) since the beginning of the school year?

In the case of parents whose eldest child is 12 years of age or younger, the median number of conferences is two.

The same figure—two—is the median for parent/teacher conferences for parents whose eldest child is 13 years of age or older.

From these findings, it appears that during an average period of eight school months, three out of five parents will talk to teachers about the progress of their child. And, on the average, these parents, during a period of eight months, will hold two such meetings.

Parents' Estimates of Time Children Spend on Television, Homework, Reading

Parents who now have children enrolled in the public or parochial and private schools were asked to give an estimate of the time spent, on a typical school day, by their eldest child on television, homework, and reading.

Since time spent is likely to vary with age, the results are reported for those whose eldest child is 12 years of age and younger, and those 13 years of age and older.

The first question:

> (For eldest child) About how much time does he/she spend looking at television after school hours and until he/she goes to bed, on a typical school day?

(Based on Those Responding)	By Children 12 Years of Age and Younger %	By Children 13 Years of Age and Older %
No time	2	5
Up to 1 hour	20	26
Over 1 hour to 2 hours	38	33
Over 2 hours to 3 hours	28	17
Over 3 hours to 4 hours	10	11
Over 4 hours	2	8

The second question:

> And about how much time on school homework on a typical school day?

(*Based on Those Responding*)	*By Children 12 Years of Age and Younger* %	*By Children 13 Years of Age and Older* %
No time	24	15
Up to 15 minutes	3	3
16 to 30 minutes	22	10
Over 30 minutes to 1 hour	29	30
Over 1 hour to 2 hours	17	32
Over 2 hours	5	10

The third question:

And about how much time on reading—not connected with schoolwork—on a typical school day?

(*Based on Those Responding*)	*By Children 12 Years of Age and Younger* %	*By Children 13 Years of Age and Older* %
No time	12	28
Up to 30 minutes	43	24
Over 30 minutes to 1 hour	33	28
Over 1 hour	12	20

What this adds up to—for children 12 years and younger—is that the typical child spends approximately:
— 2 hours viewing television on a typical school day,
— 30 minutes reading (not schoolwork), and
— 45 minutes doing homework.

Among children 13 years of age and older, the typical child spends approximately:
— 2 hours viewing television,
— 30 minutes reading (not schoolwork), and
— 1 hour doing homework.

Parental Help with Homework

To find out whether parents help their children with homework, the following question was asked of parents with school-age children about their eldest child:

Do you regularly help your child with his/her homework?

Parents who have children in the public schools and parents of children in the parochial/private schools give almost exactly the same amount of help to their children.

	Public School Parents %	Parochial School Parents %
Yes, regularly	24	17
Yes, when he/she needs help	27	32
No	44	41
Don't know/no answer	5	10

When the age of the eldest child is considered, parents respond in this way:

	Children 12 Years of Age and Under %	Children 13 Years of Age and Older %
Yes, regularly	37	16
Yes, when he/she needs help	34	26
No	27	58
Don't know/no answer	2	*

*Less than 1%

Time Limits on Television Viewing

Because the attraction of television is so great for children in most families, many educators have come to the conclusion that definite limits should be placed on the amount of time that parents permit their children to view television during the school week.

To discover how many parents already impose such rules, this question was asked (about the eldest child):

Do you place a definite limit on the amount of time your child spends viewing television during the school week?

The results:

	National Totals %	Parents Whose Eldest Child Is 12 Years and Under %	Parents Whose Eldest Child Is 13 Years and Over %
Yes, have definite time limit	35	49	28
No	60	50	70
Don't know/no answer	5	1	2

Safety of Children

One of the interesting facts turned up in the present survey is the relatively high percentage of parents (one in four) who fear for the physical safety of their children in school—and 28 percent fear for the safety of their children in their own neighborhoods. Fewer parents of children who attend parochial school worry about their children's physical safety in school, but still the figure is high—one in five.

The first question asked (about the eldest child):

When he/she is at school, do you fear for his/her physical safety?

	Public School Parents %	Parochial School Parents %
Yes, fear for safety	25	19
No	69	73
Don't know/no answer	6	8

The second question asked:

When your child is outside at play in your own neighborhood, do you fear for his/her safety?

	Public School Parents %	Parochial School Parents %
Yes, fear for safety	28	30
No	68	61
Don't know/no answer	4	9

Further Breakdowns

THE MAJOR PROBLEMS

What do you think are the biggest problems with which the PUBLIC schools in this community must deal?

	National Totals %	No Children in Schools %	Public School Parents %	Parochial School Parents %
Lack of discipline	26	26	27	29
Integration/segregation/ busing	13	13	11	18

	National Totals %	No Children in Schools %	Public School Parents %	Parochial School Parents %
Lack of proper financial support	12	11	14	14
Difficulty of getting "good" teachers	11	10	12	19
Poor curriculum	10	9	12	14
Use of drugs	7	8	6	3
Parents' lack of interest	5	5	6	7
Size of school/classes	5	4	7	11
Teachers' lack of interest	5	4	6	5
Mismanagement of funds/programs	4	4	3	5
Pupils' lack of interest	3	3	4	2
Problems with administration	3	3	3	5
Crime/vandalism	2	3	1	1
Lack of proper facilities	2	2	3	—
Transportation	2	2	1	1
Parents' involvement in school activities	1	1	1	—
Communication problems	1	1	1	—
Too many schools/ declining enrollment	1	1	1	1
School board policies	1	*	2	—
Drinking/alcoholism	1	1	*	—
There are no problems	4	2	7	3
Miscellaneous	5	4	6	7
Don't know/no answer	16	21	9	3

*Less than 1%
(Figures add to more than 100% because of multiple answers.)

WAYS IN WHICH LOCAL SCHOOLS ARE GOOD

In your own opinion, in what ways are your local PUBLIC schools particularly good?

	National Totals %	No Children in Schools %	Public School Parents %	Parochial School Parents %
The curriculum	23	17	35	28
The teachers	20	18	26	13

	National Totals %	No Children in Schools %	Public School Parents %	Parochial School Parents %
Extracurricular activities	10	8	15	9
School facilities	7	6	9	6
Equal opportunity for all students	4	3	5	8
Good administration	3	2	5	3
Parental interest/ participation	3	2	4	1
Good student/teacher relationships	3	1	6	1
Good discipline	2	2	2	1
Small school or small classes	2	2	3	3
Up-to-date teaching methods	2	2	3	2
No racial conflicts	2	1	2	3
Good lunch program	1	1	2	3
Transportation system	1	1	1	1
Kids are kept off the street	1	1	*	—
Close to home	1	1	1	—
Nothing is good	9	9	7	10
Miscellaneous	1	1	1	—
Don't know/no answer	31	39	14	29

*Less than 1%
(Totals add to more than 100% because of multiple answers.)

SMALL COMMUNITIES VS. BIG CITIES

In general, do you think that students today get a better education in schools that are located in small communities or in schools located in big cities?

	National Totals %	No Children in Schools %	Public School Parents %	Parochial School Parents %
Small communities	68	66	72	59
Big cities	11	11	10	16
Makes no difference	12	13	11	20
Don't know/no answer	9	10	7	5

GOVERNMENT-MANDATED PROGRAMS

Services for the physically and mentally handicapped student cost more than regular school services. When the local schools are required to provide these special services by the federal government, should the federal government pay the extra cost, or not?

	National Totals %	No Children in Schools %	Public School Parents %	Parochial School Parents %
Yes, government should pay extra cost	82	80	85	84
No, should not	11	12	9	14
Don't know/no answer	7	8	6	2

LOCAL CONTROL OF FEDERAL PROGRAMS

When federal agencies appropriate money for educational programs, they usually require the schools that receive this money to spend it as these agencies direct. Should, or should not, this be changed to permit local school authorities to decide how the money is to be spent?

	National Totals %	No Children in Schools %	Public School Parents %	Parochial School Parents %
Yes, change to allow local people to decide	62	60	65	67
No, should not change	29	29	29	27
Don't know/no answer	9	11	6	6

Composition of the Sample

No children in schools	66%
Public school parents	30%*
Parochial school parents	6%*

*Totals exceed 34% because some parents have children attending more than one kind of school.

Sex	%
Men	47
Women	53
	100

Race	
White	88
Nonwhite	12
	100

Occupation	
Business & professional	27
Clerical & sales	8
Farm	2
Skilled labor	19
Unskilled labor	21
Nonlabor force	20
Undesignated	3
	100

Religion

		Income	
Protestant	60	$20,000 & over	22
Roman Catholic	29	$15,000 to $19,999	18
Jewish	3	$10,000 to $14,999	23
Others	8	$7,000 to $9,999	10
	100	$5,000 to $6,999	9
		$3,000 to $4,999	10
Age		Under $3,000	7
18 to 24 years	18	Undesignated	1
25 to 29 years	10		100
30 to 49 years	35		
50 years & over	37	Political Affiliation	
	100	Republican	21
		Democrat	45
		Independent	31
		Other	3
			100
Region		Education	
East	28	Elementary grades	16
Midwest	27	High school incomplete	16
South	28	High school complete	34
West	17	Technical, trade, or	
	100	business school	5
		College incomplete	17
Community Size		College graduate	12
1 million & over	20	Undesignated	*
500,000 to 999,999	12		100
50,000 to 499,999	26		
2,500 to 49,999	16		
Under 2,500	26		
	100		

*Less than 1%

THE DESIGN OF THE SAMPLE

The sampling procedure is designed to produce an approximation of the adult civilian population 18 years of age and older, living in the United States, except for those persons in institutions such as prisons or hospitals.

The design of the sample is that of a replicated probability sample, [*so can generalize back to population*] down to the block level in the case of urban areas and to segments of townships in the case of rural areas. Approximately 300 sampling locations are used in each survey. Interpenetrating samples can be provided for any given study when appropriate.

The sample design included stratification by these four size-of-community strata, using 1970 census data: 1) cities of population 1 million and over; 2) 250,000–999,999; 3) 50,000–249,999; 4) all other population. Each of these strata was further into seven geographic regions: New England, Middle Atlantic, East Central, West Central, South, Mountain, and Pacific. Within each city-size/regional stratum, the population was arrayed in geographic order and zoned into equal-sized groups of sampling units. Pairs of localities were selected in each zone, with probability of selection of each locality proportional to its population size in the 1970 census, producing two replicated samples of localities.

Within localities so selected for which the requisite population data are reported, subdivisions were drawn with the probability of selection proportional to size of population. In all other localities, small definable geographic areas were selected with equal probability.

Separately for each survey, within each subdivision so selected for which block statistics are available, a sample of blocks or block clusters is drawn with probability of selection proportional to the number of dwelling units. In all other subdivisions or areas, blocks or segments are drawn at random or with equal probability.

In each cluster of blocks and each segment so selected, a randomly selected starting point is designated on the interviewer's map of the area. Starting at this point, interviewers are required to follow a given direction in the selection of households until their assignment is completed.

Interviewing is conducted at times when adults, in general, are most likely to be at home, which means on weekends, or if on weekdays, after 4:00 p.m. for women and after 6:00 p.m. for men.

Allowance for persons not at home is made by a "times-at-home" weighting procedure rather than by "call-backs." This procedure is a standard method for reducing the sample bias that would otherwise result from underrepresentation in the sample of persons who are difficult to find at home.

The prestratification by regions is routinely supplemented by fitting each obtained sample to the latest available Census Bureau estimates of the regional distribution of the population. Also, minor adjustments of the sample are made by educational attainment by men and women separately, based on the annual estimates of the Census Bureau (derived from their Current Population Survey) and by age.

In interpreting survey results, it should be borne in mind that all sample surveys are subject to sampling error; that is, the extent to which the results may differ from what would be obtained if the whole population surveyed had been interviewed. The size of such sampling errors depends largely on the number of interviews.

Readers interested in determining the approximate size of sampling error for any percentage given in this report should obtain a copy of *The Gallup Polls of Attitudes toward Education, 1969–1973*, which provides tables and instructions permitting such calculations for all the Gallup polls published in the *Kappan*. (Order from Director of Administrative Services, Phi Delta

Kappa, Box 789, Eighth and Union, Bloomington, IN 47401. Price, $2.25 each or $2 each for five or more copies.)

comments and questions _____

1. Discuss the merits and limitations of Gallup's approach to determining the "new issues" as a basis for developing the questionnaire. Does the panel of citizens adequately represent either the "common person" or the public school teacher? If the answer is "no," what implications, if any, does this have?
2. We commend Gallup for his thorough approach to, and discussion of, sampling.
3. How sufficient is the information regarding the training of the interviewers and the nature of the interviewing form? Why or why not is it sufficient?
4. How sufficient is the discussion of the pretesting of the questionniare? What evidence is presented that the respondents, the researcher, and the reader of the report all interpret the questions in the same way?
5. How confident can we be that the changes reported across years are statistically significant? What does this imply?
6. In what way(s) would the results of this survey be useful in local educational decision-making processes?
7. We commend the author for presenting the data according to various categories as well as in terms of an overall aggregate. This allows for meaningful interpretation.

CORRELATIONAL RESEARCH

chapter four _____

Correlational research is concerned with discovering and/or measuring the degree of relationship between two or more variables. Such research is often conducted for the purpose of making predictions. Correlational studies are also useful in exploratory research where the relationship (and the degree of relationship) between variables is unknown.

Recall that one of the goals of science is to predict behavior. In the educational arena the ability to predict accurately is very important. It has been said that all decisions involve prediction. By this it is meant that any time a person decides on a certain course of action, he is making some assumptions (predictions) concerning the outcomes of that course of action. The more accurately we are able to predict, the better decisions we should make. The prediction of future enrollments in a school district, for example, affects building decisions. Predicting the chances of college success for an individual helps in counseling that person.

Suppose that an investigator is interested in studying the relationship between scholastic aptitude and grade-point average (GPA) for third-graders. Let us assume that a research study reports a coefficient of correlation[1] of +0.90 between a scholastic aptitude test (SAT) score and grade-point average (GPA). Let us further assume that the coefficient reported is reliable. What then, does

_____

[1]A correlation coefficient is a statistic used to describe the relationship between two variables. The value of this statistic can range from +1.00 to −1.00. When an increase in one variable tends to be accompanied by an increase in the other variable (such as aptitude and achievement), the correlation is positive. When an increase in one tends to be accompanied by a decrease in the other (such as speed and accuracy), then the correlation is negative. A perfect positive correlation (1.00) or a perfect negative correlation (−1.00) occurs when a change in the one variable is always accompanied by a commensurate change in the other variable. A zero (0.00) correlation occurs when there is no relationship between the two.

a +0.90 coefficient of correlation mean? How can it be interpreted? This relationship can be interpreted in one of three ways:

1. Students' GPAs are influenced by their SAT scores.
2. Students' SAT scores are influenced by their GPA scores.
3. Some unknown third factor, such as emotional stability or socioeconomic level, influences both scores.

Occasionally, researchers forget the last possibility. Correlational research only indicates whether a relationship exists, it does *not* indicate whether existing relationships are causal.

However, whether or not a causal relationship exists, one can predict quite accurately, with a correlation of 0.90, an individual's GPA from knowledge of his SAT score or vice versa.

Correlational research is also useful in exploratory studies where it is not known what variables are related to each other and/or how they are so related. Such studies may assist the researcher to identify the relevant variables that can later be studied experimentally if one wishes to test causal hypotheses. As Sax states:

> The point to keep in mind is this: while correlations do not necessarily imply causation, a correlation of zero [that is, no relationship] does eliminate the possibility that there is a causal relationship between the two variables under consideration. (Material in brackets added.)[2]

Correlational studies are thus very useful in that they help to eliminate irrelevant variables from further consideration and permit the researcher to focus his effort on more relevant variables in the more costly experimental studies.

Although correlational studies are of considerable value to educators, ignorance of some statistical aspects may lead to pitfalls or mistakes in interpretation. Also, correlational studies do have some limitations of which the researcher should be aware.

Statistical Aspects

An introductory section in a book of readings can hardly do justice to a discussion of correlational statistics. Such techniques as partial and multiple correlation and factor analysis are not easy to explain to the uninitiated. We do, however, want to introduce three aspects of which every consumer should be cognizant: shrinkage, correction for attenuation, and the effect of sample heterogeneity.

[2]Gilbert Sax, *Empirical Foundations of Educational Research.* Englewood Cliffs, N.J.: Prentice-Hall, 1968, p. 294.

SHRINKAGE

Suppose we wish to use scholastic aptitude test scores and high-school GPA to predict college GPA. The typical approach would be to take a sample of students, obtain the values for the three variables (SAT test scores, high-school GPA, and college GPA) for each person in the sample and build an equation that gives us the best prediction of the college GPA from knowledge of the other two variables. (This equation is called a *multiple regression equation*.) The multiple correlation (multiple because we are predicting from more than one variable) between predicted college GPA and actual college GPA is, for this sample, as high as possible. However, the regression equation has taken advantage of chance relationships in the data. If the same equation were used on a new sample of students, we would expect the new coefficient to be smaller, or to have shrunk. How much it will shrink varies from situation to situation. In general the smaller the sample size and the larger the number of predictor variables the greater will be the shrinkage. Although there are equations that allow one to estimate the degree of shrinkage, it is usually considered better to actually compute the multiple correlation on a new sample, using the equation constructed from the original data. This procedure is referred to as *cross validation*. You should look for it in multiple-prediction studies. It is from the correlation coefficient for the cross-validated group that you should judge predictive accuracy. Note: Be wary of multiple-prediction studies that have no cross-validation sample (or at least some estimate of the shrinkage).

CORRECTION FOR ATTENUATION

The value of a correlation coefficient depends, in part, upon how accurately (reliably) the two sets of variables are originally measured. In many instances the reliability of the original measures are quite low, thus attenuating (lowering) the magnitude of the measure of relationship. This attenuated value can be "corrected" by a statistical technique called—naturally enough—a *correction for attenuation*. This correction tells us what the degree of relationship would be if the original measures were perfectly reliable. The correction can be applied to amend the unreliability of either measure or both. Corrections for attenuation are certainly subject to misinterpretation. Naive users may easily be led into believing that the degree of relationship between variables is higher than it actually is. When reading correlational research, be sure to notice whether a correlation has been corrected. Researchers that do correct for attenuation should definitely also report the uncorrected value. In general, when one is conducting a prediction study there should be no correction for attenuation. In studies where one is interested in estimating the critical relationships, such corrections may be appropriate.

EFFECTS OF SAMPLE HETEROGENEITY

Other things being equal, the more heterogeneous the sample with respect to the variables being correlated, the higher the correlation. Thus, when one is evaluating the degree of relationship it is important to note this variability. Some researchers choose subjects from both extremes of a distribution and run correlations on two variables for these subjects. The correlation obtained will be much higher than would be obtained if all the subjects' scores (or a random subsample) had been used. For example, suppose we were interested in studying the relationship between a teacher's judgments of students' ability and the students' scores on a scholastic aptitude test. If we used scores for our correlation coefficient only for those students whom the teacher judged as the very brightest *and* the very dullest, we would have a very heterogeneous sample. The correlation coefficient on this sample would be higher than if the teacher rated all her pupils and the correlation were run on the total sample.

On the other hand, other researchers run correlations on samples that are very homogeneous. For example, correlations between the Miller Analogies Test (MAT) and GPA are often not high for students in a Ph.D. program because, relatively speaking, we are using a group that is very homogeneous on both variables. (This is called a restriction of range.) This is particularly true if admission to the Ph.D. program is contingent upon a minimum MAT score. A low correlation between those two variables for Ph.D. candidates would not necessarily mean that the MAT is a useless *selection* tool. Had all applicants been accepted, the variability of the MAT scores would increase (and in all likelihood the variability of the GPAs) and a higher correlation would be observed.

There are equations that allow one to predict changes in the size of the correlation coefficient with changes in group heterogeneity. These can be found in most statistics and test theory texts. The major point we wish to convey to our readers is that group variability does affect the correlations obtained, so one needs to look carefully at the characteristics of the sample before making any generalizations regarding degree of relationship to other groups.

Limitations of Correlational Research

An occasionally troublesome problem in correlational (especially predictive) studies is that of criterion contamination. Criterion contamination occurs when the criterion score is influenced by the knowledge of the predictor score. Suppose that in September a ninth-grade math teacher gives and scores a test designed to predict success of his pupils in ninth-grade math. If his knowledge of these predictor scores consciously or unconsciously affects the grades (criterion scores) he assigns at the end of year, then we have criterion contamination. The best way to avoid this problem is to make sure the rater supplying the criterion scores has no knowledge of the predictor values. The producer of a research article should explain how the data were gathered so the reader of the report can discern whether or not criterion contamination may have occurred.

While correlational research can be an extremely valuable aid in decision making for the practicing educator, it does not do as well under a "science advancement" criterion. Those whose main interest is to advance the theoretical knowledge generally prefer experimental research.

As you have been told before, correlation does not indicate causation. Also, those doing correlational research will often include variables in their study even though there is no theoretical reason for including them. Throwing a lot of variables into the research design and hoping some of them will be related to each other is called a "shotgun approach." (One should not conclude that because a researcher considered a number of variables that his approach is analogous to the shotgun approach—it is only a shotgun approach if the researcher relies on "guesses" rather than critical thinking and suggestions garnered from previous research.) Spurious correlations often arise from this type of research. Without replication the researcher has no way of telling which relationships are spurious and which are real. Even if he can discern which relationships are real, he often cannot establish any theoretical reasons for them.

Some Specific Questions To Be Asked When Reading Correlational Studies

In addition to the general series of questions that should be raised when reading any and all types of research studies there are some questions that are particularly appropriate when reading correlational research. Some of these are:

1. Did the researcher imply causation in discussing his findings?
2. Was a cross-validations sample used?
3. Is the correlation coefficient misleading due to the nature of the sample? A very heterogeneous sample would result in a spuriously high correlation and a very homogeneous sample would result in a spuriously low one. Did the researcher discuss this?
4. Was the appropriate correlational technique employed?
5. Did the researcher draw his conclusions on the basis of the "corrected" value of the correlation coefficient?
6. Was there a criterion contamination problem?
7. Was a shotgun approach used? Did the variables have some theoretical rationale for being considered?

Examples of Correlational Studies

Are the following selections largely concerned with prediction or determining the degree of relationship between various constructs? How much do they advance our *understanding* of the variables investigated? While reading these studies keep in mind the questions discussed in Chapter One as well as those raised above.

PREDICTIVE VALIDITY OF THE KUDER OCCUPATIONAL INTEREST SURVEY: A 12- to 19-Year Follow-up

DONALD G. ZYTOWSKI*

More than 1,000 men and women were located 12 to 19 years after taking an early form of the Kuder Occupational Interest Survey either in high school or college. Satisfactory data were available for 882 subjects. Fifty-one percent were employed at the time of the follow-up in an occupation that would have been suggested to them had their inventory been interpreted to them. This compares favorably with other validity findings for occupationally scaled interest inventories and represents about 90% of the possible validity as derived from concurrent validity figures. College major scales from a high school level administration correctly predicted 55%. Subjects in occupations consistent with their early interest profiles did not report greater job satisfaction or success but did show greater continuance in their occupational career. Better prediction is achieved when the occupation is one named on the profile and when the person has gone to or graduated from college or entered a high-level or scientific-technical occupation.

Any test or inventory used in the guidance or counseling of young persons must be shown to possess validity, particularly of the predictive kind. Reviewers of the Kuder Occupational Interest Survey (KOIS), Brown (1971), Stahman (1971), Dolliver (1972), and Walsh (1972), agree that although the KOIS is well constructed and promising, its predictive validity needs to be investigated. The present study was undertaken to correct that lack.

Many studies, especially those using the Kuder Form B or C interest inventories, have shown that "type of interest" or homogeneous scales are predictive of occupations observed a number of years after their administration. Zytowski (1974) has summarized these studies and concluded that they provide correct identification for between 55 percent and 65 percent of their subjects. Super and Crites (1962) presented a similar review.

Although all of the interest inventories that use normative or occupational scales—the several versions of the Strong Vocational Interest Blank

*From *Journal of Counseling Psychology*, 23:3 (1976), pp. 221–233. Copyright 1976 by the American Psychological Association. Reprinted by permission. Requests for reprints should be sent to Donald G. Zytowski, Student Counseling Service, Iowa State University, Ames, Iowa 50010.

(SVIB), the Minnesota Vocational Interest Inventory (MVII), and the KOIS—
have extensive data in their manuals on their ability to distinguish between
persons in different occupations (a form of concurrent validity), really only the
SVIB has had extensive investigation of its predictive validity. The best known
is Strong's 18-year follow-up (Strong, 1955), but a number of other studies have
been performed and are reported in convenient form by Campbell (1971).
Strong concludes that persons are three times as likely to be in an occupation on
which they made a T score of 45 or higher than in an occupation on which they
scored lower than 25. Campbell concurs in his review of other follow-up
studies, although he suggests that when the inventory is taken by high school
boys, it is used more effectually to suggest general direction of career rather
than specific occupation. Berdie (1960) and Super and Crites (1962) review
much of the same material and draw similar conclusions.

Brown (1961), Dolliver (1969), and Kunce, Dolliver and Irwin (1972)
have been critical of Strong's method of expressing the predictive validity of the
SVIB. Both conclude that because of misunderstandings of Strong's qualifying
phrases, which are not usually quoted in interpretations, it is better not to use
such a statement with clients. Kunce et al. suggest that for purposes of explaining the accuracy of the SVIB to clients, a statement of the number or
percentage of persons in a given occupation who scored an A on that occupation
is sufficient. A recapitulation of six studies of the SVIB presented by Campbell
(1971) and others reviewed by Kunce et al. (1972) suggests that it is accurate to
say that about 50 percent of the persons in a given occupation, or of a group of
persons in diverse occupations, scored an A or high score on the appropriate
scale of their interest inventory, taken some years previously.

Predictive Validity of Other Inventories

The SVIB form for women has had very few tests of its predictive validity,
despite its long history. In one, identified by Campbell (1971) as the only
adequate study of predictive validity of the women's form, Harmon (1969)
concluded that among women who reported some commitment to a career, the
validity was essentially equal to that of the men's form. There is a new,
"merged" form of the SVIB, the Strong-Campbell Interest Inventory
(Campbell, 1974), which will undoubtedly suffer the same criticism as has the
KOIS.

The only other inventory possessing occupational scales, the MVII, has
been shown to predict the type of vocational training program that high school
students elected after an administration of the inventory three years previously;
it does so by combining all scale scores in a multiple discriminant functional
analysis (Silver and Barnette, 1970).

All of the foregoing studies of predictive validity used occupational membership as their criterion. Other attributes of work may also be used. According to Porter and Steers (1973), tenure appears to be predictable from interest measures. The evidence generally supports the relation between interests and job satisfaction (Kuder, 1956; Strong, 1955; Super & Crites, 1962), although Berdie (1960) believes that the relation is more reliable concurrently than predictively. A few studies have shown scores on interest scales to be related to job performance (Ghei, 1960; Nash, 1966), and Super and Crites (1962) concluded that success is predicted best in occupations characterized by one or two relatively homogeneous interest clusters.

In summary, it seems reasonable to expect an interest inventory with occupational scales to show that about half of a group of persons received a high score on their own occupational scale in a prior administration. Additionally, it is more likely that those in occupations consistent with their earlier interest scores will be more satisfied with their work, remain in the job longer, and perform better, although these latter relations are much less clear than the occupational membership criterion alone.

It is reasonable to ask whether 50 percent hits in predictive validity is a good or poor level. However, the literature on interest inventorying appears never to have addressed the question explicitly. The level found in studies of concurrent validity could suggest some upper limit against which to compare the level of predictive validity. Taking those who scored an A level of their own SVIB scale (as opposed to scoring highest), Strong (1955) points out that 69 percent of a criterion group will score A by reason of the normal distribution of *T* scores. Dolliver, Irwin, and Bigley (1972) and Dyer (1939) present data showing that less than 50 percent of an unselected group attain an A level on their own scale, and among Strong's (1955) subjects, only 58 percent had A level scores in the concurrent administration.

Kuder[1] found that 34 percent of a group of men in varied occupations scored *highest* on their own occupational scale. Campbell (1971, p. 285) says that most men are not in the occupation on which they score highest; probably not more than one third are. And Zytowski (1972) has found 35 percent and 28 percent of a varied group scoring highest on their own scales for the KOIS and the SVIB, respectively.

This suggests that the top limit for predictive validity lies at about one third scoring highest on their own scale and between one half and two thirds scoring at a level that would allow their own scale to be suggested to them as worth considering. Presumably, such factors as the maturity of interest at the time the inventory was taken and the number of years that have since elapsed, not to mention faults in the inventory itself and situational factors that prevent the expression of interests in one's employment, reduce the level of predictive validity below that which would be expected from concurrent validity.

[1]Kuder, G. F. Personal communication, March 1974.

Methodology of Assessing Predictive Validity

The methodologies used to assess the validity of occupational interest scales are quite varied and, as Kunce et al. (1972) have pointed out, tend to influence the obtained results. A survey of these methodologies follows.

There are several distinct lines of pursuit. Kuder (1966) has tended to show the accuracy with which the inventory classifies persons in their own occupations. Thus, for a group of persons in a single occupation, he reports the number who receive their highest score on their own scale and compares it with the number who receive their highest scores on one or more of the other scales of the inventory.

Strong (1955), on the other hand, has asked whether the individual is in an occupation that earlier would have been identified for him/her as worth consideration in career planning. This method is dependent on what means have been used to mark a high score, but it provides some real measure of the validity of the statement(s) used in transmitting the results of the inventory to its taker.

Campbell (1966) uses a variation of this method. He scans a large number of inventory takers to identify all those who scored high on a single scale, for example, physician, lawyer, social worker. He then traces all of that special population that he can and ascertains what percentage is in the target occupation, in related occupations, and in unrelated occupations. This procedure avoids the loss of subjects who are in occupations for which there is no exact equivalent scale.

Many validity studies use only subjects who are employed in occupations scored on the profile. So, although Strong (1955) located 884 of his inventory takers after 18 years, only 663 were used in the analysis because the remainder were in occupations for which the SVIB had no scales. To prevent the loss of many subjects in the analysis of a heterogeneous sample, such as that of the present study, some method must be used to identify the scale that is most near the occupation of the person. One technique, used by Strong (1955) in a supplementary analysis, is to present the profile of the person along with his present occupation and ask expert users of the inventory whether they consider the profile to be consistent with the occupation. Another approach is McArthur's (1954) "indirect" procedure, in which the experts are given only the person's present occupation and are required to select the appropriate predictor scale without seeing his/her profile.

Kunce et al. (1972) have shown that at least one influence affecting the level of obtained validity is the rigor of the definition of the occupation. For example, an engineer who gives his occupation as "group leader" of an aerospace design department could be identified as a technical administrator by a rigorous definition or as an engineer by a looser one.

176

Another influence on predictive validity is the number of scores or patterns a person may earn at the level that suggests "consideration," such as the top .06 for the KOIS and an A score or primary pattern for the SVIB. Clearly, the likelihood of a successful prediction is enhanced as the number of potential predictors increases. Darley and Hagenah (1955) found that 40 percent of their college students showed two or more primary patterns, but no investigator of predictive validity has taken this into account.

METHOD

The following kinds and forms of data were collected (the first five by means of a personal data questionnaire) in light of the foregoing discussion:

1. Present job title and description.
2. Job satisfaction as assessed by two questions: one asking the person to estimate his current level of satisfaction on a 7-point scale, and the other asking if the person would continue working at the same job were he/she enabled to change occupations without loss of income.
3. Job success, estimated by a parallel question to the first job satisfaction estimate, above.
4. A chronological account of the jobs, occupations, and other employment with the interval spent in each from the time the inventory was taken or from the time the person graduated from high school.
5. If the person attended college, the last college major the person studied or graduated with. (The KOIS has a number of college major scales.)
6. A contemporary administration of the KOIS from as many persons as could be persuaded to take it.

The following analyses were undertaken:

1. The level of predictive validity was assessed by (a) deciding whether the predictor scale represented a hit, near hit, or miss, and (b) examining the rank of the predictor scale among all scales.
2. Concurrent validity was assessed by the same methods to provide some estimate of the maximum level of validity that could be expected.
3. For persons who went to college, the predictive validity of the college major scales was assessed in terms of hits, near hits, and misses.
4. Levels of satisfaction were expressed in several ways, and success was compared for each condition of hit, near hit, or miss.
5. Cross tabulations were made between hit, near hit, and miss and a number of variables inherent in the method and data, such as the person's gender, age at first administration, and whether or not the predictor scale was selected by judges.

Evaluation of nominal data in various comparisons was achieved by means of the chi-square test of association. Where the data were continuously distributed, the t test was used.

Subjects

Answer sheets from the original sample were obtained from various try-out versions of what later became the KOIS. They were loaned to the investigator by G. F. Kuder. Table 1 gives information about the various sources. Those given before 1960 were never interpreted in any form resembling the KOIS. Those given after 1960 may have had information returned to the takers as reported by Form D, that is, using a different kind of score and far fewer occupational scales. Some of the Duke University engineering students were given a second, follow-up administration (Gehman & Gehman, 1968), but to

SOURCES AND CHARACTERISTICS OF SUBJECTS

table 1

GROUP	ORIGINAL N	GENDER	GRADE WHEN TESTED	YEAR FIRST INVEN-TORIED	YEARS ELAPSED	APPROXIMATE AGE AT FOLLOW-UP
Brookline, Mass.	469	M and F	8	1961	12	25
Brookline, Mass.	552	M and F	10	1961	12	27
Brookline, Mass.	414	M and F	12	1961	12	29
Forsythe County, N.C.	147	Mostly M	9–12	1955	17	31–34
Castle Heights Military Academy	278	M	high school	1954	18	34
Brooklyn Auto High School	182	M	high school	1957	16	32
Manhattan Printing High School	255	M	high school	1957	16	32
Shorter College	59	F	College jr.	1954	19	39
Medical College of Virginia, physical therapy students	39	M and F	College sr.	1955	18	39
Duke University engineers	466	M	College fr.	1954–1959	14–19	32–37
Duke University engineers		M	College sr.	1954–1959	14–19	35–40
Other Duke University students	300	M and F	College fr.	1954–1959	14–19	32–37
Other Duke University students		M and F	College sr.	1960–1961	12–13	33–34

Note. Abbreviations: M = male, F = female, jr. = junior, sr. = senior, fr. = freshman.

the investigator's knowledge, no other group was given a follow-up. It should be noted that the year of administration varies from 1954 to 1961, and that the age at administration is reflected by educational levels varying from Grade 8 to college senior. The residence of the subject pool is mainly urban, from the eastern seaboard and southern geographical regions.

Changes in the Inventory

The inventories used in the period 1954 to 1961 were identical to the present KOIS, although they could not be scored as the KOIS until 1966. One item appeared in different form in the 1954 version; it read, "Be stupid, be lazy, be mean." A series of studies by Diamond[2] established that "Have trouble learning most things, be able to loaf whenever you want to, say things to hurt people" was less objectionable and most nearly equivalent. The latter version appears in the present (1966) edition of the KOIS. The difference was presumed not to influence the comparison between the predictive and concurrent validities in the present study.

Locating Subjects

None of the early inventories were administered with the prospect of a later follow-up in mind. Thus, a variety of techniques had to be used to locate subjects in 1972–1973.

Castle Heights Military Academy, Shorter College, Medical College of Virginia Physical Therapy School, and Duke University all supplied addresses from alumni files. The Forsythe County school superintendent, who had given the original inventories 12 years previously, located subjects by personal knowledge. Brooklyn Auto and Manhattan Printing high school graduates were sought by telephone contact with persons with the same names listed in current New York metropolitan phone directories, by newspaper advertising, and by a news story in a printing trade weekly.

Brookline, Massachusetts, subjects had recorded their parents' names and addresses on their answer sheets. The parents who were still listed at the same address in the 1972 Boston telephone directory were mailed a request for their sons' or daughters' present addresses. One of the Brookline groups was having a graduating class reunion, and some data on current occupation were obtained from a reunion booklet published for the occasion.

Mailings to subjects always included lists of those who were still unlocated with a request for their current address or their occupation.

[2]Diamond, E. E. *Changes in response to a Kuder verification scale item as a result of substitution of synonymous phrasing.* Paper presented at the meeting of the National Council of Measurement in Education, October 29, 1965, New York, New York.

Selection of Predictor Scales

For each respondent, the KOIS scale that was to predict his or her present occupation (as reported in the personal data questionnaire) needed to be identified. If the respondent reported a title identical to a KOIS scale, such as elementary teacher, lawyer, or physician, that scale was identified as the predictor. If the occupation did not match (n = 439), such as investment broker, editor, or machine repairman, a panel of 3 experienced counselors (including the investigator) independently selected the most representative scale after McArthur's (1954) "indirect" method. The scale agreed on by two of the three counselors was retained. In cases in which there was no agreement (approximately 6 percent), the differences were negotiated until two counselors agreed.

The rank of a predictor scale was calculated among the scales appropriate to the gender of the respondent. For several occupations, such as architect, chemist, and engineer, women were scored and ranked among the scales originally formed on all-men groups. (Presently, all scores are reported irrespective of the gender of the respondent.) Thus, depending on the gender of the respondent, and whether his/her scale was located among the men's or women's scales, there may have been many or few scales competing for rank. This is important in light of Brown's (1961) discussion of base rates.

College majors were used as predictor scales for certain occupations. For example, managers in white-collar situations were assigned the business management major as their predictor scale, while shop managers, if it could be ascertained from their title and job description, were assigned the industrial foreman/supervisor scale.

Criterion for Deciding Hits and Misses

In accord with the method used by Strong (1955) and many other investigators, a hit was defined as a score that placed the predictor scale high enough to draw the attention of the inventory taker to it for consideration. For the KOIS, this category is defined by Kuder (1966) as all scales ranking in the highest .06 range of scores. This may include only one or a number of scales.

Since investigators of the SVIB have also used a near-hit category, such a level was arbitrarily assigned to the next .06 range of scores. A miss was defined as a scale that fell below this range.

Career Consistency

The personal data questionnaire requested a chronological list of jobs since leaving high school or since taking the inventory if it was taken after high school. Each college major and occupation reported in this list was coded with Holland's (1973) three-letter code, which also may be used to assess the similarity of any pair of occupations. The similarity between each successive pair of reported occupations and majors was derived, and the mean similarity for each subject was taken as an index of his/her career consistency or continuation in an occupation.

Results and Discussion

Approximately 2,000 valid addresses were obtained from the effort to locate subjects. Of these, 1,084 returned inventories and personal data questionnaires. There were four conditions that prevented a respondent from being used in the study of predictive validity:

1. Being employed in an occupation that was judged as inadequately reflected by any present KOIS scale, for example, bartender and diplomat.
2. Having spent more than half the time since leaving formal education as a homemaker.
3. Being unemployed. (Although these subjects showed an occupation up to the time of their unemployment, they were excluded because it was not certain that they would continue their previous occupation.)
4. A profile judged invalid by Kuder's (1966) criterion of having no scores over the level of 31. No subject was excluded on the basis of a V score under 45 unless the profile was also invalid.

Subjects excluded for these reasons totaled 202, leaving 884 subjects in the main analysis. Clearly, there was a great deal of attrition of subjects between the number of answer sheets available and the number of subjects in the study of predictive validity. Strong (1955) located 77 percent of his original sample, but Dolliver et al. (1972) based their conclusions on only 22 percent of their original group. That different studies tend to obtain relatively similar predictive validities suggests that they are united by being limited to persons who leave a trace of themselves with their school, parents, or friends. The present study, which located approximately two thirds of the original sample and obtained data from one half of that group, may be comparable with other studies on such a basis. As with other studies, the validity of the KOIS for missing subjects simply cannot be ascertained.

VALIDITY FINDINGS

Occupational scales. Table 2 presents the percentage of hits, near hits, and misses in the prediction by the 12- to 19-year-old scale scores of present occupation of subjects in each of the original groups, as well as the levels obtained from the concurrent administration. The percentage of hits and misses

table 2

GROUP	PREDICTIVE						CONCURRENT					
	Hits		Near hits		Misses		Hits		Near hits		Misses	
	n	%	n	%	n	%	n	%	n	%	n	%
Brookline, Grade 8	61	43.6	55	39.3	24	17.1	69	50	41	29	29	21
Brookline, Grade 10	58	45.3	40	31.3	30	23.4	62	52	30	25	27	23
Brookline, Grade 12	76	48.7	47	30.1	33	21.2	68	58	33	28	17	14
Forsythe County	16	27.1	23	40.0	20	33.0	26	50	21	40	5	10
Castle Heights	20	39.2	17	33.3	14	27.5	23	45	21	41	17	14
Brooklyn Auto	8	72.7	3	27.3	0	0	2	25	3	38	3	38
Manhattan Printing	4	80.0	1	20.0	0	0	1	100	0	—	0	—
Shorter College	10	52.6	5	26.3	4	21.1	12	52	7	30	4	17
Physical therapists	7	100	0	0	0	0	6	85	1	15	0	0
Duke engineers	161	66.6	48	20.2	29	12.2	146	63.8	60	26.2	23	10
Other Duke students	32	47.1	21	30.9	15	22.0	41	62.1	10	15.1	15	22.7
Total	453	51.3	260	29.5	169	19.2	456	55.4	227	27.6	140	17.0

is rather varied among the different groups, but in general, *50 percent of the total group was found in an occupation that would have been mentioned to them had the inventory been interpreted 12 to 19 years previously.*

Of special note are the extreme percentages of hits in some groups. Predictions for former engineering students (not all of whom were in engineering occupations at the time of follow-up) were more accurate than predictions for subjects tested in high school and influenced the overall predictive findings because of the large number of engineering students. Other follow-up studies also report large proportions of engineers and other professionals in their samples. Of equal interest is the lower predictive validity associated with the inventories administered in the two high schools from the southern region of the United States, Forsythe County, and Castle Heights Military Academy. The administrator of the inventories to the former group (Sarbaugh)[3] suggests that the generally modest socioeconomic status of this region might account for this finding. A higher economic status may be assumed for the Brookline, Massachusetts, group who, although inventoried while in high school, show a higher percentage of hits.

The very high percentages of hits for the small groups—the Brooklyn Auto High School, the Manhattan Printing High School and the physical therapists—appear to be the consequence of the homogeneity of their present occupations. It is also notable that the predictive validity for each of the Brookline groups increases with the advancing age of administration, suggesting the work of an age-when-inventoried factor in the validity of the scales. These

[3]Sarbaugh, R. Personal communication, December 12, 1974.

factors and others receive consideration in analyses presented and discussed below.

The data representing concurrent validity in Table 3 show for the total group an increase in hits and decrements for the near hits and misses. The high school administrations generally show the greatest improvement when the time interval is reduced to zero, but the engineers (who, it might be noted, are at mid-career) have present interests that are somewhat less likely to be in agreement with their occupations than their earlier tested interests. These observations suggest the utility of studying the maturation of interests in certain occupational groups.

The closeness of the overall percentages of hits for predictive and concurrent validity suggests that the interval of time between inventory and observation of occupational status makes only slight difference with the KOIS—that the inventory will identify the appropriate occupation in more than 50 percent of the cases, from a large and varied group of persons.

In Table 3 are presented the hit/miss rates in several predictive and concurrent validity studies, compared with the findings of the present study. All involve only the SVIB for men, because no other studies have presented their findings in a form which makes this type of comparison possible. And, although the criterion for a hit is not the same, the level of hits is surprisingly close in all.

It was suggested in the introductory discussion that a test of the con-

PROPORTION OF HITS, NEAR HITS, AND MISSES IN THE PRESENT STUDY COMPARED WITH OTHER FOLLOW-UP STUDIES

table 3

STUDY	CRITERION FOR HIT	% HITS	% NEAR HITS	% MISSES
		Predictive test		
Present study	top .06	51	30	19
Strong (1955)	As	45	19	36
Trimble (1965)	As	49	17	34
Brandt & Hood (1968)	primary pattern	47	20	23
Dolliver et al. (1972)	As	42	12	46
McArthur (1954)	As	45	20	35
		Concurrent test		
Present study	top .06	55	28	17
Strong (1955)	As	58	16	26
Dyer (1939)	As	44	21	35
Dolliver et al. (1972)	As	42	12	46

current validity of an inventory could be used to provide an estimate of the upper limit for predictive validity. In theory, concurrent validity should be near 70 percent hits, as derived from the characteristics of a normal distribution. In practice, the concurrent validity reported in the few tests performed seems to be about the same or slightly exceeding the level of predictive validity.

It might also be noted that the level of predictive validity found for the KOIS is similar to the percentage of correct classification derived by Zytowski (1974) for homogeneous scales on interest inventories, also mentioned in the introduction of the present study.

College major scales. Another criterion for which the KOIS is scored is college majors; no other interest inventory has such scales. Among the respondents who went to college, their major was noted and related to the existing scales by gender. This was done for only the high school administrations; comparisons of college major from an inventory administered during the college years would have been only a retrospective measure of concurrent validity. Results are presented in Table 4. Assuming the major to be reliable at the third year of college, the average span of prediction represented is about 5 years, with a range from 3 to 8.

The predictive validity of the college major scales of the KOIS is very slightly superior to that of the occupational scales, especially in the category of a hit compared to near hits. The Forsythe County subjects also are comparably less predictable in this situation. Nevertheless, it appears appropriate to state that more than half of the students who had decided on a major in college are correctly predicted by a scale in the top .06 of the scores on the KOIS administered during high school and about four fifths are among the top .12. Assuming some decrement associated with the early age from which prediction is made, this level is remarkably good.

PREDICTIVE VALIDITY OF KOIS COLLEGE MAJOR SCALES

table 4

GROUP	GRADE WHEN INVEN- TORIED	SPAN OF PRE- DICTION (YR.)[a]	HITS		NEAR HITS		MISSES	
			n	%	n	%	n	%
Brookline	8	8	68	56.7	29	24.2	23	19.2
Brookline	10	6	69	62.7	29	26.4	12	10.9
Brookline	12	3	64	58.7	29	26.6	16	14.7
Forsythe County	9–12	c. 5	10	27.0	13	35.1	14	37.8
Castle Heights	9–12	c. 5	18	48.6	5	13.5	14	37.8
Total			229	55.4	105	25.4	79	19.1

[a] Assumes major decided on in junior year.

Rank order. Examining validity by Kuder's method of rank of own scale (Table 5) shows the largest proportion of subjects ranking first on their own scale and slightly more than 50 percent ranking in the top 10 scales. Table 5 also presents rank data from the concurrent administration, where 66 percent fall in the top 10 ranks. This figure is somewhat less than that found by Zytowski (1972) and substantially less than that of Kuder (1966). This finding must be interpreted in light of the presumed intercorrelations between the scales and the number of scales that form the total group from which the ranking is obtained. In the former case, it may be noted that the KOIS yields scores on six kinds of engineering specialities, four psychologists, five social worker scales for women, and others. A subject might easily score higher on a related specialty than on his/her own scale by a single lambda point and thereby drive down the rank of the predictor scale. In addition a scale may compete for rank among 37 women's occupational scales, 19 women's college major scales, 20 scales normed on men but scored for women, and so on. Further, in Zytowski's (1972) study, no subjects were in occupations not actually found on the KOIS profile, and Kuder (1966) included only subjects from 30 occupations, selected in part for their independence with other scales. It is possible that the unselected nature of the subjects in the present study blurs the distinctions needed for

DISTRIBUTION OF SUBJECTS' RANKS ON OWN SCALE: PREDICTIVE AND CONCURRENT

table 5

RANK	PREDICTIVE		CONCURRENT		CONCURRENT FROM ZYTOWSKI (1972)		CONCURRENT FROM KUDER (1966)	
	n	%	n	%	n	%	n	%
1	101	11.5	108	14.6	102	35.3	1688	56
2	68	7.7	72	9.7	54	18.7	479	16
3	59	6.6	59	8.0	26	9.0	233	8
4	41	4.6	40	5.4	16	5.5	135	5
5	35	4.0	44	6.0	13	4.5	90	3
6	35	4.0	42	5.7	16	5.5	84	3
7	38	4.3	34	4.6	10	3.5		
8	33	3.7	29	3.9	9	3.1		
9	32	3.6	34	4.6	6	2.1		
10	30	3.4	22	3.0	5	1.7		
Subtotal	472	53.5	484	65.5	257	88.9	297	10
+10	410	46.5	255	34.5	32	11.1		
Total	882		739		289		3000	

Note. Top .06 cannot be located on a ranking procedure, since it varies for every subject. Some have only 1 scale in top .06, while many have more than 10. See Table 7 for means and standard deviations.

LEVELS OF SATISFACTION AND SUCCESS ASSOCIATED
WITH HITS, NEAR HITS, AND MISSES FOR
MALES AND FEMALES

table 6

MEASURE	SATISFACTION[a]			CHANGED JOBS[b]			SUCCESS		
	n	M	SD	n	M	SD	n	M	SD
				Men					
Hits	305	5.33	1.01	301	2.98	.98	138	5.17	1.02
Near hits	120	5.25	1.15	118	3.03	.99	72	5.31	.92
Misses	54	5.24	1.23	53	2.46	1.14	24	5.15	1.15
				Women					
Hits	127	5.18	1.10	123	2.78	1.01	125	5.13	.45
Near hits	114	5.08	1.25	111	2.93	1.00	107	5.13	1.22
Misses	38	5.00	1.16	37	2.53	1.08	34	5.16	.73

[a] $t_{hit/miss}$ = .508 for men and .849 for women.
[b] $t_{hit/miss}$ = 3.40 for men and 1.25 for women.

such high levels of separation of subjects reported in other studies of concurrent validity of the KOIS.

Other Criteria

The findings from other studies with respect to other criteria of predictive validity—occupational satisfaction, success, and continuance—have been very mixed. The data on these variables for the present study are given in Table 6. They succeed little in clarifying the matter. Two measures of job satisfaction were used: a direct self-report and an indirect report. No significant differences are observed in satisfaction between men and women in occupations congruent with their prior KOIS profiles. When satisfaction is represented by whether the respondent says he/she would change job or occupation, only for men is the null hypothesis rejected. As in other studies, few persons reported themselves dissatisfied.

In contrast with some studies, the job success criterion in the present study is self-reported rather than established by objective evidence of progress, such as increase in income, promotions, and the like. The data related to agreement between profile and present occupation for this criterion are random, suggesting that this variable is considerably more complex than can be represented by a single scale using self-report, since other investigators have found relationships.

It is interesting to note that the index of satisfaction involving a statement about changing jobs approaches some significant differences, and that there *is* a significant difference between the number of jobs and occupational changes reflected by the career index for the three levels of agreement between early KOIS profile and present occupation: hits $(n = 262)$—$M = 4.04$, $SD = 1.39$; near hits $(n = 186)$—$M = 3.81$, $SD = 1.51$; misses $(n = 120)$— $M = 3.74$, $SD = 1.39$; $t_{hit/miss} = 1.945$, $p < .05$.

In summary, although being in an occupation which is consistent with a 12- to 19-year-old KOIS is not related to self-reported satisfaction or success for this population, it is somewhat related to stability or continuation in that occupation, registered by two different methods.

Factors That Influence Predictive Validity

There is some decrement in validity as a result of the selection of predictor scales by the panel of judges: direct selection $(n = 450)$—55 percent hits, 29 percent near hits, and 16 percent misses; indirect selection $(n = 432)$—48 percent hits, 30 percent near hits, and 22 percent misses; $\chi^2(3) = 6.697$, $p < .10$. It is possible that this represents the judges' degree of unfamiliarity with the idiosyncracies of the KOIS. This might have been avoided by using Strong's (1955) or Campbell's (1966) procedures of simply asking the judges to report whether the profile as a whole was consistent with the present occupation, but it seems that such a procedure was not comparable with that used when there was a scale with the same name as the present occupation.

The chi-square test for association of validity with gender is not significant although the percentages of hits differ; apparently both genders are equally predictable: males $(n = 648)$—49 percent hits, 30 percent near hits, and 21 percent misses; females $(n = 234)$—57 percent hits, 28 percent near hits, and 16 percent misses; $\chi^2(3) = 4.724$, $p < .10$. It appears, then, that the KOIS is not as vulnerable as the SVIB to the reduction of validity found by Harmon (1969) when the criterion is present occupation.

Since the instructions for interpreting the KOIS suggest that all scales

RELATION OF SELECTED PROFILE CHARACTERISTICS TO LEVEL OF PREDICTIVE VALIDITY

table 7

MEASURE	NO. SCALES IN TOP .06 RANGE			SCORE OF HIGHEST SCALE		V SCORE	
	n	M	SD	M	SD	M	SD
Hits	453	12.699	6.651	52.196	10.439	50.929	4.216
Near hits	260	11.093	6.769	50.795	9.225	50.779	4.339
Misses	169	9.52	8.033	51.713	9.050	50.883	4.443

Note. $t_{hit/miss} = 4.59$, $p < .01$.

ranking in the top .06 range of scores be considered by the person, the number of such scales could be crucial to whether the person's present occupation is predicted. Table 7 presents this analysis. It appears that the average profile has about 10 scales at this level; depending on what group of scales on the profile the 10 scales are set within, this is a fairly high base rate to work with. The number of scales in the top .06 range is statistically related to the predictive validity, but nothing is known of how a person obtains many or few. The range among the subjects was from exactly 1 to more than 20 in a few cases, chiefly engineers. Table 7 also shows levels of the highest score on the profile and of V scores for level of predictive validity. The level of highest score bears no obvious relationship to whether the early administration predicts validly or not. And, although Kuder (1966) demonstrates convincingly that the V score separates between sincere and insincerely answered items, it does not appear to be associated with predictive validity. This is not to say that a low V score is as predictive as an unsuspect one, but only that there were no more low V scores among hits than among misses.

Table 8 presents an analysis of the effects of the respondents' ages when first administered and the span of time elapsing until their occupations were compared with their profiles. The data indicate that college administration yields superior results and that there is a slightly higher percentage of hits when the span of prediction is shorter. Although the chi-square test of association of these variables is very high, most of the difference appears attributable to the college group, which was heavily weighted with students who had made a commitment to engineering at the time of their KOIS administration.

This latter observation suggests a separation of the validity data by whether the subjects were enrolled in a vocational program at the time of the early administration (Table 9). It should be noted that although a person might have been in a vocational preparation program, he or she might not be in that

**RELATION OF AGE WHEN INVENTORIED
AND SPAN OF PREDICTION
TO VALIDITY**

table 8

GRADE (AGE) WHEN INVENTORIED	SPAN OF PREDICTION (YR.)	HITS		NEAR HITS		MISSES	
		n	%	n	%	n	%
Grade 8	12	61	46.9	55	19.2	24	33.8
High school	12	134	46.7	87	30.3	66	23.0
	16–18	48	41.4	44	29.3	34	29.3
College[a]	12–19	210	62.8	74	21.8	44	15.3

Note. $\chi^2(5) = 38.13, p < .01.$
[a]Heavily weighted with senior engineers.

table 9

MEASURE	HITS		NEAR HITS		MISSES		TOTAL *n*
	n	%	*n*	%	*n*	%	
In relevant curriculum	183	68.3	52	19.4	33	12.3	621
In general studies	273	44.0	208	33.5	140	22.5	268

Note. $\chi^2(3) = 720.89, p < .001$.

occupation at the time of the follow-up. An example of this is the Brooklyn Auto High School students, most of whom were located as employed by New York City's Department of Sanitation, well predicted by the Truck Driver scale selected as the indirect measure by the panel of judges. One might be able to say that the early enrollment of such persons suggests that their occupational behavior is more responsive to their interest patterns than is the occupational behavior of those who are in general studies.

Findings of high validity for persons who attended college [attended college ($n = 647$)—58 percent hits, 24 percent near hits, and 18 percent misses; did not attend college ($n = 218$, college attendance not ascertained for 17 subjects)—35 percent hits, 24 percent near hits, and 41 percent misses: $\chi^2(3) = 51.326, p < .001$] who are presently in high level occupations (presumably attained by means of a college education; see Table 10) or who are in scientific or technological occupations (Table 11) suggest an overarching influence of socioeconomic status factors on the predictive validity of the KOIS. This should not be unexpected; such factors are hypothesized by Blau, Gustad,

table 10

OCCUPATIONAL LEVEL	HITS		NEAR HITS		MISSES	
	n	%	*n*	%	*n*	%
1	60	72	16	19	7	8
2	174	57	92	30	39	13
3	83	44	61	32	46	24
4	38	53	23	32	11	15
5	11	31	16	46	8	23

Note. Total $N = 685$; 198 subjects were excluded because of difficulties in reliably coding occupational level. $\chi^2(6) = 32.908, p < .001$.

table 11

FIELD	n	HITS		NEAR HITS		MISSES	
		n	%	n	%	n	%
Service	48	21	44	17	35	10	21
Business contact	60	25	42	26	43	9	15
Organization	102	34	33	43	42	25	25
Technology	253	171	68	61	24	21	8
Outdoor	5	2	—	1	—	2	—
Science	87	49	56	27	31	11	13
General culture	142	59	42	48	34	35	35
Arts and enter- tainment	20	6	30	7	35	7	35
Total *ns*	717	367	51	230	32	120	17

Note. $\chi^2(7) = 62.239, p<.001.$

Parnes, and Wilcock (1956) and demonstrated by occupational sociologists (cf Caplow, 1954; Duncan, 1965; and Slocum, 1966, among others). Having access to and taking advantage of further education by reason of his/her socioeconomic status apparently enables a person more reliably to find expression of his/her interest pattern in his/her choice of occupation. However, careers in business organization and arts and entertainment are comparatively less accurately predicted by the KOIS.

Conclusions and Implications

A number of conclusions appear to be available from the present findings of the predictive validity of the KOIS:

1. Slightly more than every other person who takes the KOIS is in an occupation which would have been suggested to him/her as worth considering from an inventory taken 12 to 19 years previously.
2. The predictive validity of the occupational scales of the KOIS is comparable to that of any interest inventory scored for occupations when the criterion is membership in the occupation and, to an extent, continuation in the occupation. As well, the predictive validity is similar to that obtained with the use of homogeneous interest scales.
3. The predictive validity of the college major scales of the KOIS is slightly superior to that of the occupational scales.

4. As a ratio with concurrent validity, the KOIS is rather close to being as valid as possible among the population of the study, which is marked for being extremely variable in terms of socioeconomic status, consistency of career progression, and in terms of indirectly selected predictors, compared with other studies.

5. The KOIS does not predict occupational satisfaction in this population, which reports itself mainly as not dissatisfied. Neither does the KOIS predict self-reported success.

6. In counseling use, more confidence may be placed in the predictiveness of a profile when (a) the occupation under consideration is one of those listed on the profile; (b) the inventory taker has a greater number of scales listed in the top .06 range; (c) the counselee attends college; and (d) the counselee plans to enter a high level occupation or one in the science or technology areas.

references _____

Berdie, R. F. Validities of the Strong Vocational Interest Blank. In W. L. Layton (Ed.), *The Strong Vocational Interest Blank: Research and uses.* Minneapolis: University of Minnesota Press, 1960.

Blau, P. M., Gustad, J. W., Parnes, H. S., & Wilcock, R. C. Occupational choices: A conceptual framework. *Industrial and Labor Relations Review,* 1956, *9,* 531–543.

Brandt, J. E., & Hood, A. B. Effect of personality adjustment on the predictive validity of the Strong Vocational Interest Blank. *Journal of Counseling Psychology,* 1968, *15,* 547–551.

Brown, F. A note on expectancy ratios, base rates, and the SVIB. *Journal of Counseling Psychology,* 1961, *8,* 368–369.

Brown, F. G. Review of the Kuder Occupational Interest Survey. *Measurement and Evaluation in Guidance,* 1971, *4,* 122–125.

Campbell, D. P. Occupations ten years later of high school seniors with high scores on the Strong Vocational Interest Blank Life Insurance Salesman scale. *Journal of Applied Psychology,* 1966, *50,* 369–372.

Campbell, D. P. *Handbook for the Strong Vocational Interest Blank.* Stanford, Calif,: Stanford University Press, 1971.

Campbell, D. P. *Manual, Strong-Campbell Interest Inventory.* Stanford, Calif,: Stanford University Press, 1974.

Caplow, T. *The sociology of work.* Minneapolis: University of Minnesota Press, 1954.

Darley, J. G., & Hagenah, T. *Vocational interest measurement.* Minneapolis: University of Minnesota Press, 1955.

Dolliver, R. H. "3.5 to 1" on the SVIB as a pseudo-event. *Journal of Counseling Psychology,* 1969, *16,* 172–174.

Dolliver, R. H. Review of the Kuder Occupational Interest Survey. In O. K. Buros (Ed.), *The seventh mental measurements yearbook.* Highland Park, N.J.: Gryphon Press, 1972.

Dolliver, R. H., Irwin, J. A., & Bigley, S. S. Twelve-year follow-up of the Strong Vocational Interest Blank. *Journal of Counseling Psychology*, 1972, *19*, 212–217.

Duncan, O. D. Social origins of salaried and self-employed professional workers. *Social Forces*, 1965, *44*, 186–189.

Dyer, D. T. The relation between vocational interests of men in college and their subsequent histories for ten years. *Journal of Applied Psychology*, 1939, *23*, 280–288.

Gehman, W. S., & Gehman, I. H. Stability of engineering interests over a period of four years. *Educational and Psychological Measurement*, 1968, *28*, 367–376.

Ghei, S. Vocational interests, achievement, and satisfaction. *Journal of Counseling Psychology*, 1960, *7*, 132–136.

Harmon, L. W. Predictive power over ten years of measured social service and scientific interests among college women. *Journal of Applied Psychology*, 1969, *53*, 193–198.

Holland, J. L. *Making vocational choices: A theory of careers.* Englewood Cliffs, N.J.: Prentice-Hall, 1973.

Kuder, G. F. *Manual, Kuder Preference Record, Form C* (6th Ed.). Chicago: Science Research Assoc., 1956.

Kuder, G. F. *Manual, Kuder Occupational Interest Survey, Form DD.* Chicago: Science Research Assoc., 1966.

Kunce, J. T., Dolliver, R. H., & Irwin, J. A. Perspectives on interpreting the validity of the SVIB-M. *Vocational Guidance Quarterly*, 1972, *21*, 36–42.

McArthur, C. Long-term validity of the Strong interest test in two subcultures. *Journal of Applied Psychology*, 1954, *38*, 346–353.

Nash, A. N. Development of a Strong Vocational Interest Blank key for selecting managers. *Journal of Applied Psychology*, 1966, *50*, 250–254.

Porter, L. W., & Steers, K. M. Organizational, work, and personal factors in employee turnover and absenteeism. *Psychological Bulletin*, 1973, *80*, 151–176.

Silver, H. A., & Barnette, W. L. Predictive and concurrent validity of the Minnesota Vocational Interest Inventory for vocational high school boys. *Journal of Applied Psychology*, 1970, *34*, 436–440.

Slocum, W. L. *Occupational careers: A sociological perspective.* Chicago: Aldine, 1966.

Stahman, R. F. Review of the Kuder Occupational Interest Survey. *Journal of Counseling Psychology*, 1971, *18*, 191–192.

Strong, E. K., Jr. *Vocational interests eighteen years after college.* Minneapolis: University of Minnesota Press, 1955.

Super, D. E., & Crites, J. O. *Appraising vocational fitness by means of psychological tests.* New York: Harper & Row, 1962.

Trimble, J. T. *A ten-year longitudinal follow-up of inventoried interests of selected high school students.* Unpublished doctoral dissertation, University of Missouri—Columbia, 1965.

Walsh, W. B. Review of the Kuder Occupational Interest Survey, In O. K. Buros (Ed.), *The seventh mental measurements yearbook.* Highland Park, N.J.: Gryphon Press, 1972.

Zytowski, D. A concurrent test of accuracy-of-classification for the Strong Vocational Interest Blank and the Kuder Occupational Interest Survey. *Journal of Vocational Behavior*, 1972, *2*, 245–250.

Zytowski, D. G. Predictive validity of the Kuder Preference Record, Form B, over a 25-year span. *Measurement and Evaluation in Guidance*, 1974, *1*, 122–129.

comments and questions _____

1. In the section "Predictive Validity of Other Inventories" Zytowski presents a rationale for his conclusion that " . . . the top limit for predictive validity lies at about one third scoring highest on their own scale and between one half and two thirds scoring at a level that would allow their own scale to be suggested to them as worth considering." Do you understand the rationale and accept his conclusion? Defend your answer.

2. Zytowski said that the inventories administered before 1960 were *never* interpreted in any form resembling the KOIS. Why is this an important point in a predictive validity study?

3. From reading this article, it should be apparent that locating subjects in follow-up research is no easy task. We commend Zytowski for his diligence. In spite of this diligence, Zytowski's return rate was about 50 percent. Thus, he correctly concludes that "the validity of the KOIS for missing subjects simply cannot be ascertained." We wish all researchers would be similarly cautious about the generality of their data. Suppose that Zytowski had been able to obtain demographic data about both the respondents and nonrespondents. How could such data have been useful in determining whether Zytowski could generalize to the nonrespondents?

4. What do the *t*-values in the footnote of Table 6 indicate?

5. Does a high ratio of predictive validity to concurrent validity imply satisfactory predictive validity? Why?

6. Would you agree with us that to thoroughly understand this article, the reader must have considerable knowledge about previous research on interest inventories? Why or why not?

AFFECTIVE AND COGNITIVE CORRELATES OF
12   CLASSROOM ACHIEVEMENT[*,1,2,3]

ROBERT K. GABLE, ARTHUR D. ROBERTS, and STEVEN V. OWEN

This study examined the relationship between cognitive and affective variables as predictors of classroom achievement. Final social studies grades were obtained and the Watson-Glaser Critical Thinking Appraisal, Cooperative English Test, JIM Scale, and Gable-Roberts Attitude Toward School Subjects measures were administered to 431 eleventh grade students. Correlational and multiple regression procedures were employed. Significant relationships ($p < .01$) were found for both the cognitive and affective variables when correlated with course grades. A measure of motivation toward education predicted grades nearly as accurately as any of the cognitive variables.

A direct outcome of accountability in public schools is that teachers and counselors will have to bear increasing responsibility for the academic success and failure of their students. Clearly, too, there will be more stress on maximizing student academic success and minimizing failure. Any counseling program designed to reduce academic failure involves two basic steps. The first step is to identify, usually in a prediction format, those students likely to encounter academic difficulty. Once a valid and stable prediction equation has been developed, it becomes possible to identify these students quickly and efficiently. The second step employs preventive or remedial techniques by counselors and teachers to reduce the likelihood of failure among "high risk" students. Both steps seem important to the welfare of students, teachers, and counselors, The worth of traditional cognitive predictor variables has been well established (cf.

*Reprinted with permission from *Educational and Psychological Measurement,* 37:4 (1977), pp. 977–986. Copyright © 1977 by Educational and Psychological Measurement.

[1]Support from the University of Connecticut Research Foundation under the National Science Foundation Grant no. 35-235 and the Computer Center under Grant no. GJ-9 is greatly appreciated.

[2]Appreciation is extended to the following people for their assistance in this project: Ed Boland, Frank Gross, Frank Taylor, Tony Torre, Leo Yconiello, and Christine LaConte-Roberts.

[3]Reprints may be obtained from the senior author at the Bureau of Educational Research, U-4, School of Education, University of Connecticut, Storrs, Connecticut 06268.

Probability rev. of previous research! (handwritten annotation)

Lavin, 1965). Affective variables, however, have not shown such consistency in predicting academic achievement. Often, they are maintained to relate to scholastic performance.

The purpose of this research dealt with the first step, namely, increasing the accuracy of identifying selected cognitive and affective instruments as potential predictors of achievement.

General Attitudes toward School

Malpass (1953) found no relationship between attitude toward school and achievement test scores, but reported a significant relationship between overall attitude toward school and eighth grade classroom grades. Carter (1959) noted correlations near .60 between attitude toward school and grade point averages for samples of high school students. However, Jackson and Lahaderne (1967) cited negligible correlations between attitudes toward school and scholastic achievement for a sample of sixth grade pupils. These findings were part of a review of the literature by Jackson (1968), who concluded that little significant relationship has been shown to exist between attitude toward school and teacher grades.

Jackson and Getzels (1959) discovered no significant differences between satisfied and dissatisfied high school students in intellectual ability and academic achievement. They found that satisfied students were significantly higher than dissatisfied ones on several affective personality measures such as the California Personality Test and the Adjective Check List. Brodie (1964) observed that satisfied high school students, especially females, significantly outperformed dissatisfied students in several achievement areas. Williams (1970) discovered that satisfied in comparison with dissatisfied high school students scored significantly higher in the ability, achievement, and personality (Bell Adjustment Inventory and Tennessee Self-Concept) areas. After controlling for intelligence differences, Williams obtained no achievement test differences, but did find that the dissatisfied students were significantly below the satisfied students on all personality characteristics and on grade point average as well. Based on these findings, it appears that personality characteristics, as well as school achievement, are important considerations when one is studying attitudes toward school.

Attitudes toward Specific Subject Areas

Neale, Gill, and Tismer (1970) suggested that although overall attitude toward school may not be correlated with classroom achievement, attitudes toward specific school subjects may be related in specific subject areas. Although the findings are contrary to studies reported by Carter (1954) and Malpass (1953), their hypothesis of relationships of attitudes in specific subjects to achievement in those subject areas is in need of further examination. Bassham, Murphy, and Murphy (1964) found significant relationships between attitudes toward a specific school subject (mathematics) and achievement in that subject. Neale et al. (1970) reported some significant correlations between parallel attitude and achievement areas but found that pretest achievement was consistently the most valid predictor of final achievement.

It is difficult to ascertain whether overall attitudes toward school or attitudes toward specific sources was the distinguishing element in explaining the reported findings. Whereas measures of attitudes toward specific courses appear correlated with achievement performance, they explain little of the variation in the regression of attitude on achievement. Also, the studies examining overall attitude toward school are contradictory and only tend to support the hypothesized relationship. Comparisons across studies are difficult and risky, as not only different classroom achievement reinforcement models— competitive vs. non-competitive (Williams, 1970)—but also various measurement instruments and dissimilar sample characteristics have been involved.

The important consideration of the nature of the criterion measure has been supported in research by Khan (1969), who found that several affective components (e.g., achievement anxiety, attitudes, need achievement) significantly increased the predictive power of a cognitive battery. Using Metropolitan Achievement Test subscores as criteria, he showed multiple correlation coefficients as high as .90 when affective measures were added to the predictor pool. This level of prediction was substantially higher than has been commonly reported in the literature; Khan attributed the increase to the use of more reliable criteria than those reflected by classroom grades. However, in receiving considerable support from teachers, administrators, parents, and students, grades as measures of academic success have continued to be widely used. Although the reliability of classroom grades leaves room for improvement, prediction studies using grades as a criterion measure also can be improved. In addition, the complex relationship between affective components and classroom outcomes merits further investigation (Khan, 1969).

Problem

The general purpose of this study was to examine the relationships between cognitive and affective variables in the context of predicting student achievement in the classroom. The specific problem was explicated in terms of the following two-part question: To what extent and in what manner would classroom achievement (grades) be predicted from selected cognitive and affective variables?

Methods

INSTRUMENTATION

The instrumentation employed consisted of the Watson-Glaser Critical Thinking Appraisal (Watson and Glaser, 1951), the Cooperative English Tests-Reading Comprehension Section (Educational Testing Service, 1960), JIM Scale (Frymier, 1965), and the Gable and Roberts Attitude Toward School Subjects (GRASS) measure (Gable and Roberts, 1972). Final grades in social studies classes were also used. The Watson-Glaser Critical Thinking appraisal generated scores in the following areas: inference, recognition of assumptions, deduction, interpretation, and evaluation of arguments. The Cooperative English Test yielded vocabulary, level of comprehension, and speed of comprehension scores.

The JIM Scale provided a motivation toward school score which has been referred to as a measure of academic motivation, as it usually correlates around .40 with grades. Frymier also reported that JIM Scale scores have been found to be significantly higher for overachievers than for underachievers (as identified by standardized achievement tests) and for groups of students identified by teachers as being highly motivated.

The GRASS scale yielded two measures of attitude toward social studies which were generated through a factor analysis: general interest in and perceived usefulness of the subject. The alpha internal consistency reliabilities of the scores were found to be .94 and .70 for a sample of 893 high school students (Gable and Roberts, 1972).

ANALYSES

The extent of the relationship between classroom achievement in social studies and each of the cognitive and affective variables was examined by generating product moment correlations among all variables and multiple correlations for selected sets of cognitive and affective variables relative to the prediction of a criterion measure of end-of-the-year grades in social studies. Finally, the manner in which cognitive and affective variables predicted classroom achievement (grades serving as the criterion) was examined by performing a stepwise multiple regression analysis.

SAMPLE

The participants in this study consisted of 431 eleventh grade students from two high schools in an essentially white, middle class Northeastern city of approximately 46,000 people. Data were gathered on all predictor variables in September; final social studies grades were obtained in June. The classroom situation could be classified as competitive with respect to achieving grades in courses.

Results and Discussion

Table 1 contains the intercorrelations, means, and standard deviations for the cognitive and affective predictors and the criterion variable (social studies grades). Inspection of the intercorrelations among the predictors indicates that, as expected, the inter- and intracorrelations for the cognitive measures (Watson-Glaser and Cooperative English) tended to be higher than were the correlations between the cognitive and the affective measures. Moreover, although the attitude toward social studies measures (interest and usefulness) tended to be unrelated to any of the cognitive or affective predictors, motivation toward school measure was slightly related to the cognitive measures but unrelated to attitude toward social studies scores (interest and usefulness).

To examine the specific objective of this study, one must consider the relationships found between social studies grades and both the cognitive and affective predictors. Inspection of the Table 1 entries shows that the highest correlations with grades were found for the cognitive *Cooperative English* scales: speed of comprehension ($r = .41$, $p<.01$) and vocabulary ($r = .40$, $p<.01$). But the affective measure, *JIM Scale* motivation toward school, was almost equally related to grades ($r = .40$, $P<.01$). Whereas the remaining cognitive Cooperative English and Watson-Glaser scales were moderately related to social studies grades, attitude toward social studies (general interest and perceived usefulness) measures were negatively related to grades. The negative correlation is puzzling as a slightly inverse relationship ($r = -.21$, $p<.01$) occurred between perceived usefulness of social studies and classroom achievement.

Table 2 presents the results of the stepwise multiple regression analysis employed to examine the manner in which social studies grades could be predicted from the selected cognitive and affective measures. Of particular interest are the multiple correlations which indicated the extent of the relationship between social studies grades and a set of cognitive and affective variables. An observation of the combination of the increases in the multiple correlations to around .569 and the associated F values for the regression weights for variables which entered into the equation suggest that the most efficient equation would probably include the six predictors: speed of comprehension, motivation toward school, interpretation, perceived usefulness, vocabulary, and recognition of assumptions.

Since multiple regression techniques capitalize upon chance relationships among variables, it is desirable to obtain a more nearly accurate estimate

INTERCORRELATIONS, MEANS, AND STANDARD DEVIATIONS FOR PREDICTOR AND CRITERION VARIABLES[a,b]

table 1

VARIABLES	RCAS	DED	INTRP	EVARG	MOT	VOC	LVCMP	SPCMP	INT	USE	SSGRD	MEANS	STANDARD DEVIATIONS
INF	.22	.35	.43	.30	.26	.49	.45	.45	.03	-.02	.32	9.3	3.0
RCAS		.23	.29	.22	.15	.18	.18	.23	-.08	-.03	.24	9.7	3.1
DED			.41	.19	.25	.37	.38	.42	.03	-.05	.24	16.1	3.3
INTRP				.26	.29	.40	.40	.42	.04	-.04	.38	15.6	3.5
EVARG					.16	.29	.25	.29	-.02	-.05	.16	8.1	2.5
MOT						.27	.37	.34	-.01	-.12	.40	115.2	20.9
VOC							.61	.71	.03	-.11	.40	34.6	8.2
LVCMP								.82	.11	.13	.37	21.8	5.9
SPCMP									.06	.01	.41	33.6	10.7
INT										.31	-.08	33.3	4.2
USE											-.21	14.3	2.8
SSGRD												78.6	9.3

[a] Variables:

INF = Inference
RCAS = Recognition of Assumptions
DED = Deduction
INTRP = Interpretation
EVARG = Evaluation of Arguments
MOT = Motivation Toward School

VOC = Vocabulary
LVCMP = Level of Comprehension
SPCMP = Speed of Comprehension
INT = Interest
USE = Usefulness
SSGRD = Social Studies Grades

[b] A correlation of .10 was significant at $p < .05$; one of .13 was significant at $p < .01$ for a sample of $N = 431$.

STEP-WISE MULTIPLE REGRESSION, MULTIPLE CORRELATIONS AND FULL MODEL REGRESSION WEIGHTS[a]

table 2

STEP NUMBER	VARIABLE ENTERED	MULT R	SE EST.	df	F[b]	R²	INCREASE IN R²	FINAL b	FINAL SE b	FINAL F
1	SPCMP	.413	8.47	429	88.31	.171		.11	.07	2.31
2	MOT	.494	8.09	428	69.22	.244	.073	.10	.02	25.56 *
3	INTRP	.526	7.93	427	54.51	.277	.033	.41	.13	10.48 *
4	USE	.554	7.77	426	47.09	.307	.030	−.51	.15	12.03 *
5	VOC	.562	7.73	425	39.19	.316	.009	.15	.07	4.52 *
6	RCAS	.569	7.69	424	33.76	.324	.008	.28	.13	4.72 *
7	INF	.571	7.69	423	29.18	.326	.002	.21	.16	1.73
8	INT	.572	7.69	422	25.64	.327	.001	−.09	.09	.94
9	EVARG	.573	7.69	421	22.88	.328	.001	−.15	.16	.84
10	DED	.574	7.70	420	20.62	.330	.002	−.10	.13	.58
11	LVCMP	.574	7.70	419	18.74	.330	.000	.07	.12	.30
							Constant	59.17		

*p<.01.

[a]The 6 predictor regression equation was: SSGRD = .13(SPCMP) + .10(MOT) + .42(INTRP) − .52(USE) + .16(VOC) + .27(RCAS) + 55.3.

[b]All multiple correlations were significant at the p < .01 level.

of the "real" multiple correlation. Cross-validation procedures (developing a regression equation and applying the formula to a new sample) have often been supported in the literature as one means of estimating the population multiple R. However, researchers have argued persuasively that the much easier application of a "shrinkage" formula provides a satisfactory estimate of the population R. A shrinkage formula was thus applied to the R of .569 (found at the sixth step) as follows:

$$\hat{R} = \sqrt{1 - \left[(1 - R^2)\left(\frac{N - 1}{N - m - 1}\right)\right]}$$

Where $\hat{R}$ = estimate of population R
  N = sample size
and m = number of predictor variables

Applying the formula revealed that the original R, of .569 was reduced to .544. This negligible amount of shrinkage supports the stability of the regression outcomes. Nevertheless, this six predictor equation explained only 32 percent of the variation in grades. (See Table 2, R squared.)

It is important to note the manner in which the grades were predicted. The first variable was cognitive (speed of comprehension—SPCMP), but the second variable to enter the regression equation was an affective measure (motivation toward school—MOT). Thus, the contribution of affective variables in explaining the variation in classroom achievement is supported. But this conclusion must be clarified. The two affective measures employed in this study (motivation toward school and attitude toward social studies) had low negative correlations with each other (see Table 1). Thus, academic motivation toward school, which is measured by the JIM Scale, contributed to the prediction of classroom achievement. However, general interest in and perceived usefulness of the subject of social studies were found in this study to be either unrelated or inversely related to social studies grades.

Conclusions

The findings in this study lend further clarification to the prediction of classroom achievement. As expected, cognitive variables contributed to explaining variation in classroom grades. The combination of cognitive and a special type of affective variable in the six predictor equation resulted in a R of .569 which explains about 32 percent of the variation in grades. Although these findings may support the proponents of affective considerations, the conceptual significance of adding the affective measure as a predictor of grades may be in the nature of the JIM Scale. Since the JIM Scale appears to measure "academic motivation," it is not surprising that it contributes to explaining variation in grades. It should be noted that the more general attitude toward social studies (interest and usefulness) measures had low inverse correlations with grades.

The significant correlation of general "academic" motivation toward school with social studies grades lends support to the studies by Malpass (1953), Carter (1959), and Brodie (1964), but not to the findings of the Jackson and Lahaderne (1967) nor to the general trend of the findings in the review by Jackson (1968). This lack of agreement may be due to the use of measuring instruments which do not include "academic motivation" in their conceptualization of attitudes toward school. Also, the lack of any significant relationship between the measures of specific attitude toward social studies and social studies grades is generally contrary to the findings of Bassham et al. (1964), and Neale et al. (1970). Thus, the distinguishing feature in explaining differences in reported findings does not appear to be either general attitudes toward school or attitudes toward specific subjects.

Perhaps the construct of motivation or attitude toward school reflects larger personality characteristics such as those studied by Jackson and Getzels (1959) and Williams (1970). In these two studies, significant personality differences were found in favor of students satisfied with school. Perhaps one should accept the moderate relationships between cognitive measures and classroom achievement and give more thought to including several personality characteristics in studies which seek to explain differences in classroom achievement. Only by employing such multivariate research will one be able efficiently to identify indicators of academic success or failure. To be effective as counselors, individuals need to call for and support the outcomes of relevant research.

When consistent indicators of failure can be identified with a higher degree of accuracy than they have been in the past, counseling efforts may become more focused.

references _____

Bassham, H., Murphy, M., and K. Murphy. Attitude and achievement in arithmetic. *Arithmetic Teacher*, 1964, *11*, 66–72.

Brodie, T. A. Attitude toward school and academic achievement. *Personnel and Guidance Journal*, 1964, *43*, 375–378.

Carter, H. D. Improving the prediction of school achievement by use of the California Study Methods Survey. *Educational Administration and Supervision*, 1959, *45*, 255–261.

Educational Testing Service, *Cooperative English Tests*. Princeton: Educational Testing Service, Cooperative Tests and Services, 1960.

Frymier, J. R. *Development and validation of a motivation index: A sixth report.* The Ohio State University, Columbus, Ohio, 1965.

Gable, R. K. and Roberts, A. D. *The development of an instrument to measure attitudes toward school subjects.* Paper presented at the annual meeting of the Northeastern Educational Research Association, Boston, November, 1972.

Jackson, P. W. *Life in classrooms.* New York: Holt, Rinehart and Winston, 1968.

Jackson, P. W. and J. W. Getzels, Psychological health and classroom functioning: a study of dissatisfaction with school among adolescents. *Journal of Educational Psychology*, 1959, *50*, 295–300.

Jackson, P. W. and H. M. Lahaderne. Scholastic success and attitude toward school in a population of sixth grades. *Journal of Educational Psychology*, 1967, *58*, 15–18.

Khan, S. B. Affective correlates of academic achievement. *Journal of Educational Psychology*, 1969, *60*, 216–221.

Lavin, D. *Prediction of academic performance.* New York: Russell Sage Foundation, 1965.

Malpass, L. F. Some relationships between students' perceptions of school and their achievement. *Journal of Educational Psychology*, 1953, *44*, 475–482.

Neale, D. C., Gill, N., and Tismer, W. Relationship between attitudes toward school and their achievement. *Journal of Educational Research*, 1970, *63*, 232–239.

Watson, G. and Glaser, E. *Watson-Glaser Critical Thinking Appraisal.* New York: Harcourt, Brace and Jovanovich, 1951.

Williams, R. L. Personality ability, and achievement correlates of scholastic attitudes. *Journal of Educational Research*, 1970, *63*, 401–403.

comments and questions _____

1. Some critics of testing contend that predictions from tests which identify students likely to encounter academic difficulties result in more harm than good. What is the authors' position regarding this?

2. The authors used the criterion "grades" as their operational definition of achievement. These data were gathered in June. The data of predictor variables were obtained in September. Given the nature of the criterion variable what is the potential for criterion contamination?

3. The authors report a correlation of $-.21$ between social studies grades and perceived usefulness of social studies. Does this suggest that if social studies teachers wish to increase pupil achievement (grades) they should instil a negative attitude about the general usefulness of social studies?

4. Is the shrinkage formula computed by the authors an adequate substitute for a cross-validation study? Why or why not?

5. The last two sentences in this article suggest the need for further research. Are there any data in this article which would support this?

MEASURING TEACHER EFFECTS ON PUPIL ACHIEVEMENT[*][1]

DONALD J. VELDMAN and JERE E. BROPHY[2]

Several recent books and articles have concluded that only the quality of the student body, and not the quality of the school or its teaching staff, "makes a difference" on measures of student learning. These studies, however, have measured only presage variables and have used schools rather than teachers as the unit of analysis. The present study, using a sample of 115 second- and third-grade teachers with five or more consecutive years of experience teaching at their respective grade levels, showed that teachers do affect student learning to a degree that is both statistically and practically significant. Teacher effects were especially robust in the data from Title I schools serving disadvantaged populations.

Of late, several books and articles have appeared which argue that "schools don't make a difference." These statements have been based on the Coleman Report (Coleman, et al., 1966) and other investigations which shared several common characteristics that precluded drawing any such inferences. First, they have used *schools* rather than *teachers* as the unit of analysis. Schools are not appropriate units for analysis because they are staffed by teachers of varying ability, and lumping together the data from these individual teachers masks rather than reveals the effects of the quality of schooling. Only data based on the teacher as the unit of analysis can show that some teachers are better than others. Second, to the extent that teaching staffs do differ in quality, schools serving advantaged groups are likely to have better staffs than schools serving disadvantaged groups (Mood, 1970). This factor accentuated the probability of finding that "schools don't make a difference," since better students get better

[*] From *Journal of Educational Psychology*, 66:3 (1974), pp. 319–325. Copyright 1974 by the American Psychological Association. Reprinted by permission.

[1] This article is an expanded version of a paper presented at the annual meeting of the American Educational Research Association, New Orleans, February 1973. The research described was supported by National Institute of Education Contract OE 6-10-108, The Research and Development Center for Teacher Education. The opinions expressed herein do not necessarily reflect the position or policy of the National Institute of Education, and no official endorsement by that office should be inferred. For their assistance in preparing the data and manuscript, the authors wish to thank Marilyn Arnold, Carolyn Evertson, Susan Florence, Kathy Paredes, Kathleen Senior, Jane Sheffield, and John Sheffield.

[2] Requests for reprints should be sent to Jere E. Brophy, Department of Educational Psychology, University of Texas, Austin, Texas 78712.

teaching, thus increasing the achievement gap between such students and less gifted students. Third, and most important, one cannot draw conclusions about schooling without measuring it, but this is being done nevertheless. Coleman and his colleagues measured presage variables like years of teaching experience and highest degree obtained, but they did not obtain either process data on teachers' classroom performance or product data showing the student learning gains that individual teachers produced.

The latter technique, employed in this study, is best suited for demonstrating that teachers do in fact make a difference (or, more specifically, that teachers differ in their relative impact on student learning). The usefulness of such data, although seemingly obvious on a commonsense basis, has not been recognized or stressed until recently (Mood, 1970). Furthermore, its validity was seriously challenged by Rosenshine's (1970) review of stability in teacher effectiveness. Rosenshine could locate only five studies containing information on teacher stability over long periods (one semester or more). Of these, one involved recruits in an armed service training school and two others came from a study in which a new curriculum was being introduced; therefore, the teachers were not teaching in their accustomed ways. Thus, only two studies reflected teaching by typical teachers working under normal conditions. One study gave no stability coefficient but stated that stability was very low, while the other reported a coefficient of .09.

These data seemed to support the idea that teachers are not stable or consistent in the relative student learning gains they produce and that teacher effectiveness (by this definition, at least) is not a "trait" or stable quality. However, the data from these studies were from unselected teacher samples that may have included substantial proportions of new teachers and/or teachers recently shifted into a new grade. Such teachers are known to be unstable in their teaching behavior (appropriately so, since they are meeting and adjusting to new demands); therefore, they are unlikely to show much stability.

The present study investigated teacher stability in producing student learning gains in a sample of teachers with five or more years of experience teaching at the same grade level. Although few would argue that the amount of gain pupils show on standard achievement tests is the only or even the best measure of teaching effectiveness, it is being used increasingly for this purpose. The present paper concerns methodological considerations involved in obtaining unbiased estimates of teacher influence on pupil achievement and provides data related to the substantive question of whether or not (or how much) teachers "make a difference."

Samples and Measures

All second- and third-grade teachers (N = about 275) in a large Southwestern urban school system were considered for inclusion in a comprehensive investigation of teacher effectiveness, classroom behavior, and personal characteristics. All teachers were female. Teachers selected from the full sample for inclusion in the present study were those who *(a)* had at least five years of teaching experience at their grade, *(b)* had taught the same grade level during the three focal years (1967–1969), and *(c)* had at least 14 children with available data for each of these years (data on 20–30 pupils were available for most classes). The teachers represented 15 Title I (poverty area) and 35 non-Title I schools. The four samples resulting from this selection were as follows:

> 21 Grade 2, Title I teachers (1,210 pupils);
> 35 Grade 2, non-Title I teachers (2,168 pupils);
> 20 Grade 3, Title I teachers (1,216 pupils); and
> 39 Grade 3, non-Title I teachers (2,744 pupils).

Pupil records were retrieved from school files for each of four successive years of regular fall achievement testing. Grade equivalent scores were obtained for the Metropolitan Achievement Test (MAT) subscales. Different forms of the MAT battery were used with each of the four samples, necessitating separate statistical analyses.

Influences on Predictive Efficiency

It is now generally accepted that residual gain scores are superior to simple pretest–posttest difference scores as measures of teacher influence. What is not clear, however, is the importance of residualizing with more than the simple pretest variable (Cronbach & Furby, 1970). The following series of analyses were designed to explore this problem.

A series of regression models were compared, using *(a)* pretest, *(b)* squared pretest, *(c)* pupil sex, *(d)* year of testing, and *(e)* teacher[3] as predictors of posttest performance. In each comparison, one of these influences was omitted to determine its contribution to prediction of the criterion. Tables 1–4 contain the results of these comparisons, expressed as percentages of criterion variance associated with each influence. These data suggested the following conclusions:

> 1. Inclusion of a squared score variable to permit curvilinear regression added little to the precision of the estimates, although it was slightly more influential in Grade 3 than in Grade 2.
>
> 2. Inclusion of pupil sex in the model added very little to predictive efficiency, even though girls significantly outperformed boys at these grade levels.

---

[3]Teachers were represented in the equations by a set of binary variables, one per teacher. The entire set was omitted to estimate teacher influence.

table 1

MAT SUBTEST	M		INFLUENCE (%)				
	Pretest	Posttest	Pretest	Squared pretest	Sex	Year	Teacher
Word Knowledge	1.74	2.41	32.65	.14	.23	.20	6.14
Word Discrimination	1.83	2.81	42.43	.14	.30	1.71	3.55
Reading	1.77	2.52	22.34	.07	1.43	.29	6.90
Arithmetic Computation	1.87	2.79	27.80	.57	.00	1.04	4.50
Verbal average	1.78	2.58	46.77	.13	.47	1.10	5.30
Total	1.83	2.68	42.85	.09	.34	1.56	5.75

Note. Data on the Arithmetic Reasoning subtest were not available for this sample.
Abbreviation: MAT = Metropolitan Achievement Test.

table 2

MAT SUBTEST	M		INFLUENCE (%)				
	Pretest	Posttest	Pretest	Squared pretest	Sex	Year	Teacher
Word Knowledge	2.50	3.71	61.01	.30	.03	.03	2.69
Word Discrimination	2.82	3.70	58.11	.41	.31	.04	2.95
Reading	2.51	3.62	53.17	.01	.01	.04	2.97
Arithmetic Computation	2.52	3.18	29.93	.92	.16	.22	5.66
Arithmetic Reasoning	2.52	3.25	40.12	.00	.00	.07	4.22
Verbal average	2.61	3.67	71.72	.24	.00	.03	2.28
Quantitative average	2.52	3.22	42.30	.24	.03	.05	5.02
Total	2.57	3.44	70.38	.00	.02	.00	3.04

Note. Abbreviation: MAT = Metropolitan Achievement Test.

The sex difference was included in the prescores, however, so that its influence was negligible with prescores controlled.

3. Systematic differences among the three years of testing were trivial. This was expected, since there was no known reason to believe that any yearly differences in residual gain would appear.

4. Inclusion of the teacher variable usually yielded a significant, and often a substantial, increase in predictive efficiency. In short, teachers did make a difference, although pupil prescores were usually the strongest predictors by a considerable margin.

5. The influences of sex, year, and teacher appeared to be stronger in Title I than in non-Title I schools. Although the reasons for the year-effect differences were unclear, the sex- and teacher-effect differences were readily interpretable. Sex differences, including sex differences in school achievement, are more extreme in lower- than in higher-socioeconomic-status populations (Hess, 1970), so that a greater sex effect was expected in the Title I schools. Similarly, the differential teacher effect was expected on the basis of what is known about the relationship of ability and achievement differences to socioeconomic status. At a given age level, the cognitive abilities and school achievement of lower-socioeconomic-status children are less advanced than those of their higher-socioeconomic-status peers. This can be seen in the present data by comparing (a) the means of Table 1 versus those of Table 2 with (b) the means of Table 3 versus those of Table 4. Among other things, this means that the more advantaged children were better able to learn on their own and/or from one another and thus were less dependent upon the teacher for their degree of success in mastering the curriculum—hence, the greater teacher effect in Title I schools.

6. Teacher impact appeared to be stronger on verbal skills than on quantitative skills in Title I schools and vice versa in non-Title I schools. This was probably an elaboration of the factor described in Paragraph 5; socioeconomic-status differences are greatest on measures of verbal skills.

7. Teacher impact was stronger in Grade 3 than in Grade 2 in Title I schools but about equal in non-Title I schools. Again, this was probably an elaboration of the factor described in Paragraph 5; by Grade 3, the socioeconomic-group differences, and thus the opportunity for teacher impact in Title I schools, were larger than they were in Grade 2 (note the larger differences in Grade 3 postscores than in Grade 2 postscores in Tables 2 and 4).

8. Predictability of posttest scores of pupils was generally greater in Grade 3 than in Grade 2, in non-Title I than in Title I schools, and on verbal than on quantitative measures. The first and third conclusions have been discussed above. The greater predictability in non-Title I schools resulted from the higher correlations between pre- and postscores in these schools. This, in turn, was due most likely to the combined effects of (a) the great variance in scores in non-Title I schools, which made for higher correlations when coefficients were not corrected for attenuation and (b) the more advanced verbal and math skills of children in the non-Title I schools, which enabled them to answer correctly more often and to guess less often than children in Title I schools whose scores very likely contained more error variance due to guessing or other response sets.

table 3

	M		INFLUENCE (%)				
MAT SUBTEST	Pretest	Posttest	Pretest	Squared pretest	Sex	Year	Teacher
Word Knowledge	2.51	3.27	37.15	.90	.10	.33	17.64
Word Discrimination	2.82	3.34	44.33	.35	.65	1.85	4.96
Reading	2.62	3.25	34.36	.36	.21	.16	10.86
Arithmetic Computation	2.76	3.44	29.89	.03	.41	1.18	9.34
Arithmetic Reasoning	2.76	3.05	26.63	.86	.36	.36	4.04
Verbal average	2.65	3.29	51.28	1.00	.16	.94	12.44
Quantitative average	2.76	3.25	34.40	.14	.47	.87	6.31
Total	2.70	3.27	50.08	1.16	.41	1.44	9.83

Note. Abbreviation: MAT = Metropolitan Achievement Test.

table 4

	M		INFLUENCE (%)				
MAT SUBTEST	Pretest	Posttest	Pretest	Squared pretest	Sex	Year	Teacher
Word Knowledge	3.67	4.85	64.98	.67	.00	.02	2.16
Word Discrimination	3.66	4.62	67.08	.99	.03	.09	1.29
Reading	3.52	4.65	57.09	1.47	.00	.15	1.41
Arithmetic Computation	3.14	4.13	33.84	1.03	.07	.07	6.94
Arithmetic Reasoning	3.23	4.23	50.55	.00	.02	.12	4.28
Verbal average	3.62	4.71	76.04	1.16	.00	.08	1.08
Quantitative average	3.19	4.18	54.89	.14	.00	.12	5.23
Total	3.40	4.44	75.92	.39	.00	.12	2.16

Note. Abbreviation: MAT = Metropolitan Achievement Test.

Consistency of Teacher Impact

The next step of the analysis addressed the question of the degree to which individual teachers' influence on child gain was consistent across three successive years, and hence, across classes of pupils.

Residual gain scores for all pupils were obtained, using only simple pretest scores as covariates. These were then averaged for each teacher for each of her three classes. These average residual gains were then used to compute intraclass correlations among the three years for each of the four samples of teachers. Intraclass correlations (Ebel, 1951) provided indices of the consistency of pupil gain within teachers, across classes of pupils. The results of this analysis are shown in Table 5. With the exception of the second grade, Title I sample, in which none of the coefficients were statistically significant, it was apparent that three-year averages[4] were reasonably reliable estimates of teacher impact on student learning.

Conclusions

The data show that reasonably stable estimates of teacher influence can be obtained from standardized achievement measures of pupil performance when

INTRACLASS CORRELATIONS ACROSS THREE YEARS

table 5

| | GRADE 2 | | GRADE 3 | |
| | Title I | Non-Title I | Title I | Non-Title I |
MAT SUBTEST				
Word Knowledge	.43	.66 *	.78 *	.63 *
Word Discrimination	.36	.74 *	.26	.49 *
Reading	.24	.66 *	.50 *	.23
Arithmetic Computation	.00	.48 *	.63 *	.80 *
Arithmetic Reasoning	—	.61 *	.27	.64 *
Verbal average	.35	.71 *	.65 *	.38 *
Quantitative average	—	.59 *	.50 *	.75 *
Total	.19	.69 *	.54 *	.65 *

Note. Abbreviation: MAT = Metropolitan Achievement Test.
* $p < .05$.

[4]These intraclass coefficients (Ebel, 1951) concern three-year averages and are *not* averages of the three possible two-year correlations.

sample selection procedures eliminate new teachers and teachers who have recently switched grades. The increasing use of the team approach in elementary schools, however, lessens the practical interest of such measures. Also, although the stability coefficients from this study were considerably higher than those located by Rosenshine (1970), they were not high enough to justify the use of residual gains on such measures for teacher accountability purposes (Brophy, 1973).

The differences between Title I and non-Title I schools were consistent with the theoretical position that the school is relatively more important, compared to the home, in determining the achievement levels of economically disadvantaged pupils than it is for advantaged pupils. This, in turn, suggested that the quality of teaching is more crucial in such settings than in advantaged schools.

A subsample of these teachers, selected because they showed the greatest consistency across four years in the degree of student learning gains they produced, is presently being studied in an effort to establish those personal traits and classroom behaviors which are associated with teacher effectiveness in producing learning gains (Brophy & Evertson, 1973; Evertson & Brophy, 1973; Peck & Veldman, 1973). Having established that teachers have differential impacts in determining student scores on product measures, we are now attempting to identify the presage and process variables associated with these differences.

references _____

Brophy, J. Stability in teacher effectiveness. *American Educational Research Journal,* 1973, *10,* 245–252.

Brophy, J., & Evertson, C. Low inference observational coding measures and teacher effectiveness. Paper presented at the annual meeting of the American Educational Research Association, New Orleans, February 1973.

Coleman, J., et al. *Equality of Educational Opportunity.* Washington, D.C.: U.S. Office of Health, Education, and Welfare, 1966.

Cronbach, L. J., & Furby, L. How we should measure "change"—Or should we? *Psychological Bulletin,* 1970, *74,* 68–80.

Ebel, R. Estimation of the reliability of ratings. *Psychometrika,* 1951, *16,* 407–423.

Evertson, C., & Brophy, J. High inference behavioral ratings as correlates of effective teaching. Paper presented at the annual meeting of the American Educational Research Association, New Orleans, February 1973.

Hess, R. Class and ethnic influences upon socialization. In P. Mussen (Ed), *Carmichael's manual of child psychology.* (3rd ed.) Vol. 2. New York: Wiley, 1970.

Mood, A. Do teachers make a difference? In, *Do Teachers Make a Difference? A Report on Recent Research on Pupil Achievement.* (U.S. Office of Education 58042) Washington, D.C.: U.S. Government Printing Office, 1970.

Peck, R., & Veldman, D. Personal characteristics associated with effective teaching. Paper presented at the annual meeting of the American Educational Research Association, New Orleans, February 1973.

Rosenshine, B. The stability of teacher effects upon student achievement. *Review of Educational Research*, 1970, *40*, 647–662.

comments and questions _____

1. Why should teachers rather than schools be used as the unit of analysis if one wishes to make inferences about teacher effects on pupil achievement? Do you think many researchers and readers of such reports have drawn incorrect inferences about teacher effects from school mean data?

2. Is the sample described in sufficient detail? What is the general socioeconomic level of the non-Title I schools? Does the conclusion that there are differential influences between the Title I and non-Title I schools permit one to draw inferences about teacher effects in high socioeconomic suburban schools? Support your answer.

3. We do not fault the authors for only using female teachers. However, does this seriously limit the generalizability of the data?

4. Would one expect the squared pretest score (in addition to the nonsquared score) to contribute anything to the prediction of a criterion? Why?

5. The authors of this article conclude that teacher effect is stronger in Title I than in non-Title I schools. They also draw other conclusions about differential influences between the two types of schools. Do they present any inferential statistics to corroborate these conclusions? Would another type of statistical analysis have been more powerful in comparing Title I and non-Title I schools? If yes, which one(s)?

6. Does the fact that "the more advantaged children were better able to learn on their own and/or from one another. . . " account for "the greater teacher effect in Title I schools"? Are there other possible explanations for the findings of differential effects? What would one expect to find if, for some reason, the quality of teachers was more homogeneous in the non-Title I schools?

7. What are some possible reasons for the apparent lack of consistency of pupil gains within teachers across classes for the Grade 2, Title I sample given that the other three samples show reasonably high consistency?

SOME CORRELATES OF NET GAIN RESULTANT FROM ANSWER CHANGING ON OBJECTIVE ACHIEVEMENT TEST ITEMS*

14

DANIEL J. MUELLER and ALLAN SCHWEDEL

Few teachers include test-taking strategies as part of their curricula. Nevertheless, students do acquire strategies to use against their recurring enemy—the objective achievement test. One tactic of test-taking strategy deals with answer-changing behavior; whether to change a response after deliberation, or not to change it, is the student's dilemma. Many students do change answers, but research indicates that students generally believe that changing answers is an unwise tactic (Foote & Belinky, 1972; Mathews, 1929). In a graduate level educational measurement course, the authors found that 64 percent of the students believed that changing answers would tend to lower a student's total score; 36 percent believed that changing answers would neither raise nor lower total score. None believed that changing answers would increase scores. Contrary to students' expectations, research studies report that most students gain in total score by changing answers (Bath, 1967; Jacobs, 1972; Reiling & Taylor, 1972). A small percentage of the students in the above mentioned studies did, however, decrease their total scores as a consequence of changing answers.

The purpose of this study was to determine the relationship of sex, answer-changing incidence, and total score to net changes in total score resulting from changing answers, by examining the answer-changing behavior of a large number of graduate students responding to achievement test items.

Method

Data were collected from test results of 471 graduate students enrolled in an educational measurement course. The examinations, given over a period of several semesters, covered descriptive statistics, basic measurement princi-

*From *Journal of Educational Measurement*, 12:4 (Winter 1975), pp. 251–254. Copyright 1975, National Council on Measurement in Education, Inc., East Lansing, Mich. Reprinted by special permission.

213

ples, and concepts relevant to test construction and interpretation. The test items were in multiple-choice and true-false formats. The internal consistency coefficients of these exams, as determined by Kuder-Richardson Formula 20, ranged from .78 to .92.

Students were given no special instructions regarding answer changing, although they were advised that there would be no penalty for guessing. Since these exams were designed primarily to test power, students were given liberal time allocations, and consequently the opportunity to reexamine their answers if they so desired. Students recorded their answers on optical scanning answer forms. The number and type of answer changes were determined by checking each answer sheet for erasures. Answer changes were classified into the following categories:

1. Wrong answer changed to right answer;
2. Wrong answer changed to another wrong answer;
3. Right answer changed to wrong answer.

Findings

Answer-changing behavior was widespread; 80 percent of the students in this group changed at least one of their initial answers. Yet the percent of total answers changed was relatively small—only 3.7 percent. Sixty-five percent of the students profited by the answer changes which they made; seventeen percent lost points, and eighteen percent of those who changed answers experienced no net score change. Of the answers changed, 5.3 times as many were changed from wrong to right as from right to wrong. The mean point gain for all students who changed answers was .98.

Six variables were intercorrelated in order to clarify the statistical relationships among them:

1. Sex
2. Number of Wrong to Right changes;
3. Number of Wrong to Wrong changes;
4. Number of Right to Wrong changes;
5. Total Test Score;
6. Net Score Change, i.e., Number of Wrong to Right changes minus Number of Right to Wrong changes.

Table I shows the intercorrelations among these variables.

Both Total Test Score and Net Score Change varied independently of Sex, as indicated by correlations of .03 and .02, respectively. The correlation between the number of Right to Wrong changes and Sex (.09) was significant

CORRELATES OF NET SCORE CHANGE

Total scores will be always changed

table 1

(N = 377)

	SEX	TOTAL SCORE	WRONG TO RIGHT	RIGHT TO WRONG	WRONG TO WRONG
Total Score	.03				
Wrong to Right	.08	.18 **			
Right to Wrong	.09 *	−.18 **	.13*		
Wrong to Wrong	.00	−.22 **	.12*	.11 *	
Net Score Change	.02	.26 **	.84**	−.43**	.05

more to right = when \8 here & he scores

Is a relationship here?

* p < .05
** p < .01

only significant one but low — so conclude sex had the rel. to answ. changing patterns.

(p < .05), with males making more Right to Wrong changes than did females. Nevertheless, the ratio of gains to losses remained nearly equal for both sexes since males also made more Wrong to Right changes than did females.

The significant positive correlation between Total Score and Net Score Change (.26) indicated that by changing answers, higher-scoring students gained more points than did lower-scoring students. Unfortunately, this correlation is somewhat confounded since Total Score is, in part, a function of the students' answer-changing behavior. Such confounding existed also in the significant positive correlation of Total Score with number of Wrong to Right changes (.18), and the significant negative correlation of Total Score with number of Right to Wrong changes (− .18).

Another way to view the relationship between answer-changing behavior and Total Score is to correlate Total Score with the number of Wrong to Wrong changes. Although Total Score is influenced by Net Score Change (the combination of Wrong to Right and Right to Wrong changes), no such causal relationship exists between Total Score and the number of Wrong to Wrong changes. A significant negative correlation was found between Total Score and number of Wrong to Wrong changes (−.22), with higher-scoring students making fewer Wrong to Wrong changes. This finding suggests a fundamental difference in answer-changing behavior between high- and low-scoring students.

A special effort was made to characterize those students who experienced net score losses as a result of changing answers. A one-way analysis of variance, comparing students experiencing net score gains (N = 313), with those experiencing net score losses (N = 64), indicated that these groups could not be differentiated on the basis of sex. However, when Total Test Score was used as the dependent variable a significant difference was found between net score losers and net score gainers, with net score losers having lower mean Total Test Scores than net score gainers (F = 12.59, df = 1,375, p < .001).

A separate analysis, in which Net Score Change was the dependent variable and Total Test Score the independent variable, indicated that while the low-scoring third of the students did not experience net gains as large as did the middle- and high-scoring groups, they did experience a mean net gain of .47 points. Furthermore, construction of a frequency distribution of Total Test Scores of the 64 net score losers indicated that while not many losers earned *extremely* high scores, there were net score losers across the entire range of the Total Test Score distribution. Of the students experiencing net score losses, the mean loss was 1.3 points, with only three of these 64 students losing more than 2 points.

Conclusions

The results of this study are in agreement with the results of previous studies, which report net gains in total score for most students as a result of answer-changing behavior (See Mueller and Wasser, 1975, for a review of studies in this area). Sex differences were not found to be related to net score changes, although males did make a greater number of answer changes than did females. While a few students across the entire total test score distribution experienced net score losses as a result of changing answers, there was a clear tendency for more lower-scoring students than higher-scoring to experience such losses.

For teachers who want to give their students advice about test taking strategies, the results of this study suggest that careful answer changing frequently improves one's score on an objective test. But these results should not be over-generalized. In this study answer-changing behavior was examined only with college students. These results may not be replicated with younger students. Furthermore, no attempt was made, in this study, to examine systematically the relationships of test-specific variables to answer-changing behavior. The examinations used in this study were unit exams (three per semester) in an educational measurement course. The exams were about an hour in length; were composed entirely of true-false and multiple-choice items; and tested knowledge, understanding, and application. Future studies should control for item type, test length, level of learning, subject matter, and grade level, and examine the differential effect of these variables on answer-changing behavior and net score change.

In addition, it is important to study further other variables which may relate to successful answer-changing behavior. It is possible, for instance, that certain personality variables such as impulsivity or anxiety, and aptitude variables such as critical thinking ability may correlate with the incidence and effectiveness of answer-changing behavior. Another potentially fruitful area of investigation would be to study *directly* the answer-changing tactics used by students. It may be possible to differentiate effective from ineffective tactics and thus instruct students in effective test-taking behavior.

references _____

Bath, J. A. Answer-changing behavior on objective examinations. *The Journal of Educational Research*, 1967, *61*, 105–107.

Foote, R., & Belinky, C. It pays to switch? Consequences of changing answers on multiple-choice examinations. *Psychological Reports*, 1972, *31*, 667–673.

Jacobs, S. S. Answer changing on objective tests: Some implications for test validity. *Educational and Psychological Measurement*, 1972, *32*, 1039–1044.

Mathews, C. O. Erroneous first impressions on objective tests. *Journal of Educational Psychology*, 1929, *20*, 280–286.

Mueller, D., & Wasser, V. Implications of changing answers on objective test items. Submitted for publication, 1975.

Reiling, E., & Taylor, R. A new approach to the problem of changing initial responses to multiple choice questions. *Journal of Educational Measurement*, 1972, *9*, 67–70.

comments and questions _____

1. Why do you suppose so many people incorrectly believe that changing answers is an unwise tactic?

2. Would graduate students in an educational measurement course (the sample in this study) be more astute in test-taking skills than the average student? Would one expect similar findings in a less sophisticated group of students? Discuss.

3. The authors forthrightly discuss the confounding effects of some of the correlations. But couldn't they have eliminated the confounding by correlating, for example, the net score change with the total score of the unchanged items? What would be the advantages and disadvantages of such an approach? Are there other statistical techniques that would eliminate the confounding? If yes, what are they?

4. Are the findings about the correlates of net gain studied in this article useful with respect to giving students *differential* advice regarding answer-changing strategies? Why or why not?

PRESCHOOL MEASURES OF SELF-ESTEEM AND ACHIEVEMENT MOTIVATION AS PREDICTORS OF THIRD-GRADE ACHIEVEMENT*

BRENT BRIDGEMAN and **VIRGINIA C. SHIPMAN**

Longitudinal data on 404 children from predominantly low-income areas in three regionally distinct sites were used to determine (a) the relation of preschool, kindergarten, and first-grade measures of self-esteem and achievement motivation (primarily the Brown IDS Self-Concept Referents Tests and Gumpgookies) to reading, mathematics, and problem-solving (Raven Coloured Progressive Matrices) performance in the third grade and (b) whether such measures can improve on predictions made solely from an early achievement measure (Caldwell's Preschool Inventory). Although the early self-esteem scores had a strong negative skew, they contributed significantly to predictions of third-grade performance. However, the predictive variation in the scores may have represented differences in task understanding and attentiveness rather than differences in self-esteem. Achievement motivation scores, especially in the year prior to entrance into first grade, contributed significantly to predictions of later achievement. Results varied somewhat by sex, socioeconomic status, and geographical site.

Standard preschool achievement tests have been found to be only somewhat predictive of later academic performance. Since children's school performance is influenced not only by what they know but by their attitudes and motives, consideration of variables from the affective domain (e.g., achievement motivation, self-esteem) should improve predictions of academic success. If such variables were found to be important predictors, either by themselves or in combination with other variables, they might be valuable in the early identification of children likely to experience difficulties in academic achievement. Furthermore, more complete knowledge of the relation of these affective-social variables to later school achievement should help guide the implementation of Head Start and other preschool programs designed to facilitate later achievement by encouraging the child's development in these areas.

*From *Journal of Educational Psychology*, 70:1 (1978), pp. 17–28. Copyright 1978 by the American Psychological Association, Inc. Reprinted by permission.

This research was supported by Grant H-8256 from the Office of Child Development, and this article is based on a larger report submitted to that agency. Portions of this article were presented at the meeting of the American Psychological Association, Washington, D.C., September 1976.

Requests for reprints should be sent to Brent Bridgeman, Educational Testing Service, Princeton, New Jersey 08540.

For example, the finding that individual differences in early measures of self-esteem are predictive of later academic achievement would provide additional support for increased and systematic efforts to raise self-esteem. Similarly, a preschool program that claimed it was successful because it increased children's achievement motivation might be considered truly successful only if measured achievement motivation could actually be shown to predict subsequent achievement.

Since preschool children's performances on achievement measures are themselves influenced by affective states of the child while taking the test (Zigler & Butterfield, 1968), it is unclear whether independent assessment of relevant affective variables would increase predictions to later achievement. One would expect such independent predictions for newly emerging affective feelings that have not had an opportunity to influence the early achievement scores. Indeed, a number of investigations report significant incremental validities for affective measures over what could have been predicted solely from aptitude or achievement tests (e.g., Cattell, Barton, & Dielman, 1972; Khan, 1969). Nearly all such studies, however, involve children from the third-grade level or beyond.

There is some research, however, that assesses the ability of measures of self-esteem at the preschool or kindergarten level to predict later school achievement. One example is a study by Wattenberg and Clifford (1964), who related ratings of self-concept made at the beginning of kindergarten with reading test scores 2½ years later. Self-concept scores were obtained from judges' ratings of tape-recorded remarks made by children while drawing pictures of their families and while responding to a specially constructed incomplete-sentences test. For their measure of self-esteem (Quantified Self-Concept [good–bad]), significant predictions to the reading score (at the .05 level, one-tailed) were found in only 4 of the 14 subgroups in their analysis; the magnitude of the correlations was not reported.

Research relating early indicators of achievement motivation to actual early elementary school achievement also has been very limited, due largely to a lack of adequate measuring instruments of early motivation. Assessment procedures that work well with older children and adults may not be feasible or valid with young children. One attempt to assess achievement motivation directly in preschool and kindergarten children is an objective-projective technique known as Gumpgookies that is designed to elicit choices between alternative behaviors that reflect differences in motivation (Adkins & Ballif).[1] While the authors provide some evidence of concurrent validity, evidence on predictive validity is lacking. A commercial version of Gumpgookies, Animal Crackers, is currently being nationally marketed in a "research edition," although no information is yet available on its ability to predict school achievement.

---

[1]Adkins, D.C., & Ballif, B. L. *Final report: Motivation to achieve in school* (Report to the Office of Economic Opportunity). Honolulu: Head Start Research Center, University of Hawaii, 1970.

Another approach to the assessment of affective and social functioning in young children is the use of teacher or observer ratings. For example, Kohn and Rosman (1974) found that kindergarten teacher ratings of 209 lower- and middle-class boys on three social-emotional variables (apathy–interest, anger–cooperation, and task orientation) were significantly related to achievement in second grade, especially for the task orientation score. However, when kindergarten measures of cognitive functioning were included first in the prediction equations, the affective-social variables did not significantly add to prediction of arithmetic or word knowledge and contributed only an additional 3 percent of the variance for predictions of reading achievement. Pusser and McCandless (1974), with a longitudinal sample of economically disadvantaged children, used a number of factor analytically derived "socialization dimensions" to predict achievement at the end of second grade from data obtained while the children were in prekindergarten classes. After entering scores from the verbal facility factor in a multiple regression, a factor called "coping with anxiety by aggression" contributed significantly to the multiple correlation for girls. This factor was defined largely by the preschool teacher's rating of aggression. For boys, only the "alienation" factor added significantly to the prediction.

Previous investigations of the relation of affective-social behaviors to later academic performance were necessarily limited by the lack of a longitudinal data base that was relatively comprehensive with respect to children sampled or variety of measures included. For example, Kohn and Rosman's (1974) sample was limited to boys living in New York City, and possible sex or location differences obviously could not be discussed. Further, Kohn and Rosman's affective-social measures were limited to teacher ratings, and no self-report measures were used. Pusser and McCandless (1974), with their sample limited to low-income Atlanta children, had no measure of achievement motivation either from an individual child test or from teacher ratings.

The current analyses address two major questions: (a) the relation of measures of self-esteem and achievement motivation obtained in the Head Start year, kindergarten, and first grade to reading and mathematics achievement in the third grade and (b) whether in the preschool years such measures can improve predictions made solely from a preschool achievement measure. A criterion measure of problem-solving ability also was included in order to investigate possible differential predictions when compared with the more directly school-oriented achievement measures.

Method

SUBJECTS

The sample for the current report is a subsample from an extensive longitudinal investigation of young children, most of whom come from economically disadvantaged families. Sample selection procedures and initial sample characteristics have been presented elsewhere (Shipman, 1973). Briefly, in the fall of 1968 four regionally distinct communities were selected which (a) had sufficient numbers of children in grade school and in the Head Start program, (b) appeared feasible for longitudinal study, given expressed community and school cooperation and expected mobility rates, and (c) offered variation in preschool and primary grade experiences. The study sites chosen were Lee County, Alabama; Portland, Oregon; St. Louis, Missouri; and Trenton, New Jersey; however, the St. Louis site had to be dropped in the third year of the study, and children there were lost for further longitudinal analyses. Within these communities, elementary school districts with a substantial proportion of the population eligible for Head Start were selected. In each school district an attempt was made to test all nonphysically handicapped, English-speaking children who were expected to enroll in first grade in the fall of 1971 (i.e., children of approximately 3½–4½ years of age).

In 1969 mothers were interviewed and children were tested prior to their enrollment in Head Start or any other preschool program. For this initial four-site sample, at least partial data were obtained on a total of 1,875 children of whom 62 percent were black and 53 percent were male. The current analysis focused on children from the longitudinal sample (i.e., children originally tested in 1969) who had complete data and valid scores on Year 6[2] Cooperative Primary Tests plus at least one of the self-esteem or achievement-motivation measures from the first 4 years of the study. A substantial number of children from the original sample, though located for individual testing, were no longer in target classrooms (i.e., classrooms containing 50 percent or more children who had been previously tested) and therefore were not given the group achievement tests necessary for the current analysis. In addition to simply moving out of the district, the most frequent reasons for no longer being in target classrooms were being retained in or skipping a grade, enrollment in a private/parochial school, and, in Portland, exercising the option available there to be bussed to a different elementary school.

Given the similarity of preliminary findings for Portland and Trenton, data from these two sites were pooled to form a combined urban/northern sample. Lee County is a basically rural southern county in which, given the absence of a public kindergarten program, Head Start was a kindergarten-level program rather than a prekindergarten program as it was in the urban sites. Therefore, Lee County was treated separately in all analyses. For simplicity of presentation, Portland and Trenton are referred to as the urban sites and Lee County is referred to as the rural site; however, the reader should remember

---

[2]Throughout this article "Year" refers to year of the Longitudinal Study: Year 1 = January to August 1969 (child age 3½–4½); Year 2 = September 1969 to August 1970 (child age 4½–5½); Year 3 = September 1970 to August 1971 (child age 5½–6½); Year 4 = September 1971 to August 1972 (child age 6½–7½); Year 5 = September 1972 to August 1973 (child age 7½–8½); Year 6 = September 1973 to August 1974 (child age 8½–9½).

that Lee County differs from Portland and Trenton in more than just its level of urbanization. Because of the small number of white children with the necessary scores who had attended Head Start and the fact that this small group of white children had somewhat different background characteristics, they were excluded from the current Head Start samples. A white middle-socioeconomic-status (SES) sample from Lee County that attended private schools or kindergartens was included, however, to permit race/SES (race and SES are totally confounded) comparisons in the rural site. In the urban Head Start sample there were 90 boys and 77 girls; in the rural Head Start sample, 89 boys and 72 girls; and in the rural "other preschool" group, 41 boys and 35 girls.

On one common SES index (Census Bureau classification of head-of-household occupation [from professional = 0 to laborer = 9, plus an additional category unemployed = 10]), the two Head Start samples were quite comparable (urban $M = 7.51$, $SD = 2.35$ and rural $M = 7.31$, $SD = 1.78$), although on a second index (the highest grade in school attained by the mother) the urban sample was slightly higher ($M = 10.39$ vs. 9.32 with SDs of 2.25 and 2.38, respectively). As intended, the Lee County "other preschool" sample was of substantially higher SES, with a mean head-of-household occupational level of 1.78 ($SD = 2.38$) and a mean mother's educational level of 13.54 ($SD = 2.54$).

MEASURES OF SELF-ESTEEM

Brown IDS Self-Concept Referents Test. This task attempts to assess children's attitudes and feelings about their general ability, appearance, physical state, affective tone, and fears (Brown).[3] A full-length color Polaroid photograph of the child is taken, and after the tester verifies that the child recognizes herself/himself in the picture the child is asked to respond to 14 bipolar items (e.g., "Is (child's name) happy or is she/he sad?"). After the 14 items are administered, the child is asked to respond to the same items again, this time answering as she/he thought her/his teacher would respond in describing how she/he felt. Thus, the task attempts to assess the child's perception of "self-as-object." The Brown was administered in Years 1, 2, 3, and 4, although in Year 1 no teacher-referent items were included and in Year 2 these items were administered only to children attending a preschool.

Perceived school success. In this interview item, four stick figures printed on a page are shown to the child, and he/she is asked to "point to the one that is most like you." The tester explains that the first one is doing "very good work in school," the second one "pretty good work," the third "not too good work," and the fourth "very bad work in school." This item was adminis-

[3]Brown, B. *The assessment of self-concept among four-year-old Negro and white children: A comparative study using the Brown IDS Self-Concept Referents Test.* Paper presented at the Meeting of the Eastern Psychological Association, New York City, April 1966.

tered in Years 4 and 6 of the study as part of a longer school-perception inter-view, but only the Year 4 score was used in the current predictive analyses.

Coopersmith Self-Esteem Inventory (CSEI). Although first adminis-tered in Year 6, the CSEI was included in the current analysis in order to permit comparisons to correlations from the earlier measures. This instrument was designed to provide a general index of the child's feeling of self-worth and self-esteem (Coopersmith, 1967). After the tester reads the item, the child is asked to make a mark on an answer sheet after either "like me" or "unlike me." The items include such statements as "I'm proud of my school work" and "I often feel upset in school." The version of the CSEI used in the present study contained 42 items.

MEASURES OF ACHIEVEMENT MOTIVATION

Gumpgookies. Gumpgookies consists of dichotomous items designed to measure academic achievement motivation (Adkins, Payne, & Ballif, 1972; Adkins & Ballif, Note 1). The child is told that she/he has her/his very own imaginary figure called a Gumpgookie that shares her/his feelings and behaves exactly as she/he does. Each item shows two Gumpgookies engaged in different activities or having different attitudes (e.g., "This one likes to learn. This one likes to play all the time."), and the child is asked to pick which Gumpgookie is hers/his. For each item, the response indicating greater motivation to achieve in school was predetermined by agreement among a group of judges.

A 75-item version was used in Years 2 and 3. In Year 4 it was replaced by a new 60-item version wherein items having low biserial correlations with total test score in the Year 3 Longitudinal Study data and in Adkin's Head Start sample (Adkins)[4] were eliminated.

School enjoyment. This child interview item relates to the affective component of achievement motivation. The item states, "Some kids like school a lot, other kids don't like school very much. How much do you like school?— very much, a little bit, or not so much?" It was administered in Year 4 and, with an additional response choice, in Year 6, but only the Year 4 score was analyzed for the current report.

Schaefer Classroom Behavior Inventory (CBI)—Task Orientation Score. The task orientation score on the short form of the CBI (Schaefer, Aaronson, & Small)[5] is defined as perseverance and concentration and may be viewed as an indication of the child's achievement motivation as perceived by

---

[4]Adkins, D.C. Personal communication, November 2, 1971.
[5]Schaefer, E.S., Aaronson, M.R., & Small, V. *Classroom behavior inventory, short form.* Un-published manuscript 1970. (Available from E. S. Schaefer, Department of Maternal and Child Health, University of North Carolina, Chapel Hill, North Carolina 27514.)

the teacher. For this score, the child's teacher is asked to rate the frequency of occurrence of five behaviors (e.g., "Stays with a job until she/he finishes it.") on a 5-point scale from "almost never" to "almost always." The CBI scores for first grade (Year 4) were included in the predictive analyses, and third-grade (Year 6) scores were included for comparison purposes.

MEASURES OF COGNITIVE PERFORMANCE

Preschool Inventory (PSI). The PSI, developed by Caldwell for use in Project Head Start as a general achievement test for preschool children, taps a range of verbal, quantitative, and perceptual—motor skills defined by teachers as expected of children in kindergarten.

Cooperative Primary Tests—Reading and Math. The Cooperative Primary Tests are nationally standardized achievement tests designed for use in first through third grade.

Raven Coloured Progressive Matrices (booklet version). Compared with the measures listed above, this task is more a measure of problem-solving ability and less a measure of specific school learning. It assesses the individual's ability to make perceptual discriminations, to compare, and to reason by analogy.

DATA COLLECTION PROCEDURES

Individual child measures (Brown, individual Gumpgookies, PSI, Raven, and child interview items) were administered by specially trained local women, most of whom were black housewives with limited work experience. After their training by the local study coordinator, Year 6 Cooperative Primary Tests were group administered by the regular classroom teachers to target classes in all three sites. Local project staff, rather than the children's teachers, administered the Coopersmith Self-Esteem Inventory to all third-grade target classrooms in order to enhance the child's feeling of confidentiality in the information obtained. In addition to data from child tests, information was obtained from teacher ratings of study children and their classmates in target classrooms with the Schaefer Classroom Behavior Inventory.

Because of budgetary constraints data collection was not always uniform across sites. The most intensive testing coincided with the year of children's attendance in Head Start programs in each site. Thus, testing was limited in Lee County in Year 2 and in Portland and Trenton in Year 3. Of the measures relevant for this report, the Preschool Inventory was not administered in the urban sites in Year 3, and Gumpgookies was not administered in Lee County in Year 2. In Year 2 Gumpgookies was administered individually, but in Year 3 it was group administered in target classrooms. In Year 4 the funds available permitted individual administration of Gumpgookies in both Lee County and Portland but only group administration in target classes in Trenton (which had been selected as the site for reduced testing in Year 4 because it contained the fewest longitudinal subjects).

Results

SELF-ESTEEM

Since young children sometimes failed to choose either of the bipolar alternatives on the Brown IDS Self-Concept Referents Test, an adjusted self-concept score was created which was the proportion of positive responses for those items clearly answered in either a positive or negative manner. The means and standard deviations of these adjusted scores plus scores for the first-grade "perceived school success" item are presented in Table 1. Since the mean levels and correlational patterns for the teacher-referent and self-referent scores were highly similar, only the latter scores are reported here.

Consistent with previous findings (Walker, 1973; Brown, Note 3), preschool self-esteem scores on the Brown were uniformly high. Scores at the end of the first grade also were very high, with 86 percent of the total sample responding positively to 12 or more of the 14 items. Similarly, responses to the perceived school-success item were highly positive, with 75 percent of the total sample indicating they thought they were doing "very good work in school."

Before using the highly skewed Brown scores in correlational analyses they were normalized with an area transformation. Correlations of these normalized scores with the third-grade cognitive-perceptual scores are presented in Table 1; correlations with the Preschool Inventory (PSI) that was administered in the same year as the Brown and correlations with the third-grade Coopersmith Self-Esteem Inventory (CSEI) scores are included also for comparison purposes. Means, standard deviations, and correlations among the third-grade measures are presented in Table 2. For a variety of reasons (e.g., child absence, tester error) a child occasionally would not receive a valid score on a particular instrument, which caused the exact n on which each correlation was based to vary slightly. For the purpose of simplifying presentation, only the minimum value of n for a particular row of correlations is presented.

With the exception of the urban males, correlations in the Head Start sample from the Brown to the third-grade cognitive scores were generally positive and significant in Years 1 and 2 but absent in Years 3 and 4. The relatively high predictions from the Year 1 score indicate that the Brown administered at ages 3½ to 4½ was measuring something that had implications for future cognitive performance; however, the low correlations with the third-grade Coopersmith Self-Esteem score suggest that it was not assessing a stable general self-esteem personality dimension.

Correlational Research

MEANS, STANDARD DEVIATIONS, AND CORRELATIONS
FOR THE MEASURES OF SELF-ESTEEM

table 1

Measure	Group	Mini-mum n	M	SD	Concurrent PSI	Read	Math	Raven	CSEI
							Year 6 (third grade)		
Year 1 Brown	UHSM	70	.85	.14	−.04	−.14	−.17	−.12	.19
	UHSF	50	.82	.15	.38 **	.19	.29 **	.25 *	.16
	RHSM	59	.79	.15	.13	.28 *	.44 **	.28 *	.25 *
	RHSF	52	.72	.17	.17	.36 **	.48 **	.26 *	.11
	ROPM	23	.86	.14	.34 **	.28	.38 *	.34 *	.00
	ROPF	21	.88	.15	.20	.11	.25	.04	.08
Year 2 Brown	UHSM	67	.88	.12	.04	−.07	−.01	.08	−.08
	UHSF	61	.86	.12	.38 **	.29 *	.23 *	.33 *	.25 *
	RHSM	76	.80	.13	.31 *	.14	.27 **	.02	.38 **
	RHSF	63	.81	.13	.40 **	.21	.36 **	.22 *	.08
	ROPM	25	.88	.11	.27	.18	.29 *	.23	−.09
	ROPF	22	.91	.08	−.44	−.31	−.25	−.42	.15
Year 3 Brown	UHSM	74	.91	.08	—	.28 **	.12	.16	.15
	UHSF	66	.89	.11	—	−.13	−.11	.03	−.14
	RHSM	81	.88	.11	.12	−.02	−.02	.09	.04
	RHSF	66	.88	.12	.11	.03	−.05	−.10	.14
	ROPM	25	.89	.10	.29	.24	.30 *	.54 **	−.06
	ROPF	.21	.92	.08	.21	.33 *	.29	.33 *	.17
Year 4 Brown	UHSM	78	.91	.10	—	−.08	−.21	−.09	.07
	UHSF	70	.90	.08	—	.03	.14	.00	−.08
	RHSM	88	.90	.11	—	.08	.02	.06	.28 *
	RHSF	68	.89	.12	—	−.13	−.12	−.14	−.03
	ROPM	29	.89	.11	—	.19	.20	.22	.01
	ROPF	22	.89	.09	—	−.02	.13	.06	.46 **
Year 4 Perceived School Success	UHSM	79	3.70	.69	—	.09	.29 **	−.11	.07
	UHSF	70	3.76	.59	—	.03	.13	.10	−.07
	RHSM	88	3.84	.45	—	.18	.05	−.10	−.13
	RHSF	67	3.74	.61	—	.16	−.29	−.11	.02
	ROPM	29	3.35	.83	—	.23	.36 *	.31 *	.28
	ROPF	22	3.59	.56	—	−.12	−.21	−.19	.20

Note. PSI = Preschool Inventory; CSEI = Coopersmith Self-Esteem Inventory; UHSM = urban Head Start male; UHSF = urban Head Start female; RHSM = rural Head Start male; RHSF = rural Head Start female; ROPM = rural other preschool male, ROPF = rural other preschool female.

*$p < .05$, one-tailed.
**$p < .01$, one-tailed.

It is possible that true variation in early self-esteem is unrelated to variation in later self-esteem, even though it is related to variation in later achievement, for example, by affecting the acquisition of preacademic skills. However, it seems at least as likely that variation on the Year 1 Brown represented something other than variation in self-esteem. For example, it might

**MEANS, STANDARD DEVIATIONS, AND CORRELATIONS
FOR THE THIRD-GRADE CRITERION MEASURES**

table 2

Measure	Group	Minimum n	M	SD	Math	Raven	CSEI	CBI
Cooperative	UHSM	75	24.65	7.93	.56 **	.34 **	.31 **	.28 **
Primary	UHSF	67	29.97	8.43	.67 **	.57 **	.42 **	.59 **
Reading	RHSM	72	23.11	8.10	.67 **	.51 **	.44 **	.51 **
	RHSF	63	26.34	8.58	.66 **	.37 **	.40 **	.50 **
	ROPM	30	37.22	7.48	.74 **	.41 **	.09	.53 **
	ROPF	22	42.06	5.27	.56 **	.61 **	.17	.19
Cooperative	UHSM	72	28.47	8.07		.12	.20 *	.31 **
Primary	UHSF	67	30.46	9.19		.30 **	.47 **	.49 **
Math	RHSM	72	27.62	8.60		.35 **	.38 **	.43 **
	RHSF	66	28.55	7.72		.34 **	.30 **	.38 **
	ROPM	30	45.24	9.28		.70 **	.30	.54 **
	ROPF	23	46.46	8.51		.63 **	.31	.37 *
Raven	UHSM	77	20.20	4.31			−.06	.02
Coloured	UHSF	71	2.83	5.32			.43 **	.39 **
Progressive	RHSM	72	18.26	4.31			.20 *	.30 **
Matrices	RHSF	67	17.28	3.95			.08	.10
	ROPM	30	24.80	4.59			.15	.29 *
	ROPF	23	26.34	5.21			−.03	.29
Coopersmith	UHSM	76	24.68	6.60				.24 *
Self-Esteem	UHSF	70	25.81	6.01				.43 **
Inventory	RHSM	70	25.31	5.98				.39 **
	RHSF	66	26.33	6.16				.27 *
	ROPM	29	28.30	6.17				.32 *
	ROPF	22	30.78	6.38				.58 **
Schaefer	UHSM	78	13.29	5.24				
CBI Task	UHSF	73	15.85	6.15				
Orientation	RHSM	84	14.92	5.97				
	RHSF	71	17.77	6.31				
	ROPM	38	19.07	4.84				
	ROPF	33	22.38	3.38				

Note. CSEI = Coopersmith Self-Esteem Inventory; CBI = Classroom Behavior Inventory; UHSM = urban Head Start male; UHSF = urban Head Start female; RHSM = rural Head Start male; RHSF = rural Head Start female; ROPM = rural other preschool male; ROPF = rural other preschool female.
*$p < .05$, one-tailed.
**$p < .01$, one-tailed.

have reflected intrinsic task motivation or attentiveness. Some children might have listened carefully to each item and considered both alternatives before responding, whereas others might have quickly chosen either the first or the last alternative that they heard. Reports from the testers in the field indicated that in fact many children did appear to be responding in the latter manner. On the assumption that true self-esteem was high in both groups, children in the former (attentive) group would receive higher scores than children in the latter (inattentive) group (since the position of positive responses was counterbalanced), thus accounting for the correlation of the self-esteem (attentiveness) scores with later cognitive performance. Consistent with this interpretation, the low correlation of the Year 1 Brown scores with concurrent PSI scores in the rural Head Start sample might reflect the relatively minor influences of intrinsic motivation on the easier items of the PSI, which were the discriminating items in Year 1. These items primarily require only recall of basic information. The correlations of the Year 1 Brown with Year 2 PSI scores in this rural Head Start sample were somewhat higher (*r*s to Year 2 PSI of .46 and .32 for boys and girls, respectively, and *r*s of .47 and .44 to Year 3 PSI), which suggests the increased importance of intrinsic motivation when the discriminating items required more than simple recall.

To assess the extent to which performance on the Brown added to the prediction of performance on the third-grade cognitive measures made solely from the children's PSI scores, we ran multiple correlations, first entering the PSI then adding the Brown (except in the supplementary middle-SES "other preschool" sample where the *n*s were too small). In the urban sites, adding the Brown to the Year 1 PSI did not significantly increase the multiple correlation, but in the rural site the multiple correlation with third-grade math as the criterion significantly increased from .43 to .58 for boys and from .26 to .51 for girls. In Year 2 with the higher concurrent correlations of the Brown and PSI, the Brown contributed little to predictions of third-grade math performance, with the only significant increase for the sample of rural girls (*R* increased from .47 to .53). The perceived school-success scores were so skewed as to make any interpretation of correlational patterns highly questionable.

ACHIEVEMENT MOTIVATION

Means and standard deviations for the achievement motivation scores are presented in Table 3. (Since Gumpgookies was first administered during the Head Start year, there are no Year 2 Gumpgookies scores in the rural site. Note also that the *n* was reduced in the urban sites in Year 3 because Gumpgookies in that year was group administered only in target classrooms.) Although Adkins et al. (1972) reported results based on a total score plus four scores derived from a factor analysis of the items, attempts to replicate their factors, even after partialing for response bias, were unsuccessful. Further, alpha coefficients in the high .80s and low .90s for the total score suggested that subscores were unnecessary. Although Adkins et al. found a correlation of .34 between age (which ranged from 39 to 76 months in their sample) and total score, in the current sample with its more restricted age range, the correlation of age with total score was only .17 in Year 2, .07 in Year 3, and .08 in Year 4. Hence, the conversion to age-normed Z scores described by Adkins et al. was not necessary in this sample.

MEANS, STANDARD DEVIATIONS, AND CORRELATIONS FOR THE MEASURES OF ACHIEVEMENT MOTIVATION

table 3

| | | | | | | CORRELATIONS | | | |
| | | | | | Concurrent | Year 6 (third grade) | | | |
Measure	Group	Mini-mum n	M	SD	PSI	Read	Math	Raven	CBI
Year 2	UHSM	64	52.70	10.87	.13	.36 *	.04	.17	.14
Gumpgookies	UHSF	60	52.29	9.89	.32 **	.22 *	.13	.29 *	.18
Year 3	UHSM	44	56.85	10.56	—	−.18	−.06	−.09	.13
Gumpgookies	UHSF	40	54.42	11.35	—	.35 *	.31 *	.34 *	.13
	RHSM	74	53.73	11.14	.42 **	.24 *	.59 **	.42 **	.16
	RHSF	57	56.28	10.48	.33 **	.39 **	.55 **	.16	.42 **
Year 4	UHSM	72	49.87	9.12	—	.14	.12	.14	.20
Gumpgookies	UHSF	64	52.93	6.65	—	.01	.16	.14	−.11
	RHSM	88	53.31	5.29	—	.22 *	.31 **	.11	.12
	RHSF	68	54.34	5.13	—	.06	.24 *	−.02	.09
	ROPM	40	50.00	7.65	—	.04	.01	.12	−.10
	ROPF	33	52.91	6.24	—	.01	−.14	−.20	.13
Year 4	UHSM	77	16.23	5.69	—	.11	.18	.20 *	.28 *
CBI Task	UHSF	64	18.67	5.52	—	.58 **	.53	.40 **	.52 **
Orientation	RHSM	88	14.88	6.58	—	.33 **	.29 **	.20 **	.30 **
	RHSF	66	18.47	5.63	—	.26 *	.34 **	.16	.37 **
	ROPM	39	20.77	4.95	—	.47 **	.56 **	43 **	.16
	ROPF	33	20.65	5.22	—	.12	.08	.31	.00
Year 4	UHSM	76	2.61	.71	—	−.17	.04	−.10	.19
school	UHSF	69	2.59	.76	—	−.16	.08	−.10	.04
enjoyment	RHSM	86	2.36	.84	—	.25 **	.26 **	.21 *	.19
	RHSF	67	2.49	.83	—	.00	.08	−.10	.26 *
	ROPM	39	1.95	.92	—	.20	.29 *	.12	.12
	ROPF	31	2.21	.93	—	.21	.10	.02	.20

Note. PSI = Preschool Inventory; CBI = Classroom Behavior Inventory; UHSM = urban Head Start male; UHSF = urban Head Start female; RHSM = rural Head Start male; RHSF = rural Head Start female; ROPM = rural other preschool male; ROPF = rural other preschool female.

*p < .05, one-tailed.
**p < .01, one-tailed.

Consistent with previous findings (Adkins & Ballif, Note 1), the means during the preschool and kindergarten years were relatively high and increased with age, although they did not approach the maximum possible score of 75. However, on the 60-item first-grade version, scores were approaching ceiling levels. Similarly, in first grade, responses to the item on self-reported school enjoyment were close to the maximum of 3.0. However, in first grade, teacher perceptions were not so uniformly positive as were the self-reports. Average teacher ratings of task orientation, while generally positive, were closer to the midpoint value of 15 than to the maximum possible score of 25. In both the urban and rural Head Start samples, girls were rated significantly higher in task orientation: in the urban sites, $t(151) = 2.69$, $p < .01$; in the rural site, $t(156) = 3.69$, $p < .01$. Previously reported findings on the same sample (Emmerich, 1971) indicated similar sex differences when trained observers rated children's task orientation during free play in urban Head Start classes.

Since Year 3 Gumpgookies was group administered in target Head Start classrooms, no scores on it were available for the white middle-SES "other preschool" sample. In Year 4 there were no race/SES differences for rural girls, but for boys, first-grade Gumpgookies scores were significantly higher in the rural Head Start sample than in the rural "other preschool" sample, $t(126) = 2.45$, $p < .05$. This is in direct opposition to previous findings on the relation of SES to achievement motivation (e.g., Adkins et al., 1972). However, the Year 4 Gumpgookies scores in the "other preschool" sample did not correlate with teacher ratings of Year 4 task orientation in first grade and were not predictive of later achievement; the score apparently has different meanings in the two groups.

Self-reported school enjoyment was higher for children in the Head Start sample, with the differences for boys reaching statistical significance, $t(123) = 2.37$, $p < .05$. On the ratings of task orientation made by the first-grade teachers, mean scores were significantly higher for the white middle-SES "other preschool" boys than for the black lower-SES boys in the rural Head Start sample, $t(126) = 5.58$, $p < .01$, although the difference for girls was not significant, $t(101) = 1.93$, $p > .05$. Unlike the Head Start sample, in the "other preschool" sample there was no significant sex difference in the task orientation ratings.

To correct for the moderate skew of the Gumpgookies scores, we normalized them prior to the correlational analyses reported in Table 3. In the urban sites, Gumpgookies scores in Year 2 were predictive of third-grade reading for boys and girls, and Raven scores for girls only. They were significantly correlated with concurrent PSI performance only for girls. By the kindergarten year in the urban sites (Year 3), Gumpgookies was no longer predictive of any of the third-grade scores for boys, although for girls it continued to predict reading and Raven scores, and in addition was predictive of math performance. In the rural site, Year 3 Gumpgookies scores were significantly related to third-grade performance in both reading and math and, for boys only, to Raven scores. Furthermore, the correlations with math scores were fairly substantial, accounting for 30%–35% of the variance.

In the urban sites, neither of the first-grade self-report measures (Gumpgookies and school enjoyment) was significantly related to the third-grade cognitive-perceptual scores. In the rural site, reported school enjoyment by boys was significantly related to the cognitive-perceptual scores, although the largest correlation accounted for less than 7 percent of the variance. First-grade Gumpgookies scores in the rural site were still significantly related to third-grade math performance for boys and girls, although to a significantly lesser extent than were the scores from Gumpgookies administered during the previous year. Gumpgookies scores were significantly related to reading scores only for boys and were not related to Raven scores for either boys or girls. Thus, for children similar to those in this sample, the age period 4–5½ (i.e., prior to entry into first grade) appears to be a critical time for the administration of Gumpgookies since there is a notable drop in its predictive validity the following year.

In the urban sites, task orientation ratings were predictive of reading and math performance only for girls, but in the rural site these teacher ratings were predictive for both boys and girls. Low but statistically significant correlations with Raven scores were obtained for all groups except rural girls. In the urban sites, the statistically significant differences between boys and girls in the predictions of both reading ($z = 3.18$, $p < .01$) and math ($z = 2.43$, $p < .05$) may reflect greater variability over time of achievement-related behaviors for boys or it may reflect a greater difficulty on the part of first-grade teachers in identifying predictive achievement-related behaviors in urban boys. The lack of prediction for boys was apparently not caused by a lack of variability in the teacher ratings since the standard deviations of the ratings were almost identical in the two sex groups.

In the urban sample, adding Year 2 Gumpgookies scores to the PSI significantly improved predictions of reading scores only for boys (R increased from .29 to .43) and added nothing to predictions of math and Raven scores for either urban boys or urban girls. Gumpgookies scores in Year 3 added nothing for the urban sample, but for the rural sample they significantly improved predictions of third-grade reading for girls (R increased from .42 to .50) and Raven scores for boys (R increased from .27 to .43). Gumpgookies performance contributed most in the rural site for predictions of math scores. It added significantly to predictions for both boys and girls, accounting for an additional 18 percent–19 percent of the math variance; for boys, R increased from .45 to .62, and for girls from .45 to .62.

Discussion

The high mean scores on both the Brown IDS Self-Concept Referents Test and the "school success" item suggest that in both middle- and low-SES samples self-esteem is quite high in the preschool years and through the first grade. By third grade more variation in self-esteem was noted, and these third-grade scores were more strongly related to concurrent achievement measures. The current results are thus consistent with previous suggestions (Calsyn, 1973; Kifer, 1975) that differences in academic self-esteem develop as a reaction to school success and failure rather than act as a cause of such school performance. An implication for education appears to be that teachers in the early elementary grades should be alert to the behaviors of themselves and others in the school setting which may decrease a child's initially high level of self-esteem.

The correlational analyses with the Brown indicated the predictive value of this measure with children under age 5, although the predictive variation may be related to differences in task motivation and understanding rather than differences in self-esteem. This illustrates the critical point that the predictive validation of a measuring instrument must not be confused with establishing the predictive validity of a theoretical construct. The hypothesis that these scores are actually reflecting differences in attentiveness and task motivation could be assessed in future studies by including tester ratings of these behaviors obtained immediately after the child finished the task; scores of the inattentive children could then be treated separately in the analyses. However, if inattentive children were truly low in self-esteem, this information would be lost.

The drop in predictive validity beyond age 5 indicates an apparent critical period for the Brown to assess whatever it is that it is measuring. It also demonstrates that measures close in time need not correlate more highly than the same measures with a greater interval between assessments, especially at young ages when developmental changes in children and the way they respond to test items occur fairly rapidly.

Gumpgookies scores, especially in Year 3 in the rural site, were significantly related to the third-grade cognitive measures. Not all the predictive variation in Gumpgookies was already reflected in concurrent cognitive measures since it added significantly to predictions from the concurrent PSI. Thus, Gumpgookies apparently assesses achievement-related attitudes that are important for later school achievement but are not yet totally reflected in concurrent achievement measures. Since natural variation in achievement motivation as defined by the Gumpgookies test (i.e., liking school activities, feeling positive about one's self as a learner, expecting to succeed, persevering in attempts to succeed, and knowing mechanisms/tools that will enable one to succeed) appears to make a substantial independent contribution to predictions of academic achievement, preschool programs designed to develop these attitudes might make a substantial contribution to the child's later success in school.

Although there were a number of significant predictions from preschool Gumpgookies scores, especially in the rural site, by first grade Gumpgookies scores were less predictive of later achievement. As with the Brown, there is apparently a critical time for the administration of Gumpgookies. Perhaps as children get older they are more likely to take time to think of the socially desirable response, which results in scores near the ceiling level that are necessarily less predictive. If this hypothesis is correct, future modifications of Gumpgookies to improve the apparent social desirability of the nonachievement response might be useful (e.g., this Gumpgookie works at his/her own paper on his/her desk, and this Gumpgookie helps the teacher clean the blackboard). Thus the child motivated to achieve social acceptance from the teacher could be distinguished from the child motivated to achieve academically. Another hypothesis for superior predictions from the earlier scores is that Gumpgookies is more differentiating during the period when achievement attitudes are in their formative stage and children are first exposed to a major emphasis on school-oriented achievement; thus scores may reflect also the child's readiness to assume such motivation.

Self-reports by low-SES black children in first grade indicated that stereotypes of these children as disliking school and being disinterested in academic achievement are incorrect; however, these positive attitudes were not reflected in their basic reading and math skills or, especially in boys, in task-oriented behaviors as perceived by their teachers. Thus, although developing positive attitudes may be necessary for school success, it is obviously not sufficient; teachers also must provide adequate instruction on the appropriate task-related behaviors. Also, the school environment must reinforce and sustain such interest and motivation.

Further analyses are needed to explore a number of specific issues. For example, the apparently stronger association of achievement motivation to math performance than to reading or Raven performance needs to be explained. It may be that this relation is found because math is less intrinsically motivating, instruction in math is less individualized, and/or a greater complexity of skills is involved in reading and the items on the Raven, thus leading to more reliance on general cognitive-perceptual abilities and previously acquired skills; or it may be something unique to the particular achievement measures used in this study. Since the reliance of the Brown on children's ability to verbalize their conception of self emphasizes the cognitive components of self-esteem, different techniques for assessing self-esteem at the preschool level (e.g., observer ratings instead of a self-report measure) should also be explored. Although the focus of this report is on its relation to school achievement, that is obviously not the sole reason for studying self-esteem; the development of self-esteem in preschool children deserves further study whether or not it can be shown to predict later achievement. To nurture it, however, we must be able to recognize its many manifestations.

The variations in correlational patterns across the various subsamples also need to be explored, especially the general lack of significant correlations found for the urban Head Start males. The poor predictions cannot be ascribed solely to the sex, race, or SES of this group because of the fairly substantial correlations found for the rural children of the same sex, race, and approximately the same (or slightly lower) SES. In an attempt to unravel the complex sex and site variations, differences in the home and school environments of these children need to be more closely examined. For example, Follow Through programs were available only in the urban sites. If these programs were especially helpful for the least motivated boys, the lower correlations for that group would make sense and could even be seen as a positive program impact. This could be clarified by comparing children from the same site who were or were not exposed to Follow Through. Better yet would be the use of classroom observations that identified differential teacher reinforcements of achievement-related behaviors. Presently planned analyses will investigate the extent of differential classroom experiences according to the child's sex, race, and site and cognitive, affective, and social characteristics at time of entry into grade school.

The current analyses provide only a hint of the vast complexity in the relations among affective, social, and cognitive processes. There is a strong need for further analyses of these data as well as future replication efforts in order to more clearly define these complex processes.

references _____

Adkins, D. C., Payne, F. D., & Ballif, B. L. Motivation factor scores and response set scores for ten ethnic-cultural groups of preschool children. *American Educational Research Journal,* 1972, *9,* 557–572.

Calsyn, R. *The causal relationship between self-esteem, locus of control, and achievement: A cross-lagged panel analysis.* Unpublished doctoral dissertation, Northwestern University, 1973.

Cattell, R. B., Barton, K., & Dielman, T. E. Prediction of school achievement from motivation, personality, and ability measures. *Psychological Reports,* 1972, *30,* 35–43.

Coopersmith, S. *The antecedents of self-esteem.* San Francisco: Freeman, 1967.

Emmerich, W. *Disadvantaged children and their first school experiences: Structure and development of personal-social behaviors in preschool settings* (ETS PR 71–20). Princeton, N.J.: Educational Testing Service, 1971. (ERIC Document Reproduction Service No. ED 013 371)

Khan, S. B. Affective correlates of academic achievement. *Journal of Educational Psychology,* 1969, *60,* 216–221.

Kifer, E. Relationships between academic achievement and personality characteristics: A quasi-longitudinal study. *American Educational Research Journal,* 1975, *12,* 191–210.

Kohn, M., & Rosman, B. L. Social-emotional, cognitive, and demographic determinants of poor school achievement: Implications for a strategy of intervention. *Journal of Educational Psychology,* 1974, *66,* 267–276.

Pusser, H. E., & McCandless, B. R. Socialization dimensions among inner-city five-year-olds and later school success: A follow-up. *Journal of Educational Psychology,* 1974, *66,* 285–290.

Shipman, V. C. Disadvantaged children and their first school experiences, ETS-Head Start longitudinal study. In J. C. Stanley (Ed.), *Compensatory education for children, ages 2 to 8.* Baltimore, Md.: Johns Hopkins University Press, 1973.

Walker, D. K. *Socioemotional measures for preschool and kindergarten children.* San Francisco: Jossey-Bass, 1973.

Wattenberg, W. W., & Clifford, C. Relation of self-concepts to beginning achievement in reading. *Child Development,* 1964, *35,* 461–467.

Zigler, E., & Butterfield, E. C. Motivational aspects of changes in IQ test performance of culturally deprived nursery school children. *Child Development*, 1968, *39*, 1–14.

comments and questions _____

1. Do you feel that the authors have described their sample and method in sufficient detail? Why are race and SES totally confounded?
2. Does the article provide any evidence for the construct validity of the self-esteem and achievement motivation inventories? If not, should there be such evidence?
3. What psychometric and/or psychological rationale could be advanced for the authors normalizing the highly skewed Brown self-concept scores?
4. While the "minimum n" is explained following the reference to Table 2, we believe it should have been presented at least two paragraphs earlier.
5. How would the fact that attentive students receive higher scores on the Year 1 Brown than nonattentive students account "for the correlation of the self-esteem (attentiveness) scores with later cognitive performance"?
6. If the Gumpgookies and the Brown have an apparent critical period for maximum predictive validity, what does this connote regarding the measures' construct validities or their usefulness in attempting to upset negative predictions?
7. The authors recognize the large variations in correlational patterns across the various subsamples. Could this be due to the fact that "data collection was not always uniform across sites"? If the variations across subsamples are not due to methodological factors, then we surely agree that "The current analyses provide only a hint of the vast complexity in the relations among affective, social, and cognitive processes."
8. How did the authors account for the effects of chance relationships on the size of the multiple R?

EX=POST=FACTO RESEARCH

chapter five ─────────────────────────────

For the most part, historical research is concerned with "what was"; descriptive research with "what is"; and correlational research with "what will be." Experimental research, which will be discussed in greater detail in the next chapter, is concerned primarily with the attempt to explain "why what is, really is." In other words, experimental research is concerned with ascertaining causal relationships. *Ex-post-facto* research (sometimes called causal-comparative) has characteristics of descriptive, correlational, and experimental research. It is descriptive because the researcher must describe his findings as he observed them. It is an extension of correlational research in that it attempts to ascribe causal relationships to the observed phenomena. You will recall that correlational research does not, and is not designed to, demonstrate cause-and-effect relationships. In fact, the authors have attempted to inculcate the philosophy that "correlation does *not* imply causation." Unlike correlation research, the ex-post-facto method attempts to deduce, or discover *how* and *why* a particular phenomenon occurs. In this it is akin to experimental research. However, ex-post-facto research does not *prove* cause-and-effect relationships. Kerlinger defines ex-post-facto research as follows:

> Ex-post-facto research is systematic empirical inquiry in which the scientist does not have direct control of independent variables because their manifestations have already occurred or because they are inherently not manipulable. Inferences about relations among variables are made, without direct intervention, from concomitant variation of independent and dependent variables.[1]

[1] Fred N. Kerlinger, *Foundations of Behavioral Research* (2d ed.). New York: Holt, Rinehart and Winston, 1973, p. 379.

The independent variables Kerlinger speaks of are those variables whose effects are being evaluated. The dependent (criterion) variables are those that are being predicted, or those that are affected by the independent variables.

Only in experimental research can one actually establish cause-and-effect relationships, for only in experimental research can the independent variables (or at least one of the independent variables) be manipulated by the researcher. This manipulated independent variable is referred to as a *treatment*. Manipulating a treatment is vital in attempting to establish causal relationships and will be discussed in greater detail in an ensuing section. Because of this lack of a treatment, ex-post-facto or causal-comparative research is sometimes referred to as *quasi-experimental* research.

Correlational, ex-post-facto, and experimental research are all concerned with the advancement of knowledge but in a slightly different way. Correlation-type studies, concerned with studying the *relationship* between two or more variables, *may suggest* causes of observed behavior whereas experimental and ex-post-facto studies try to isolate causes. Possibly the following example will help clarify the situation.

There is considerable controversy today concerning whether or not smoking causes lung cancer. The only research evidence that has been presented is of either a correlation type, such as studying the relationship between the degree of smoking and the incidence of lung cancer; or an ex-post-facto type of study, where, after an individual has died and a postmortem has been performed, the researcher attempts to deduce the fact that smoking contributed to the cause of death (lung cancer). Now, in order for this question to be studied experimentally, it would be necessary to obtain two groups of individuals (who are hopefully comparable), submit one group to the treatment (smoking) and withhold the treatment from the other group.[2] Other than having one group smoke and the other group not smoke, both groups of individuals would have identical experiences and exposures. Then, after the study had been completed, and a period of time had elapsed, the lungs of the individuals in each group would be examined. If a greater incidence of lung cancer is found in the smoker group (experimental group) than in the nonsmoker group (control group), one might conclude that smoking does in fact cause lung cancer.

Basically, the major difference between ex-post-facto and experimental studies is that in the *ex-post-facto* the researcher begins with two (or more) groups of subjects—one in which the variable he is interested in studying, say, mental retardation or lung cancer, is *already present;* the other in which this variable is absent. Then, retrospectively, he attempts to identify other variables that are plausible explanations for this observed variable; that is, he attempts to determine what factor(s) causes lung cancer or mental retardation. Unfortu-

---

[2]A restrictive definition of experimental research would demand that the subjects be randomly assigned to the two groups. Under a less restrictive definition one would call this study experimental whether or not the groups had been assigned at random since the independent variable was under the control of the experimenter. This will be discussed more fully later.

nately, the researcher is unable to be as certain of his statement "If x, then y, or x causes y" as he would had he conducted a true experiment. This is due to a lack of control over other relevant variables (that is, because of a lack of control of other plausible explanations for the observed phenomenon).

The reader at this point may inquire "If experimental research is the only way to prove cause and effect, *why* conduct ex-post-facto research?" The answer is quite simple. Experimental research can be quite costly in time, effort, and money, Also, there are many instances in educational research where it is not possible for the researcher to manipulate the independent variable because it is in principle beyond control or because such manipulation might prove injurious or even lethal to the subject. For example, let us assume that a researcher is interested in studying whether brain damage affects a second-grade student's learning of simple arithmetic concepts. It should be readily obvious that to conduct such a study in an experimental fashion, the researcher would have to select a group of subjects (Ss), assign them to either an experimental (E) group in which each subject will be exposed to a treatment that induces brain damage; or a control (C) group that is not subjected to this treatment, and then conduct his study. How far do *you* think a researcher would be able to go in conducting this study?

In an ex-post-facto study, the researcher looks for a group of subjects (Ss) who are already brain-damaged and another group of Ss who are "normal." Then, in a post-hoc, or after the fact, fashion the researcher determines whether there is any difference between the two groups in their ability to learn simple arithmetic concepts. Then he tries to learn what factors are responsible for causing this difference. He may conclude that the *only* factor is brain damage. But is it? As we shall see in a subsequent discussion, it need not be.

The ex-post-facto method, therefore, is used in those instances where an experiment cannot or should not be conducted. Some areas that are most amenable to ex-post-facto research are the study of delinquency,[3] the study of riots,[4] the study of student activists,[5] the Authoritarian Personality Studies,[6] the study of the influence of social class on learning,[7] and the numerous studies on the Equality of Educational Opportunity.[8] These studies are just some examples where the experimental approach was not feasible and still the values accrued from these studies were significant.

[3]Sheldon Glueck and Eleanor Glueck, *Physique and Delinquency*. New York: Harper & Row, 1956.

[4]See, for example, Seymour M. Lipsit and Sheldon S. Wolin (eds.), *The Berkeley Student Revolt: Facts and Interpretations*. Garden City, N.Y.: Doubleday, 1965. Martin Myerson, "The Ethos of the American College Student: Beyond the Protests." In Robert Morrison (ed.), *The American University*. Boston: Houghton Mifflin, 1967.

[5]See the *Report of the National Commission on Civil Disorders*. New York: Bantam, 1968.

[6]Theodore W. Adorno et al., *The Authoritarian Personality*. New York: Harper & Row, 1950.

[7]See Allison Davis, *Social Class Influences upon Learning*. Cambridge, Mass.: Harvard University Press, 1948.

[8]James Coleman et al., *Equality of Educational Opportunity*. Washington, D.C.: U.S. Government Printing Office, 1966.

There is no denying that the ex-post-facto approach to studying educational problems may not be as neat as the experimental method. However, the ex-post-facto method can and does provide the educational research with valuable clues concerning the nature of phenomena. If we were to "shy away from" ex-post-facto research because of its limitations, there would be a large vacuum in our knowledge about human behavior. We should not and cannot avoid ex-post-facto research. As Kerlinger aptly states, "If a tally of sound and important studies in psychology, sociology, and education were made, it is likely that ex post facto studies would outnumber and outrank experimental studies."[9]

The ex-post-facto method has certain unique problems and limitations associated with it—as do the historical, descriptive, correlational, and experimental methods. Among these problems, the more important ones relate to (1) lack of a treatment, (2) self-selection of subjects, and (3) interpretability of findings. Both the *researcher* and the *consumer* of research must be attuned to and cognizant of these limitations.

Problems Associated with Ex-Post-Facto Research

The most generally recognized difference between the ex-post-facto and experimental methods is one of treatment control. Since, as has been mentioned, one cannot control the treatment, it is obvious that one has no control over which subjects (Ss) will receive which treatments. Ideally, we would like to randomly select a sample of subjects from a larger population, and randomly assign the subjects to treatment groups. In ex-post-facto studies we must classify the Ss as we find them. (This is often referred to as *self-selection*.) Possibly the following example will help the reader.

A researcher is interested in studying the relationship between achievement and anxiety. In an ex-post-facto study the researcher identifies Ss who do and do not possess the anxiety syndrome and obtains achievement results for them. Now if we find that the low anxious group exceeds the high anxious group in achievement, it may be tempting to conclude that high anxiety results in decreased achievement. But this is a tenuous conclusion. There are too many opportunities for other extraneous variables to enter into the study and hence influence the results obtained. (An extraneous variable is any variable that impedes attributing all differences in the dependent variables to the independent variables.) Since the Ss selected themselves into one of two groups, one is always plagued with the very real possibility that the groups differ in ways other than level of anxiety. For example they may differ in intelligence, health, and/or socioeconomic status.

[9]Fred N. Kerlinger, *Foundations of Behavioral Research* (2d ed.). New York: Holt, Rinehart and Winston, 1973, p. 392.

Because treatment and randomization are not possible in ex-post-facto research, and, because of the lack of control inherent in such research, it is most difficult to conclude that "if a, then b." Before the researcher can conclude "if a, then b," or "a causes b," he should be convinced that there are no other factors such as x or y that may have caused b. How can the researcher be fairly certain that neither x nor y caused b? The best method would be to conduct an experiment where one randomly assigns subjects to the treatment groups. Then, any difference between the two groups of Ss on the dependent variable is considered to be caused by the difference in the independent variable since both groups are considered to be comparable in all respects except that one group has, *a priori*, been exposed to or afflicted with the independent variable while the other group has not.

The following example illustrates the difficulty in identifying and isolating the single factor responsible for a particular behavior. Let us assume that six children in the Jones family went to the circus. Let us further assume that three of the children went with Mr. Jones and three went with Mrs. Jones. When the children came home from the circus, the three who went with Mrs. Jones said they didn't feel well. The next morning, the three children were very ill. When the doctor arrived, he asked Mr. and Mrs. Jones as well as the children a number of questions. He learned that each of the three ill children had a chocolate sundae. The other three children (those who went with Mr. Jones and were *not* ill) did not have a chocolate sundae. From the questions asked, the doctor ascertained that this was the only difference between the two groups of children—they went on the same bus, on the same rides, and to the same sideshows. Hence, the one known difference between the two groups of children (healthy and sick) was that only the sick children had had a chocolate sundae. Using the ex-post-facto approach, one might be apt to conclude, as did the doctor, that it was the chocolate sundae and only the chocolate sundae that caused the illness.[10] This is a plausible explanation and may well be correct. But need it be? Not necessarily! Another explanation might be that this reflects a self-selection factor (lack of randomization of subjects to treatments). Perhaps the three children who were with Mrs. Jones purposely chose to go with their mother because of their predisposition to nausea and their knowledge of their mother's greater nurturance.

As was mentioned earlier, the ex-post-facto method differs from the experimental method in that in a "true" experiment, the researcher can manipulate the treatment, and has the power (ability) to employ randomization procedures in the selection of his subjects and/or assignment of treatments. Because of this, it is *possible* for a researcher studying the chocolate sundae illness in a "true" experimental fashion to take into consideration some or many of the factors that make interpretation tenuous when an ex-post-facto study is

---

[10]If we were to conduct an experiment, eating or not eating the chocolate sundae would be the *independent* variable and the illness would be the *dependent* variable.

conducted. In other words, we do not mean to imply that the problems encountered by the doctor in arriving at a definitive decision (was it the sundae only or a combination of the sundae with some other factor(s) that caused the illness) would not also be present if one were to conduct an experiment. Rather, we are saying that in an experiment the researcher could have done something about some of the factors that make interpretation difficult. For example, he could have decided *a priori* which of the three children would accompany Mr. Jones and which three would go with Mrs. Jones. The researcher has the power to determine whether it was Mr. or Mrs. Jones' group that would receive the treatment. Also, if the experimenter felt that it was a combination of, say, overexhaustion and the sundae that caused the illness, he could have controlled the degree of exhaustion in the study.

At this point, the reader should not interpret some of the weaknesses in the ex-post-facto method as reason(s) for avoiding this type of research. It is true that the ex-post-facto researcher does not have as much control as the researcher engaged in experimental research, but there are still some controls that the ex-post-facto researcher can exercise in a post-hoc fashion. However, because his controls are after-the-fact, he is more restricted as to what he can and cannot do. Hence, his conclusions may not be as definitive as those reached by the experimentalist. Kerlinger says, "Where one must be careful with experimental results and interpretations, one must be doubly careful with ex post facto results and interpretations."[11]

Some Specific Questions To Be Asked When Reading Ex-Post-Facto Research Studies

Heretofore, we have considered some of the most important limitations of the ex-post-facto method that should and must be considered by both the producer and the consumer of research. In the light of these limitations, here are some questions that both doers and readers of research must consider.

1. How are the subjects classified? Are the criteria for classification clearly and concisely described? Are the classifications such that they will permit one to deduce (or will they demonstrate) similarities, differences, and relationships?
2. How comparable were the groups on extraneous variables? (Note: We did not say *identical*—why?) If the groups were not comparable, what effect might this have on the findings? Did the researcher state the lack of comparability as a limitation of his study?
3. Did the researcher clearly describe his sample (or population) if a sample was used? If a sample was used, how were the Ss selected?

[11]Fred N. Kerlinger, *Foundations of Behavioral Research* (2d ed.). New York: Holt, Rinehart and Winston, 1973, p. 392.

4. Has the researcher *really* attempted to probe for and did he demonstrate causal relationships or is the study purely descriptive and conjectural?
5. What extraneous factors, if any, might have influenced the outcome of the study? Did the researcher attempt to control for these factors? How? If not, should he have controlled for them? Which ones should he have controlled? Why?
6. Were any "leads" turned up in the study that might be the basis for an experimental study? If so, what were some of these "leads"?
7. Did the researcher exercise care and judiciousness in his interpretation of the findings? If not, where did he err? Were any alternative hypotheses advanced? Should any have been generated?

In conclusion, the writers strongly urge you, the reader, regardless of whether you are a user or producer of research, not to be hypercritical (that is, to avoid "nit-picking") and eager to condemn the ex-post-facto method. As mentioned earlier, there are certain types of problems that can be studied only by this method. Also, it is of great importance to do ex-post-facto research if for no other reason than to obtain "leads" for future experimental research. Without a doubt, research in the social sciences can benefit greatly by using a combination of *both* experimental and ex-post-facto methods.

Examples of Ex-Post-Facto Research

Selections 16–20 all use the ex-post-facto method but study different types of problems. As you read each article, consider the specific questions raised above as well as the general questions raised in Chapter I.

META-ANALYSIS OF PSYCHOTHERAPY OUTCOME STUDIES*

MARY LEE SMITH
GENE V. GLASS

ABSTRACT: Results of nearly 400 controlled evaluations of psychotherapy and counseling were coded and integrated statistically. The findings provide convincing evidence of the efficacy of psychotherapy. On the average, the typical therapy client is better off than 75 percent of untreated individuals. Few important differences in effectiveness could be established among many quite different types of psychotherapy. More generally, virtually no difference in effectiveness was observed between the class of all behavioral therapies (systematic desensitization, behavior modification) and the nonbehavioral therapies (Rogerian, psychodynamic, rational-emotive, transactional analysis, etc.).

Scholars and clinicians have argued bitterly for decades about the efficacy of psychotherapy and counseling. Michael Scriven proposed to the American Psychological Association's Ethics Committee that APA-member clinicians be required to present a card to prospective clients on which it would be explained that the procedure they were about to undergo had never been proven superior to a placebo ("Psychotherapy Caveat," 1974). Most academics have read little more than Eysenck's (1952, 1965) tendentious diatribes in which he claimed to prove that 75 percent of neurotics got better regardless of whether or not they were in therapy—a conclusion based on the interpretation of six controlled studies. The perception that research shows the inefficacy of psychotherapy has become part of conventional wisdom even within the profession. The following testimony was recently presented before the Colorado State Legislature:

*From *American Psychologist*, 32:9 (1977), pp. 752–760. Copyright 1977 by the American Psychological Association. Reprinted by permission.

The research reported here was supported by a grant from the Spencer Foundation, Chicago, Illinois. This paper draws in part from the presidential address of the second author to the American Educational Research Association, San Francisco, April 21, 1976.

Requests for reprints should be sent to Gene V Glass, Laboratory of Educational Research, University of Colorado, Boulder, Colorado 80302.

Are they [the legislators] also aware of the relatively primitive state of the art of treatment outcome evaluation which is still, after fifty years, in kind of a virginal state? About all we've been able to prove is that a third of the people get better, a third of the people stay the same, and a third of the people get worse, irregardless of the treatment to which they are subjected. (Quoted by Ellis, 1977, p. 3)

Only close followers of the issue have read Bergin's (1971) astute dismantling of the Eysenck myth in his review of the findings of 23 controlled evaluations of therapy. Bergin found evidence that therapy is effective. Emrick (1975) reviewed 72 studies of the psychological and psychopharmacological treatment of alcoholism and concluded that evidence existed for the efficacy of therapy. Luborsky, Singer, and Luborsky (1975) reviewed about 40 controlled studies and found more evidence. Although these reviews were reassuring, two sources of doubt remained. First, the number of studies in which the effects of counseling and psychotherapy have been tested is closer to 400 than to 40. How representative the 40 are of the 400 is unknown. Second, in these reviews, the "voting method" was used; that is, the number of studies with statistically significant results in favor of one treatment or another was tallied. This method is too weak to answer many important questions and is biased in favor of large-sample studies.

The purpose of the present research has three parts: (1) to identify and collect all studies that tested the effects of counseling and psychotherapy; (2) to determine the magnitude of effect of the therapy in each study; and (3) to compare the effects of different types of therapy and relate the size of effect to the characteristics of the therapy (e.g., diagnosis of patient, training of therapist) and of the study. Metaanalysis, the integration of research through statistical analysis of the analyses of individual studies (Glass, 1976), was used to investigate the problem.

Procedures

Standard search procedures were used to identify 1,000 documents: *Psychological Abstracts, Dissertation Abstracts,* and branching off of bibliographies of the documents themselves. Of those documents located, approximately 500 were selected for inclusion in the study, and 375 were fully analyzed. To be selected, a study had to have at least one therapy treatment group compared to an untreated group or to a different therapy group. The rigor of the research design was not a selection criterion but was one of several features of the individual study to be related to the effect of the treatment in that study. The definition of psychotherapy used to select the studies was presented by Meltzoff and Kornreich (1970):

> Psychotherapy is taken to mean the informed and planful application of techniques derived from established psychological principles, by persons qualified through training and experience to understand these principles and to apply these techniques with the intention of assisting individuals to modify such personal characteristics as feelings, values, attitudes, and behaviors which are judged by the therapist to be maladaptive or maladjustive. (p. 6)

Those studies in which the treatment was labeled "counseling" but whose methods fit the above definition were included. Drug therapies, hypnotherapy, bibliotherapy, occupational therapy, milieu therapy, and peer counseling were excluded. Sensitivity training, marathon encounter groups, consciousness-raising groups, and psychodrama were also excluded. Those studies that Bergin and Luborsky eliminated because they used "analogue" therapy were retained for the present research. Such studies have been designated analogue studies because therapy lasted only a few hours or the therapists were relatively untrained. Rather than arbitrarily eliminating large numbers of studies and losing potentially valuable information, it was deemed perferable to retain these studies and investigate the relationship between length of therapy, training of therapists, and other characteristics of the study and their measured effects. The arbitrary elimination of such analogue studies was based on an implicit assumption that they differ not only in their methods but also in their effects and how those effects are achieved. Considering methods, analogue studies fade imperceptibly into "real" therapy, since the latter is often short term, or practiced by relative novices, etc. Furthermore, the magnitude of effects and their relationships with other variables are empirical questions, not to be assumed out of existence. Dissertations and fugitive documents were likewise retained, and the measured effects of the studies compared according to the source of the studies.

The most important feature of an outcome study was the magnitude of the effect of therapy. The definition of the magnitude of effect—or *"effect size"*—was the *mean difference between the treated and control subjects divided by the standard deviation of the control group*, that is, $ES = (\bar{X}_T - \bar{X}_C)/s_C$. Thus, an "effect size" of $+1$ indicates that a person at the mean of the control group would be expected to rise to the 84th percentile of the control group after treatment.

The effect size was calculated on any outcome variable the researcher chose to measure. In many cases, one study yielded more than one effect size, since effects might be measured at more than one time after treatment or on more than one different type of outcome variable. The effect-size measures represent different types of outcomes: self-esteem, anxiety, work/school achievement, physiological stress, etc. Mixing different outcomes together is defensible. First, it is clear that all outcome measures are more or less related to "well-being" and so at a general level are comparable. Second, it is easy to imagine a Senator conducting hearings on the NIMH appropriations or a college president deciding whether to continue funding the counseling center asking, "What kind of effect does therapy produce—on anything?" Third, each primary researcher made value judgments concerning the definition and direction of positive therapeutic effects for the particular clients he or she studied. It is reasonable to adopt these value judgments and aggregate them in the present study. Fourth, since all effect sizes are identified by type of outcome, the magnitude of effect can be compared across type of outcome to determine whether therapy has greater effect on anxiety, for example, than it does on self-esteem.

Calculating effect sizes was straightforward when means and standard deviations were reported. Although this information is thought to be fundamental in reporting research, it was often overlooked by authors and editors. When means and standard deviations were not reported, effect sizes were obtained by the solution of equations from t and F ratios or other inferential test statistics. Probit transformations were used to convert to effect sizes the percentages of patients who improved (Glass, in press). Original data were requested from several authors when effect sizes could not be derived from any reported information. In two instances, effect sizes were impossible to reconstruct: (a) nonparametric statistics irretrievably disguise effect sizes, and (b) the reporting of no data except the alpha level at which a mean difference was significant gives no clue other than that the standardized mean difference must exceed some known value.

Eight hundred thirty-three effect sizes were computed from 375 studies, several studies yielding effects on more than one type of outcome or at more than one time after therapy. Including more than one effect size for each study perhaps introduces dependence in the errors and violates some assumptions of inferential statistics. However, the loss of information that would have resulted from averaging effects across types of outcome or at different follow-up points was too great a price to pay for statistical purity.

The effect sizes of the separate studies became the "dependent variable" in the metaanalysis. The "independent variables" were 16 features of the study described or measured in the following ways:

1. The type of therapy employed, for example, psychodynamic, client centered, rational-emotive, behavior modification, etc. There were 10 types in all; each will be mentioned in the Results section.

2. The duration of therapy in hours.

3. Whether it was group or individual therapy.

4. The number of years' experience of the therapist.

5. Whether clients were neurotics or psychotics.

6. The age of the clients.

7. The IQ of the clients.

8. The source of the subjects—whether solicited for the study, committed to an institution, or sought treatment themselves.

9. Whether the therapists were trained in education, psychology, or psychiatry.

10. The social and ethnic similarity of therapists and clients.

11. The type of outcome measure taken.

12. The number of months after therapy that the outcomes were measured.

13. The reactivity or "fakeability" of the outcome measure.

14. The date of publication of the study.

15. The form of publication.

16. The internal validity of the research design.

Definitions and conventions were developed to increase the reliability of measurement of the features of the studies and to assist the authors in estimating the data when they were not reported. The more important conventions appear in Table 1. Variables not mentioned in Table 1 were measured in fairly obvious ways. The reliability of measurement was determined by comparing the codings of 20 studies by the two authors and four assistants. Agreement exceeded 90 percent across all categories.[1]

Analysis of the data comprised four parts: (1) descriptive statistics for the body of data as a whole; (2) descriptive statistics for the comparison of therapy types and outcome types; (3) descriptive statistics for a subset of studies in which behavioral and nonbehavioral therapies were compared *in the same study;* and (4) regression analyses in which effect sizes were regressed onto variables descriptive of the study.

Findings

DATA FROM ALL EXPERIMENTS

Figure 1 contains the findings at the highest level of aggregation. The two curves depict the average treated and untreated groups of clients across 375 studies, 833 effect-size measures, representing an evaluation of approximately 25,000 control and experimental subjects each. On the average, clients 22 years of age received 17 hours of therapy from therapists with about 3½ years of experience and were measured on the outcome variables about 3¾ months after the therapy.

---

[1]The values assigned to the features of the studies, the effect sizes, and all procedures are available in Glass, Smith, and Miller. (Glass, G. V., Smith, M. L., & Miller, T. I. *The benefits of psychotherapy.* Book in preparation, 1977)

CONVENTIONS FOR MEASUREMENT OF THE FEATURES OF STUDIES

table 1 _____

STUDY FEATURE	VALUE
Experience of therapist (when not given)	Lay counselor (0 years) MA candidate (1 year) MA counselor (2 years) PhD candidate or psychiatric resident (3 years) PhD therapist (4 years) Well-known PhD or psychiatrist (5 years)
Diagnosis of client (neurotic or psychotic)	Neurotic unless symptoms or Labels clearly indicate otherwise.
IQ of client (low, average, high)	Average unless identified as otherwise by diagnostic labels (e.g., mentally retarded) or institutional affiliation (college attendance).
Source of subjects	Clients solicited for purpose of the study. Clients committed to institution, hence to therapy. Clients recognized existence of problem and sought treatment.
Similarity of therapist and client ("very similar" to "very dissimilar")	College students: very similar Neurotic adults: moderately similar Juveniles, minorities: moderately dissimilar Hospitalized, chronic adults, disturbed children, prisoners: very dissimilar
Type of outcome measure	Fear, anxiety: Spielberger & Cattell anxiety measures, behavioral approach tests. Self-esteem: inventories, self-ideal correlations, ratings by self and others. Adjustment: adjustment scales, improvement ratings, rehospitalization, time out of hospital, sobriety, symptomatic complaints, disruptive behavior.

STUDY FEATURE	VALUE	
	Work/school achievement: grade point average, job supervisor ratings, promotions. Personality traits: MMPI or other trait inventories, projective test results. Social behavior: dating, classroom discipline, public speaking, information-seeking behavior, sociometrics. Emotional-somatic disorder: frigidity, impotence. Physiological stress: galvanic skin response, Palmer Sweat Index, blood pressure, heart rate.	
Reactivity of measurement	1 (low):	Physiological measures; grade point average
	2	Projective device (blind); discharge from hospital (blind)
	3	Standardized measures of traits (MMPI, Rotter)
	4	Experimenter-constructed questionnaires; client's self-report to experimenter; discharge (nonblind); behavior in presence of therapist
	5 (high):	Therapist rating; projective device (nonblind)
Form of publication	Journal Book Thesis Unpublished document	
Internal validity (high, medium, low)	High: Randomization, low mortality Medium: More than one threat to internal validity Low: No matching of pretest information to equate groups	

figure 1

Effect of therapy on any outcome. (Data based on 375 studies; 833 data points.)

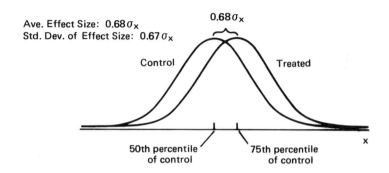

Ave. Effect Size: $0.68\,\sigma_x$
Std. Dev. of Effect Size: $0.67\,\sigma_x$

$0.68\,\sigma_x$

Control

Treated

50th percentile of control

75th percentile of control

x

For ease of representation, the figure is drawn in the form of two normal distributions. No conclusion about the distributions of the scores within studies is intended. In most studies, no information was given about the shape of an individual's scores within treated and untreated groups. We suspect that normality has as much justification as any other form.

The average study showed a .68 standard deviation superiority of the treated group over the control group. Thus, the average client receiving therapy was better off than 75 percent of the untreated controls. Ironically, the 75 percent figure that Eysenck used repeatedly to embarrass psychotherapy appears in a slightly different context as the most defensible figure on the efficacy of therapy: The therapies represented by the available outcome evaluations move the average client from the 50th to the 75th percentile.

The standard deviation of the effect sizes is .67. Their skewness is +.99. Only 12 percent of the 833 effect-size measures from the 375 studies were negative. If therapies of any type were ineffective and design and measurement flaws were immaterial, one would expect half the effect-size measures to be negative.

The 833 effect-size measures were classified into 10 categories descriptive of the type of outcome being assessed, for example, fear and anxiety reduction, self-esteem, adjustment (freedom from debilitating symptoms), achievement in school or on the job, social relations, emotional-somatic problems, physiological stress measures, etc. Effect-size measures for four outcome categories are presented in Table 2.

Two hundred sixty-one effect sizes from over 100 studies average about 1 standard deviation on measures of fear and anxiety reduction. Thus, the average treated client is better off than 83 percent of those untreated with respect to the alleviation of fear and anxiety. The improvement in self-esteem is

EFFECTS OF THERAPY ON FOUR TYPES OF OUTCOME MEASURE

table 2

TYPE OF OUTCOME	AVERAGE EFFECT SIZE	NO. OF EFFECT SIZES	STANDARD ERROR OF MEAN EFFECT SIZE[a]	MDN TREATED PERSON'S PERCENTILE STATUS IN CONTROL GROUP
Fear-anxiety reduction	.97	261	.15	83
Self-esteem	.90	53	.13	82
Adjustment	.56	229	.05	71
School/work achievement	.31	145	.03	62

[a]The standard errors of the mean are calculated by dividing the standard deviation of the effect sizes (not reported) by the square root of the number of them. This method, based on the assumption of independence known to be false, gives a lower bound to the standard errors (Tukey, J. W. Personal communication, November 15, 1976.) Inferential techniques employing Tukey's jackknife method which take the nonindependence into account are examined in Glass (in press).

nearly as large. The effect sizes average .9 of a standard deviation. Improvement on variables in the "adjustment" outcome class averages considerably less, roughly .6 of a standard deviation. These outcome variables are measures of personal functioning and frequently involve indices of hospitalization or incarceration for psychotic, alcoholic, or criminal episodes. The average effect size for school or work achievement—most frequently "grade point average"—is smallest of the four outcome classes.

The studies in the four outcome measure categories are not comparable in terms of type of therapy, duration, experience of therapists, number of months posttherapy at which outcomes were measured, etc. Nonetheless, the findings in Table 2 are fairly consistent with expectations and give the credible impression that fear and self-esteem are more susceptible to change in therapy than are the relatively more serious behaviors grouped under the categories "adjustment" and "achievement."

Table 3 presents the average effect sizes for 10 types of therapy. Nearly 100 effect-size measures arising from evaluations of psychodynamic therapy, that is, Freudianlike therapy but *not* psychoanalysis, average approximately .6 of a standard deviation. Studies of Adlerian therapy show an average of .7 sigma, but only 16 effect sizes were found. Eclectic therapies, that is, verbal, cognitive, nonbehavioral therapies more similar to psychodynamic therapies than any other type, gave a mean effect size of about .5 of a standard deviation.

EFFECTS OF TEN TYPES OF THERAPY ON ANY OUTCOME MEASURE

table 3

TYPE OF THERAPY	AVERAGE EFFECT SIZE	NO. OF EFFECT SIZES	STANDARD ERROR OF MEAN EFFECT SIZE	MDN TREATED PERSON'S PERCENTILE STATUS IN CONTROL GROUP
Psychodynamic	.59	96	.05	72
Adlerian	.71	16	.19	76
Eclectic	.48	70	.07	68
Transactional analysis	.58	25	.19	72
Rational-emotive	.77	35	.13	78
Gestalt	.26	8	.09	60
Client-centered	.63	94	.08	74
Systematic desensitization	.91	223	.05	82
Implosion	.64	45	.09	74
Behavior modification	.76	132	.06	78

Although the number of controlled evaluations of Berne's transactional analysis was rather small, it gave a respectable average effect size of .6 sigma, the same as psychodynamic therapies. Albert Ellis's rational-emotive therapy, with a mean effect size of nearly .8 of a standard deviation, finished second among all 10 therapy types. The Gestalt therapies were relatively untested, but 8 studies showed 16 effect sizes averaging only .25 of a standard deviation. Rogerian client-centered therapy showed a .6 sigma effect size averaged across about 60 studies. The average of over 200 effect-size measures from approximately 100 studies of systematic desensitization therapy was .9 sigma, the largest average effect size of all therapy types. Implosive therapy showed a mean effect size of .64 of a standard deviation, about equal to that for Rogerian and psychodynamic therapies. Significantly, the average effect size for implosive therapy is markedly lower than that for systematic desensitization, which was usually evaluated in studies using similar kinds of clients with similar problems—principally, simple phobias. The final therapy depicted in Table 3 is Skinnerian behavior modification, which showed a .75 sigma effect size.

Hay's ω^2, which relates the categorical variable "type of therapy" to the quantitative variable "effect size," has the value of .10 for the data in Table 3. Thus, these 10 therapy types account for 10 percent of the variance in the effect size that studies produce.

The types of therapy depicted in Table 3 were clearly not equated for duration, severity of problem, type of outcome, etc. Nonetheless, the differences in average effect sizes are interesting and interpretable. There is probably a tendency for researchers to evaluate the therapy they like best and to pick clients, circumstances, and outcome measures which show that therapy in the best light. Even so, major differences among the therapies appear. Implosive therapy is demonstrably inferior to systematic desensitization. Behavior modification shows the same mean effect size as rational-emotive therapy.

EFFECTS OF CLASSES OF THERAPY

To compare the effect of therapy type after equating for duration of therapy, diagnosis of client, type of outcome, etc., it was necessary to move to a coarser level of analysis in which data could be grouped into more stable composites. The problem was to group the 10 types of therapy into classes, so that effect sizes could be compared among more general types of therapy. Methods of multidimensional scaling were used to derive a structure from the perceptions of similarities among the 10 therapies by a group of 25 clinicians and counselors. All of the judges in this scaling study were enrolled in a graduate-level seminar. For five weeks, the theory and techniques of the 10 therapies were studied and discussed. Then, each judge performed a multidimensional rank ordering of the therapies, judging similarity among them on whatever basis he or she chose, articulated or unarticulated, conscious or un-

figure 2 ────────────────────────────

Multidimensional scaling of 10 therapies by 25 clinicians and counselors.

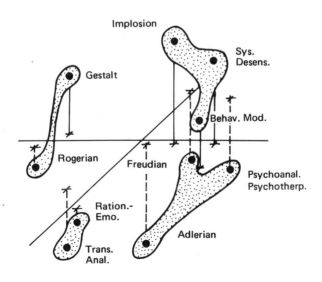

conscious. The results of the Shepard-Kruskal multidimensional scaling analysis appear as Figure 2.

In Figure 2 one clearly sees four classes of therapies: the ego therapies (transactional analysis and rational-emotive therapy) in front; the three dynamic therapies low, in the background; the behavioral triad, upper right; and the pair of "humanistic" therapies, Gestalt and Rogerian. The average effect sizes among the four classes of therapies have been compared, but the findings are not reported here. Instead, a higher level of aggregation of the therapies, called "superclasses," was studied. The first superclass was formed from those therapies above the horizontal plane in Figure 2, with the exception of Gestalt therapy for which there was an inadequate number of studies. This superclass was then identical with the group of behavioral therapies: implosion, systematic desensitization, and behavior modification. The second superclass comprises the six therapies below the horizontal plane in Figure 2 and is termed the *nonbehavioral superclass*, a composite of psychoanalytic psychotherapy, Adlerian, Rogerian, rational-emotive, eclectic therapy, and transactional analysis.

Figure 3 represents the mean effect sizes for studies classified by the two superclasses. On the average, approximately 200 evaluations of behavioral therapies showed a mean effect of about $.8\sigma_x$, standard error of .03, over the control group. Approximately 170 evaluations of nonbehavioral studies gave a mean effect size of $.6\sigma_x$, standard error of .04. This small difference ($.2\sigma_x$) between the outcomes of behavioral and nonbehavioral therapies must be considered in light of the circumstances under which these studies were con-

figure 3 _____

Effect of Superclass #1 (behavioral) and Superclass #2 (non-behavioral)

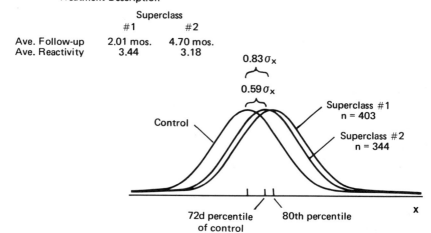

	Treatment Description	
	Superclass	
	#1	#2
Ave. Follow-up	2.01 mos.	4.70 mos.
Ave. Reactivity	3.44	3.18

$0.83\sigma_x$

$0.59\sigma_x$

Control

Superclass #1
n = 403

Superclass #2
n = 344

x

72d percentile   80th percentile
of control

ducted. The evaluators of behavioral superclass therapies waited an average of 2 months after the therapy to measure its effects, whereas the postassessment of the nonbehavioral therapies was made in the vicinity of 5 months, on the average. Furthermore, the reactivity or susceptibility to bias of the outcome measures was higher for the behavioral superclass than for the nonbehavioral superclass; that is, the behavioral researchers showed a slightly greater tendency to rely on more subjective outcome measures. These differences lead one to suspect that the $.2\sigma_x$ difference between the behavioral and nonbehavioral superclasses is somewhat exaggerated in favor of the behavioral superclass. Exactly how much the difference ought to be reduced is a question that can be approached in at least two ways: (1) examine the behavioral versus nonbehavioral difference for only those studies in which one therapy from each superclass was represented, since for those studies the experimental circumstances will be equivalent; (2) regress "effect size" onto variables descriptive of the study and correct statistically for differences in circumstances between behavioral and nonbehavioral studies.

Figure 4 represents 120 effect-size measures derived from those studies, approximately 50 in number, in which a behavioral therapy and nonbehavioral therapy were compared simultaneously with an untreated control. Hence, for these studies, the collective behavioral and nonbehavioral therapies are equivalent with respect to all important features of the experimental setting, namely, experience of the therapists, nature of the clients' problems, duration of therapy, type of outcome measure, months after therapy for measuring the outcomes, etc.

The results are provocative. The $.2\sigma_x$ "uncontrolled" difference in

figure 4 ————————————————————

Effect of Superclass #1 (behavioral) and Superclass #2 (nonbehavioral). (Data drawn only from experiments in which Superclass #1 and Superclass #2 were simultaneously compared with control.)

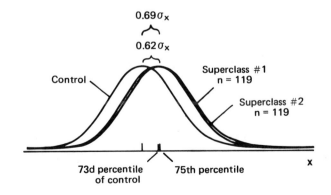

Figure 3 has shrunk to a $.07\sigma_x$ difference in average effect size. The standard error of the mean of the 119 different scores (behavioral effect size minus nonbehavioral effect size in each study) is $.66/\sqrt{119} = .06$. The behavioral and nonbehavioral therapies show about the same average effect.

The second approach to correcting for measurable differences between behavioral and nonbehavioral therapies is statistical adjustment by regression analysis. By this method, it is possible to quantify and study the natural covariation among the principal outcome variable of studies and the many variables descriptive of the context of the studies.

Eleven features of each study were correlated with the effect size the study produced (Table 4). For example, the correlation between the duration of the therapy in hours and the effect size of the study is nearly zero, $-.02$. The correlations are generally low, although several are reliably nonzero. Some of the more interesting correlations show a positive relationship between an estimate of the intelligence of the group of clients and the effect of therapy, and a somewhat larger correlation indicating that therapists who resemble their clients in ethnic group, age, and social level get better results. The effect sizes diminish across time after therapy as shown by the last correlation in Table 4, a correlation of $-.10$ which is closer to $-.20$ when the curvilinearity of the

CORRELATIONS OF SEVERAL DESCRIPTIVE VARIABLES WITH EFFECT SIZE

table 4

VARIABLE	CORRELATION WITH EFFECT SIZE
Organization (1 = individual; 2 = group)	$-.07$
Duration of therapy (in hours)	$-.02$
Years' experience of therapists	$-.01$
Diagnosis of clients (1 = psychotic; 2 = neurotic)	$.02$
IQ of clients (1 = low; 2 = medium; 3 = high)	$.15^{**}$
Age of clients	$.02$
Similarity of therapists and clients (1 = very similar; . . . ; 4 = very dissimilar)	$-.19^{**}$
Internal validity of study (1 = high; 2 = medium; 3 = low)	$-.09^{*}$
Date of publication	$.09^{*}$
"Reactivity" of outcome measure (1 = low; . . . ; 5 = high)	$.30^{**}$
No. of months posttherapy for follow-up	$-.10^{*}$

$^{*}p < .05.$
$^{**}p < .01.$

relationship is taken into account. The largest correlation is with the "reactivity" or subjectivity of the outcome measure.

The multiple correlation of these variables with effect size is about .50. Thus, 25 percent of the variance in the results of studies can be reduced by specification of independent variable values. In several important subsets of the data not reported here, the multiple correlations are over .70, which indicates that in some instances it is possible to reduce more than half of the variability in study findings by regressing the outcome effect onto contextual variables of the study.

The results of three separate multiple regression analyses appear in Table 5. Multiple regressions were performed within each of three types of therapy: psychodynamic, systematic desensitization, and behavior modification. Relatively complex forms of the independent variables were used to account for interactions and nonlinear relationships. For example, years' experience of the therapist bore a slight curvilinear relationship with outcome, probably because more experienced therapists worked with more seriously ill clients. This situation was accommodated by entering, as an independent variable, "therapist experience" in interaction with "diagnosis of the client." Age of client and follow-up date were slightly curvilinearly related to outcome in ways

REGRESSION ANALYSES WITHIN THERAPIES

table 5

	UNSTANDARDIZED REGRESSION COEFFICIENTS		
INDEPENDENT VARIABLE	Psychodynamic (n = 94)	Systematic Desensitization (n = 212)	Behavior (n = 129)
Diagnosis (1 = psychotic; 2 = neurotic)	.174	−.193	.041
Intelligence (1 = low; . . . ; 3 = high)	−.114	.201	.201
Transformed age[a]	.002	−.002	.002
Experience of Therapist × Neurotic	−.011	−.034	−.018
Experience of Therapist × Psychotic	−.015	.004	−.033
Clients self-presented	−.111	.287	−.015
Clients solicited	.182	.088	−.163
Organization (1 = individual; 2 = group)	.108	−.086	−.276
Transformed months posttherapy[b]	−.031	−.047	.007
Transformed reactivity of measure[c]	.003	.025	.021
Additive constant	.757	.489	.453
Multiple R	.423	.512	.509
s_e	.173	.386	.340

[a]Transformed age = $(\text{Age} - 25)(|\text{Age} - 25|)^{1/2}$
[b]Transformed months posttherapy = $(\text{No. months})^{1/2}$
[c]Transformed reactivity of measure = $(\text{Reactivity})^{2.25}$

most directly handled by changing exponents. These regression equations allow estimation of the effect size a study shows when undertaken with a certain type of client, with a therapist of a certain level of experience, etc. By setting the independent variables at a particular set of values, one can estimate what a study of that type would reveal under each of the three types of therapy. Thus, a statistically controlled comparison of the effects of psychodynamic, systematic desensitization, and behavior modification therapies can be obtained in this case. The three regression equations are clearly not homogeneous; hence, one therapy might be superior under one set of circumstances and a different therapy superior under others. A full description of the nature of this interaction is elusive, though one can illustrate it at various particularly interesting points.

In Figure 5, estimates are made of the effect sizes that would be shown for studies in which simple phobias of high-intelligence subjects, 20 years of age, are treated by a therapist with 2 years' experience and evaluated immediately after therapy with highly subjective outcome measures. This verbal description of circumstances can be translated into quantitative values for the independent variables in Table 5 and substituted into each of the three regression equations. In this instance, the two behavioral therapies show effects superior to the psychodynamic therapy.

In Figure 6, a second prototypical psychotherapy client and situation are captured in the independent variable values, and the effects of the three types of therapy are estimated. For the typical 30-year-old neurotic of average IQ seen in circumstances like those that prevail in mental health clinics (individual therapy by a therapist with 5 years' experience), behavior modification is estimated to be superior to psychodynamic therapy, which is in turn superior to systematic desensitization at the 6-month follow-up point.

figure 5 _____

Three within-therapy regression equations set to describe a prototypic therapy client (neurotic) and therapy situation.

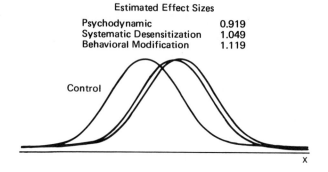

Estimated Effect Sizes

Psychodynamic	0.919
Systematic Desensitization	1.049
Behavioral Modification	1.119

Control

figure 6 _____

Three within-therapy regression equations set to describe a prototypic therapy client (phobic) and therapy situation.

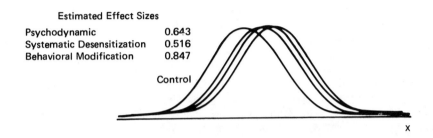

Estimated Effect Sizes

Psychodynamic	0.643
Systematic Desensitization	0.516
Behavioral Modification	0.847

Control

X

Besides illuminating the relationships in the data, the quantitative techniques described here can give direction to future research. By fitting regression equations to the relationship between effect size and the independent variables descriptive of the studies and then by placing confidence regions around these hyperplanes, the regions where the input-output relationships are most poorly determined can be identified. By concentrating new studies in these regions, one can avoid the accumulation of redundant studies of convenience that overelaborate small areas.

Conclusions

The results of research demonstrate the beneficial effects of counseling and psychotherapy. Despite volumes devoted to the theoretical differences among different schools of psychotherapy, the results of research demonstrate negligible differences in the effects produced by different therapy types. Unconditional judgments of superiority of one type or another of psychotherapy, and all that these claims imply about treatment and training policy, are unjustified. Scholars and clinicians are in the rather embarrassing position of knowing less than has been proven, because knowledge, atomized and sprayed across a vast landscape of journals, books, and reports, has not been accessible. Extracting knowledge from accumulated studies is a complex and important methodological problem which deserves further attention.

references _____

Bergin, A. E. The evaluation of therapeutic outcomes. In A. E. Bergin & S. L. Garfield (Eds.), *Handbook of psychotherapy and behavior change.* New York: Wiley, 1971.

Ellis, R. H. Letters. *Colorado Psychological Association Newsletter*, April 1977, p. 3.

Emrick, C. D. A review of psychologically oriented treatment of alcoholism. *Journal of Studies of Alcohol*, 1975, *36*, 88–108.

Eysenck, H. J. The effects of psychotherapy: An evaluation. *Journal of Consulting Psychology*, 1952, *16*, 319–324.

Eysenck, H. J. The effects of psychotherapy. *Journal of Psychology*, 1965, *1*, 97–118.

Glass, G. V. Primary, secondary, and meta-analysis of research. *The Educational Researcher*, 1976, *10*, 3–8.

Glass, G. V. Integrating findings: The meta-analysis of research. *Review of Research in Education*, in press.

Luborsky, L., Singer, B., & Luborsky, L. Comparative studies of psychotherapies. *Archives of General Psychiatry*, 1975, *32*, 995–1008.

Meltzoff, J., & Kornreich, M. *Research in psychotherapy.* New York: Atherton, 1970.

Psychotherapy caveat. *APA Monitor*, December 1974, p. 7.

comments and questions _____

1.   Meta-Analysis is a new approach to data analysis. We think that it has a great deal of promise. It is definitely more informative than the typical review of literature. We urge you to read Glass (1976) referenced at the end of this article.

2.   Do you agree that this article be classified under ex-post-facto research? If not, where would you classify it and why?

3.   Does the statement "an effect size of +1 indicates that a person at the mean of the control group would be expected to rise to the 84th percentile. . . " assume anything regarding the shape of the distribution?

4.   Discuss the analogy "analysis: *T*-test as Meta-Analysis: *F*-test."

5.   Is there any bias in the findings given the procedure for identifying the documents? Discuss.

6.   Given a correlation of −.09 between internal validity of the study and "effect size" (see Table 4), what implications, if any, can be drawn with respect to the importance of rigor in research?

7.   It is readily obvious that Smith and Glass' task was time consuming and complex. Would you agree with us that the scholarly contribution warrants such efforts? Explain.

THE AFFECTIVE AND COGNITIVE CONSEQUENCES OF AN OPEN EDUCATION ELEMENTARY SCHOOL[*,1]

17

ROBERT J. WRIGHT

One hundred fifth grade children, enrolled in one of two suburban elementary schools (one traditionally organized and the other with an open orientation), were used to compare various pupil outcome dimensions in two different educational environments. Subjects used in this ex post facto study were balanced with respect to several dimensions of socioeconomic status, ability, and previous achievement prior to assignment to one of the two groups. Differences in school environments were quantified using two instruments. After two and one half years, overall differences were found between the two on several achievement variables. No differences were noted with respect to three measures of personality and three measures of cognition.

In this country today there is an educational trend toward a less structured, more child-oriented, type of curriculum. A variety of names have been applied to this general movement. The term which seems to have become most commonly associated with this trend in both the popular and professional literature is "open education" (Walberg, 1971).

While a large body of literature has recently evolved which describes open educational practices (Bartel, 1972), little has been published describing the overall effect that these programs have on children. Friedlander (1965) proposes that caution must be used with educational innovations lest they become universally accepted as a new orthodoxy without detailed and firm evidence that they can fulfill the expectations for improvement held for them. Walberg and Thomas (1972) noted in reference to the growing move toward open schools, "There has been very little research and evaluation on Open Education, aside from the testimonials by exponents and reporters."

*From *American Educational Research Journal,* 12:4 (1975), pp. 449–465. Copyright 1975, American Educational Research Association, Washington, D.C.

[1] Data for this study were collected as part of a doctoral dissertation in the Department of General Educational Psychology, College of Education, Temple University.

This new movement has not been received with universal acceptance by either the parents who must send their children to an open school, or by all psychologists and educators. A critical review of the proposals of many of the most popular authors of texts proposing alternative educational programs has recently been published (Troost, 1973).

One of the ways for advocates of open education to be able to respond to their critics is to show systematic evidence concerning the effects of this model. Such efforts must go beyond the confines of standardized achievement tests. Teachers using an open education model are believed to hold goals for pupil growth which may be beyond the measurement scope of such tests (Plowden, 1967; Silberman, 1971). Consequently a thorough evaluation of an open program would need to measure dimensions of social-personal growth and cognitive development as well as the mastery of academic skills.

During the past ten years at least three major studies have been reported which have attempted to isolate specific pupil outcomes on a wide range of personality, cognitive and achievement variables which were influenced by teaching style or school environment. Robert Spaulding (1965) used a sample of teachers and pupils from twenty-one fourth and sixth grade classes selected from an upper middle class school district near San Francisco. This study reported the inter-relationships among achievement, creativity, pupil self-concept and teacher-pupil transactions. Robert Soar (1966) in a two-year study of 57 third, fourth, fifth and sixth grade classes studied the relationships among psychological and behavioral teacher variables, and the achievement, anxiety, dependency, and creativity of their students.

A more recently reported study by Patricia Minuchin and her co-workers (Minuchin, Biber, Shapiro & Zimiles, 1969) went beyond the familiar design which uses classroom teachers' variables as the only salient issue in determining the classroom environment.

These three studies, and the general literature of open education, suggest several pupil outcome variables which may be differentially effected by a shift in the school environment from a more traditional structure to an open education approach. One such area involves the various dimensions of academic achievement in the skill oriented subject areas. Others include cognitive variables such as creativity and cognitive development. Several pupil personality factors have also been demonstrated to be potentially sensitive to modifications in the educational environment. Three such personality constructs which may be influenced by the school environment include self-esteem, locus of control, and school related anxiety.

This study was undertaken to investigate the impact upon pupils of one open school program with respect to several dimensions of achievement, cognition, and personality development.

Method

SCHOOLS

Two suburban elementary schools which are located in the same school district and are only two miles apart were used in this study. One of these schools which was opened in the fall of 1970 was designed as an open architecture school. All the teachers who staff this school were volunteers. Prior to the opening of this school the administration of the school district made a commitment to the development of the faculty of the open school. During the summer prior to the opening of this school the district conducted a six day inservice training session for these teachers. Five more days of inservice training were scheduled during the first year of operation. During each summer since the informally organized school opened, the school district has provided an additional week of inservice training for the teachers of this school.

The open school was designed with three learning areas, "pods," within which as many as ten professional and paraprofessional staff members work with about 200 children. As there are no walls or partitions within the pods, teachers and children can be seen working together in small clusters around the pod as well as in many other areas of the school. For more than half of the school day children of the open school work together in family groups which include children of all grade levels.

The second elementary school was opened in the fall of 1965 and represents a more traditional approach to education. The building is arranged with a series of hallways along which individual self-contained classrooms are located. Children are divided for instruction into the typical grade levels. At each grade level children are grouped by ability and achievement for instruction in subject disciplines such as reading and mathematics.

SUBJECTS

In 1970 when the informally organized school first opened, students were transferred to it from two nearby schools. Over ninety per cent of the students at this new school came from the traditional school included in this study. Assignment to the open school was done on a geographic basis. Parents were given no option as to which school their children would attend. In an effort to insure parental understanding of the program of the new school, the school district instituted a public relations effort even before that building was opened. A parents council was formed which served both in an advisory capacity with the school administration, and as a public relations vehicle with other parents. This parents council held evening meetings with the other parents of children who were scheduled to be transferred to the open school. After the school was in session they continued to hold periodic meetings with other parents to explain programs and answer questions. During the first three years this council gave parents guided tours of the school on a monthly basis.

Thus, for the most part the subjects used in this study attended classes together in a traditional school through the second grade. The educational experiences of the two groups of children became very different with the opening of the informally organized school in 1970. At that time the children used in this study were entering the third grade. This study focused on these two groups of children two and a half years later when they were enrolled in the fifth grade. The two samples included children who were enrolled in one of these two schools for a minimum of three years. Those children who transferred into either of the two schools within the last three years were not included.

School enrollment data were examined to determine if there were any differences between the two groups with respect to ability or self-reported socioeconomic characteristics. Small, but systematic differences in the levels of attained education of the parents of children of these two schools were found.

MEANS AND *F* RATIOS FOR THE DIMENSIONS OF ABILITY, AGE, NUMBER OF SIBLINGS, ACHIEVEMENT SCORES, AND ATTENDANCE FOR FIFTH GRADE STUDENTS USED IN THE TWO SAMPLES

table 1

DIMENSION	OPEN SCHOOL	TRADITIONAL SCHOOL	*F*[a] RATIO
Ability (IQ)	107.0	111.0	3.27
Age (as of 12/31/72 in months)	116.2	115.3	.79
Number of Siblings	2.0	2.0	.06
Stanford Achievement Test[a]			
Word Meaning	51.5	51.9	.00
Paragraph Meaning	53.6	51.6	.14
Vocabulary	60.1	57.8	.20
Spelling	44.6	40.2	.60
Word Skills	53.4	49.2	.54
Arithmetic Comprehension	54.0	50.1	.53
Arithmetic Concepts	52.8	50.1	.58
Social Studies and Science	53.2	52.5	.91
Attendance (number of days present)	172.1	171.9	.88

[a]Achievement scores are reported as normative percentiles.
[b]An *F* ratio of 3.91 with 1 and 100 degrees of freedom is significant at the .05 confidence level. Wilks lambda = .89 (F = .88; df = 12, 87)

The direction of these differences indicated higher levels among the parents of children in the traditional school.

In an effort to control this nonequivalency of the groups, subjects were selected for inclusion in this study by a pairwise matching technique which balanced the samples with respect to parental education. The resultant sample consisted of fifty pairs of subjects. This final sample was found to consist of thirty boys and twenty girls from the traditional school, and twenty-eight boys and twenty-two girls from the open school.

To test the equivalency of the two samples, prior to third grade, second grade attendance data, age, number of siblings, achievement test scores, and IQ, were examined. These twelve indices were tested by a two group multivariate T test. Table 1 presents the means and univariate F ratios for these twelve variables. None of these twelve indices were observed to be significantly different. The overall multivariate test was also found to be insignificant ($F = .88$, $df = 12; 87$).

SCHOOL ENVIRONMENT

To evaluate the differences of educational programs at the two schools, two instruments were selected, the teacher questionnaire Dimensions of Schooling (Traub, Weiss, Fisher & Mussella, 1972) and the Flanders Interaction Analysis (Amidon & Flanders, 1971).

The Dimensions of Schooling Questionnaire was administered to the teachers of the two schools a month before the study began. This instrument was specifically developed to elicit information about several aspects of school life hypothesized to be important in the implementation of open education programs. This instrument had an advantage over most teacher questionnaires in that it investigates the ongoing educational program in terms of specific, non-judgmental, operationally defined questions.

Overall differences between the faculties of the two schools on the total scores on the Dimensions of Schooling Questionnaire were analyzed by a univariate test. The maximum score on the Dimensions of Schooling Questionnaire is 30 and the minimum is zero. Higher scores indicate greater emphasis on "open approaches" to teaching. Table 2 presents a summary of this analysis. The mean scores (open school = 15.86, traditional school = 11.07) were found to be significantly different ($t = 3.46$, $df = 35$, $p < .01$). The direction of this difference indicates that teachers of the open school reported behaviors more congruent with open education than did teachers of the traditional school.

Classroom observations were conducted using the system developed by Flanders and his associates (Amidon & Flanders, 1971). This system is one of the most widely accepted classroom observational techniques, and its use has been well supported in the literature (Medley & Mitzel, 1963). The Flanders

**MEANS, STANDARD DEVIATIONS, AND UNIVARIATE *t* RATIO
FOR THE TOTAL RESPONSES OF THE OPEN AND TRADITIONAL
SCHOOL TEACHERS ON THE DIMENSIONS OF SCHOOLING QUESTIONNAIRE[a]**

table 2

	OPEN SCHOOL (N = 20)	TRADITIONAL SCHOOL (N = 17)
Mean	15.86	11.07
Standard Deviation	3.52	2.38

[a]*t* ratio = 3.46; *df* = 35; *p*<.01

system provided descriptive information regarding the teacher's verbal interactions with students.

Observations were carried out in the two schools at random times over a two week period in the fall of 1973. The interactions of eight teachers with their students in each school were recorded by the Flanders technique for three, twenty minute intervals. The eight teachers in each school were selected as being those who had the most contact with fifth grade children.

The difference in the proportion of observations in each category across the two schools were tested by a series of z tests. The results of these analyses are presented in Table 3. Of the ten observation categories, eight were found to differ significantly for the teachers of the two schools.

Thus, the results of the teacher questionnaire administered in the two

**PROPORTION OF RESPONSES AND RELATED SIGNIFICANCE TESTS
FOR OBSERVATIONS USING THE INTERACTION ANALYSIS
TECHNIQUE IN THE TRADITIONAL AND OPEN SCHOOL**

table 3

INTERACTION ANALYSIS CATEGORY	PROPORTION OF OBSERVATIONS			
	Open School	Traditional School	z Ratio	p
Accepts feelings	.0015	.0011	.89	ns
Praises or encourages	.0301	.0290	.45	ns
Accepts & uses ideas of students	.0307	.0204	6.83	<.01
Asks questions	.0940	.1164	−5.03	<.01
Lecturing	.1617	.3567	−30.76	<.01
Giving directions	.1331	.0610	16.72	<.01
Criticizing or justifying authority	.0148	.0252	−5.17	<.01
Student talk—response	.1078	.1449	−7.70	<.01
Student talk—initiation	.1141	.0727	9.81	<.01
Silence or confusion	.3059	.1726	21.48	<.01

schools, and of the observations made in the two schools, indicated that the two schools did differ significantly on these teacher controlled dimensions.

INSTRUMENTATION

School achievement was measured by the nine subtests of the Stanford Achievement Test, Intermediate Battery II, Form W (Kelley, Madden, Gardner, & Rudman, 1964). These nine subscales include measures of Word Meaning; Paragraph Meaning; Spelling; Language; Arithmetic Computation, Arithmetic Concepts; Arithmetic Applications, Social Studies; and Science.

The development of formal operational thought was measured by a modified form of Eric Lunzer's instrument, How Clearly Can You Think? (Lunzer, 1965). The modifications with this measure of cognitive development were designed to make it more appropriate for a younger population. These modifications included the removal of about fifty per cent of the original items which were judged as being beyond a young preadolescent population. Five items involving combinatorial reasoning were added to the measure bringing the total number of items to 25. These 25 items included ten verbal analogies, ten number sequence problems, and five combinatorial reasoning problems. There is some indication that success on this type of instrument is correlated with Piaget's description of formal reasoning (Lunzer, 1973).

Creativity was tested using the verbal and figural battery of the Torrance Tests of Creative Thinking (Torrance, 1966). This instrument is one of the most widely used creativity measures in the literature (Beatty, 1969). Torrance (1966) has suggested that this instrument may be potentially useful in the assessment of the differential effects of various kinds of experimental programs and new curricular arrangements.

Three measures of pupil personality were used in this study. With each of these instruments small modifications were required to remove references to the child's home life. This was a requirement imposed on the study by the cooperating school system. These instruments included: the short form of B. N. Phillips' (1968) measure of school related anxiety, the Coopersmith's (1967) measure of self-esteem, and a measure of locus of control, the Intellectual Achievement Responsibilities Scale by Crandall, Katkovsky, and Crandall (1965).

PROCEDURE

All student testing was directed by the experimenter and conducted in large group settings at the two schools. The Stanford Achievement Test Intermediate Battery II, Form W, was administered at the traditional school during the third week of October. All fifth graders were tested simultaneously in testing sessions of about two hours in length. Testing was carried out over a three day period. The entire fifth grade at the open school was tested under similar testing conditions, with the same instrument, during the first three days of the first whole week of November. The time lag of over two weeks between the testing at the two schools was provided to reduce possible contamination which may have resulted if achievement testing was carried out the week preceding Halloween.

As the school system routinely administered the Stanford Achievement Test in the second, third and fifth grades, the children of both schools were familiar with the testing procedures. This also reduced the possibility that the children were aware of the special nature of the testing.

During the last two days of the second week of November, measures of cognition, creativity, and personality were administered to students of the traditional school. The first testing session included the entire fifth grade of the traditional school being tested with the Torrance Tests of Creative Thinking. The testing was carried out according to the standard instructions provided by the test author. The figural subtest was administered before the verbal subtest. Due to the scheduling requirements of the school, both subtests were given in one sitting. A short recess period was scheduled between the administration of the two subtests.

The second testing session at the traditional school included only the fifty-one subjects of the study. During this test session the measures of self-esteem, locus of control, school anxiety, and formal operations were administered in the foregoing sequence. To reduce experimental contamination, no teachers were used to proctor during the administration of these measures. The children were told that the experimenter was writing a report which would tell how the typical fifth grade student felt about certain things. The children were assured that while their teachers would learn what the average responses were, they would not know, nor ever be shown, the individual answers given by the students. The students were also told that fifth graders in other schools would also answer the same questions. To help reduce the test like nature of these instruments, the students were assured that there were no right or wrong answers on the first three instruments. This nonjudgmental quality, and the anonymity of their responses, were discussed before the administration of each of the measures with the students.

These instruments were not administered with the students of the open school until the first week of December. This delay provided time for make-up testing at the traditional school, and also avoided giving these tests close to the Thanksgiving Day holiday. This second phase of testing at the open school involved only the subsample of fifth grade children used in the study. The testing was done in a large group setting over three sessions of about an hour and a half in length each. The schedule of the open school did not provide a block of time of sufficient length to administer both sections of the Torrance Tests together on the same day. Thus, three testing sessions on consecutive days were required to complete this phase of the testing. The same sequence for administration of the tests was used in both schools. In the open school, as in the traditional school, faculty proctors were not used when the measures of self-esteem, locus of control, school anxiety, and formal operations were administered. During the final testing session when these last four instruments were administered, the children were given the same assurances about the nonjudgmental nature of the questions, and the protection of their anonymity, which were given to the children of the traditional school.

Results

Means and variances for the fifteen variables by school are presented in Table 4. The nine achievement scores from the Stanford Achievement Test are preported in grade equivalency form based on national averages. Formal Operational Thought was scored on the basis of number of correct responses out of a possible maximum of 25 items. Locus of Control was scored on the basis of the number of internal locus responses out of a maximum of thirty. The Coopersmith Self-Esteem Inventory was scored for positive self-esteem on a scale with a maximum of fifty. The Phillips' School Anxiety Questionnaire was scored for high anxiety responses on a scale with a maximum anxiety score of 23.

Pupil outcome differences as a result of the two educational approaches were assessed by two 2 × 2 (school by sex) multivariate analyses of variance procedures. Sex was included as a second independent variable in these analyses to account for a possible systematic sex by educational environment interaction. The nine achievement test scores were used as dependent measures in the first analysis. The multivariate F ratio for overall achievement differences between the two schools was significant ($F = 2.56$, $df = 9$; 88, $p < .01$). Six of the nine univariate F ratios for these variables were significantly different for the two school samples. These variables include the measures of: Word Meaning, Paragraph Meaning, Arithmetic Concepts, Arithmetic Application, Social Studies, and Science. An examination of the achievement means by school indicated that achievement was higher in all nine areas for the traditional school students.

The multivariate test for a main effect by sex was also significant ($F = 3.87$, $df = 9$; 88, $p < .001$). None of the univariate tests reached significance. The test for a multivariate interaction of sex by school was not significant.

The second multivariate analysis included six pupil outcome variables as the dependent measures. These included: Formal Operations, Locus of Control, Self Esteem, School Anxiety, Verbal Creativity and Figural Creativity. Table 6 presents the results of this analysis. The multivariate F ratio for overall differences on these six variables was not significant ($F = 1.07$, $df = 9$; 88). The only univariate difference to reach significance on this vector was

table 4

| VARIABLE | TRADITIONAL SCHOOL | | | | | | OPEN SCHOOL | | | | | |
| | Boys (N = 30) | | Girls (N = 20) | | Combined (N = 50) | | Boys (N = 28) | | Girls (N = 22) | | Combined (N = 50) | |
	Mean	SD	Mean	SD	Mean	SD	Mean	SD	Mean	SD	Mean	SD
Achievement												
Word Meaning	4.91	1.36	4.74	.95	4.84	1.19	4.58	.85	4.05	.70	4.35	.78
Paragraph Meaning	5.13	1.68	5.20	1.22	5.16	1.48	4.53	1.07	4.76	1.03	4.63	1.04
Spelling	4.13	1.35	4.75	1.35	4.40	1.35	4.18	1.03	4.34	1.19	4.25	1.09
Language	4.67	1.35	4.93	1.24	4.78	1.29	4.43	1.08	4.73	1.01	4.56	1.04
Arith. Computation	4.38	1.29	4.74	.87	4.54	1.11	3.63	.81	4.02	.80	3.80	.81
Arith. Concepts	5.43	1.25	5.43	1.00	5.43	1.14	5.32	1.01	4.82	.86	5.10	.94
Arith. Applications	5.36	2.19	5.22	1.22	5.30	1.81	4.56	.91	4.64	1.08	4.60	.98
Social Studies	5.02	1.24	4.90	.87	4.97	1.08	4.54	.88	4.23	.63	4.40	.77
Science	4.73	1.29	4.92	1.18	4.81	1.23	4.33	.96	4.18	.85	4.26	.90
Formal Operations	6.79	3.4	7.14	2.6	6.94	3.1	5.50	3.0	6.41	2.6	5.90	2.9
Locus of Control	20.24	3.4	21.38	3.2	20.72	3.4	20.21	3.7	20.23	4.3	20.22	3.9
Self-Esteem	33.21	8.6	31.14	7.1	32.34	8.0	32.43	7.5	28.32	7.7	30.62	7.7
School Anxiety	8.62	4.5	12.38	4.0	10.20	4.6	11.11	4.8	13.36	5.2	12.10	5.1
Creativity												
Verbal	127.72	20.0	145.95	24.3	135.38	23.5	127.82	16.3	131.86	22.7	129.60	19.2
Figural	207.10	27.7	220.29	35.8	212.64	31.7	199.82	24.2	214.59	38.1	206.32	31.6

MULTIVARIATE ANALYSIS OF VARIANCE FOR SEX AND TWO SCHOOL TYPES ACROSS NINE ACHIEVEMENT VARIABLES

table 5

SOURCE OF VARIATION	df	F	p
School	9;88	2.56	.01
Sex	9;88	3.87	.0004
School × Sex	9;88	1.16	.33

UNIVARIATE ANALYSES

		School		Sex		School × Sex	
Source of Variation	df	F	p	F	p	F	p
Word Meaning	1;96	5.73	.02	2.85	.09	.77	.38
Paragraph Meaning	1;96	4.15	.04	.34	.56	.10	.75
Spelling	1;96	.40	.53	2.50	.12	.86	.36
Language	1;96	.88	.35	1.36	.24	.01	.93
Arithmetic Computation	1;96	13.84	.00	3.62	.06	.01	.94
Arithmetic Concepts	1;96	2.50	.12	1.38	.24	1.41	.24
Arithmetic Applications	1;96	5.82	.02	.01	.93	.14	.71
Social Studies	1;96	8.79	.00	1.26	.26	.24	.63
Science	1;96	6.43	.01	.01	.92	.59	.44

School Anxiety. An examination of the direction of this difference indicates that students of the open school have higher levels of school anxiety.

A significant multivariate main effect by sex was found ($F = 3.94$, $df = 6$; 91, $p < .002$). Four significant univariate F tests for this main effect indicate that girls tend to have higher levels of creativity and school anxiety, and lower levels of self-esteem than boys. The multivariate test for an interaction between school type and sex was not significant.

Discussion

One part of the overall hypothesis of this study predicting that students from the two schools would differ on the nine achievement test variables were supported. The direction of the differences on each of these achievement variables indicates that the children of the open school have a conspicuous deficiency in these academic skill areas. The importance of this finding should be emphasized in light of the relatively brief duration of the treatment condition. There are several possible explanations for this difference in overall achievement. One of these explanations includes the issue of curriculum and teaching objectives. An analysis of the responses of the faculty of the open school to the items of the Dimensions of Schooling questionnaire indicated that they saw their educational objectives and curriculum as being flexible, and open to periodic modifications and student input. The responses from the traditional

table 6

SOURCE OF VARIATION	df	F	p
School	6;91	1.07	.38
Sex	6;91	3.94	.00
School × Sex	6;91	1.26	.28

UNIVARIATE ANALYSIS							
		School		Sex		School × Sex	
Source of Variation	df	F	p	F	p	F	p
Formal Operations	1;96	3.05	.08	1.10	.30	.22	.64
Locus of Control	1;96	.47	.50	.60	.44	.58	.45
Self-Esteem	1;96	1.23	.27	3.89	.05	.43	.52
School Anxiety	1;96	4.18	.04	10.25	.00	.64	.43
Verbal Creativity	1;96	1.96	.17	7.07	.01	2.89	.09
Figural Creativity	1;96	1.03	.31	4.92	.03	.02	.90

school faculty indicated that they saw the curriculum as being more rigid and less open to modifications. They also tended to see the educational objectives of the school as being more rigid, and predetermined by the school administration. Thus, these data indicate that this consistent and more structured approach to the educational process may be related to better achievement in the content areas as measured by standard achievement tests. When students are given greater freedom to explore their own interests, they may not use these opportunities to develop the basic skills which are needed for success on achievement tests.

Teachers of the open school have also reported using a more flexible and less content oriented type of student evaluation. Without the extrinsic motivation provided by periodic classroom tests, children of the open school may expend less effort toward the mastery of difficult areas of knowledge such as arithmetic.

The second part of the overall hypothesis, that the two schools would differ on six cognitive and personality variables, was not supported. Only one of the nonachievement variables, School Anxiety, was different for the two schools. Students of the open school reported higher levels of school anxiety than students of the traditional school. This unexpected difference may be related more to the nature of the instrument than to differences between the two schools. Many items of this instrument are related to the evaluation of students, and are phrased in terms of the traditional school environment. Such items included: "When the teacher says that she is going to find out how much you have learned, does your heart begin to beat faster?" and, "Do you worry a lot before you take a test?" According to the responses of the teachers of the open school, student evaluation tends to be less formal, and more individualized than it is in the traditional school. Thus, questions phrased in the terms used with this anxiety scale may not be a part of the typical experiences that open school students have had with their teachers. If such unusual experiences were to occur, they might be more anxiety provoking than if such occurrences were a typical part of the school experience.

To assess the overall influence of this open education program it is necessary to take careful note of these student variables which did not show significant differences for the two school groups. Contrary to the prevailing literature of this field (Haddon & Lytton, 1968, 1971; Rogers, 1969; Weber, 1968), students in the open school did not have higher levels of tested creativity. Also, no differences between groups were found on such variables as self-esteem, locus of control, and cognitive development. Thus, it would appear from these data that the open school environment does not have a profound influence on either the cognitive or affective development of children.

The area of greatest impact associated with the implementation of this open education program was found with the various facets of pupil achievement. Specifically, after four and a half semesters in this environment, the students of the open school had significantly lower overall levels of academic achievement. These differences were especially noticeable in arithmetic computation, as well as in reading, and the other reading related achievement areas.

Rathbone (1972) has recently expressed the belief that the ultimate academic goals of open education should be the same as they are for the more traditional form of education. In many respects these goals are very conventional and involve the mastery of basic skills in such areas as reading and arithmetic. He feels that while the daily achievement expectations that open school teachers hold for their students may not be as rigid as they are for the teachers in the traditional setting, their long term goals are very similar. The data of this study indicates that this open school has not been able to meet these long term academic objectives.

The results of this study tend to support the concerns expressed by several authors (Friedlander, 1965; Troost, 1973) about the recent trend in American education away from the more structured type of curriculum. Authors who have supported the movement toward open education in this country (Rogers, 1972; Silberman, 1971) have emphasized the importance of understanding the process of education as well as the final products. These authors have suggested that children should be given the opportunity to explore their own interests, and the freedom to pursue those areas of knowledge to which their natural motivation and curiosity will lead them. It is possible that educational practices founded on these principles do not necessarily lead to mastery of basic skills in the standard content areas. Yet, mastery of the basic skills such as reading may be even more essential to the child who is attempting to work independently than they are to the child who is working in a more fixed learning environment.

The general expectancy that the faculties of the two schools would have different approaches to teaching was supported. Using a self-report instrument, teachers of the open school reported classroom behaviors and procedures more congruent with those which were hypothesized to be a part of an open approach to education than did the teachers of the traditional school.

Direct observations of the teacher-student interactions in the two schools also supported the expectancy that the teaching approach used in the two schools was different. While the time spent by teachers in praising child and in accepting and clarifying the feelings of children was found to be about the same in the two schools, open school teachers used student ideas in their interactions with students about fifty percent more frequently than did the traditional school teachers. Teachers of the open school also asked fewer direct questions of students and therefore received fewer direct responses to questions from students than the traditional school teachers. Open school teachers also participated in more student initiated exchanges than did their traditional school counterparts.

The expectation that the traditional school teachers would spend a greater proportion of time lecturing to students and criticizing students was also supported. Teachers of the traditional school spent more than twice as much time lecturing than did the open school teachers. Traditional school teachers also criticized students, or justified their position to students, more frequently than did the open school teachers.

Open school teachers were unexpectedly found to spend more than twice as much time giving directions to students than did the traditional teachers. This difference may reflect teacher responses to the greater amount of student initiated questions in the open classroom. This difference may also reflect a greater dependence on student projects and other self-directed learning experiences which are an integral part of the teaching process in the open school. Such student initiated learning activities would possibly need more direction from the teacher than is normally required in a more structured learning environment.

references _____

Amidon, E. J., & Flanders, N. A. *The role of the teacher in the classroom: A manual for understanding and improving teacher classroom behavior.* (rev. ed.) Minneapolis: Association for Productive Teaching, 1971.

Bartel, H. Bibliography on open education. Unpublished bibliography, Temple University, 1972.

Beatty, W. (Ed.) *Improving educational assessments and an inventory of measures of active behavior.* Washington. D.C.: Association for Supervision and Curriculum Development, 1969.

Coopersmith, S. *Antecedents of self-esteem.* San Francisco: W. H. Freeman, 1967.

Crandall, V. C., Katkovsky, W., & Crandall, V. J. Children's beliefs in their own control of reinforcements in intellectual-academic achievement situation. *Child Development,* 1965, *36,* 91–109.

Friedlander, B. Z. A psychologist's second thoughts on concepts, curiosity, and discovery in teaching and learning. *Harvard Education Review,* 1965, *35,* 18–38.

Haddon, F. A., & Lytton, H. Teaching approach and the development of divergent thinking abilities in primary schools. *British Journal of Educational Psychology,* 1968, *38,* 171–180.

Haddon, F. A., & Lytton, H. Primary education and divergent thinking abilities—four years on. *British Journal of Educational Psychology,* 1971, *41,* 136–147.

Kelley, T. L., Madden, R., Gardner, E. F., & Rudman, H. C. *Stanford Achievement Test: Intermediate II Battery.* New York: Harcourt, Brace, & World, 1964.

Lunzer, E. A. Formal reasoning: A re-appraisal. Paper presented at the third annual symposium of the Jean Piaget Society, Philadelphia, May, 1973.

Lunzer, E. A. Problems of formal reasoning in test situations. In P. H. Mussen (Ed.), European research in cognitive development. *Monographs of the Society for Research in Child Development,* 1965, *30,* 19–46.

Medley, D. M., & Mitzel, H. E. Measuring classroom behavior by systematic observation. In N. L. Gage (Ed.), *Handbook of research on teaching.* Chicago: Rand McNally, 1963.

Minuchin, P., Biber, B., Shapiro, E., & Zimiles, H. *The psychological impact of school experience.* New York: Basic Books, 1969.

Phillips, B. N. The nature of school anxiety and its relationship to children's school behavior. *Psychology in the Schools,* 1968, *3,* 195–204.

Plowden, B., et al. *Children and their primary schools: A report of the Central Advisory Council on Education.* London: Her Majesty's Stationery Office, 1967.

Rathbone, C. H. Examining the open education classroom. *School Review,* 1972, *80,* 521–550.

Rogers, C. R. *Freedom to learn.* Columbus: Charles E. Merrill, 1969.

Rogers, V. R. An American reaction. In E. B. Nyquist & G. R. Hawes (Eds.), *Open education.* New York: Bantam, 1972.

Silberman, C. E. *Crisis in the classroom.* New York: Random House, 1971.

Soar, R. S. *An integrative approach to classroom learning* (Final report, Public Health Service Grant No. 5-R11-MH 01096 and National Institute of Mental Health Grant No. 7-R11-MH 02045). Philadelphia: Temple University, 1966. |ED 033 749|.

Spaulding, R. L. Achievement, creativity, and self-concept correlates of teacher-pupil transactions in elementary school classrooms. (Cooperative Research Project 1352). New York: Hofstra University, 1965.

Torrance, E. P. *Torrance tests of creative thinking: Norms-technical manual.* Princeton, N.J.: Personnel Press, 1966.

Traub, R. E., Weiss, J., Fisher, C. W., & Musella, D. Closure on openness: Describing and quantifying open education. *Interchange,* 1972, *3,* 69–83.

Troost, C. J. (Ed.) *Radical school reform: Critique and alternatives.* Boston: Little, Brown, 1973.

Walbert, H. J. Characteristics of open education: a look at the literature for teachers. (USOE Title IV Program, Contract No. OEC 1-7-062805-3963) Newton, Mass.: Education Development Center, 1971. [ED 058 164].

Walberg, H. J., & Thomas, S. C. Open education: an operational definition and validation in Great Britain and United States. *American Educational Research Journal*, 1972, 9, 197–208.

Weber, W. A. Relationship between teacher behavior and pupil creativity in the elementary school. Paper presented at the annual meeting of the American Educational Research Association, Chicago, February, 1968, [ED 028 150].

17 a   SOME REMARKS ON "OPEN EDUCATION"*

BERNARD Z. FRIEDLANDER

Wright's study, "The Affective and Cognitive Consequences of an Open Education," makes a double contribution to progress on an important problem of educational policy and practice. His data are valuable in their own right, and his challenge to the assumptions and ideology of open education is bound to stimulate others to sharpen their wits in pursuing the debate between tradition and innovation. This stimulation should help elevate the discourse to the level of demonstration and findings, so it will not simply continue in terms of allegiance and aspiration.

One recognizes, of course, that this report is not a final statement in favor of traditional classrooms over open classrooms. It is simply a factual finding that in this particular setting these children in the open classrooms did less well than other children in traditional classrooms on certain generally accepted measures of progress and performance in school. These results seem to point in the direction of general value statements about the relative effectiveness of fundamentally different approaches to school organization. However, they cannot be taken as a final answer to a problem that calls for much larger accumulations of data in a variety of settings, and for a broader base for generalization and inference.

Granting that Wright's work is just a step toward judgment, and not a final judgment in and of itself, it appears to lead to a critical three-layer "either/or" confrontation with some very uncomfortable thoughts:

Either the open classrooms in this study were indeed less effective than the traditional ones in conveying some fundamental skills and values, *or*

*Reprinted from *American Educational Research Journal*, 12:4 (1975), pp. 465–468.
Copyright 1975; American Educational Research Association, Washington, D.C.

(a)   the tests which indicated less competent performance among the open classroom children were not as valid as they ought to be in measuring student capability and states of being, or

(b)   the aspects of pupil performance which these tests tap are less important for the children's developmental experience than some unmeasured and unidentified benefits which the children can be hoped or presumed to have gained from having been in the open rather than the traditional classrooms.

Any way we look at them, these propositions raise conceptual, policy, and practical issues of the first magnitude. If the test data mean what they say, and if the open classrooms really *are* less effective instruments for fostering development than the traditional classrooms, what are we to say to those who have agitated so strongly for open classroom principles and open classroom architecture? Perhaps more important, what shall we ask the open classroom advocates to say to children, teachers, parents, school boards, and taxpayers who willingly or unwillingly responded to their enthusiastic advocacy? And if further assessments support Wright's findings at higher levels of generalizability, what is to be done with the expensive innovative architecture that is highly resistive to reconversion to traditional classroom organization?

On the other hand, if the tests *don't* mean what they say, where does that leave the professional community that relies on such tests to produce meaningful data as a basis for policy and practical decisions? And where does that leave the larger society that has been led to believe that educational research could be counted upon to provide a basis for important social action and social change?

Finally, where are we if we find ourselves accepting *decrements* in scholastic performance in the basic school skills as the price to be paid for undemonstrable, hoped-for gains that we cannot find a way to identify in some measurable fashion? Also, how are we to interpret Wright's findings of *increased* anxiety among the open classroom children, when we have been led to expect that the open classroom provides affective advantages that might outweigh the traditional significance of scholastic skills? Every college sophomore who has taken a competent course in child psychology is aware that increased anxiety is perhaps the least acceptable side effect of the pursuit of some other developmental objective.

I am very glad that I am in a position that I can raise questions like these without being obliged to answer them. If I were called upon to try, I simply don't know what I would do. I have been in some open classrooms that seemed like the blessed ideal of what schools should be like in terms of superior, humane teaching and learning; and I have been in open classrooms that could be compared only to the back wards of an unreformed mental hospital. Likewise, I have also been in traditional classrooms that could be described in very much the same fashion, at both ends of the scale.

Ultimately, the process of formulating, conducting, and interpreting open education research must come to grips with the question of values. It is inadequate to think that data can be obtained in a value vacuum. From the standpoint of the children, the critical values call for a balance between instructional objectivity and rigor on one hand in transmitting the skills that are indispensable for competent adaptation, and on the other hand, the desire to let children cultivate their powers in an atmosphere that fosters confident individuality. From the standpoint of the educators, the critical values often turn on a pivot of personality and careerist considerations in which some thrive on stability and certainty, and others thrive on change and ambiguity.

Values such as these are often looked upon as being simply contaminants to research. Yet in this question of the relative merits of traditional versus open classrooms, it is probably true that these values hold the key to the realities which the research is supposed to study. If the open classroom is intended, among other things, to cultivate children's sense of their own individuality in the exercise of intelligence and interpersonal dealings, it must take account of the fact that children differ greatly in their needs for structured environments and specified expectations.

It is a gross oversight of available knowledge in psychology to assume that looser structure in the environment of the classroom is of some benefit for all children, just because it is a great benefit for some children. It is predictable that children who have a low tolerance for ambiguity and uncertainty would find an open classroom that operates very successfully for some children extremely threatening and anxiety-provoking. It is also predictable that personality configurations among administrators and teachers who seek out the challenge of innovation in developing the open classroom would tend to be unmindful of the valid needs for order, predictability, and specificity for persons unlike themselves.

Where open classrooms are established as a school-wide policy without offering a choice, they are an invitation to disappointment. Without *individual* selection for one program or the other, and freedom to move back and forth on the basis of experience, it can almost be forecast that there would probably be as many children who lose as there are those who gain. Since innovators and ambiguity seekers are usually in the minority among adults, it may even be probable that there would be *more* losers than winners among children when structured lattices of expectation, performance, and evaluation give way to the more fluid give and take of spontaneity and imagination.

Perhaps the worst mistake that could be made would be for opponents of the open classroom idea to use Wright's report as a basis for arguing against the value of open classrooms all across the board. If they try, they shouldn't be allowed to get away with it. However, the open classroom advocates must now recognize that the burden is increasingly upon them to accommodate their enthusiasm to these data, and that they must find improved ways to substantiate the values their vision proposes to advance. In my view, they will have increased hopes for doing this if they take individual differences into account in planning their programs and conducting their research.

When means are found to identify *temperaments* that thrive in the more open classroom environment and those that thrive in the more traditional ones, it will probably be discovered that these distinctions can confer great benefits on a great many children in both of these general categories. This might be one of the great breakthroughs to meeting individual children's *real* needs on a more individual basis that educational innovators have been looking for.

comments and questions

1. Wright states that "Assignment to the open school was done on a geographic basis." Does this suggest that this study is really experimental rather than ex post facto? Why?

2. To test the equivalency of the two groups prior to third grade, Wright performed *both* multivariate and univariate tests. Given that the overall multivariate test was not significant, what was the purpose of the univariate tests? Given that the F ratio for ability approached significance (see Table 1) do you think that Wright should have performed an Analysis of Covariance? Is the F ratio of 3.91 with 1 and 100 *df* (significant at the .05 level) for a *one* or *two*-tailed test? If the former, was this appropriate?

3. We commend Wright on his thorough description of the educational program at the two schools. However, given the heterogeneity of "open" and "traditional" classroom environments, can one reasonably generalize Wright's findings? Does Friedlander comment on this aspect?

4. Discuss the implication(s) of the fact that only volunteer teachers were used in the "open" school.

5. Friedlander presents a "three-layer 'either/or' confrontation." Which 'either/or' do you find most convincing? Why?

6. We commend Wright for his thorough description of the Method and the clarity with which he presented his Results. In addition, it should be noted that Wright attempts to relate his Findings to previous authors' positions.

A THIRTY-YEAR FOLLOW-UP
OF TREATMENT EFFECTS*

18

JOAN McCORD*

ABSTRACT: Over 500 men, half of whom had been randomly assigned to a treatment program that lasted approximately 5 years, were traced 30 years after termination of the project. Although subjective evaluations of the program by those who received its benefits would suggest that the intervention had been helpful, comparisons between the treatment and control groups indicate that the program had negative side effects as measured by criminal behavior, death, disease, occupational status, and job satisfaction. Several possible processes are suggested in explanation of these findings.

In 1935, Richard Clark Cabot instigated one of the most imaginative and exciting programs ever designed in hopes of preventing delinquency. A social philosopher as well as physician, Dr. Cabot established a program that both avoided stigmatizing participants and permitted follow-up evaluation.

Several hundred boys from densely populated, factory-dominated areas of eastern Massachusetts were included in the project, known as the Cambridge-Somerville Youth Study. Schools, welfare agencies, churches, and the police recommended both "difficult" and "average" youngsters to the program. These boys and their families were given physical examinations and were

*From *American Psychologist*, 33:3 (1978), pp. 284–289. Copyright 1978 by the American Psychological Association. Reprinted by permission.

This study was supported by U.S. Public Health Service Research Grant No. 5 R01 MH26779, National Institute of Mental Health (Center for Studies of Crime and Delinquency). It was conducted jointly with the Department of Probation of the Commonwealth of Massachusetts.

An earlier version of this paper was presented at the 28th annual meeting of the American Association of Psychiatric Services for Children, San Francisco, California, November 10–14, 1976.

The author wishes to express appreciation to the Division of Alcoholism, to the Cambridge & Somerville Program for Alcoholism Rehabilitation, to the National Institute of Law Enforcement (through Grant NI 74–0038 to Ron Geddes), to the Massachusetts Departments of Mental Health, Motor Vehicles, and Correction, and to the many individuals who contributed to this research.

Requests for reprints should be sent to Joan McCord, 1279 Montgomery Avenue, Wynnewood, Pennsylvania 19096.

interviewed by social workers who then rated each boy in such a way as to allow a selection committee to designate delinquency-prediction scores. In addition to giving delinquency-prediction scores, the selection committee studied each boy's records in order to identify pairs who were similar in age, delinquency-prone histories, family background, and home environments. By the toss of a coin, one member of each pair was assigned to the group that would receive treatment.[1]

The treatment program began in 1939, when the boys were between 5 and 13 years old. Their median age was 10½. Except for those dropped from the program because of a counselor shortage in 1941, treatment continued for an average of 5 years. Counselors assigned to each family visited, on the average, twice a month. They encouraged families to call on the program for assistance. Family problems became the focus of attention for approximately one third of the treatment group. Over half of the boys were tutored in academic subjects; over 100 received medical or psychiatric attention; one fourth were sent to summer camps; and most were brought into contact with the Boy Scouts, the YMCA, and other community programs. The control group meanwhile, participated only through providing information about themselves. Both groups, it should be remembered, contained boys referred as "average" and boys considered "difficult."

The present study compares the 253 men who had been in the treatment program after 1942 with the 253 "matched mates" assigned to the control group.

Method

Official records and personal contacts were used to obtain information about the long-term effects of the Cambridge–Somerville Youth Study.[2] In 1975 and 1976, the 506 former members of the program were traced through court records, mental hospital records, records from alcoholic treatment centers, and vital statistics in Massachusetts. Telephone calls, city directories, motor-vehicle registrations, marriage and death records, and lucky hunches were used to find the men themselves.

Four hundred eighty men (95 percent) were located; among these, 48 (9 percent) had died and 340 (79 percent) were living in Massachusetts.[3] Questionnaires were mailed to 208 men from the treatment group and 202 men from

[1]An exception to assignment by chance was made if brothers were in the program; all brothers were assigned to that group which was the assignment of the first brother matched. See Powers and Witmer (1951) for details of the matching procedure.
[2]A sample of 200 men had been retraced in 1948 (Powers & Witmer, 1951), and official records had been traced in 1956 (McCord & McCord, 1959a, 1959b).
[3]Two hundred forty-one men from the treatment group and 239 men from the control group were found; 173 from the treatment group and 167 from the control group were living in Massachusetts.

the control group. The questionnaire elicited information about marriage, children, occupations, drinking, health, and attitudes. Former members of the treatment group were asked how (if at all) the treatment program had been helpful to them.

Responses to the questionnaire were received from 113 men in the treatment group (54 percent) and 122 men in the control group (60 percent). These responses overrepresent men living outside of Massachusetts, $\chi^2(1) = 10.97$, $p < .001$.[4] Official records, on the other hand, provide more complete information about those men living in Massachusetts.

Comparison of Criminal Behavior

The treatment and control groups were compared on a variety of measures for criminal behavior. With the exception of Crime Prevention Bureau records for unofficial crimes committed by juveniles, court convictions serve as the standard by which criminal behavior was assessed. Although official court records may be biased, there is no reason to believe that these biases would affect a comparison between the matched groups of control and treatment subjects.

Almost equal numbers in the treatment and control groups had committed crimes as juveniles—whether measured by official or by unofficial records (see Table 1).

It seemed possible that the program might have benefited those referred as "difficult" while damaging those referred as "average." The evidence, however, failed to support this hypothesis. Among those referred as "difficult," 34 percent from the treatment group and 30 percent from the control group had official juvenile records; an additional 20 percent from the treatment group and 21 percent from the control group had unofficial records. Nor were there differences between the groups for those who had been referred as "average."[5]

As adults, equal numbers (168) had been convicted for some crime. Among men who had been in the treatment group, 119 committed only relatively minor crimes (against ordinances or order), but 49 had committed serious crimes against property (including burglary, larceny, and auto theft) or against persons (including assault, rape, and attempted homicide). Among men from the control group, 126 had committed only relatively minor crimes; 42 had committed serious property crimes or crimes against persons. Twenty-nine men from the treatment group and 25 men from the control group committed serious crimes after the age of 25.

---

[4]Among those sent the questionnaire, the response rate for men living in Massachusetts was 53 percent; for men living outside Massachusetts, the response rate was 74 percent. A similar bias appeared for both groups.

[5]For the treatment group, 18 percent had official records and an additional 13 percent had unofficial records. For the control-group "average" referrals, the figures were 19 percent and 13 percent, respectively.

JUVENILE RECORDS

table 1 ───

RECORD	TREATMENT GROUP	CONTROL GROUP
No record for delinquency	136	140
Only unofficial crimes	45	46
Official crimes	72	67
Total	253	253

Reasoning that the Youth Study project may have been differentially effective for those who did and did not have records as delinquents, it seemed advisable to compare adult criminal records while holding this background information constant. Again, there was no evidence that the treatment program had deflected people from committing crimes (see Table 2).

The treatment and control groups were compared to see whether there were differences (a) in the number of serious crimes committed, (b) in age when a first crime was committed, (c) in age when committing a first serious crime, and (d) in age after which no serious crime was committed. None of these measures showed reliable differences.

Benefits from the treatment program did not appear when delinquency-prediction scores were controlled or when seriousness of juvenile record and juvenile incarceration were controlled. Unexpectedly, however, a higher proportion of criminals from the treatment group than of criminals from the control group committed more than one crime, $\chi^2(1) = 5.36$, $p < .05$.

JUVENILE DELINQUENCY AND ADULT CRIMINAL RECORDS

table 2 ───

RECORD	TREATMENT GROUP	CONTROL GROUP
Official juvenile record		
No adult record	14	15
Only minor adult record	33	27
Serious crimes as adults	25	25
No official juvenile record		
No adult record	71	70
Only minor adult record	86	99
Serious crimes as adults	24	17
Total	253	253

Among the 182 men with criminal records from the treatment group, 78 percent committed at least two crimes; among the 183 men with criminal records
from the control group, 67 percent committed at least two crimes.

Comparison of Health

Signs of alcoholism, mental illness, stress-related diseases, and early death
were used to evaluate possible impact of the treatment program on health.

   A search through records from alcoholic treatment centers and mental
hospitals in Massachusetts showed that almost equal numbers of men from the
treatment and the control groups had been treated for alcoholism (7 percent
and 8 percent, respectively).

   The questionnaire asked respondents to note their drinking habits and
to respond to four questions about drinking embedded in questions about
smoking. The four questions, known as the CAGE test (Ewing & Rouse, Note
1), asked whether the respondent had ever taken a morning eye-opener, felt
the need to cut down on drinking, felt annoyed by criticism of his drinking, or
felt guilty about drinking.[6] The treatment group mentioned that they were
alcoholic or responded *yes* more frequently, as do alcoholics, to at least three of
the CAGE questions: 17 percent compared with 7 percent, $\chi^2(1) = 4.98$,
$p < .05$.

   Twenty-one members of each group had received treatment in mental
hospitals for disorders other than alcoholism.[7] A majority of those from the
treatment group (71 percent) received diagnoses as manic-depressive or
schizophrenic, whereas a majority of those from the control group (67 percent)
received less serious diagnoses such as "personality disorder" or
"psychoneurotic," $\chi^2(1) = 4.68$, $p < .05$.

   Twenty-four men from each group are known to have died. Although
the groups were not distinguishable by causes of death, among those who died,
men from the treatment group tended to die at younger ages, $t(94) = 2.19$,
$p < .05$.[8]

   The questionnaire requested information about nine stress-related diseases: arthritis, gout, emphysema, depression, ulcers, asthma, allergies, high
blood pressure, and heart trouble. Men from the treatment group were more

---

   [6]This test was validated by comparing the responses of 58 acknowledged alcoholics in an alcoholism rehabilitation center with those of 68 nonalcoholic patients in a general hospital: 95
percent of the former and none of the latter answered *yes* to more than two of the four questions
(Ewing & Rouse, Note 1). Additional information related to alcoholism is being gathered through
interviews.
   [7]An additional five men from the treatment group and three men from the control group had
been institutionalized as retarded.
   [8]The average age at death for the treatment group was 32 years ($SD = 9.4$) and for the control
group, 38 years ($SD = 7.5$).

likely to report having had at least one of these diseases, $\chi^2(1) = 4.39$, $p < .05$.[9] In particular, symptoms of stress in the circulatory system were more prevalent among men from the treatment group: 21 percent, as compared with 11 percent in the control group, reported having had high blood pressure or heart trouble, $\chi^2(1) = 4.95$, $p < .05$.

Comparison of Family, Work, and Leisure Time

A majority of the men who responded to the questionnaire were married: 61 percent of the treatment group and 68 percent of the control group. An additional 15 percent of the treatment group and 10 percent of the control group noted that they were remarried. Fourteen percent of the treatment-group and 9 percent of the control-group respondents had never married. The remaining 10 percent of the treatment group and 13 percent of the control group were separated, divorced, or widowed. Among those ever married, 93 percent of each group had children. The median number of children for both sets of respondents was three.

About equal proportions of the treatment- and the control-group respondents were unskilled workers (29 percent and 27 percent, respectively). At the upper end of the socioeconomic scale, however, the control group had an advantage: 43 percent from the control group, compared with 29 percent from the treatment group, were white-collar workers or professionals, $\chi^2(2) = 4.58$, $p < .05$. For those whose occupations could be classified according to National Opinion Research Center (NORC) ranks, comparison indicated that the control-group men were working in positions having higher prestige, $z = 2.07$, $p < .05$ (Mann-Whitney U test).

The questionnaire inquired whether the men found their work, in general, to be satisfying. Almost all of the men who held white-collar or professional positions (97 percent) reported that their work was satisfying. Among blue-collar workers, those in the treatment group were less likely to report that their work was generally satisfying (80 percent, compared with 95 percent among the control group), $\chi^2(1) = 6.60$, $p < .02$.

The men described how they used their spare time. These descriptions were grouped to compare the proportions who reported reading, traveling, doing things with their families, liking sports (as spectators or participants), working around the house, watching television, enjoying music or theater or photography, doing service work, enjoying crafts or tinkering, and participating in organized group activities. The treatment and control groups did not differ in their reported uses of leisure time.

[9]Thirty-six percent of those in the treatment group and 24 percent of those in the control group reported having had at least one of these diseases.

Comparison of Beliefs and Attitudes

The men were asked to evaluate their satisfaction with how their lives were turning out, their chances for living the kinds of lives they'd like to have, and whether they were able to plan ahead.[10] Men from the treatment and the control groups did not differ in their responses to these questions.

A short form of the F scale (Adorno, Frenkel-Brunswik, Levinson, & Sanford, 1950) developed by Sanford and Older (Note 2) was included in the questionnaire. Men were asked whether they agreed or disagreed with the following statements: "Human nature being what it is, there must always be war and conflict. The most important thing a child should learn is obedience to his parents. A few strong leaders could make this country better than all the laws and talk. Most people who don't get ahead just don't have enough willpower. Women should stay out of politics. An insult to your honor should not be forgotten. In general, people can be trusted."

Despite diversity in opinions, neither answers to particular questions nor to the total scale suggested that treatment and control groups differed in authoritarianism. Both groups selected an average of 2.9 authoritarian answers; the standard deviation for each group was 1.7.

Each man was asked to describe his political orientation. About one fifth considered themselves liberals, two fifths considered themselves conservatives, and two fifths considered themselves as middle-of-the-road. No one considered himself a radical. Treatment and control groups did not differ reliably.

The men also identified the best periods of their lives, and, again, there was little difference between control and treatment groups.

Subjective Evaluation of the Program

Former members of the treatment group were asked, "In what ways (if any) was the Cambridge-Somerville project helpful to you?"

Only 11 men failed to comment about this item. Thirteen noted that they could not remember the project. An additional 13 stated that the project had not been helpful—though several of these men amplified their judgments by mentioning that they had fond memories of their counselors or their activities in the project.

Two thirds of the men stated that the program had been helpful to them. Some wrote that, by providing interesting activities, the project kept

[10]This set of questions was developed at the University of Michigan Survey Research Center as a measure of self-competence. It has an index of reproducibility as a Guttman Scale of .94 (see Douvan & Walker, 1956).

them off the streets and out of trouble. Many believed that the project improved their lives through providing guidance or teaching them how to get along with others. The questionnaires were sprinkled with such comments as "helped me to have faith and trust in other people"; "I was put on the right road"; "helped prepare me for manhood"; "to overcome my prejudices"; "provided an initial grasp of our complex society outside of the ghetto"; and "better insight on life in general."

A few men believed that the project was responsible for their becoming law-abiding citizens. Such men wrote that, had it not been for their particular counselors, "I probably would be in jail"; "My life would have gone the other way"; or "I think I would have ended up in a life of crime."

More than a score requested information about their counselors and expressed the intention of communicating with them.

Summary and Discussion

This study of long-term effects of the Cambridge-Somerville Youth Study was based on the tracing of over 500 men, half of whom were randomly assigned to a treatment program. Those receiving treatment had (in varying degrees) been tutored, provided with medical assistance, and given friendly counsel for an extended period of time.

Thirty years after termination of the program, many of the men remembered their counselors—sometimes recalling particular acts of kindness and sometimes noting the general support they felt in having someone available with whom to discuss their problems. There seems to be little doubt that many of the men developed emotional ties to their counselors.

Were the Youth Study program to be assessed by the subjective judgment of its value as perceived by those who received its services, it would rate high marks. To the enormous credit of those who dedicated years of work to the project, it is possible to use objective criteria to evaluate the long-term impact of this program, which seems to have been successful in achieving the short-term goals of establishing rapport between social workers and teenage clients.

Despite the large number of comparisons between treatment and control groups, none of the objective measures confirmed hopes that treatment had improved the lives of those in the treatment group. Fifteen comparisons regarding criminal behavior were made; one was significant with alpha less than .05. Fifteen comparisons for health indicated four—from three different record sources—favoring the control group. Thirteen comparisons of family, work, and leisure time yielded two that favored the control group. Fourteen comparisons of beliefs and attitudes failed to indicate reliable differences between the groups.

The objective evidence presents a disturbing picture. The program seems not only to have failed to prevent its clients from committing crimes—

thus corroborating studies of other projects (see, e.g., Craig & Furst, 1965; Empey, 1972; Hackler, 1966; Miller, 1962; Robin, 1969)—but also to have produced negative side effects. As compared with the control group,

1. Men who had been in the treatment program were more likely to commit (at least) a second crime.

2. Men who had been in the treatment program were more likely to evidence signs of alcoholism.

3. Men from the treatment group more commonly manifested signs of serious mental illness.

4. Among men who had died, those from the treatment group died younger.

5. Men from the treatment group were more likely to report having had at least one stress-related disease; in particular, they were more likely to have experienced high blood pressure or heart trouble.

6. Men from the treatment group tended to have occupations with lower prestige.

7. Men from the treatment group tended more often to report their work as not satisfying.

It should be noted that the side effects that seem to have resulted from treatment were subtle. There is no reason to believe that treatment increased the probability of committing a first crime, although treatment may have increased the likelihood that those who committed a first crime would commit additional crimes. Although treatment may have increased the likelihood of alcoholism, the treatment group was not more likely to have appeared in clinics or hospitals. There was no difference between the groups in the number of men who had died before the age of 50, although men from the treatment group had been younger at the age of death. Almost equal proportions of the two groups of men had remained at the lowest rungs of the occupational structure, although men from the treatment group were less likely to be satisfied with their jobs and fewer men from the treatment group had become white-collar workers.

The probability of obtaining 7 reliably different comparisons among 57, with an alpha of .05, is less than 2 percent. The probability that, by chance, 7 of 57 comparisons would favor the control group is less than 1 in 10,000.[11]

At this juncture, it seems appropriate to suggest several possible interpretations of the subtle effects of treatment. Interaction with adults whose values are different from those of the family milieu may produce later internal conflicts that manifest themselves in disease and/or dissatisfaction.[12] Agency

[11]This estimate is conservative: The count of 57 comparisons includes comparisons that are not independent (e.g., adult criminal record and crimes after the age of 25), but only 7 independent significant relationships have been counted. If comparisons for any stress-related disease, for NORC ranking of occupation, and for job satisfaction without controlling work status are counted, 10 out of 60 comparisons were significant.

[12]Such conflicts seem to have been aroused by intervention in the lives of hard-core, unemployables (Padfield & Williams, 1973).

intervention may create dependency upon outside assistance. When this assistance is no longer available, the individual may experience symptoms of dependency and resentment. The treatment program may have generated such high expectations that subsequent experiences tended to produce symptons of deprivation. Or finally, through receiving the services of a "welfare project," those in the treatment program may have justified the help they received by perceiving themselves as requiring help.

There were many variations to treatment. Some of these may have been beneficial. Overall, however, the message seems clear: Intervention programs risk damaging the individuals they are designed to assist. These findings may be taken by some as grounds for cessation of social-action programs. I believe that would be a mistake. In my opinion, new programs ought to be developed. We should, however, address the problems of potential damage through the use of pilot projects with mandatory evaluations.

reference notes _____

1. Ewing, J. A., & Rouse, B. A. *Identifying the "hidden alcoholic."* Paper presented at the 29th International Congress on Alcohol and Drug Dependence, Sydney, New South Wales, Australia, February 3, 1970.
2. Sanford, F. H., & Older, J. J. *A short authoritarian-equalitarian scale* (Progress Report No. 6, Series A). Philadelphia, Pa.: Institute for Research in Human Relations, 1950.

references _____

Adorno, T. W., Frenkel-Brunswik, E., Levinson, D. J., & Sanford, R. N. *The authoritarian personality.* New York: Harper, 1950.

Craig, M. M., & Furst, P. W. What happens after treatment? A study of potentially delinquent boys. *Social Service Review,* 1965, *39,* 165–171.

Douvan, E., & Walker, A. M. The sense of effectiveness in public affairs. *Psychological Monographs,* 1956, *70* (22, Whole No. 429).

Empey, L. T., & Ericson, M. L. *The provo experiment: Evaluating community control of delinquency.* Lexington, Mass.: Lexington Books, 1972.

Hackler, J. C. Boys, blisters, and behavior: The impact of a work program in an urban central area. *Journal of Research in Crime and Delinquency,* 1966, *12,* 155–164.

McCord, J., & McCord, W. A follow-up report on the Cambridge-Somerville youth study. *Annals of the American Academy of Political and Social Science,* 1959, *322,* 89–96. (a)

McCord, W., & McCord, J. *Origins of crime.* New York: Columbia University Press, 1959. (b)

Miller, W. B. The impact of a "total community" delinquency control project. *Social Problems*, 1962, *10*, 168–191.

Padfield, H., & Williams, R. *Stay where you were: A study of unemployables in industry*. Philadelphia, Pa.: Lippincott, 1973.

Powers, E., & Witmer, H. *An experiment in the prevention of delinquency: The Cambridge-Somerville youth study*. New York: Columbia University Press, 1951.

Robin, G. R. Anti-poverty programs and delinquency. *Journal of Criminal Law, Criminology, and Police Science*, 1969, *60*, 323–331.

THROWING THE BABY OUT
WITH THE BATHWATER

The Hazards of Follow-up Research*

SUZANNE B. SOBEL

ABSTRACT: This article is a critique of the foregoing article by McCord (1978). It is suggested that McCord's conclusions are too strong and may lead policy makers astray. Although the idea of a 30-year follow-up is good, McCord's variables are not strong enough to justify the conclusions drawn.

Follow-up studies of intervention programs with delinquent youths are often greatly lacking. Although the preceding article by McCord (1978) confirms the previously reported negative results of the Cambridge–Somerville Study (McCord & McCord, 1959a, 1959b; Powers & Witmer, 1951), one can only admire McCord's continued pursuit of this type of research and analysis. Today, with the impact of the increased number of intervention programs in all areas of mental health, research documenting that intervention was not sufficient to deter future criminal behavior merits our careful attention. Although the Powers and Witmer (1951) study addressed "treatment," it is important to remember that it did not address the "psychotherapeutic treatment" of today's standards. Knowledge of psychotherapy has come a long way since the social casework model of the late 1930s. However, the techniques of subject selection were quite detailed, and one wonders whether a more productive study could be designed and executed today.

The data presented by McCord (1978) bring to light many important

*From *American Psychologist*, 33:3 (1978), pp. 290–291. Copyright 1978 by the American Psychological Association. reprinted by permission.

Requests for reprints should be sent to Suzanne B. Sobel, 230 F Street, N.E., Washington, D.C. 20002.

issues involved with the design and evaluation of studies of treatment outcome. The present article focuses on a few issues directly related to McCord's work.

McCord has not investigated whether the data conform to the "deterioration effect" of treatment, a phenomenon documented by Bergin (1967, 1971). The omission in the analysis of a breakdown of the subjects into "improved" and "not-improved" groups may lead to erroneous and misleading conclusions. Such conclusions become potentially dangerous when utilized to justify planning and programming in the delinquency field that effectively excludes the active involvement of mental health professionals. McCord's view is literal and simplistic. It lacks an appreciation of intrapsychic processes that are affected by treatment. One wonders what her preconceived notions regarding this research may have been and whether or not they were borne out.

McCord reports seven measures that significantly discriminate the treatment and control groups. The relevance of some of these measures is questionable, especially the variable of age at death. Whether the 113 men in the treatment group were judged as improved, worse, or unchanged by their counselors is unknown. If the treatment group had been broken down into these categories and then analyzed with their controls, some differences favoring the "improved" treatment subjects might have appeared. Although it is speculative, but highly possible, that the reported negative effects of treatment might not persist or might remain only for those who had shown no improvement or who had seemed to get worse as time went on, the globalness of the data comparisons leads one to speculate that perhaps the differences may have been washed out.

However, there are some interesting results from a psychological point of view that McCord appears to overlook or discount. That the treatment group was more likely to report having had a stress-related disease is an important result. It is highly possible that the study had a positive impact on the treatment group by getting these men, who traditionally may not have consulted medical facilities, to seek assistance in times of stress, whereas the control subjects were not predisposed to do so since they did not have the relevant experiences and familiarity with the agencies that the treatment group did. Another interesting result was that the treatment group seemed to report more negative self-characteristics; perhaps this resulted because of their involvement in intrapsychically oriented counseling. However, the consistently positive subjective reports of the treatment group about their experiences must have some pervading impact on their lives today. Inquiry into how the subjects relate their experiences with their counselors to their current lives would have been revealing.

McCord's speculation that interaction with adults with different value systems and social statuses may have produced internal conflicts that later manifested in disease or dissatisfaction may be inaccurate. Rather, interaction with these professionals may have led those in the treatment group to develop an awareness of differences and thus a consequently more realistic self-image that may have been negative.

If McCord's speculation about internal conflicts is correct, then professionals involved in intervention programs must be careful to resolve this tension and internal conflict before the termination of a study. Does this then bind us to working with patients for their whole life spans or for the life spans of the psychotherapists or intervention researchers? Perhaps the internal conflict that McCord is speculating about may only be the result of the abrupt termination of the program, thus reflecting only the effects of incomplete treatment.

The wealth of data from the Cambridge–Somerville Youth Study has not yet been put to adequate use by investigators designing prevention programs. With the abundance of funds spent on intervention programs today, and with assessment occurring only at the cessation of programs, it is a highlight that McCord has continued to assess and reassess these results. Few studies exist in this area. Notable exceptions are the 5- and 10-year follow-ups by Shore and Massimo (1969, 1973) of their studies of the use of vocationally oriented psychotherapy to prevent delinquency. Our data banks on the assessment of the effectiveness of such intervention are incomplete. McCord's analysis challenges the increased use of psychotherapy and psychological input in the rehabilitation and treatment of criminal offenders, especially juvenile ones.

How tragic that this study can be interpreted as showing negative results and, therefore, as indicating extreme caution in the design of intervention programs. While McCord seems to be overconcerned about the potential damage of intervention programs of a social-action nature and desires to mandate pilot projects with mandatory evaluation, it is questionable whether one could pilot a longitudinal study that would insure only positive results. Her conclusion lacks realism.

The legacy that the Cambridge–Somerville Youth Study leaves us is one of careful intervention, constant evaluation, and longitudinal follow-up. The importance of this is emphasized by McCord's work, which guides us toward follow-up studies rather than evaluations solely during the implementation phase. Whether or not the Cambridge–Somerville project prevented crime is an academic question. Certainly the data do not indicate success. But were we to analyze the data systematically in order to structure intervention programs based on them, we might then be in a position to prevent crime, at least as a result of some of the variables that Powers and Witmer (1951) have delineated. The Cambridge–Somerville study and McCord's (1978) follow-up 30 years later should be appreciated and used as guideposts for continuing research on the outcome of intervention.

references _____

Bergin, A. E. Further comments on psychotherapy research and therapeutic practice. *International Journal of Psychiatry,* 1967, *3,* 317–323.

Bergin, A. E. The evaluation of therapeutic outcomes. In A. Bergin & S. Garfield (Eds.), *Handbook of psychotherapy and behavior change.* New York: Wiley, 1971.

McCord, J. A thirty-year follow-up of treatment effects. *American Psychologist*, 1978, *33*, 284–289.

McCord, J., & McCord, W. A follow-up report on the Cambridge–Somerville youth study. *Annals of the American Academy of Political and Social Science*, 1959, *322*, 89–96.(a)

McCord, W., & McCord, J. *Origins of crime.* New York: Columbia University Press, 1959. (b)

Powers, E., & Witmer, H. *An experiment in the prevention of delinquency.* New York: Columbia University Press, 1951.

Shore, M. F., & Massimo, J. L. Five years later: A follow-up study of comprehensive vocationally oriented psychotherapy. *American Journal of Orthopsychiatry*, 1969, *39*, 769–773.

Shore, M. F., & Massimo, J. L. After ten years: A follow-up study of comprehensive vocationally oriented psychotherapy. *American Journal of Orthopsychiatry*, 1973, *43*, 128–132.

comments and questions

1. Cabot's program was experimental in nature. Because McCord did a follow-up of Cabot's subjects thirty years later and did not herself manipulate treatments, we have classified the study as ex post facto.

2. McCord points out that there is disproportionate representation for subjects residing in and outside of Massachusetts. Why did she not comment on the representation on other factors such as "average" or "difficult" boys?

3. There are instances where McCord states that there were no differences between treatment and control groups without presenting the actual data. Is this a legitimate way to report research? If data are not reported do researchers have an obligation to maintain a data file and make it available for secondary or metaanalysis purposes? Can and/or should data files be maintained? Is it legal? Should it be?

4. Much descriptive data are presented in text form (e.g., comparing the two groups on such measures as alcoholism, mental disorders, symptoms of stress, etc.). Would it have been useful to present this material in tabular form?

5. Sobel suggests that "the 'psychotherapeutic treatment' of today's standards" is better than that of the 1930s. Does Sobel reference any study to support this?

6. Sobel states that: "Such conclusions become potentially dangerous when utilized to justify planning and programming in the delinquency field that effectively excludes the active involvement of mental health professionals." What conclusions is she referring to? Does McCord utilize the conclusions in such a fashion?

7. Sobel suggests that the "treatment" group should have been analyzed separately for "improved" and "not improved" subjects. If this were done, and if significant differences were found between the "improved" and control group, would this allow us to draw any inferences about the overall effect of the treatment?

8. The subjective reports (judgments) about the treatment were generally positive.

The objective data were negative. Sobel argues that "the consistently positive subjective reports of the treatment group about their experiences *must have some pervading impact on their lives today*" (italics added). Can this be supported? Couldn't the positive subjective responses have been a manifestation of a social desirability response set and indeed be almost completely invalid?

9. Do you think that Sobel was overly critical of McCord?

VOCATIONAL INDECISION
More Evidence and Speculation*

19

JOHN L. HOLLAND and JOAN E. HOLLAND

This study was planned to clarify the controversy about the characteristics attributed to students who are decided or undecided about a vocational goal. Samples of 1,005 high school juniors and 692 college juniors were assessed with measures of personality, decision-making ability, interests, and vocational attitude. Comparisons of undecided and decided students indicate that they are alike on most measures, but substantial and significant differences were found for the Identity and Vocational Attitude scales. In addition, student explanations of indecisiveness form an internally consistent scale. This scale is, in turn, significantly correlated with measures of Anomy (positive), Identity (negative), Interpersonal Competency (negative), and some Career Maturity (Career Maturity Inventory) variables. The pattern of present and past significant findings implies that it may be useful to interpret some kinds of indecision as the outcome of a proposed indecisive disposition. The chief practical application appears to be the need to see undecided students as multiple subtypes who need different personal–vocational treatments.

Attempts to comprehend the vocational decisiveness of some students and the indecisiveness of others are characterized by conflicting findings, negative findings, or negligible findings. Although vocationally decided and undecided students have been assessed in many ways and with a vast range of variables (Ashby, Wall, & Osipow, 1966; Baird, 1968, 1969; Elton & Rose, 1971; Holland & Nichols, 1964; Lunneborg, 1975; Nelson & Nelson, 1940; Osipow, Carney, & Barak, 1976), few clear or compelling differences emerge. Instead, the most striking outcomes of these studies are that decided and undecided high school and college students are much more alike than different and that the relatively few differences found are conflicting and confusing.

The confusing evidential situation is compounded by divergent speculations about the origins of vocational indecision (Crites, 1969; Galinsky & Fast,

*From *Journal of Counseling Psychology*, 24:5 (1977), pp. 404–414. Copyright 1978 by the American Psychological Association. Reprinted by permission.

The authors are indebted to Gary D. Gottfredson and Linda S. Gottfredson for editorial and data-processing assistance.

Requests for reprints should be sent to John L. Holland, Department of Social Relations, Johns Hopkins University, Baltimore, Maryland 21218.

1966; Goodstein, 1965; Holland, 1973; Osipow et al., 1976; Rose & Elton, 1971; Tyler, 1961). In addition, there is some experimental support for each of these diverse ideas. And, without being clear about our characterizations of undecided people or the origins of their difficulty, a wide range of treatments are being applied (Crites, 1973; McGowan, 1974; Mendonca & Siess, 1976) with some success observed for each.

The present study is another attempt to characterize "decided" and "undecided" high school and college students by assessing the participants with scales, inventories, and a questionnaire concerned with decision making. The data were analyzed to answer four questions:

1.   In what ways are decided and undecided people alike or different?

2.   What are the most and least popular "explanations" of indecision given by students who say they are undecided about or dissatisfied with their vocational aspiration?

3.   Is the number of explanations expressed by undecided students related to any competency, personality, or interest variables?

4.   Is the number of explanations expressed by students who are unsure, dissatisfied, or undecided related to any competency, personality, or interest variables?

By using measures of new and old variables to answer these questions, it was assumed that a clearer interpretation of vocational indecision might become possible.

Method

Samples of 1,005 high school juniors and 692 college juniors were administered the Life Plans Inventory, which asked about vocational decisions and contained the following scales: the Vocational Attitude and the Occupational Information scales from Crites' (1973) Career Maturity Inventory (CMI), the Interpersonal Competency Scale (Holland & Baird, 1968a); the Preconscious Activity Scale (Holland & Baird, 1968b), the Anomy Scale (McClosky & Schaar, 1965), and the Identity Scale (Holland, Gottfredson, & Nafziger, 1975). All students also took the Self-Directed Search (SDS; Holland, 1972), which was the source of several indexes and scales: Consistency and Differentiation of the SDS profile, Profile Similarity (the average correlation among the five SDS subprofiles), the Sum of the Self-Estimates score (the sum of the numerical values indicated by a participant on the 12 self-ratings), and the Average Translation score (an index of the degree to which a person's vocational aspirations agree with the SDS assessment—shown in Holland, 1972; see Table 3). A subsample of high school juniors (216 boys and 161 girls) also took the entire CMI and the Life Plans

Inventory. The tables in this study contain fewer students than the total sample assessed earlier, because many students failed to respond to one or more items about undecidedness and dissatisfaction, or failed to indicate their sex. In every instance, all available data have been used.

These assessment devices and the sampling have been more fully described elsewhere (Holland, Gottfredson, & Nafziger, 1975), and a technical report (Holland, Gottfredson, & Nafziger, 1973) provides additional information. The samples are not representative of any well-defined population. The goal was to secure persons broadly distributed across personality types and geographical locations. Samples came from eight high schools in four states and eight colleges in six states. School means for fathers' educational level varied from 2.2 to 5.2 on a 7-point scale, ranging from completion of eighth grade or less (1) to obtaining a graduate or professional degree (7).

In the following analyses, it appeared useful to try two different definitions of indecision: The first was a simple true–false criterion and the second was a multiple-choice or more differentiated criterion. The two groups formed by these criteria have a 75 percent overlap among high school students but only a 50 percent overlap among college students. The analyses indicate that the two criteria of indecision produced similar results.

Results

As a first step, *decided* and *undecided* students were compared on all variables. In these comparisons, decided equals saying "true" to the following statement: "I have made a tentative occupational choice or I am currently employed full time." Tables 1 and 2 show the results for high school and college students.

Tables 1 and 2 indicate that undecided and decided students are alike on most variables. Despite the large samples, only the Identity, Short Vocational Attitude, and Artistic Summary scales produce statistically significant differences for both boys and girls in the high school sample; and only the Interpersonal Competency and Identity scales yield significant differences for both men and women in the college sample. Finally, only differences in the Identity Scale replicate across all four groups.

The results imply that undecided students lack a clear sense of identity. In responding to the items in the 15-item Identity Scale, they said: "I change my opinion of myself a lot" (true). "I can't really say what my interests are" (true). "If someone asked, I could describe my personality with considerable accuracy" (false). "I have a clear picture of my abilities and talents—what I am good at" (false). "I know what kind of life I want for myself" (false). "I never feel the same about myself from week to week" (true). These and similar items express a shifting self-picture and an inability to assess oneself accurately or to relate personal characteristics to occupational possibilities.

The other differentiating variables—Vocational Attitude (CMI), Inter-

PERSONAL CHARACTERISTICS OF DECIDED
AND UNDECIDED HIGH SCHOOL STUDENTS

table 1

VARIABLE	DECIDED			UNDECIDED		
	M	SD	n	M	SD	n
Boys						
Consistency[a]	2.11	.80	143	2.19	.74	139
Differentiation[a]	11.23	2.28	143	10.72	2.39	139
Interpersonal Competency[b]	12.14	3.30	139	11.98	3.22	137
Preconscious Activity[b]	16.91	5.18	132	17.84	5.25	131
Identity[b]	11.80**	2.69	139	9.98	3.11	139
Anomy[b]	4.73	2.19	132	4.92	2.18	135
Short Vocational Attitude[b]	12.20*	1.96	140	11.72	1.99	139
Long Vocational Attitude[c]	35.53	5.78	58	33.95	5.41	83
Self-Appraisal[c]	12.10	4.37	58	12.53	3.79	83
Occupational Information[c]	16.59	3.76	58	16.04	3.35	83
Goal Selection[c]	11.30	4.04	57	11.00	3.86	82
Planning[c]	12.86	4.38	57	12.43	4.52	81
Problem Solving[c]	10.58	3.69	57	9.42	3.66	81
Occupational Information[b]	16.01	3.55	140	16.12	3.04	139
Realistic Summary score[a]	9.10	4.50	143	8.27	4.05	139
Investigative Summary score[a]	7.24	4.20	143	7.29	4.09	139
Artistic Summary score[a]	3.82	3.17	143	4.73*	3.80	139
Social Summary score[a]	8.52	3.21	143	9.45*	2.85	139
Enterprising Summary score[a]	6.33	3.38	143	6.96	3.35	139
Conventional Summary score[a]	3.97	3.07	143	4.46	3.69	139
Sum of self-estimates score[a]	47.75	8.91	142	47.24	9.32	136
Average translation score[b]	2.62	1.03	136	2.38	.93	127
Profile similarity[a]	.45	.23	143	.45	.22	139
Father's education	2.76	1.69	143	2.99	1.86	139
Girls						
Consistency[a]	2.42	.56	303	2.46	.58	219
Differentiation[a]	11.83	2.06	303	11.54	2.03	219
Interpersonal Competency[b]	12.26*	3.26	287	11.69	3.04	206
Preconscious Activity[b]	21.36	5.18	272	20.87	5.06	192
Identity[b]	11.74**	2.67	295	9.68	3.38	207
Anomy[b]	3.97	2.36	282	4.25	2.10	199
Short Vocational Attitude[b]	13.26**	1.77	296	12.66	1.86	214
Long Vocational Attitude[c]	39.67**	3.66	61	36.22	4.84	59
Self-Appraisal[c]	15.28	2.48	61	14.63	2.16	59
Occupational Information[c]	17.80	1.97	61	17.17	2.06	59
Goal Selection[c]	14.21	2.80	61	13.38	3.50	58
Planning[c]	15.18	2.76	61	14.54	2.87	59
Problem Solving[c]	12.88	2.62	61	12.27	'2.44	59
Occupational Information[b]	16.79	2.75	302	16.43	2.90	218
Realistic Summary score[a]	2.57	2.51	303	2.83	2.42	219
Investigative Summary score[a]	6.16	3.89	303	5.55	3.26	219
Artistic Summary score[a]	6.43	3.58	303	7.11*	3.68	219

VARIABLE	DECIDED			UNDECIDED		
	M	*SD*	*n*	*M*	*SD*	*n*
	Girls					
Social Summary score[a]	11.80	2.59	303	12.08	2.40	219
Enterprising Summary score[a]	5.28	2.77	303	5.32	2.80	219
Conventional Summary score[a]	5.60	4.55	303	5.78	4.26	219
Sum of self-estimates score[a]	49.16**	7.60	295	47.25	7.47	215
Average translation score[b]	2.73*	1.03	287	2.50	.91	200
Profile similarity[a]	.52	.21	303	.50	.20	219
Father's education	3.53	2.02	303	3.58	1.98	219

Note. Indicated are the significant *t*-test results between decided and undecided students of the same sex.
[a]Scales or derivatives included in the Self-Directed Search.
[b]Scales included in the Life Plans Inventory.
[c]Scales included in the Career Maturity Inventory.
*$p < .05$.
**$p < .01$.

personal Competency, Sum of the Self-Estimates score (SDS), and Artistic Summary Scale (SDS)—usually appear consonant with this interpretation. Positive associations are expected between identity, maturity, interpersonal competency, and self-confidence, but why a high Artistic Summary score is associated with being undecided is not clear.

The next analyses were performed for students who expressed uncertainty, dissatisfaction, or indecision according to the following item:

> How satisfied are you with your present job or your choice of an occupation?
> (Check one of the following.)
> — 1. Well satisfied with choice
> — 2. Satisfied, but have a few doubts
> — 3. Not sure
> — 4. Dissatisfied, but intend to remain
> — 5. Very dissatisfied and intend to change
> — 6. Undecided about my future career

In the questionnaire, only those students who checked alternatives 3, 4, 5, or 6 were asked to respond true or false to each of the statements shown in Table 3 (potential explanations of their indecision or dissatisfaction). Table 3 indicates the percentage of the student samples responding true to each statement.

Males and females endorse these explanations in about the same rank order. Many of the statements in these tables resemble the items in the Identity Scale—especially the expressions of doubt about self-perceptions of abilities, strengths, and weaknesses, lack of occupational knowledge, and deci-

PERSONAL CHARACTERISTICS OF DECIDED
AND UNDECIDED HIGH SCHOOL STUDENTS

table 2

VARIABLE	DECIDED			UNDECIDED		
	M	SD	n	M	SD	n
Men						
Consistency[a]	2.51	.68	275	2.42	.72	67
Differentiation[a]	11.84	2.18	275	11.49	2.26	67
Interpersonal Competency[b]	13.16*	3.29	271	12.08	3.85	65
Preconscious Activity[b]	17.54*	5.80	256	19.27	5.66	60
Identity[b]	12.69**	2.30	266	11.15	2.56	65
Anomy[b]	2.45	2.10	262	2.92	2.09	63
Short Vocational Attitude[b]	13.59**	1.57	269	12.82	1.80	65
Occupational Information[b]	19.08	1.62	275	18.78	1.79	67
Realistic Summary score[a]	7.52	4.56	275	6.76	4.34	67
Investigative Summary score[a]	7.81	4.23	275	7.63	4.35	67
Artistic Summary score[a]	3.57	3.57	275	4.88**	3.44	67
Social Summary score[a]	8.38	3.55	275	9.40*	3.47	67
Enterprising Summary score[a]	6.46	4.04	275	6.84	3.98	67
Conventional Summary score[a]	4.37	3.87	275	3.57	3.38	67
Sum of self-estimates score[a]	52.35	7.32	273	50.98	7.27	66
Average translation score[b]	2.50	.98	256	2.30	.94	62
Profile similarity[a]	.52	.20	275	.49	.20	67
Father's education	3.72	1.66	275	4.00	1.78	67
Women						
Consistency[a]	2.58	.54	307	2.68	.52	41
Differentiation[a]	11.93	1.91	307	11.73	2.58	41
Interpersonal Competency[b]	13.13**	3.10	294	10.85	3.46	40
Preconscious Activity[b]	20.84	6.04	281	21.79	5.90	38
Identity[b]	12.86**	2.38	298	10.82	2.98	40
Anomy[b]	2.42	1.92	286	2.81	1.76	37
Short Vocational Attitude[b]	14.07	1.43	299	13.72	1.62	40
Occupational Information[b]	19.03*	1.47	305	18.54	1.58	41
Realistic Summary score[a]	2.62	2.48	307	3.29	2.92	41
Investigative Summary score[a]	6.09	3.87	307	5.85	3.40	41
Artistic Summary score[a]	7.36	3.58	307	8.44	3.47	41
Social Summary score[a]	12.15	2.53	307	11.32	2.64	41
Enterprising Summary score[a]	4.73	2.86	307	4.27	3.26	41
Conventional Summary score[a]	4.51	3.70	307	4.44	3.79	41
Sum of self-estimates score[a]	50.52**	6.90	303	46.71	7.14	41
Average translation score[b]	2.87*	.87	295	2.57	.81	38
Profile similarity[a]	.53	.20	307	.49	.22	41
Father's education	4.12	1.74	307	4.58	1.87	41

Note. Indicated are the significant *t*-test results between decided and undecided students of the same sex.

[a]Scales or derivatives included in the Self-Directed Search.
[b]Scales included in the Life Plans Inventory.
[c]Scales included in the Career Maturity Inventory.
*p < .05.
**p < .01.

STUDENTS' EXPLANATIONS FOR BEING UNSURE, DISSATISFIED,
OR UNDECIDED ABOUT A VOCATIONAL CHOICE

table 3

EXPLANATION	HIGH SCHOOL		COLLEGE	
	Boys (n = 115–119)	Girls (n = 182–200)	Men (n = 84–86)	Women (n = 67–72)
I am not sure that my present occupational choice or job is right for me.	77.39	71.43	85.53	76.12
I don't know enough about employment opportunities.	73.95	77.00	61.63	73.61
I don't know enough about the special kinds of people who enter different occupations.	73.11	73.20	58.82	64.28
I don't know enough about what workers do in various occupations.	71.43	64.82	50.00	58.33
I am uncertain about the occupation I could perform well.	67.80	78.89	47.67	70.83
I am uncertain about the occupations I would enjoy.	65.55	70.71	77.91	74.65
I am sometimes interested in occupations which I am not qualified to do well.	63.02	61.14	70.93	63.38
I don't have to make a decision right now.	62.71	56.34	67.44	58.57
I doubt if I have the ability to make a good vocational decision right now.	52.94	57.65	34.52	44.28
I don't know what my major strengths and weaknesses are.	52.94	45.68	31.76	41.67
I don't have the money to do what I would really like to do.	52.94	34.18	40.70	24.28
If I had to make an occupational choice right now, I am afraid I would make a bad choice.	42.02	48.95	29.41	22.86
I am uncertain about my ability to finish the necessary education or training.	38.14	32.65	19.77	22.22

Note. Numbers given are percentages. Values for *n* vary from item to item, because students did not always respond to every item.

sion-making ability. Table 3 also suggests that there are many competent but undecided people whose environmental situation does not require a decision at this time: Of the students polled, 56 percent to 67 percent said, "I don't have to make a decision right now."

The next analyses were performed to learn if the variables used to distinguish decided from undecided students would also serve to distinguish degrees of indecision *among* students who were undecided by the true–false criterion. In this instance the sheer number of "explanations" indicated by an

CORRELATIONS BETWEEN INDIVIDUAL AND TOTAL NUMBER
OF REASONS FOR BEING UNSURE, DISSATISFIED,
OR UNDECIDED ABOUT A VOCATIONAL CHOICE

table 4

	TOTAL NO. REASONS			
	High school		College	
EXPLANATION	Boys	Girls	Men	Women
	(n = 146–176)	(n = 186–229)	(n = 84–94)	(n = 62–79)
I am not sure that my present occupational choice or job is right for me.	.52*	.43*	.33*	.35*
I don't know enough about employment opportunities.	.40*	.40*	.62*	.35*
I don't know enough about the special kinds of people who enter different occupations.	.46*	.43*	.60*	.52*
I don't know enough about what workers do in various occupations.	.42*	.43*	.57*	.42*
I am uncertain about the occupations I could perform well.	.58*	.48*	.51*	.67*
I am uncertain about the occupation I would enjoy.	.36*	.52*	.41*	.35*
I am sometimes interested in occupations which I am often not qualified to do well.	.29*	.33*	.40*	.31*
I don't have to make a decision right now.[a]	.09	.17*	.12	.00
I doubt if I have the ability to make a good vocational decision right now.	.41*	.55*	.46*	.42*
I don't know what my major strengths and weaknesses are.	.50*	.44*	.56*	.30*
I don't have the money to do what I would really like to do.[a]	.06	.11	.17	−.01
If I had to make an occupational choice right now I am afraid I would make a bad choice.	.48*	.57*	.57*	.43*
I am uncertain about my ability to finish the necessary education or training.	.30*	.34*	.37*	.36*

Note. Values for *n* vary from item to item, because students did not always respond to every item.
[a]The omission of these items should increase the reliability of this scale.
*p < .05.

undecided student was used to measure degrees of indecision. Table 4 shows how the 13 reasons correlate with the total number of reasons across the samples of male and female high school and college students. The Kuder-Richardson 20 values for this scale across the four samples of high school and college males and females are .86, .84, .78, and .63, respectively.

CORRELATIONS BETWEEN THE NUMBER OF EXPLANATIONS
AND ASSESSMENT VARIABLES FOR "UNDECIDED" STUDENTS

table 5

VARIABLE	HIGH SCHOOL				COLLEGE			
	Boys		Girls		Men		Women	
	r	n	r	n	r	n	r	n
Consistency[a]	01	139	01	219	01	67	22	41
Differentiation[a]	04	139	04	219	−01	67	−03	41
Interpersonal Competency[b]	−21**	137	−15*	206	−09	65	−27	40
Preconscious Activity[b]	01	131	09	192	14	60	06	38
Identity[b]	−43**	139	−39**	207	−57**	65	−35*	40
Anomy[b]	19*	135	02	199	−07	63	41*	37
Short Vocational Attitude[b]	−15	139	−10	214	−12	65	−12	40
Long Vocational Attitude[c]	−17	83	−05	59				
Self-Appraisal[c]	−07	83	07	59				
Occupational Information[c]	−07	83	27*	59				
Goal Selection[c]	−18	82	44**	58				
Planning[c]	02	81	17	59				
Problem Solving[c]	−02	81	26*	59				
Occupational Information[b]	08	139	19**	218	08	67	40**	41
Realistic Summary score[a]	02	139	−04	219	−06	67	−15	41
Investigative Summary score[a]	12	139	09	219	02	67	10	41
Artistic Summary score[a]	01	139	−01	219	02	67	38*	41
Social Summary score[a]	−04	139	04	219	−05	67	−35*	41
Enterprising Summary score[a]	−13	139	02	219	01	67	−10	41
Conventional Summary score[a]	03	139	−09	219	06	67	−11	41
Sum of self-estimates score[a]	−15	136	−09	215	−18	66	−10	41
Average translation score[b]	03	127	01	200	−20	62	06	38
Profile similarity[a]	09	139	08	219	−08	67	01	41
Father's education	02	139	10	219	03	67	23	41

Note. Decimals are omitted.
[a]Scales or derivatives included in the Self-Directed Search.
[b]Scales included in the Life Plans Inventory.
[c]Scales included in the Career Maturity Inventory.
*p < .05.
**p < .01.

Table 5 shows the correlations between the number of explanations and the assessment variables used earlier. The Identity Scale correlates with total reasons across all four groups. The greater the number of explanations a student offers for undecidedness, the lower the Identity score (rs range from −.35 to −.57). Again, the Interpersonal Competency and Occupational Information (CMI) scales differentiate for some but not all samples. The Interpersonal Competency Scale is negatively correlated with the number of rationalizations a student gives for undecidedness. The Occupational Information Scale (CMI) correlates positively and unexpectedly with the number of student explanations of indecision. Similarly, the number of student explanations also cor-

**CORRELATIONS BETWEEN THE NUMBER OF EXPLANATIONS
AND ASSESSMENT VARIABLES FOR UNSURE,
DISSATISFIED, OR UNDECIDED STUDENTS**

table 6 _____

VARIABLE	HIGH SCHOOL				COLLEGE			
	Boys		Girls		Men		Women	
	r	n	r	n	r	n	r	n
Consistency[a]	03	123	−14*	201	−10	86	−07	72
Differentiation[a]	−06	123	−01	201	−19	86	−16	72
Interpersonal Competency[b]	−18*	119	−26**	183	−32**	84	−40**	68
Preconscious Activity[b]	10	115	05	171	−03	77	02	63
Identity[b]	−35**	123	−41**	186	−60**	83	−45**	70
Anomy[b]	30**	120	11	179	34**	81	32*	61
Short Vocational Attitude[b]	−16	123	−14*	194	−09	82	−29*	69
Long Vocational Attitude[c]	−29*	69	−30*	54				
Self-Appraisal[c]	−12	69	−10	54				
Occupational Information[c]	−19	69	39**	54				
Goal Selection[c]	−01	68	34*	54				
Planning[c]	02	68	15	54				
Problem Solving[c]	−13	68	30*	54				
Occupational Information[b]	02	122	20**	199	−06	86	13	72
Realistic Summary score[a]	06	123	−01	201	03	86	−01	72
Investigative Summary score[a]	−04	123	03	201	00	86	09	72
Artistic Summary score[a]	−04	123	−14	201	05	86	06	72
Social Summary score[a]	−07	123	−01	201	−03	86	−16	72
Enterprising Summary score[a]	−08	123	−01	201	−20	86	−05	72
Conventional Summary score[a]	05	123	−01	201	10	86	23	72
Sum of self-estimates score[a]	−10	122	−17*	196	−27*	86	−21	70
Average translation score[b]	−21*	113	07	183	−28*	81	−08	67
Profile similarity[a]	−01	123	−03	201	−26*	86	−14	72
Father's education	07	123	05	201	14	86	−05	72

Note. Decimals are omitted.
[a]Scales or derivatives included in the Self-Directed Search.
[b]Scales included in the Life Plans Inventory.
[c]Scales included in the Career Maturity Inventory.
*$p < .05$.
**$p < .01$.

relates positively with several other CMI scales in some samples: Goal Selection and Problem Solving. These latter results are puzzling.

The correlations in Table 5 were then recomputed for students who were unsure, dissatisfied, or undecided about a career (the same criterion used to define the samples in Tables 3 and 4) to form Table 6.

The use of a differentiated definition of dissatisfaction and indecision in Table 6 results in 25 rather than 15 statistically significant correlations. Equally important, the trends are more readily interpretable. In three of four groups, the correlations between the Identity Scale and the number of explanations are larger. The Interpersonal Competency Scale now replicates across all four groups; three of four correlations are larger than before and statistically significant. The Anomy Scale is now significantly related to the number of student explanations in three of four groups. Likewise, the Sum of Self-Estimates (SDS) and the Average Translation scores are negatively correlated with the number of explanations; whereas earlier, both variables had insignificant correlations with the number of explanations. The CMI scales appear to be unaffected by the redefinition of the undecided group.

Discussion

The results suggest that high school and college students who characterize themselves as "decided" or "undecided" differ in terms of their sense of identity and vocational maturity, but they do not differ consistently on most other characteristics. This main finding is strengthened by the explanations that students give for their undecided state. These explanations are reminiscent of some items in the Identity and Vocational Attitude scales. In addition, and perhaps most importantly, the correlations between the degree of indecision (the number of explanations a student checked) for undecided or dissatisfied students (Table 6) and the Identity, Interpersonal Competency, Anomy, Vocational Attitude, Sum of Self-Estimates, and the Average Translation scores, scales, or indexes form a consistent cluster.

This cluster is compatible with the outcomes of many earlier studies and much speculation. In a closely related study, Kelso (1976) compared decided and undecided high school students (1,015 boys and 1,247 girls), using the 10 items of the Identity Scale included in the present 15-item scale in this study along with the other scales of the Psychosocial Maturity Inventory (Greenberger, Josselson, Knerr, & Knerr, 1975) and found that the Identity Scale discriminated between choosers and nonchoosers. In addition, other scale comparisons imply that nonchoosers lack work involvement, self-reliance, and communication skills. According to other scales, they were also less involved with peers, family, and schools.

Other studies indicate that the Vocational Attitude Scale is usually positively related to being decided, involved, and concerned with planning (Crites, 1973). The content of the Identity Scale is concerned with a clear and stable self-picture of personality, interests, and talents; the Identity Scale also has moderately positive correlations with the Interpersonal Competency Scale and moderately negative correlations with the Anomy Scale (Holland, Note 1). In their validation of the Anomy Scale, McClosky and Schaar (1965) have provided substantial evidence that their scale taps a broad range of personal variables associated with alienation and pathology including its correlations with the Manifest Anxiety Scale. Consequently, the moderately high anxiety scores obtained for undecided students (Kimes & Troth, 1974) are consistent with the present results. Likewise, the findings that undecided students tend to drop out, earn fewer credits, and get lower grades (Elton & Rose, 1971; Lunneborg, 1975) seem consistent with our findings of Anomy and the low involvement observed among undecided students by other investigators.

In an earlier study, Holland et al. (1975) found no relation between the quality of student decision making and being decided or undecided—an unexpected finding. In the present study, the quality of decision making (described earlier as translation ability) for males is related to the number of student explanations of decision-making difficulties when only uncertain or dissatisfied students are considered.

Most recently, Osipow et al. (1976) developed a 19-item scale of educational-vocational undecidedness that resembles the 13-item scale formed here from student explanations of undecidedness or dissatisfaction. A review of both scales suggests substantial common content—lack of confidence about decision-making skills and lack of self- and environmental information—although some items are unique to each scale. Osipow et al. developed explanations of undecidedness by a factor analysis of student self-reports that results in four factors: need for structure, perceived external barriers, positive choice conflict, and personal conflict. The present study complements this earlier work by tying undecidedness, and student self-reports thereof, to a wide range of psychological variables with substantial explanatory value. Our results suggest that the student explanations form a single internally consistent scale; the factor analysis by Osipow et al. of a similar scale implies multiple scales.

Finally, and unfortunately, the vocational indecision literature is littered with other findings that are not easily integrated with the present results. A review of the whole literature is required to put everything in place, although reviews by Crites (1969) and Osipow (1973) are largely consistent with the present findings.

Perhaps we have been too concerned with finding a few explicit variables and too little concerned with discovering the broad patterns suggested by a host of poorly defined variables. It may be useful to consider undecided people as comprising multiple subtypes rather than a single type (Crites, 1969).

For example, more than 50 percent of the undecided students (see Table 3) reported. "I don't have to make a decision right now." In an earlier study (Holland, Note 2), 42 percent and 54 percent of the males and females in a national sample of 2-year college students ($N = 22,000$) said: "The main reason I am undecided about my vocation is: It doesn't seem important to make a decision yet." In an Australian study, Kelso (1975) found that realism about vocational choice was clearly related to how soon a high school student had to go to work. In short, a large proportion of undecided students are doing what intelligent adults do—delaying some decisions until reality arrives. Such a strategy is not necessarily stupid, uninformed, or immature.

Two other subgroups may exist among undecided people and require special vocational assistance. The first group has a slight to moderate dose of immaturity, interpersonal incompetency, anxiety, and alienation. Perhaps they comprise a quarter of the undecideds. Finally, another quarter of the undecideds may have moderate to severe cases of immaturity, incompetency, anxiety, and alienation.

Taken together, the results have stimulated the following speculations about the character of undecided students, the relations of their personal dispositions to decision-making processes, and some plausible explanations why diverse vocational treatments help some people but not others. The correlates of student difficulties in making vocational choice expressed in Table 6 imply the following complex but consistent cluster of personal traits, attitudes, and skills: interpersonal incompetency, lack of self-confidence, lack of involvement, anxiety, an unclear and shifting identity, and poor decision-making skills.

The rationale for the Anomy Scale resembles this syndrome. McClosky and Schaar (1965) conceptualize anomy as a state of mind caused by personal factors that impair learning and socialization. Using a large state sample ($N = 1,082$) and a large national sample ($N = 1,484$), McClosky and Schaar demonstrate that the Anomy Scale has moderate positive relations with intolerance of ambiguity, rigidity, lack of self-confidence, passivity, anxiety, disorganization, as well as other variables including a low level of educational attainment.

Unfortunately, the concept of anomy has a long and controversial history so that its connotations are ambiguous and conflicting for many. Consequently, it may be useful for vocational purposes to relabel this speculative syndrome as *the indecisive disposition*. This disposition is seen as the outcome of a life history in which a person has failed to acquire the necessary cultural involvement, self-confidence, tolerance for ambiguity, sense of identity, self- and environmental knowledge to cope with vocational decision making as well as with other common problems.

Consequently, when treatments such as tests, workshops, counseling, vocational decision-making training, and occupational information are applied to students expressing indecision, many students make decisions or feel better because a large portion have little or no trace of the indecisive disposition. Those students who are not helped are more likely to have some or many of the personal characteristics associated with the indecisive disposition. Such people should be especially difficult to help because they suffer from a complex cluster of maladaptive attitudes and coping behaviors that are probably not amenable to brief vocationally oriented treatments. We may have been misled by assuming that indecisiveness is due to anxiety and tension rather than a host of additional unfavorable personal and situational forces. Likewise, immaturity fails to capture the wide array of personal and situational deficiencies implied by our results and those of others.

The practical applications of the results and our speculations appear to be several: (a) It is probably a mistake to treat all undecided students as if they had the indecisive disposition. Only a very small percentage could be expected to have such characteristics to an incapacitating degree. In terms of the evidence, it is more reasonable to assume that most undecided students do not have any special negative characteristics and to treat them accordingly. (b) Some undecided students do not want or need assistance. They will cope with their decisions when the realities demand it. (c) Counselors can identify indecisive students with special needs by using the brief scale used here or the scale developed by Osipow et al. (1976). Likewise, the personal histories of undecided students with special problems should be characterized by a general failure to make decisions at culturally approved times. The Vocational Attitude and Identity scales should also be helpful in identifying the small percentage of students with many of the characteristics of the indecisive disposition.

reference notes _____

1. Holland, J.E. *The Identity Scale.* Unpublished manuscript, Center for Social Organization of Schools, Johns Hopkins University, 1976.
2. Holland, J. L. *A descriptive study of two-year college students.* Unpublished manuscript, 1969. (Available from the author, Department of Social Relations, Johns Hopkins University, Baltimore, Maryland 21218.)

references _____

Ashby, J. D., Wall, H. W., & Osipow, S. H. Vocational certainty and indecision in college freshmen. *Personnel and Guidance Journal,* 1966, *44,* 1037–1041.

Baird, L. L. The Indecision Scale: A reinterpretation. *Journal of Counseling Psychology,* 1968, *15,* 174–179.

Baird, L. L. The undecided student—how different is he? *Personnel and Guidance Journal,* 1969, *47,* 429–434.

Crites, J. O. *Vocational psychology.* New York: McGraw-Hill, 1969.

Crites, J. O. *Theory and research handbook for the Career Maturity Inventory.* Monterey, Calif.: CTB/McGraw-Hill, 1973.

Elton, C. F., & Rose, H. A longitudinal study of the vocationally undecided male student. *Journal of Vocational Behavior,* 1971, *1,* 85–92.

Galinsky, M. D., & Fast, I. Vocational choice as a focus of the identity search. *Journal of Counseling Psychology,* 1966, *13,* 89–92.

Goodstein, L. D. Behavior theoretical views of counseling. In B. Stefflre (Ed.), *Theories of counseling.* New York: McGraw-Hill, 1965.

Greenberger, E., Josselson, R., Knerr, C., & Knerr, B. The measurement and structure of psychosocial maturity. *Journal of Youth and Adolescence,* 1975, *4,* 127–143.

Hilgard, E. R., & Bower, G. H. *Theories of learning.* Englewood Cliffs, N.J.: Prentice-Hall, 1975.

Holland, J. L. *Professional manual for the Self-Directed Search.* Palo Alto, Calif.: Consulting Psychologists Press, 1972.

Holland, J. L. *Making vocational choices: A theory of careers.* Englewood Cliffs, N.J.: Prentice-Hall, 1973.

Holland, J. L., & Baird, L. L. An interpersonal competency scale. *Educational and Psychological Measurement,* 1968, *28,* 503–510. (a)

Holland J. L., & Baird, L. L. The Preconscious Activity Scale: The development and validation of an originality measure. *Journal of Creative Behavior,* 1968, *2,* 217–225. (b)

Holland, J. L., Gottfredson, G. D., & Nafziger, D. H. *A diagnostic scheme for specifying vocational assistance* (Research Rep. No. 164). Baltimore, Md.: Johns Hopkins University, Center for the Social Organization of Schools, 1973. (ERIC Document Reproduction Service No. ED 087 833.)

Holland J. L., Gottfredson, G. D., & Nafziger, D. H. Testing the validity of some theoretical signs of vocational decision-making ability. *Journal of Counseling Psychology,* 1975, *22,* 411–422.

Holland, J. L., & Nichols, R. C. The development and validation of an indecision scale: The natural history of a problem in basic research. *Journal of Counseling Psychology,* 1964, *11,* 27–34.

Kelso, G. I. The influences of stage of leaving school on vocational maturity and realism of vocational choice. *Journal of Vocational Behavior,* 1975, *7,* 29–39.

Kelso, G. I. *Explorations of the developmental antecedents of Holland's occupational types.* Unpublished doctoral dissertation, Johns Hopkins University, 1976.

Kimes, H. G., & Troth, W. A. Relationship of trait anxiety to career decisiveness. *Journal of Counseling Psychology,* 1974, *21,* 277–280.

Lunneborg, P. W. Interest differentiation in high school and vocational indecision in college. *Journal of Vocational Behavior,* 1975, *7,* 297–303.

McClosky, H., & Schaar, J. H. Psychological dimensions of anomy. *American Sociological Review,* 1965, *30,* 14–40.

McGowan, A. S. Vocational maturity and anxiety among vocationally undecided and indecisive students: The effectiveness of the Self-Directed Search (Doctoral dissertation, Fordham University, 1974). *Dissertation Abstracts International,* 1974, *35,* 2691A–2692A. (University Microfilms No. 74–25, 105).

Mendonca; J. D., & Siess, T. F. Counseling for indecisiveness: Problem-solving and anxiety-management training. *Journal of Counseling Psychology,* 1976, *23,* 339–347.

Nelson, E., & Nelson, N. Student attitudes and vocational choices. *Journal of Abnormal and Social Psychology,* 1940, *35,* 279–282.

Osipow, S. H. *Theories of career development* (2nd ed.). Englewood Cliffs, N.J.: Prentice-Hall, 1973.

Osipow, W. H., Carney, C. G., & Barak, A. A scale of educational-vocational undecidedness: A typological approach. *Journal of Vocational Behavior,* 1976, *9,* 233–243.

Rose, H. A., & Elton, C. F. Attrition and the vocationally undecided student. *Journal of Vocational Behavior,* 1971, *1,* 99–103.

Tyler, L. *The work of the counselor* (2nd ed.). New York: Appleton-Century-Crofts, 1961.

comments and questions _____

1. The questions to be studied by Holland and Holland are clearly stated. Do you think that questions 3 and 4 (see p. 298) were *both a priori* questions?

2. As pointed out in the introduction to descriptive research (p. 81), the purpose of the study helps determine the classification. If the purpose is primarily to describe existing conditions we have classified it as descriptive. If the purpose is to help answer causal questions (but is nonexperimental in design) we have classified it as ex post facto. Do you agree with our classification of this study?

3. What psychometric explanations can you advance to explain the greater number of significant correlations in Table 6 than in Table 5? Do the authors provide any explanations?

4. The authors are to be commended for the manner in which they have attempted to relate their findings to those of previous researchers.

5. Do the authors address the question of the validity of students' self-reports?

EFFECT OF EARLY FATHER ABSENCE ON SCHOLASTIC APTITUDE*,[1]

20

LYN CARLSMITH

This article reports the results of an investigation into the effect of father absence on young children in terms of the patterns of math and verbal aptitude scores which these children later attain on college entrance examinations. The author relates the findings to sex-identification theory.

Theories of identification, whatever their form, usually agree on two points: for the boy to identify successfully with the father, the father must be present during at least some portion of the boy's childhood; development of an appropriate masculine identity or self-concept is predicated upon the success of this early identification with the father. One of the most direct methods of investigating these general propositions is to study boys whose fathers were absent during their childhood. The present study, by considering a sample of boys whose home life was presumably normal in every respect except for the temporary absence of the father in World War II, seeks to answer two questions. First, are there lasting measurable effects due to the absence of the father at an early age? Second, is the age of the child during the father's absence an important variable in determining these effects?

Previous studies on the effect of father absence during the first years of life represent three different approaches: 1) studies of the fantasy and behavior of children (Bach, 1946; Sears, 1946; Stolz, 1954; Lynn & Sawrey, 1959; Tiller, 1957; D'Andrade, 1962); 2) retrospective accounts from the case histories of

*Carlsmith, L., "Effect of Early Father Absence on Scholastic Aptitude," *Harvard Educational Review*, 34, 1964, No. 1, 3–21 with the permission of the publisher and author. Copyright 1964 by the President and Fellows of Harvard College.

[1]The research for this paper was done at the Laboratory of Human Development at Harvard University. It is a part of a larger project on sex identity being carried on at the Laboratory under the direction of John W. M. Whiting. A more extensive report of this study appears in a Ph.D. thesis of the same title under the author's former name, Karolyn Gai Kuckenberg, which was accepted by the Department of Social Relations in June, 1963. The author is grateful to John W. M. Whiting, Beatrice B. Whiting, and J. Merrill Carlsmith for their generous assistance in the planning and execution of this research.

delinquents (Zucker, 1943; Glueck & Glueck, 1950; Rohrer & Edmonson, 1960); 3) studies of other cultures (Burton & Whiting, 1961). Each of these sources suggests that absence of the father significantly affects personality development and behavior in certain ways. The results of all these studies are generally consistent: father-absent boys show more underlying feminine traits and, at least in lower or working class families, they attempt to compensate by demonstrating extreme masculinity. However, the effect of the early experience of father absence on later development under normal circumstances has not been studied in this culture.

The study to be reported in this paper stems from an early and serendipitous finding that aroused considerable interest at the outset of this research on the effects of father absence. The finding was this: boys who experienced early separation from their fathers had a different pattern of aptitude scores on the College Board tests than boys who were not separated. Since the finding concerned the differential development of Mathematical and Verbal ability, it dovetailed into the current interest and research on the learning of mathematical or analytical modes of thought. It seemed possible that we had hit upon an unexpected antecedent variable—the presence or absence of the father in early childhood. Although the finding was initially based on a very small sample of Harvard students, it seemed sufficiently intriguing to explore further with a much larger group of students.

Whiting's (1960) theory of cross-sex identification provided the framework from which this study developed. This theory provides a set of explicit hypotheses concerning the development of cross-sex identification. However, it should be pointed out that the present study was not designed to discriminate between theories of identification; rather, it provides evidence relevant to any general theory of identification by showing certain strong effects of father absence at various ages.

Let us now consider the relevance of aptitude scores to sex-role identification. Accumulated evidence from a large number of studies on Math and Verbal aptitudes clearly demonstrates that females are generally superior to males in Verbal areas, while males are superior to females in quantitative pursuits, particularly numerical reasoning (e.g., McCarthy, 1954; Samuels, 1943; Heilman, 1933). These differences are well replicated and seem to hold over a broad age range, increasing from the elementary school years. Preferences for school subjects follow the same pattern. A particularly relevant study by Milton (1957) indicates a striking correlation between the problem-solving ability of adolescents and their scores on masculinity-femininity scales (MMPI and Terman-Miles). That is, both boys and girls who obtain a high masculinity score show superior problem-solving ability. In a retrospective study of the autobiographies of professional mathematicians, Plank and Plank (1954) report that female mathematicians have a "strong identification with a masculine figure in their lives. Parallel with it, seems to go a lack of feminine identification . . ." (p. 268). The lives of male mathematicians are characterized by a "loss of relationship to the mother."

These findings suggest that superior ability in mathematics reflects a typically masculine way of thinking or "conceptual approach." For the purposes of this study, the pattern of Math and Verbal aptitude scores from the College Entrance Examination Board seemed to provide a clear, objective measure of this sex-typed ability. That is, students who score relatively higher on Math aptitude than on Verbal aptitude tests have an aptitude pattern that is typical of a masculine conceptual approach; students who score relatively higher on Verbal aptitude tests have a more feminine conceptual approach.

Finally, there is considerable evidence that aptitude is a fairly stable characteristic, showing little variation with time (College Board Score Reports, 1960). A special mathematics teaching program which followed school children from fourth to seventh grade (Alpert, 1963) indicates that aptitude for mathematics is fairly well established by fourth grade and is highly resistant to change during subsequent school training. These data suggest that aptitude patterns are a useful index for the measurement of primary sex-role identity since they are apparently little influenced by the external pressures or expectations that occur in the subject's later experience. That is, while we would expect many indices of personality and behavior to be strongly influenced by our cultural norms for males and females, it is likely that aptitude patterns are both relatively free from and impervious to such expectations and that they are therefore a good indicator of the primary or underlying identity.

Children who were born during the war years (1941 to 1945) and whose fathers were away during their first years of life are now finishing high school or attending college. This group offers a number of advantages for a study of the effects of early father absence on subsequent development. It is possible to locate students from stable families who have shared this common experience, the reason for father absence was socially acceptable and even desirable, the exact periods of father absence may usually be ascertained, and all other background factors (except the wartime separation) can be matched in the two groups studied. The present study includes only boys from intact families (both parents living and not divorced) of middle or upper-middle class background. The majority of students were sophomores at Harvard College; one small sample includes high school seniors who planned to attend college the next year. Thus all students have achieved a relatively high level of academic success and have also made a reasonably satisfactory adjustment in terms of our social and cultural norms.

Samples

Both college and high school students were subjects in this study. The college population consists of 881 Harvard freshmen in the class of 1963 and 307 Harvard freshmen in the class of 1964. The high school sample includes 137 boys and 135 girls from the 1961 senior classes at Concord, Lexington, and Newton South Public High Schools. All students in both the college and high

table 1

LENGTH OF TIME FATHER WAS ABSENT AFTER CHILD'S BIRTH	HARVARD CLASS OF 1963	HARVARD CLASS OF 1964
Over 3 years	38	3
2–3 years	53	36
Less than 2 years	124	44
Not absent	666	224
	HIGH SCHOOL BOYS	*HIGH SCHOOL GIRLS*
1–5 years	19	14
Less than 1 year	19	12
Not absent	99	109

school samples are American-born and are from intact families (i.e., natural parents are not separated, divorced, or deceased). The high school sample is limited to those students on whom aptitude scores from the College Entrance Examination Board were available.

All students in the study were born during the war years, 1941 to 1945. Approximately one-third of their fathers served overseas and were separated from their wives and young children for varying lengths of time. Table 1 presents this distribution.

Methodology

In March, 1961, I administered a simple questionnaire on father absence to 450 Harvard freshmen (Class of '64) who were voluntarily taking a series of interest-aptitude tests through facilities of the Harvard Testing Service. On this form, three questions were asked: was your father in the service during World War II; was he overseas during this time; if so, estimate the dates that he was overseas. Verbal and Math aptitude scores from the College Entrance Examination Board tests were then obtained on all students whose fathers had served overseas. Students whose fathers were in the service but did not go overseas were eliminated from the study because I felt it would be too difficult to ascertain the periods of father-separation for this group. Foreign-born students and those from broken homes (due to death, separation, or divorce) were also excepted. Finally, the median College Board aptitude scores for the entire freshman class were obtained.

A similar procedure was used with the high school students, except that the father-absence questionnaire was addressed to the parents to increase accuracy of the dates of the father's military service. Math and Verbal aptitude scores were then obtained for all students who had taken the College Entrance Examination Board tests. Since no other aptitude test had been uniformly administered in the high schools, the majority of high school students could not be included in this survey.

To further test the relationship between father-absence and aptitude, I studied a second group of Harvard freshmen (Class of '63). Questions on the father's military service had been included in the medical history record filled out by all entering students. Data on these students were provided by Dr. Stanley King from material collected in the Harvard Student Study.

Scholastic Aptitude Test (SAT)

This test is administered to high school juniors and seniors by the College Entrance Examination Board. The test yields two scores: a Verbal score and a Mathematical score. Norms for the test were established nationally over a period of years, and it is possible to make direct comparisons between students taking the test in different years. The reported reliability coefficient for the test is .91. In *College Board Score Reports* (1961), the average aptitude scores achieved by all high school seniors taking the test in a recent year are reported.

	AVERAGE SAT SCORES	
	Math	Verbal
Boys	527	479
Girls	467	486

The booklet also states: "In general girls do less well than boys on the Mathematical parts of the test and should not be surprised if their Mathematical scores are noticeably lower than their Verbal" (p. 8).

Data Analysis

In addition to mean Math and Verbal aptitude scores, a single Math-minus-Verbal score was computed for each subject. In this paper, the Math-minus-Verbal difference score will be represented by the term M-V. This single difference score is preferred for all comparisons between groups since it controls to some extent for general level of ability. That is, by considering only the relative superiority of Math to Verbal aptitude for each individual, differences in absolute level of ability between individuals are not weighted. For this reason, the single M-V difference score is used for all statistical comparisons between the Father-absent and Father-present groups. Several methods were used to test the significance of the difference between groups; these will be described with the presentation of results.

Results

The independent variables considered here are: 1) length of the father's absence and 2) age of the child when the father left. Since each of the three samples included in this survey represents a different class year in school and different age group (by year of birth), there is considerable variation in the periods of father-absence between groups. In addition, data on both independent variables were not available for one of the samples. Because of these limitations, it is not possible to combine groups or to present uniform tables on the dates of father-absence for all groups. In the data analysis, father-absent categories for each sample are determined by the distribution of dates of father absence, sample size, and the information available for that group. All Math and Verbal scores presented in these tables are from the Scholastic Aptitude Test (SAT) of the College Entrance Examination Board.

HARVARD CLASS OF 1964

For the entire Harvard class of 1964 (n = 1180), the median Math aptitude score was 695; the median Verbal score was 677. Clearly the students in this class scored higher on the Math aptitude test than on the Verbal aptitude test. The first evidence to be presented on the effects of father absence comes from an attempt to compare as extreme groups as possible. Twenty students whose fathers went overseas before they were six months old and were away for at least two years were chosen as the father-absent group. A matched sample of twenty students whose fathers were not in the service at all were selected as the control group. The two groups were matched on the basis of father's occupation, education, marital status (both parents living and not divorced), and on the student's previous academic experience (public or private school). Table 2A shows the breakdown on these background variables which are identical in both groups. Table 2B gives the mean age and ordinal position of subjects as well as the age of parents in the father-absent and father-present groups.[2] Except for the wartime separation of the father-absent group, none of the students in either group had been separated from his father for more than two months during his childhood or adolescence. Five students in each group attended boarding prep schools; all other students lived at home with both parents until college. During the wartime period, no other adults lived as permanent members in any of the family households of either group.

[2]Additional background information was obtained on this sample of students as part of a more intensive interview study reported in Kuckenberg, Karolyn G., Effect of Early Father Absence on Scholastic Aptitude.

**BACKGROUND VARIABLES ON WHICH
TWO GROUPS OF STUDENTS WERE MATCHED**

table 2A

FATHERS' OCCUPATIONS	FATHERS' EDUCATION
8 Physicians	14 Advanced degrees
2 Architects	5 Attended college 1–4 years
1 Lawyer	1 High school only
1 Minister	
1 Professor	
4 Business, managerial	
3 Business, sales	

SUBJECTS' EDUCATION

5 Prep school–Boarded at school
5 Prep school–Lived at home
10 Public school–Lived at home

**OTHER BACKGROUND VARIABLES:
SUBJECTS' AGE, ORDINAL POSITION, AND PARENTS' AGE**

table 2B

	FATHER ABSENT	FATHER PRESENT
Mean Age of Subjects	19.3	19.4
Only Child	4	4
Oldest Child	11	8
Second or Third Child	5	8
Mean Age of Fathers	53	55
Mean Age of Mothers	49	51
Age Range of Fathers	40–70	45–68
Age Range of Mothers	39–62	43–57

Table 3 compares these two matched groups, indicating the number of cases in which Verbal aptitude is superior to Math aptitude.

As Table 2 suggests, many doctors were sent overseas early in the war, and it is interesting to look at the findings for this single occupational group. A total of 18 doctors' sons were found to be included in the original sample of 450 students; 9 of these boys were separated from their fathers during the war years and 9 were not separated. Table 4 compares these two groups of doctors' sons, again showing the number of cases in which Verbal aptitude is superior to Math aptitude.

In these matched samples, the performance of the control group is representative of the relative aptitude scores typically obtained by males, both nationally and at Harvard (i.e., Math superior to Verbal). However, the per-

**RELATIONSHIP OF MATH TO
VERBAL APTITUDE FOR A SELECTED GROUP OF 20
MATCHED PAIRS OF SUBJECTS, HARVARD CLASS OF 1964**

table 3 ───

	APTITUDE SCORES	
	Verbal Higher Than Math	Math Higher Than Verbal
Father Absent	13	7
Father Not Absent	2	18

formance of the father-absent group is similar to the pattern typically achieved by girls (Verbal superior to Math).

To further explore the relationships between father absence and aptitude, the scores for the 83 students in the father-absent sample were analyzed. In Figure 1 the relationships between length of father absence, age of son when father left, and relative superiority of Math or Verbal aptitude are presented graphically. These drawings clearly show that both independent variables are systematically related to aptitude: the relative superiority of Verbal to Math aptitude increases steadily the longer the father is absent and the younger the child is when the father left. This effect is strongest for students whose fathers were absent at birth and/or were away for over 30 months.

The interaction of the two independent variables with aptitude is presented in Table 5, which shows the mean Math and Verbal scores and the mean M-V difference scores for these students. The table employs a two-way break: age of the child when his father left (horizontal axis); total length of time the father was away after his son's birth (vertical axis). A minus sign preceding any of the M-V scores indicates that the mean Verbal score is higher than the mean Math score for that group.

To test the significance of the relationships shown here, a regression analysis was performed. This analysis showed that each variable was

**RELATIONSHIP OF MATH TO VERBAL APTITUDE
FOR 9 MATCHED PAIRS OF DOCTORS'
SONS, HARVARD CLASS OF 1964**

table 4 ───

	APTITUDE SCORES	
	Verbal Higher Than Math	Math Higher Than Verbal
Father Absent	8	1
Father Not Absent	2	7

figure 1

Father-Absent Students, Harvard Class of 1964. Relationship of
Math to Verbal Aptitude (SAT)(n = 83).

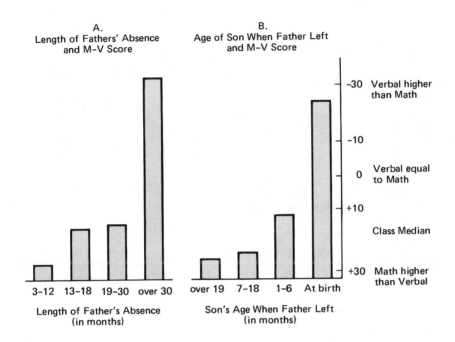

A.
Length of Fathers' Absence
and M-V Score

B.
Age of Son When Father Left
and M-V Score

-30 Verbal higher
     than Math

-10

0   Verbal equal
     to Math

+10

Class Median

+30 Math higher
     than Verbal

3-12   13-18   19-30   over 30

over 19   7-18   1-6   At birth

Length of Father's Absence
(in months)

Son's Age When Father Left
(in months)

significantly related to the M-V aptitude scores (p < .05 for each). That is, in
Table 5 each variable considered alone shows a significant effect on the M-V
score. Because of the high correlation between age at absence and length of
absence ($r = -.59$), neither variable added significantly to prediction of the
M-V score when the other had already been taken into account.

High School Class of 1961

A similar method of analysis was used for the sample of high school boys. Table
6 again shows a two-way break for length of father absence and age of son when
father left.

There are two striking differences to be seen in this table. If the father
left when his son was very young (0–12 months) and was away for a long time
(1–5 years), the relative superiority of Math to Verbal aptitude shows a sharp
decrease. This is consistent with the finding for the Harvard sample. However,

321

FATHER-ABSENT STUDENTS, HARVARD CLASS OF 1964
MEAN MATH, VERBAL, AND M-V APTITUDE SCORES (SAT)
(n = 83)

table 5

LENGTH OF FATHER'S ABSENCE (IN MONTHS)		SON'S AGE WHEN FATHER LEFT (IN MONTHS)				
		over 19	7–18	1–6	At Birth	Total
3–12	n	10	1		4	15
	Math	687	601		702	685
	Verbal	643	685		694	660
	M-V	44	−84		8	25
13–18	n	3	3	4	1	11
	Math	595	761	691	609	677
	Verbal	623	704	670	615	661
	M-V	−28	57	21	−6	16
19–30	n	1	22	8	9	40
	Math	708	696	697	665	689
	Verbal	731	668	669	693	675
	M-V	−23	28	28	−28	14
over 30	n		4	3	10	17
	Math		680	653	656	661
	Verbal		685	696	690	690
	M-V		−5	−43	−34	−29
Total	n	14	30	15	24	
	Math	669	697	687	665	
	Verbal	645	674	674	689	
	M-V	24	23	13	−24	

if the father left late in the boy's childhood and was gone for only a brief time, a reverse effect apparently takes place. The other two conditions show no strong effect. An analysis of variance shows the differences between the groups (on the M-V score) to be significant beyond the .001 level.

While this sample is too small and unstable to draw any firm conclusions, the second finding of a sharp increase in Math aptitude, relative to Verbal aptitude, for one of the father-absent groups is intriguing. Returning to Table 5, there are ten cases in a somewhat comparable cell in the upper left corner: again the father left relatively late in the boy's childhood (after he was 18 months old) and was gone for only a brief time (3–12 months). These ten cases show a noticeable superiority in Math ability and are the chief contributors to the mean Total scores for their column. The mean M-V difference score for these 10 cases is 44; the comparable score for the entire class is 18. Although

CONCORD, LEXINGTON, NEWTON
HIGH SCHOOL BOYS, CLASS OF 1961
MEAN MATH, VERBAL, AND M-V APTITUDE SCORES (SAT)
(n = 137)

table 6

LENGTH OF FATHER'S ABSENCE	SON'S AGE WHEN FATHER LEFT	MEAN APTITUDE SCORES			
		n	Math	Verbal	M-V
3–12 months	1–5 years	12	633	536	97
	0–12 months	7	568	517	51
1–5 years	1–5 years	7	555	499	56
	0–12 months	12	517	505	12
Not Absent		99	576	529	47

RELATIONSHIP BETWEEN LENGTH OF FATHER'S
ABSENCE AND APTITUDE FOR BOTH THE
COLLEGE AND HIGH SCHOOL SAMPLES

table 7

LENGTH OF FATHER'S ABSENCE	HARVARD CLASS OF 1964				HIGH SCHOOL CLASSES OF 1961			
	Mean Aptitude Scores				Mean Aptitude Scores			
	n	math	verbal	m-v	n	math	verbal	m-v
3–12 months	15	685	660	25	19	609	529	80
More than 12 months	68	680	677	3	19	532	503	29
Control Group[a]	1180	695	677	18	99	576	529	47

[a]See Table 8, p. 324.

many more cases in this experimental condition are needed, these two findings suggest that there may be a reverse effect operating if the child first knows his father and then is briefly separated from him.

To summarize these findings in comparable form for both the high school and college samples, a simple breakdown on each of the independent variables is shown in Tables 7 and 8. These tables are a condensation of the data already presented for the two groups.

Despite the sizeable difference between the groups in range of aptitude scores, the effect of father absence is similar for both groups. Comparing the father-absent students with the control groups, these data indicate that if the father leaves early (before his son is 12 months old) and if he is gone for more than a year, the son's Verbal aptitude is relatively superior to his Math

table 8

SON'S AGE WHEN FATHER LEFT	HARVARD CLASS OF 1964				HIGH SCHOOL CLASSES OF 1961			
	Mean Aptitude Scores				Mean Aptitude Scores			
	n	math	verbal	m-v	n	math	verbal	m-v
More than 12 months	21	683	658	25	19	604	522	82
0–12 months	62	682	679	3	19	536	509	27
Control Group[a]	1180	695	677	18	99	576	529	47

[a]For the Harvard Class of 1964, the scores for the Control group are the median aptitude scores obtained by the *entire* class, and therefore include both father-absent and father-present students. For the high school classes, the Control group includes only students who were not separated from their fathers at any time.

aptitude. However, both late and brief separation from the father are associated with a relative increase in Math ability.

Although the independent variables are presented separately in these tables, it should be noted that for both samples of students there is a high negative correlation between length of father's absence and son's age when father left. Thus the findings presented here should be considered as resulting from an interaction of the two variables, rather than as the result of either variable taken alone.

In addition to the high school boys, a small sample of girls from Lexington, Concord, and Newton High Schools (class of 1961) were also included in this survey. In general, the effect of father absence on aptitude appears to be the same for girls as for boys, with both early and long separation from the father being positively related to a relatively higher Verbal aptitude.

HARVARD CLASS OF 1963

As a further replication, available data on the Harvard class of 1963 were analyzed. This sample includes the entire freshman class with the exception of (1) foreign students, (2) students from broken homes, and (3) students whose fathers were in the service but did not go overseas. For this class, since it was not possible to determine the age of the child when the father left, only the duration of the father's absence will be considered here.

Table 9 compares the mean aptitude scores obtained by the father-absent and father-present groups; it also shows the relative superiority of Math to Verbal aptitude (M-V) for each group. As for the previous sample, the M-V difference score shows an orderly progression with length of time father was

table 9				
LENGTH OF FATHER'S ABSENCE	N	MATH	VERBAL	M-V
Less than 2 years	124	669	660	9
2 to 3 years	53	671	663	8
Over 3 years	38	649	646	3
Not Absent	666	680	656	24

absent, indicating that father absence is related to relatively lower Math ability.[3]

Throughout this paper, emphasis has been placed on the M-V difference scores rather than on the independent Math or Verbal scores. Although it is interesting to speculate whether a decrease in Math or an increase in Verbal ability is the chief contributor to the observed differences in the M-V scores of the father-absent students, it is impossible to tell from these data. In Table 9 the main effect of father absence seems to be a progressive depression of the Math score. However, for the first Harvard sample presented in Table 5, the principal effect of father absence appears to be an increase in Verbal ability. A careful study of these two tables strongly suggests that this discrepancy is an artifact resulting from different levels of ability between groups rather than a contradictory statement about the effects of father absence. For example, in Table 9 the group that was father-absent for over three years is considerably lower in both Math and Verbal aptitude than any of the other groups, which suggests a generally lower level of ability for this group. If we attempt to compensate for the lower ability of this group by adding 20 points to *both* their Math and Verbal aptitude scores, the M-V difference score remains unchanged, and the discrepancy between Tables 5 and 9 disappears.

This discrepancy between the two Harvard groups points up the danger of comparing Math or Verbal aptitude scores between groups, unless absolute level of ability is partialed out. From the data at hand, there is no reason to argue that father absence is consistently related to a lower level of intelligence.[4] The results do indicate however that father absence is consis-

---

[3]Since only the distribution of Math and Verbal aptitude scores were available for this sample, it was not possible to determine the M-V score for each individual subject, and thus an analysis of various test could not be performed on these data.

[4]Data from a recent study at Dartmouth College (Landauer & King, personal communication, 1963) indicate that the father-absent students (early wartime separation) scored *higher* than the class average on both the Math and Verbal aptitude tests of the College Entrance Examination Board. In the Dartmouth study, the M-V discrepancy between matched groups of father-absent and father-present control students is consistent with the findings reported here.

tently related to a discrepancy between Math and Verbal abilities and that the father-absent boys have a lower Math aptitude, relative to their Verbal aptitude, than do their father-present peers.

Discussion

Two major questions were asked at the outset of this paper. First, are there lasting measurable effects due to the absence of the father at an early age? Second, is the age of the child during the father's absence an important variable in determining these effects? The evidence presented provides clearly affirmative answers to both questions.

Stated concisely, the results of the aptitude survey of father-absent and father-present students indicate: (1) early and long separation from the father results in relatively greater ability in Verbal areas than in Mathematics; (2) no separation produces relatively greater ability in Mathematics; and (3) late brief separation may produce an extreme elevation in Mathematical ability (relative to Verbal ability).

The first two findings are consistent with predictions derived from any general theory of sex-role identification. Although the third finding has intriguing theoretical implications, it is based on a small sample and therefore must be considered less reliable than the other two findings. Since we have no additional information on this latter group, further pursuit seems unprofitable until more stable findings are obtained on a larger sample.

While the findings reported here are provocative, they leave several questions unanswered. For example, is the principal effect of early separation from the father an acceleration of Verbal ability or a depression of Math ability? This question cannot be answered from the data presented here. However, the studies of problem-solving techniques used by children (e.g., Seder, 1955; Milton, 1957; Bieri, 1960) suggest that this may be an inappropriate question. More specifically, these studies suggest that Math and Verbal aptitude scores may simply reflect two aspects of a single, more general characteristic: conceptual style or approach to problem solving. In these studies, two styles of conceptualization are usually differentiated: an "analytic approach" which is characterized by clear discrimination between stimuli, a direct pursuit of solutions, and a disregard for extraneous material; a "global approach," characterized by less clear discrimination of stimuli and a greater influence from extraneous material. The first approach is more typically used by boys while the second is more typical of girls. It seems reasonable to assume that boys using the analytic approach to problem solving would score relatively higher on Math aptitude than on Verbal aptitude tests; boys using the global approach would show relatively greater ability on Verbal comprehension tests. Thus the relative superiority of Math or Verbal aptitude is, in effect, a single measure of the boy's conceptual style or approach to problem solving. It follows that any antecedent variable, such as presence or absence of the father, may directly influence conceptual approach (i.e., aptitude pattern), but only indirectly influences performance on a particular test.

A second query that is sometimes raised in response to the data reported here concerns the possible influence of anxiety on the Math aptitude of father-absent boys. It is argued that the early experience of father-absence produces high anxiety and that anxiety has a more debilitating effect on proficiency in Mathematics than on Verbal skills. Data in support of this argument are drawn largely from studies of emotionally disturbed individuals which indicate that some aspects of Verbal ability are less vulnerable to stress and are therefore used as indicators of the "premorbid" level of intellectual functioning (e.g., Mayman et al., 1951). Contrary to this position is a directly relevant study by Alpert (1957) which relates a number of anxiety scales[5] with the Math and Verbal aptitude scores obtained on the College Board tests by a large sample of Stanford males. While most of the anxiety scales correlate negatively with both aptitude scores, the author states that "in *every* instance in which the data were significant, the correlations with mathematical aptitude were in the same direction as those with verbal aptitude but in no instance were they of as large magnitude" (p. 46). Several of the correlations between anxiety and Verbal aptitude are fairly high, but not one of the correlations with Math aptitude reaches an acceptable level of significance. Since none of the father-absent students in this study can be considered severely emotionally disturbed, there is no reason to suspect that extreme stress or anxiety is responsible for the observed differences in their aptitude scores. If anxiety had any effect at all, the Alpert study indicates that Verbal aptitude, rather than Math aptitude, would be expected to show the greater decrement. This is clearly contrary to the data reported here.

What other variables or conditions might be considered possible contributors to the aptitude differences between the father-absent and father-present groups? In the large high school and college samples, no attempt was made to match subjects on background variables (except, of course, that all subjects were from intact homes, academically successful, and from a reasonably homogeneous population). In the small matched samples, however, such variables as age, occupation and education of parents, number and age of siblings, and high school experience of subject were considered and controlled for (*cf.* Table 2). Whether there may be some further variable correlated with father absence in World War II and capable of producing such large effects on Mathematical and Verbal aptitude cannot be answered from these data. It should be borne in mind, however, that any such variable would have to account not only for differences between father absence and father presence but also for the effects due to the age of the child at the time the father

[5]Taylor Manifest Anxiety Scale; Welsh Anxiety Index; Freeman Anxiety Scale; Mandler-Sarason Test Scale; Achievement Anxiety Scale.

departed, as reported in this paper. Thus, such an explanatory variable would have to be correlated with the exact age of the child when the father was called into active duty as well as with the gross fact that the father was called overseas.

A final puzzling question is why conceptual approach or pattern of aptitudes should be so clearly sex-typed in our culture. An adequate explanation of this recurrent finding is not available, but several studies suggest that the masculine analytical approach is acquired through close and harmonious association with the father. Seder (1955) found that boys who used the global approach to problems had fathers who spent little time with them or who were very passive in their interaction with their sons. Bieri (1960) reports that boys who willingly accept authority and describe themselves as more similar to their mothers are poor performers on differentiation-analytic tasks. Levy (1943) reports the same finding for "maternally over-protected" boys. Finally, Witkin (1960) reports that boys who perform poorly on analytic problems perceive their fathers as dominating and tyrannical.

A study of male college students at Stanford University relates College Board aptitude scores with certain childhood experiences reported by the students (Maccoby, 1962). Boys who achieve a more feminine pattern of aptitudes (i.e., Math aptitude relatively lower than Verbal aptitude) than their peers report that in their childhood: (1) their fathers were away from home for one to five years; (2) they almost never talked about personal problems with their fathers; (3) they were often fearful of their fathers; and (4) they were punished exclusively by their mothers.

All of these studies consistently point to close, positive relationships between father and son as a prerequisite for development of a masculine conceptual approach. However, they still do not explain why the relationship exists or how this approach develops. Milton (1957), who reports a striking correlation between problem-solving skill and sex-role identification in both boys and girls, suggests simply that girls typically won't learn the necessary skills since problem solving is inappropriate to the female sex-role. This reasoning suggests that a conceptual approach is developed fairly consciously and probably not until after the child enters school. The accumulated evidence on learning of sex-role identity suggests that this occurs quite early in childhood through a largely unconscious process of imitation or identification with one of the parents. Whether the conceptual approach develops later as a result of sex-role identity (as Milton suggests) or early along with sex-role identity (through a similar process of identification) cannot be ascertained from the information available. However, studies of the problem-solving behavior of very young children may be designed to answer this part of the question. Studies of the interaction of mothers and fathers with their young children may also give us some ideas about the direct roles parents play in the development of a conceptual approach. At the present time, we can only say that aptitude patterns or conceptual approaches are related to both sex-role identity and to father-son relationships and that absence of the father during certain early periods of the child's life has an important effect on later cognitive development.

references _____

Alpert, R. School mathematics study group: a psychological evaluation. 1963, in press.

Alpert, R. Anxiety in academic achievement situations: its measurement and relation to aptitude. Unpublished Ph.D. thesis, Stanford University, 1957.

Bach, G. R. Father-fantasies and father-typing in father-separated children. *Child Developm.*, 1946, *17*, 63–80.

Bieri, J. Parental identification, acceptance of authority, and with n-sex differences in cognitive behavior. *J. abnorm. soc. Psychol.*, 1960, *60*, 76–79.

Burton, R. V., and Whiting, J. W. M. The absent father and cross-sex identity. *Merrill-Palmer Quarterly*, 1961, *7*, 85–95.

College board score reports. Princeton: Educational Testing Service, College Entrance Examination Board, 1960.

D'Andrade, R. G. Father-absence and cross-sex identification. Unpublished Ph.D. thesis, Harvard University, 1962.

Dember, W. N., Nairne, F., and Miller, F. J. Further validation of the Alpert-Haber achievement anxiety test. *J. abnorm. soc. Psychol.*, 1962, *65*, 427–428.

Glueck, S., and Glueck, E. *Unravelling juvenile delinquency*. New York: The Commonwealth Fund, 1950.

Heilman, J. D. Sex differences in intellectual abilities. *J. educ. Psychol.*, 1933, *24*, 47–62.

Hill, J. P. Sex-typing and mathematics achievement. Unpublished thesis prospectus, Harvard University, 1962.

Landauer, T. K., and King, F. W. Personal communication, 1963.

Lynn, D. B., and Sawrey, W. L. The effects of father-absence on Norwegian girls and boys. *J. abnorm. soc. Psychol.*, 1959, *59*, 258–262.

Maccoby, Eleanor E., and Rau, Lucy. *Differential cognitive abilities*. Final report, U.S. Office of Education, Cooperative Research Project No. 1040, 1962.

Mayman, M., Schafer, R., and Rapaport, D. Interpretation of the Wechsler-Bellevue Intelligence Scale in personality appraisal. In H. H. Anderson and G. L. Anderson (eds.) *An introduction to projective techniques*. Englewood Cliffs, N.J.: Prentice-Hall, 1951.

McCarthy, Dorothea. Language development in children. In L. Carmichael (ed.), *Manual of child psychology*. New York: Wiley, 1954, pp. 492–630.

Milton, G. A. The effects of sex-role identification upon problem-solving skill. *J. abnorm. soc. Psychol.*, 1957, *55*, 208–212.

Milton, G. A. Five studies of the relation between sex-role identification and achievement in problem-solving. Technical Report, Office of Naval Research, Contract Nonr 609 (2) (NR150–166). New Haven, Yale University, 1958.

Munroe, Ruth. The role of the father in the development of the child: a survey of the literature. Unpublished report, Harvard University, 1961.

Plank, Emma N., and Plank, R. Emotional components in arithmetical learning as seen through autobiographies. *The psychoanalytic study of the child.* Vol. IX, New York: International Universities Press, 1954.

Rohrer, J. H., and Edmonson, M. S. *The eighth generation.* New York: Harper & Row, 1960.

Samuels, F. Sex differences in reading achievement. *J. educ. Res.*, 1943, *36*, 594–603.

Sears, Pauline S. Doll play aggression in normal young children: influence of sex, age, sibling status, father's absence. *Psychol. Monogr.*, 1951, *65*, 1–43.

Sears. R. R., Pintler, M. H., and Sears, Pauline S. Effect of father separation on pre-school children's doll play aggression. *Child Developm.*, 1946, *17*, 219–243.

Seder, Joan A. The origin of difference in the extent of independence in children: developmental factors in perceptual field dependence. Senior Honors Thesis, Social Relations, Radcliffe College, 1955. (As reported by Witkin, H. A., The problem of individuality in development. *loc. cit.*)

Stolz, Lois M. *Father relations of war-born children.* Stanford, Calif.: Stanford University Press, 1954.

Tiller, P. O. Father absence and personality development of children in sailor families: a preliminary research report. Part II. In N. Anderson (ed.), *Studies of the family.* Vol. 2. Gottingen: Vandenhoeck and Ruprecht, 1957, pp. 115–137.

Tukey, J. W. The future of data analysis. *Annals Math Stat.*, 1962, *33*, 1–67.

Whiting, J. W. M. Social structure and child rearing: a theory of identification. Unpublished lectures presented at Tulane University as part of the Mona Bronsman Scheckman Lectures in Social Psychiatry, March, 1960.

Witkin, H. A. The problem of individuality in development. In Kaplan, B., and Wapner, S. (eds.), *Perspectives in psychological theory.* New York: International Universities Press, 1960.

Zucker, H. J. Affectional identification and delinquency. *Arch. Psychol.*, 1943, *40*, No. 286.

comments and questions _____

1. The questions to be studied are clearly stated.
2. This study seems to have a stronger theoretical rationale than many educational studies. (In fact one of the major criticisms of much educational research is the lack of theoretical bases.)
3. Carlsmith's research design has been well thought out in the sense of trying to control or eliminate as many potential confounding factors as possible. For example, her sample was relatively homogeneous, consisting only of students from stable families, whose fathers were absent for honorable reasons, from homes of middle or upper-middle class, with relatively high academic aptitude. What does this control do to the generalizability of her findings? Is the title of the article somewhat misleading regarding this generalizability? In terms of the practical implications of father absence, wouldn't a study of nonintact, unstable homes have been more relevant? Would using those types of families have confounded the theoretical question?
4. How accurately do you think Harvard students can report the length and dates of father absence during their early childhood?

5. Was the matching procedure Carlsmith used appropriate? Would random selection have been preferred? Why or why not?
6. Plot the interactions portrayed in Tables 5 and 6. Is interaction suggested? Are you satisfied with the statistical analysis performed with regard to the interaction question? Does regression analysis tell us anything about interaction?
7. In the discussion section, the relationship of the data to the theory was well portrayed.

EXPERIMENTAL RESEARCH

chapter six _____

As discussed in earlier sections, all research has a general method of inquiry associated with it. However, experimental research differs from other types of research in terms of *manipulation*. For any experimental study, there has to be an independent variable (treatment) that is manipulated by the experimenter and this independent variable must be under his control. Subjects should be randomly assigned to the groups also.

Some researchers insist that randomized assignment of subjects to treatment groups (or levels of treatment) is a *necessary* part of the definition of experimental research. Others say that randomization is very desirable in experimental research but need not be a part of the definition. In this book, we shall accept the latter position. Under the classification scheme we are using, we have no other category in which to place those many research studies in which the treatment is manipulated but randomized assignment of subjects is not carried out. The matters of randomization and manipulation will be discussed in greater detail later on. Nevertheless, the reader must be cognizant that manipulation of the treatment is the minimum requirement of an experimental study.

Although we know that the experimental method is the *sine qua non* for establishing cause-and-effect relationships, it should be understood at the outset that experimental research is not the panacea to our educational ills. Recognizing that the experimental method can give the researcher more meaningful data than, say, the ex-post-facto or correlational study, one might well ask "Why isn't there more experimentation in education?" As previously discussed, conducting experimental research can be very costly and time consuming. Moreover, in education, we are concerned with human behavior, which is most difficult, and sometimes impossible, to control and manipulate.

For example, let us assume that a researcher is interested in studying the relationship between the "need for" the cerebral cortex and learning. In an "ideal" experimental study, the researcher would have to randomly assign his subjects to two groups and then remove (or make inoperative) the cerebral cortex of subjects in one of the groups. Now, then, how far do you think this researcher would be able to go in conducting his research? Do you think that he would be able to obtain subjects for his study?

There are also critics of experimental research, especially as it relates to education, who contend that experimental studies lack realism and involve problems with results that have little practical significance to the classroom setting. Also, in contrast to experimental research in the physical sciences, educational experimental research is said to lack scientific rigor. The authors contend that these faults should not be blamed on the type of research conducted. Rather, they are the faults of the naive researcher. Admittedly, the control of the independent variable(s) and/or extraneous variables (which might influence the outcome of the study) are indeed difficult when dealing with human behavior. This is not to say, however, that the problems are insurmountable.

Definition of Terms

There are some terms used in experimental research—"treatment," "independent variable," "dependent variable," "extraneous variable," "experimental and control groups"—that should be in the working vocabulary of all persons involved in both the consumption and conduct of experimental research. Although some of these terms have been previously defined, we shall now briefly describe them as they are used in experimental research.

TERMS FOR THE WORKING VOCABULARY

Treatment. The experimental condition imposed in an experimental study is referred to as the *treatment* (T). It is the variable(s) that is being manipulated. A treatment is a type of *independent variable*, that is, all treatments are independent variables, but the converse need not be true. An independent variable is a treatment *only* if it is manipulated by the researcher. There may be a multitude of independent variables (IV's) all in the same study, although all are not necessarily manipulated by the researcher. The treatment may be a drug, teaching method, type of textbook, color of ink, or size of print. One cannot describe the IV or T without looking at a study because they depend upon the variable being studied. If we are studying the relationship between learning and drug X, the drug is both an IV and the treatment. Also, we may, depending upon the nature of the problem, be interested in studying not only the effect of drug X on learning, but the effects of varying amounts of drug X on the learning process. In an experimental study, the researcher may manipulate either the type and/or degree of treatment.

Dependent Variable (DV). The criterion or the variable that is being predicted; the variable that is affected or influenced by the treatment is called the *dependent variable*. In the example above, the measure of learning (usually a test score) would be the dependent variable. Just as there may be more than one independent variable, there may be more than one dependent variable.

Extraneous Variables.[1] Those variables (either something in the subject's environment *or* some characteristic or trait of the subject such as his ability, intelligence, sex, age, or personality) not explicitly taken into account in the research design that impede attributing all differences in the dependent variable(s) to the independent variable are referred to as *extraneous variables*. For example, a researcher is interested in learning whether Method A is better than Method B for teaching ninth-grade algebra. He randomly assigns his ninth-grade students to one of two classes. He teaches one class by method A and the other by method B. After testing the pupils in both classes, he finds that the students taught by Method A had higher scores (on the average) than the pupils taught by Method B. Can the researcher conclude that it was the method of teaching that resulted in one group achieving higher test scores than the other? Not necessarily. It is conceivable that the pupils in one group also differed from those in the other group in terms of their ability or aptitude to learn ninth-grade algebra. This difference in ability or aptitude is referred to as an *extraneous variable* since it conceivably could have played a large part in bringing about the observed differences. Had one considered ability in the research design, it would be an Independent Variable, *not* an Extraneous Variable, and *not* a Treatment.

Experimental Group(s)(E). The group(s) exposed to a particular treatment.

Control Group (C). A group of subjects that is comparable (but not necessarily identical) to the (E) but that is not exposed to the treatment.

Let us now attempt to clarify the terminology employed and defined above by making specific reference to an example.

> Miss Smith is interested in studying the relative efficiency of the lecture method as compared to the demonstration method in teaching eleventh-grade chemistry. She randomly selects three of her six eleventh-grade chemistry classes and teaches them by the lecture method; the other three classes are taught by the demonstration method. At the end of the term, she administers a test to all the students.

In the above example, the treatment (T) refers to the method of teach-

---

[1]Extraneous variables are often called *intervening* or *confounding variables*. There are some researchers (see Meehl, Paul E. "Nuisance Variables and the Ex-Post-Facto Design," *Minnesota Studies in the Philosophy of Science, 4,* 1970, 373–402) who feel that there is more damage done controlling for "nuisance" or extraneous variables than the damage done by the extraneous variable(s) itself.

ing—lecture vs. demonstration. The dependent variable (DV)—that is, the variable that is being predicted—is class performance on the chemistry test. In this example, there is really no experimental and control group (as we have defined these terms) inasmuch as each group was subjected to a different treatment. You will recall that an extraneous variable(s) can, and often does, influence the results of an experiment (for that matter, extraneous variables can, and often do, influence the results of ex-post-facto and correlational studies). If this is the case, and observed differences are attributed to the treatment rather than the extraneous variable(s), then the conclusion is wrong. Do you think that extraneous variables could be operating in the example above? (Some examples of possible extraneous variables in the study described above are: age, sex, aptitude to learn chemistry, teacher motivation, and teacher ability.) It is therefore very conceivable that one or more extraneous variables *could* have been operating in the study and therefore could have influenced the findings obtained. For example, if a larger proportion of the students in the "lecture" group than in the "discussion" group were motivated to achieve, it could well be that any observed difference in chemistry test scores between the two groups was the result of a difference in motivation rather than *only* a difference in teaching method. It should be readily obvious that such sources of "unwanted" variation should be removed wherever possible, or at least brought under the control of the researcher. Otherwise, it would be most difficult, if not impossible, to draw definitive conclusions.

Equating Groups

A question frequently raised is "Does an experimental study have to have both a control (C) and an experimental (E) group?" Is a study improved by having an (E) and a (C)? There is no easy answer to these questions. It all depends on the purpose of the study. In our previous example—teaching eleventh-grade chemistry—there was no (C); rather, each group received a different treatment. However, in a pharmacological study, where one is interested in studying whether or not a particular drug is effective in combating a specific disease, the group of individuals who are administered the drug are called the experimental group whereas the group of individuals who are administered no drug or a placebo are considered the control group. In experimental studies where a "true" control group is used, both groups are treated identically except for the fact that the control group is not exposed to the treatment under study.

In any experiment, it is essential that we make comparisons between two or more groups that are basically similar or comparable. (Exceptions are time-series studies and path-analysis studies.) However, it should be recognized that the control group, as previously defined (a group that receives no treatment), is not an essential ingredient in the experimental method. There are many instances where we are concerned with comparing the efficiency of, say, two methods of instruction—"A versus B." In this case, a control group would serve no useful purpose. We would only need a control group in such a study of teaching method if our hypothesis were such that we were studying whether method A or method B were superior to having no instruction. In conclusion, then, the decision of whether or not to employ a control group is dictated by the hypothesis being studied.

Whether an experiment uses a control group that receives no treatment or two experimental groups each receiving a different treatment, one should attempt to make the two groups comparable in all aspects with the exception of the treatment being administered. Therefore, we have to concern ourselves with methods of equating the different groups. We shall discuss four ways in which such equating can be done: *randomization, matching, statistical procedures,* and *repeated measures.* By no means are these procedures mutually exclusive. In fact, there are many instances where a combination of them is employed by the researcher in his attempt to equate his groups.

PROCEDURES FOR EQUATING GROUPS

1. Randomization. The purpose of randomization is to insure, or at least try to insure, against the possibility that bias will enter into the experiment and make meaningful, definitive conclusions impossible. When and what kind of randomization should be used is left to the discretion of the researcher for only he can ascertain whether (1) subjects should be randomly selected, and/or (2) groups should be randomly assigned to treatments, and/or (3) treatments should be randomly assigned to groups.

In our example of drugs and learning, there are a number of extraneous variables, such as sex, intelligence, interest, age, and SES, which *might* affect the relationship found between drugs and learning. Before we are able to conclude that the drug (and only the drug) does or does not affect the learning process, we have to be reasonably certain that the groups are comparable in all relevant characteristics before the treatment (drug) is introduced. There are many instances where bias may occur without the researcher knowing it. One way of insuring that the extraneous variables have been controlled is to randomly assign subjects to groups. (It is assumed that if our sample size is sufficiently large, extraneous variable influence will be equated in the groups.)

Randomization is the simplest and most economical way of assigning subjects to groups or groups to treatments. If the researcher employs randomization, he can protect himself from the intrusion of unusual events that may introduce bias into his study.

2. Matched Groups. Although researchers could try to match subjects in their groups on relevant variables, matching or matched groups procedures are *not* the most efficient to use in equating subjects in the (E) and (C) and/or (E) and (E). This is true for a variety of reasons. First, matching is a very complex procedure. In order to make groups as comparable as possible, one would have to match on more than one variable because of the composite of human traits. Generally, a large number of subjects should be in the initial pool because the matching process usually results in many subjects being removed from consideration and hence the groups finally constituted may not adequately represent the population. For example, let us assume that a researcher has available a "pool" of 150 Ss that he can use to study the relationship between drugs and learning. These 150 Ss will differ (or conceivably could differ) in their sex, scholastic aptitude, and reading ability—extraneous variables that the researcher would like to control. Now, imagine that the first subject selected is a boy, with a scholastic aptitude percentile score of 85, and a reading test score of 93. To find a "match," the researcher looks through the remaining 149 Ss to see if he can find another boy with similar test scores. Assume further that the researcher cannot find another boy who is comparable enough to be considered a "match." (We say "comparable" rather than "identical" because the researcher may, *a priori*, have decided to accept scores within a range of, say, plus or minus 3.) This means that, with these constraints, the first subject would have to be excluded from the study. In a similar fashion, the researcher might only have been able to match 20 of the original 150 Ss. Because of this rejection, the final group of 20 may well be markedly dissimilar from the parent population of 150 Ss. Naturally, the researcher need not try for "perfect or near-perfect" matches, but if he does not, he sacrifices group comparability. One could argue that if the original pool were larger than 150, more matches could have been made. Even if this were true, it would be a costly way of obtaining comparable groups. Wouldn't much time and energy be lost in the discarding of subjects?

Second, and possibly more important, is the fact that in many instances the researcher does not know what characteristics are relevant and hence *what* variables should be matched; and he doesn't always know how many variables should be used in the matching. Unfortunately, we know less about the social sciences than we do about the physical sciences. Because of the lack of a complete, thorough body of theory that enables us to understand how humans behave, researchers in the social sciences in general, and education in particular, are faced with the dilemma of not knowing what variable(s) they should control (minimize, or try to eliminate) in their study. In time this problem should lessen.

A variety of procedures may be used to match subjects or equate groups. Each, however, has certain problems and limitations associated with it. Because of the many problems associated with matching, we strongly urge researchers (and hence readers) to consider approaches other than matching to equate groups. Matching can be used as an adjunct to randomization to gain statistical precision but unless absolutely necessary, matching, per se, without randomization should be avoided. It goes without saying that matching is no substitute for randomization.

3. *Statistical Procedures.* Procedures such as analysis of covariance (ANCOVA) can be used to "equate" the groups on certain relevant factors observed prior to the study. However, before covariance techniques can be used, the researcher has to have available for each subject measures (called *covariates*) that correlate with the dependent variable. It is upon these latter measures that adjustments are made.

4. *Repeated Measures.* In a repeated measurement design, each subject has been given both a pretest and a post-test. Therefore, differences between the groups can be eliminated as a source of error. In a repeated measurement design fewer subjects are needed, because the researcher has two or more measures for each. One major assumption that is made in this design is that there is no differential transfer of training or learning occurring on the post-test as a result of the pretest. If this is not so, then we are unable to separate the effects of the treatment from the effects of the pretest. The repeated measurement design also unfortunately may make it very difficult to eliminate such extraneous variables as maturation, instrument decay, testing, and history. These terms will be discussed in greater detail later in the chapter.

Treatment Control

Treatment control, without a doubt, is or should be of primary concern in the experimental method. And it is often the most difficult control to achieve, even in the most well-planned and well-designed experiments, because of the researcher's inability to manipulate and maintain control of the treatment.

If a researcher is interested in studying the effects of a particular drug on the learning process, he should be able to administer the drug to one group of subjects and withhold it from another group of subjects and/or he should be able to vary the amount of the drug administered to certain subjects. This latter type of control we shall refer to as *treatment control (a specific type of independent-variable control)*. Being able to subject a particular group to a particular treatment on the surface may appear to be easy. However, this is not always the case. There are many instances where because of moral, ethical, or health reasons it is neither possible nor feasible to introduce a particular treatment. For example, let us assume that we were interested in studying the relationship between learning and some type of hallucinogenic drug. The problem could be very valuable and could make a significant contribution to education. However, because of the potential physical and/or mental danger to the subject, the researcher would not be able to introduce this treatment and hence could not conduct his experiment.

Maintaining Control. One of the major difficulties in any type of experiment where there are two groups is the situation where it may be possible for members to "leak" information from one group to the other. For example, let us assume that we have a controlled experiment designed to ascertain which of two methods is the more effective procedure for teaching simple arithmetic concepts to third-graders. We might have two groups of children, each taught by a particular teaching method. In the classroom we are able to prevent most communication among the subjects. Possibly during the school day we are able to minimize communication among the subjects. However, once the children have left school it is indeed difficult to maintain a situation of control where there is no leakage and/or cooperation among the subjects in the various groups.

Experimental Validity

Campbell and Stanley[2] have provided those engaged in experimental research with possibly the most expository treatment of *experimental validity*. They consider experimental validity to be of two types: *external* and *internal*. *External* validity provides us with an answer to the question "How far can we generalize our findings?" or "How far can we stick out our necks?" That is, to what populations, samples, situations, events, or variables can the observed effect be generalized? *Internal* validity answers the question "Did the treatment really make a difference?" "Can we be sure that it was the treatment, and *only* the treatment, that resulted in a difference in performance between the groups?"

Unfortunately, in experimental research, as in many other areas of research, we are faced with a dilemma: By emphasizing maximum internal validity, we often decrease our attempts to obtain maximum external validity. Naturally, we would like to employ an experimental design that allows for *both* maximum external and internal validity. However, we can try to be judicious in our "trade-off" so that we are able to exercise sufficient control to make the findings interpretable (internal validity) and yet have a design that permits us to generalize the findings to a population that is more inclusive than the sample of subjects studied (external validity). Recognizing that attainment of both maximum internal and maximum external validity is not possible with even the most judicious experimental design, the writers feel that *in the long run, internal validity* is more important than external validity.

INFLUENCE OF EXTRANEOUS VARIABLES

Campbell[3] designates seven classes of extraneous variables that must be controlled: history, maturation, testing, instrument decay, regression, selection,

[2]Donald T. Campbell and Julian C. Stanley. "Experimental and Quasi-experimental Designs for Research on Teaching." In N. L. Gage (ed.), *Handbook of Research on Teaching.* Skokie, Ill.: Rand McNally, 1963, pp. 171–246.

[3]Actually, there are 12 classes but we shall consider only those that are most important. See Donald Campbell, "Factors Relevant to the Validity of Experiments in Social Settings," *Psychological Bulletin,* LIV (1957), 297–312 for a more thorough discussion.

and experimental mortality. Any one of these factors can affect the internal validity. The interaction effects of some of these with the treatment variables in general can affect the external validity of experimental results. Conventional experimental designs vary in their ability to control extraneous variables and hence it is difficult to determine at the outset which is the optimal design to be employed. Let us briefly consider each of the seven major factors to see how they may influence experimental findings.

1.   *History.* In the one-group pretest–post-test design, a treatment is introduced between the pre- and post-tests. Then any gain in test score between pre- and post-tests is often attributed to the treatment. But are we justified in making this interpretation? It is conceivable that some event or action or situation intervened between the pre- and post-test in addition to the treatment that may have influenced the final observed level of performance. The introduction of this extra-experimental uncontrolled stimulus(i) is referred to as the *confounding* effect upon the treatment. If this confounding effect is a specific event, it is referred to as *history.* Let us use the following example to illustrate our point. Assume that a researcher is interested in studying attitudes of whites to blacks. Let us assume that the treatment given the whites is a film about atrocities towards blacks. Naturally, we would expect the attitudes of the whites to change after they have seen the film if we are assuming that the film (treatment) has some merit. Let us assume, however, that between the pretest and the post-test an announcement was made the five blacks were lynched by a band of whites. Let us further assume that the attitudes of the whites toward the blacks were more positive after the film than before. Are we sure that it was the film that changed the attitudes of the whites? What role did the information about the lynchings play in changing the attitudes? What about the possible interaction between the effects of the film and the effects of the information on the lynchings? As you can see, this confounding effect (history) makes it very difficult to interpret the results of the experiment.

2.   *Maturation.* Let us assume that we have the same type of one-group pre-test–post-test design. This time, however, we are concerned with studying the relationship between a particular method of instruction and mental age. In this design we would administer an intelligence test as a pretest, then introduce over a period of time a particular instructional method, and then administer the same test as a post-test. Now in the example illustrating the effect of history we saw that it was a function of a specific event, that is, information about the lynchings. In maturation, however, we are concerned with those effects that are systematic and orderly over a period of time, such as mental age, height, weight, hunger, etc. What we are trying to illustrate here is that it is conceivable that in certain types of situations it is difficult to ascertain whether the improvement observed over a period of time is due to the treatment, or to maturation, or an interaction of the treatment with maturation.

3. *Testing.* Testing in itself can confound the findings of a study. Although it is often desirable to administer both a pretest and a post-test, it is possible that the pretest in itself may have influenced performance on the post-test. We should mention at this time that the testing may be either in terms of a *reactive* or *nonreactive* measure. A *reactive* measure is one that alters, modifies, or affects the variable(s) that we are interested in studying. A *nonreactive* measure is one that does not modify the variable(s) that we are studying. For example, retesting on an interest or personality inventory may result in a change on the second testing even though only a few hours may have elapsed between the two tests. If so, the interest and/or personality inventory is referred to as a reactive measure. Measuring a person's height or the length of his carpal bone or the length of his tibia would be a nonreactive measure since the first measure could not influence the value(s) we would obtain on the second measurement.

4. *Instrument Decay.* A fourth uncontrolled source of variation is *instrument decay.* This phenomenon is operative primarily when we are using instruments such as scales, balances, or weights that may wear out in the process of being used and hence any observed differences between the pre- and post-test may well be the result of a faulty scale or a faulty balance rather than the effect of the treatment. Instrument decay is also prevalent in studies using interviewers and/or observers, especially if they become fatigued during the study and as a result may not provide valid and reliable information. To compensate for instrument decay, the researcher should only use materials that are in excellent condition.

5. *Regression.* Regression is a statistical artifact that may confound the results and make them difficult to interpret. Subjects who score at the extreme points (on the pretest), such as very brilliant or very dull, very masculine or very feminine, have a tendency to score closer to the mean on the post-test. This phenomenon is referred to as regression. Inasmuch as the regression effect manifests itself most when groups have been selected because of their extreme scores, one must, in such cases, pay particular attention to interpreting changes in performance and not confuse "true" change with observed change.

6. *Selection of Subjects.* With possibly the exception of controlling for extraneous variables (remember variables must be relevant; otherwise they need not be controlled), the selection of subjects is the *most* important factor in designing good experimental research studies. As we mentioned earlier, some form of randomization—initial assignment of subjects to the groups, the assignment of groups, or the assignment of treatments—is desirable. However, if this is not possible, *matching* can be used to make the groups comparable.

7. *Experimental Mortality.* Experimental mortality is another extraneous variable insofar as the effect of the treatment is concerned. Let us assume that the groups were equal to begin with. But, if any subjects drop out of the groups, we do not know what kind of members dropped out. Hence, any differences between the two groups on the post-test may be due to the biased composition of the remaining members. Both cross-sectional and longitudinal research are susceptible to experimental mortality.

Types of Experimental Design

As we have noted throughout our discussion, research is concerned with studying the relationship between the dependent and independent variables. Research design is analogous to a blueprint that a builder uses in that it suggests the kinds of observations (measurements) to be made, how to make these observations, and how to analyze the quantified measures. An adequate research design tells us what variable(s) is to be manipulated and how this variable is to be manipulated; it tells us what statistical analysis to use to analyze the data; and, indirectly, it tells us the kinds of conclusions and inferences that can be made from the data.

Needless to say, a goal of all researchers using the experimental method is to select an experimental design that maximizes the precision (the extent to which random error can be reduced) of an experiment, and controls for systematic bias. Fundamentally, the research design has as its major purpose the control of as many sources of variation as possible *except* the variation accounted for by the treatment. Precision of an experiment is accomplished by reducing the effects of random error. One way to reduce random error effects is by reducing the variability among the subjects used. Another way is to increase the size of the sample studied. The *best* procedure for increasing the precision of any experimental study is to try to improve the experimental design. The researcher may choose from a variety of experimental designs. He should use the one that will provide him with the most meaningful information. That is, he should choose a design that will enable him to ascertain what proportion of the total variance is caused by the treatment effect and what proportion is due to error.

The control for systematic bias or systematic error (a nonrandom mean difference between true and obtained effects) is another necessary ingredient for an "adequate" experimental design. It should be readily evident that even though manipulation was employed (you will remember that we said this distinguishes the experimental method from other research methods), a researcher could obtain differences between his groups for reasons other than the treatment afforded one group and denied the other group. For example, the two groups might not have been comparable. In an experiment designed to determine whether method A is better than method B, an overabundance of bright pupils taught by "A" could have "caused" this difference just as much as the superiority of method A. Or, if a pre- and post-test were used, practice effects might be operating, which could result in systematic error. There are many ways of generating systematic error. The *best* way to try to eliminate it is to use randomization—in assigning subjects to treatments.

It is imperative that the type of research design to be used be decided upon before any data are collected. The reason that this decision should be made early is to guarantee that certain conditions that may be inherent in a particular design are met. For example, if a particular design calls for both a pre- and post-test, the researcher should be cognizant of this before he conducts the study. He can't very well administer a pretest after the study has been completed.

In a way, the problem being studied plays an extremely important role in determining the type of experimental design to be used (naturally, such factors as cost, availability of subjects, precision, etc. are also important). Let us consider the following example to illustrate our point.

> Example: We are interested in learning whether the discussion method is better (that is, whether students learn more as manifested by higher test scores) than the lecture method to teach 11th-grade poetry. Furthermore, we have a strong feeling, based upon previous research, that the discussion method will be better for nonauthoritarian subjects; and the lecture method will be better for the more authoritarian type of student.

Before discussing some of the factors to be considered when selecting a particular type of experimental design, we should define some of the variables involved in this study.

VARIABLES IN EXAMPLE

Dependent Variable. The test scores achieved by the subjects on a test designed to measure knowledge of grade 11 poetry.

Independent Variable. The treatment, which in this example is the method of teaching. (Note: The discussion and lecture methods are *not* two different treatments; rather, they are two levels of the *same* treatment—teaching method.) There is also another independent variable—degree of authoritarianism—even though it is not physically manipulated.

Extraneous Variables. There are many variables other than the method of teaching and degree of authoritarianism which might, and could, influence the dependent variable. Some of these extraneous variables are sex, aptitude, ability, and interest of both students and teacher(s). As was mentioned earlier, the researcher and *not* the design or statistical method must decide on *what* to control and *how* to control for extraneous sources of variation. (Remember:

Maximize the variance of the dependent variable; *minimize* that portion of the DV's variance due to errors—error variance may result from errors of measurement, unreliable measures—and *control* for extraneous, systematic variance.)

Without at this time discussing the type of experimental design to be employed, we can say that the problem under study suggests the following:

1. We need two kinds of subjects: one authoritarian, the other nonauthoritarian. We shall require a fairly large number of subjects because, in essence, we have four different groups:[4] (1) authoritarians taught by the lecture method, (2) authoritarians taught by the discussion method, (3) nonauthoritarians taught by the lecture method, and (4) nonauthoritarians taught by the discussion method.
2. We need two teaching methods.
3. We need a research design that will consider the following sources of variance: (1) variance due to authoritarianism, (2) variance attributable to the teaching method employed, (3) variance accounted for by the interaction of authoritarianism and teaching method, and (4) error variance.
4. Because of possible extraneous sources of variance, we should randomly assign our subjects to the treatment.
5. We need a valid and reliable 11th-grade poetry test.
6. We have to determine whether we want all teachers to employ both levels of the treatment or whether we want each teacher to be randomly assigned to only one level.
7. We have to decide whether we want the results to be generalized beyond the sample studied.

The factors mentioned above are by no means mutually exclusive and exhaustive. They are just some illustrations of how the purpose of the study strongly influences the type of research design to be employed and guides the researcher in his approach to the solution of the problem. We shall now consider, albeit briefly, some of the different types of research designs.

EXAMPLES OF POOR RESEARCH DESIGNS

In all experimental research, poor design, as you might expect, refers to poor control or lack of control over the independent variables. Although there are several examples of poor research design, we shall consider at this time only the two most frequently occurring types: (1) the one-shot case study, and (2) the one-group pretest–post-test design.

---

[4]Actually, we have only two groups of subjects, each taught by a different method. However, in our analysis, we shall have four subgroups; each group of subjects is taught by each method.

1. The One-Shot Case Study. Here, a single group is exposed to a treatment. After the treatment, an observation is made on the dependent variable. Then the researcher tries to interpret his findings. But what can he interpret? For example, let us assume the researcher is interested in studying the effects of smoking on spelling achievement of eighth-graders. He has a group of subjects smoke and then take a spelling test. He then counts the number of errors made on the spelling test. Suppose that the average number of errors on a 50-item spelling test was eight. What can the researcher conclude? Nothing, unless he knows the average number of errors that would have been made before the group smoked; or, how many errors would be made by a group of subjects who did not smoke. Because we do not know the level of performance before the treatment was introduced, we are unable to evaluate the effect of the treatment. Also, there is no control for any extraneous variable(s), such as ability, interest, and aptitude, that might have affected spelling achievement.

2. The One-Group Pretest–Post-test Design. This is an extension of the one-shot case study. A pretest is given, a treatment administered, and then a post-test is given. Next the researcher looks at the average performance on the pretest, the average performance on the post-test, and makes the assumption that if there are any gains between the pre- and post-test, the gains are attributable to the treatment. As we mentioned earlier, how do we know that the pretest did not influence performance on the post-test? We do not know. Also, how do we know whether performance did not improve because some students decided to do extra homework? We do not know. Also, how do we know whether or not the improvement between the pre- and post-test was not related to the instrument used? We do not know. The major deficiency inherent in this design is *not* that the extraneous variables, such as history, reactive measures, maturation, or regression, are operating. The problem is that we do not know, nor can we ascertain, whether they have influenced the outcome of the experiment.

EXAMPLES OF GOOD RESEARCH DESIGNS

Fortunately, there are many good designs available to the researcher. For example, the researcher can choose (1) a post-test only control-group design, (2) a pretest–post-test control-group design, (3) the Solomon four-group design, (4) factorial designs, and (5) counterbalanced designs. The first four designs are often referred to as *true* experimental designs whereas the counterbalanced design is referred to as a *quasi-experimental* design.

1. Post-test Only Control-Group Design. In this design, both a control and experimental group are used. The dependent variable is measured at the conclusion of the experiment. Ss are randomly assigned to the (E) and (C).

This design is very efficient from the standpoint of time and economy. It does not require a pretest. Random assignment of subjects *prior* to the experiment should help make the groups equivalent; the influence of extraneous variables should be balanced in the (E) and (C). (Note: Even though the extraneous variables may not interact with the treatment, they may still affect external validity.) This design may be susceptible to low internal validity because of subject mortality, especially if subject mortality is differential—that is, the characteristics of dropouts and nondropouts may be different and these characteristics may be relevant to the dependent variable and the treatment. (If you expect to encounter mortality, consider another type of design.) This design's lack of control may result in relevant, extraneous variables influencing the results.

2. *Pretest–Post-test Control-Group Design.* This design is an extension of the pretest–post-test design in that the subjects are randomly assigned to the (E) and (C). Because the subjects have been randomly assigned to the groups, the problem of selection bias is minimized. If there is any suspicion that the groups are not comparable, analysis of covariance can be used (with the pretest being the covariate) to adjust for any initial differences between the groups. The pretest can also be used to see if there are any differences between those who continue in the study and those who leave (differential mortality). The design has strong internal validity, but making generalizations with this design introduces some problems. Since both groups were pretested, we do not know whether or not the same findings would hold for subjects who were selected from the same population but who were not pretested. The problem here is not lack of control, because both groups were pretested; rather, it is a problem of generalization. The results can be generalized only to other groups of subjects who have been pretested. It should be recognized that the pretesting effects are dependent to a large degree on the nature of the study. For example, in a study on values, pretest effects may be marked whereas in a study on achievement they may be minimal. Observer bias can be controlled by having the *same* observers for both groups. It is essential, however, that the observers do *not* know whether they are observing the (E) or the (C).

3. *Solomon Four-Group Design.* In this design, there are two control groups and two experimental groups. Subjects are randomly assigned to groups and treatments. Pretesting effects are controlled since only one (C) and one (E) are pretested but all groups are post-tested. By only pretesting one-half of the groups, the researcher can ascertain the influence of the pretest; he can determine the influence of the treatment when the pretest is given and when it is not administered; and he can observe the interaction effects of pretest and treatment.

4. *Factorial Designs.*[5] These are really a misnomer since they are not designs in the conventional sense. Rather, they are methods of analyzing data.

---

[5] Factorial designs are not unique to the experimental method. The three designs just discussed as well as ex-post-facto research could be factorial.

Whenever a researcher is interested in studying the effect of two or more variables simultaneously, he employs a factorial design. This type of design requires a minimum of two independent variables. If each independent variable has only two levels, we have a 2 × 2 factorial design. The number of digits indicates the number of independent variables being considered. The numerical value of the digits indicates the number of levels for each independent variable. For example, an experiment using four different teaching methods, three ability levels (bright, average, and dull), and six grade levels (grades 6, 7, 8, 10, 11, 12) would be represented as a 4 × 3 × 6 factorial design. As the number of independent variables is increased, the number of groups increases markedly since all levels of one independent variable are taken in combination with all levels of the other independent variables.

There are many advantages to the factorial design. First, we can treat as independent variables what otherwise would be extraneous variables. Second, this design has high internal validity. Third, several independent variables may be considered simultaneously in a single experiment which should be more economical than conducting many single experiments. Finally, the interaction effects of many variables can be studied at the same time.

5. *Counterbalanced Designs.* In this design, all subjects are exposed to all treatments. One type of counterbalanced design is the *Latin-square* design. Because of the complexity of this design, we shall end our discussion here.

Questions To Be Asked When Reading Experimental Research

In addition to those questions that must be considered in reading any type of research study or article, there are some questions that are unique to the experimental method and/or are so important in experimental research that they are presented as specific points to be considered by the reader.

1. Were experimental and control groups used? Was it necessary to have a control group in this study? Why? If an (E) and (C) were used, how were the subjects selected? Were the subjects in the (E) and (C) selected from the same population in the same manner? How were the two groups made comparable? Is any evidence presented to demonstrate the comparability of the groups?
2. Was the sample selected by groups or individuals? How might this affect the results of the study?
3. Has the best design been employed? Will it adequately answer the questions proposed in the hypothesis?
4. How were extraneous sources of variation controlled?

A Concluding Statement

To conduct good research of any type is indeed a very difficult, complex, and sometimes frustrating task. This is especially true of experimental research because of the multiplicity of problems inherent in the various kinds of research designs and because of the complex nature of human behavior. There are certain problems, errors, and deficiencies that are common in the design of most experiments and we have attempted to discuss these, albeit briefly.

Good experimental research designs begin with good problems. Another way of saying this is that research findings are never better than the questions posed. A well-designed experiment must be free from bias; it must be designed in such a way that the researcher can determine that the observed differences are the result of the treatment and only the treatment; it must be sufficiently precise to answer the questions raised; and it must be relevant for the educational arena. Manipulation and control are essential in well-designed, well-conceived, and well-executed experimental studies. The findings should be such that they can be generalized to a larger population. No amount of statistical "tomfoolery" can compensate for an inadequate research design, a trivial problem, invalid data, or inappropriate analysis. By the same token, no one type of research is better than another to rectify such errors. The important thing to remember is that after the research has been completed, one should be able to do more than just say, "so what?"

Examples of Experimental Research

Selections 21–25 are examples of experimental research. All have involved a treatment manipulation but not all have employed randomization. Some of the selections in this chapter are not research, per se, but are comments on research articles we have included. Also, there are research articles presented here that show contradictory results. As you read each selection, you should refer to the specific questions raised in this chapter's introduction as well as the more general questions posited in Chapter 1.

(handwritten annotations at top of page): Examined for internal validity = controlled internal variables "n" "A good + group experiment" so pre + postest was caused by treatment

PROGRAMED INSTRUCTION VERSUS USUAL CLASSROOM PROCEDURES IN TEACHING BOYS TO READ[*],[1]

21

JOHN D. McNEIL

Introduction

It is commonly observed that more boys than girls are unsuccessful in beginning reading (Gates, 1961; Alden, Sullivan & Durrell, 1941). Although the real cause for the failure of boys to achieve as much as girls is unknown, various theories have been proposed. Factors of growth, maturation, and development are considered most critical by some (Gallagher, 1948; Monroe, 1932). Others have stated that the reading interests of boys and girls differ and that existing instructional content appeals more to girls (Heilman, 1961). Negative treatment of male learners by female teachers has been suggested as another explanation for the slow progress of boys in reading (St. John, 1932; Davidson & Lang, 1960).

(handwritten margin annotation): Rev. of lit

A previously untried approach to the collection of evidence regarding the inferiority of boys in beginning reading is through programed instruction. This technique offers increased control by standardizing the conditions under which reading material is presented to boys and girls and insuring that all have equal opportunities to respond. The present study compares the learning of boys and girls under the controlled conditions of programed instruction with the learning of these same children under direct instruction by female teachers. The possibility is explored that classroom teachers treat boys and girls differently and that this difference in treatment is associated with differences in early reading achievement. The specific hypothesis: whereas boys excel in beginning

(handwritten margin annotation): Problem Statement

*Reprinted from *American Educational Research Journal*, 1:2 (1964), pp. 113–119, with the permission of the publisher and author. Copyright 1964 American Educational Research Association, Washington, D.C.

[1]This study was performed as part of Cooperative Research Project No. 1413, U.S. Office of Education, Evan R. Keislar, co-investigator. Appreciation is expressed to Janis S. Stone, who assisted in the design and conduct of the study.

351

reading under the neutral conditions of programed instruction, these same boys will not maintain their superiority when placed under the direction of female teachers. Further, it is hypothesized that (a) boys will be perceived by their classmates as receiving more negative comments from teachers and as having fewer opportunities to respond in their reading groups than girls and (b) reading progress will be related to teachers' comments and to opportunities to respond.

Design of the Study

The study was conducted in two phases: first, an auto-instructional program in reading was presented to kindergarten children, followed by a criterion test of word recognition (program-taught words); second, there was a follow-up study of these same children, who were subsequently enrolled as first graders under the direction of seven female teachers. Data regarding the progress of the boys and girls under teacher direction were collected by administering a similar criterion test of word recognition (teacher-taught words) after four months of instruction. Evidence of differential treatment of boys and girls and the relation of this treatment to progress in reading was gathered by means of a questionnaire to teachers and a taped interview schedule individually administered to the children.

Subjects

One hundred and thirty-two children completed the auto-instructional program as kindergartners, 72 boys and 60 girls. These children constituted the total kindergarten populations in two public schools. These children had an average chronological age of 5 years, 6 months and an average intelligence quotient of 107 with a range of 72–138 as measured by the *Kuhlmann-Anderson Test of Intelligence*. The schools represented those found in American upper-middle-class and lower-middle-class communities. From among the original sample of 132, 49 boys and 44 girls were present for instruction by the 7 female teachers. These children were the subjects during the second phase of the study: the measurement of progress under teacher direction and the search for evidence of differential treatment.

A pretest of reading readiness, which measured knowledge of letters and words to be taught by the auto-instructional program and ability to recognize likenesses in letter configurations, was given to the subjects before the study began. The performance of boys was not different from girls on this test.

Phase One: Progress of Boys and Girls under Programed Instruction

AUTO-INSTRUCTIONAL MATERIALS

The programed materials consisted of 17 daily lessons that took slightly over three weeks to administer. Each lesson was made up of approximately 35 questions or frames. Forty words were taught during the program. These words represented terms commonly found in the vocabulary of young children of both sexes and included both function words (i.e., and, with) and those with a direct referent (i.e., mother, father). A complete description of the material has been reported elsewhere (McNeil, 1963). For present purposes, it is important to know that the program was administered through apparatus that instructed 10 or fewer children at a time. Each child sat in an individual laboratory-type cubicle equipped with headphones, through which he heard a taped commentary. The cubicle contained a response and confirmation panel. The response panel consisted of three buttons by which the child answered multiple-choice questions. Confirmation of the correct answer was by light; a green light showed when the learner made a correct response, and a red one when he erred.

A single 6' × 8' screen at the front of the room was visible from each cubicle. On this screen, learners saw the daily sequence presented by film strip, while simultaneously hearing the accompanying taped commentary.

Relevant features of the auto-instructional procedures were: (1) boys and girls made individual responses and received individual confirmations, (2) because the pupils were in individual cubicles, interaction among them was not encouraged, (3) boys and girls were presented with identical frames at a common pace and received the same taped comments of encouragement, and (4) boys and girls were given equal opportunity to respond; the same number of responses was demanded daily from all learners.

PERFORMANCE ON THE CRITERION TEST FOLLOWING AUTO-INSTRUCTION

The post-test consisted of 51 multiple-choice items, each with three or four alternatives, similar in format to the frames in the auto-instructional program except that the items appeared in individual printed booklets, one item per page. Instructions for each item were given orally. No item in the post-test was identical with any frame in the program. The context and the arrangement of alternatives had not been seen previously by the pupils although the correct response called for recognition or recall of a word taught in the program. The test was administered to groups of 12 children at a time, boys and girls together.

Contrary to the usual results from studies of beginning reading, performance on the post-test by the kindergarten children revealed that the boys earned significantly higher scores: Boys (N = 72) M = 30.3, SD = 9.2; Girls (N = 60) M = 24.4, SD = 9.1) t = 3.65, p < .01.

At this stage of the investigation, three explanations for the unusual results were possible: (1) that under customary classroom conditions, boys receive inequities in treatment that do not occur under the neutral conditions of programed instruction, (2) that the sample departed from a normal distribution of boys and girls, and (3) that the mechanical gadgetry of the teaching machine was responsible for more effective stimulation of the boys' desire to learn to read. The last explanation was weakened by information collected regarding the preferences of the children for the instruction. Children were asked individually whether they would prefer to continue the program or to engage in the following activities: (1) listening to records, (2) listening to a story, (3) painting, or playing in the sandbox. Boys and girls did not differ in their preference for auto-instruction. Over 72 per cent of them preferred the programed instruction to one or more of the other activities. Evidence against the second explanation and in favor of the first explanation was collected during the next phase of the study.

Phase Two: Progress of Boys and Girls under Teacher Direction

CLASSROOM INSTRUCTION BY TEACHERS

The study did not affect the instructional procedures customarily used in the classrooms of the teachers concerned. Teachers were unaware of the nature of the investigation, having been told merely that inasmuch as some of their pupils had participated previously in a study of programed learning, a follow-up of the reading performance of the children was desirable. In general, classroom instruction consisted of a teacher assigning children to ability groups on the basis of an informal assessment of the child's readiness for reading. Three reading groups were formed in most classes. During a period of four months, each reading group was given approximately 20 minutes of direct instruction daily by the teacher and 20 minutes of daily follow-up or "seat work." Instruction usually consisted of the procedures recommended to accompany the reading materials used, which were those produced by Scott Foresman or Ginn and Company. However, the teachers were free to supplement and modify these materials.

PERFORMANCE ON THE CRITERION TEST
FOLLOWING INSTRUCTION BY TEACHERS

The word-recognition test given after classroom instruction was similar in format and number of items to the test given at the end of auto-instruction and was administered in the same manner. The correlation of scores earned on the two sets was .512 (a value significantly different from zero at the .01 level). The items selected for the second test represented a sample of the words taught by the teachers. Results obtained from both tests are shown in Table 1.

Following the auto-instructional program, boys showed a superiority to girls on a word-recognition test measuring familiarity with words taught in the program. After instruction by female teachers, these same boys were inferior to girls on a similar test covering teacher-taught words.

An examination of changes in rank order on the test of word recognition revealed that 67 per cent of the boys dropped in rank in contrast to 27 per cent

was not maintained under teacher direction indicated that there might be variables in the classroom that militated against maximum performance by young male learners.

Evidence That Women Teachers Fail To Adjust
Their Procedures to Boys

It was hypothesized that boys would be perceived by their classmates as receiving more negative comments from teachers and as receiving fewer opportunities to respond in their reading groups than girls (conditions that were absent under auto-instruction). It was also hypothesized (a) that female teachers

**SEX DIFFERENCES IN ACHIEVEMENT ON WORD RECOGNITION
FOLLOWING TWO CONDITIONS OF TEACHING**

table 1

	FOLLOWING AUTO-INSTRUCTIONAL PROGRAM		FOLLOWING INSTRUCTION BY FEMALE TEACHER	
	Mean	SD	Mean	SD
Boys (N = 49)	26.4	9.0	31.7	11.0
Girls (N = 44)	23.6	8.4	38.3	11.9
	(t = 2.24, p < .05 in two-tailed test)		(t = 2.75, p < .01 in two-tailed test)	

would assess boys as less motivated and less ready for reading than girls and (b) that there exists a positive relationship between children's perceptions of negative comments, opportunities to respond, and the variable of reading progress.

DATA FROM PUPILS AND TEACHERS

A taped interview schedule was administered individually to each of the children in the seven classrooms. The schedule consisted of statements and questions such as the following: "Name the children in your reading group." "Pretend you are in your reading group. Who is the teacher talking to when she says, 'Sit up and pay attention'?" "Who else?" (measure of negative comments) "Who doesn't get to read very much in your reading group?" (measure of opportunity to read). Children could name themselves if they wished. Children responded individually to the taped interview in an isolated room. Responses to the taped questions were recorded by the assistant who operated the audio equipment.

Teachers were asked to indicate on a 5-point check sheet each child's readiness and motivation for reading, considering the child's ability to "pay close attention to explanations, stay with a task, and ask relevant questions."

The results of the statistical nominations of those receiving negative comments showed that boys received more negative admonitions than girls ($\chi^2 = 13.2$, $p < .01$). With respect to opportunity for reading, it was found that boys were seen as given less opportunity to read ($\chi^2 = 5.7$, $p < .05$). Tabulation of the number of pupils identified by teachers as having little or no motivation or readiness for reading showed that boys were assessed more negatively than girls ($\chi^2 = 6.74$, $p < .01$).

Drop in rank order from the first to the second criterion test was correlated with the number of times an individual pupil was perceived as receiving negative comments from the teacher. The drop in rank correlated .313, $p < .01$, with number of negative comments, indicating that those who received such comments did not maintain progress in learning to read. Likewise the drop in rank order was correlated with perceived deprivation of opportunity to read. The correlation of these two indexes was .238, $p < .05$.

These results support the hypothesis that teachers treat boys and girls differently and suggest an association between teacher behavior and performance in beginning reading.

Summary and Conclusion

Evidence was sought to support the hypothesis that the inferiority of young males in learning to read might be the result of certain behavior tendencies of boys to which teachers do not adjust their procedures as well as they do to the behavior tendencies of girls.

The boys included in the study were not inferior in learning to read after auto-instructional procedures that provided frequent and equal opportunities to respond and insured identical presentation of reading lessons to boys and girls (including words of praise). However, these same boys were inferior in a similar learning task administered after ordinary classroom instruction. Also, data were presented that indicated that these boys did not receive equal classroom treatment with the girls in the group.

The findings suggest that a study of the features of auto-instruction may be useful in developing teaching procedures more appropriate for boys than those now commonly used. The reduction in peer-group interaction brought about by a self-teaching device, for example, may result in better performance on the part of those male learners who, under the stimulation of peers and teacher, display aggression or for other reasons fail to attend to the lesson at hand.

references _____

Alden, Clara; Sullivan, Helen B.; and Durrell, Donald D. "The Frequency of Special Reading Disabilities." *Education* 62: 32–36; September 1941.

Davidson, Helen H., and Lang, Gerhard. "Children's Perceptions of Their Teachers' Feelings Toward Them Related to Self-Perception, School Achievement, and Behavior." *Journal of Experimental Education* 29: 107–18; December 1960.

Gallagher, J. Roswell. "Can't Spell, Can't Read." *Atlantic* 181: 35–39; June 1948.

Gates, Arthur I. "Sex Differences in Reading Ability." *The Elementary School Journal* 61: 431–34; May 1961.

Heilman, Arthur W. *Principles and Practices of Teaching Reading.* Columbus, Ohio: Merrill, 1961. 465 pp.

McNeil, John D. "Programed Instruction as a Research Tool in Reading: An Annotated Case." *The Journal of Programed Instruction* 1: 37–42; January 1963.

Monroe, Marion. *Children Who Cannot Read.* Chicago: University of Chicago Press, 1932. 205 pp.

St. John, Charles W. "The Maladjustment of Boys in Certain Elementary Grades." *Educational Administration and Supervision* 18: 659–72; December 1932.

A CRITIQUE OF A RESEARCH REPORT:
Programed Instruction versus Usual Classroom Procedures in Teaching Boys To Read*,[1]

21a

ROBERT B. INGLE and WILLIAM J. GEPHART

Introduction

Professional journals in the field of education devote considerable attention to the reporting of educational research. Although the editors of these journals screen articles to be published, a systematic analysis of reported research is not presented to the reader. A research project conducted by one of the co-authors found that published reports of research vary significantly in value (Gephart, 1964). Thus, it is believed that critiques of published research are vitally needed in the professional literature.

The project analyzed in the following discussion was chosen to satisfy two criteria: recency of publication and quality of the research. The first criterion is self-explanatory. The second, however, requires some comment. It was decided to initiate this research-analysis series with a study that the authors believe was apparently well conceived and carefully conducted. This analysis discusses sequentially the hypothesis, evidence, and inference components of the study.

The Hypothesis

The title and some of the concluding comments in McNeil's research report lead the reader toward a focus on programed instruction in teaching boys to read. Programed instruction is an integral component of this study. However,

---

*Reprinted from *American Educational Research Journal*, 3:1 (1966), pp. 49–53, with the permission of the publisher and authors. Copyright 1966, American Educational Research Association, Washington, D.C.
[1]See McNeil (1964).

McNeil's hypotheses and introductory comments suggest that this study focuses on the problem of possible sex differentiation in instructional behavior on the part of teachers and not on a contrast between programed learning and traditional instruction. If the latter were the case, the two modes of instruction, programed learning and traditional, should occur concurrently rather than sequentially. Further, his hypothesis implies that successful learning via auto-instruction is a *fait accompli*.

> The specific hypothesis is: whereas boys excel in beginning reading under the neutral conditions of programed instruction, these same boys will not maintain their superiority when placed under the direction of female teachers. Further, it is hypothesized that (a) boys will be perceived by their classmates as receiving more negative comments from teachers and as having fewer opportunities to respond in their reading groups than girls and (b) reading progress will be related to teachers' comments and to opportunities to respond. (McNeil, 1964; p. 113)

Analysis of these hypotheses, the procedures of the study, and the conclusions suggest that the hypothesis tested is contained in his statement, " . . . classroom teachers treat boys and girls differently, and that this difference in treatment is associated with differences in early reading achievement." With this as the hypothesis, the "Whereas . . ." clause and the further hypotheses (a) and (b) become vital and creative components of the research design in which programed learning is used only as a procedure to establish the equality of the learning potential of the two sexes.

The Evidence

Testing the hypothesis of differential treatment and association of these treatment differences with reading achievement requires two types of data: (a) descriptive data on the treatment of children, and (b) data on reading achievement. Children were individually interviewed and tapes of these interviews were analyzed to identify the students most often involved in negative interaction with the teachers.

The use of children's perceptions as a data base is accepted by some and rejected by others, but resolution of this debate is not vital here. What is important is that student perceptions were the basis for these data and that other data-accumulation techniques were not used (e.g., tape recordings of classroom sessions, observation of teaching behaviors, sociometric techniques, etc.). McNeil does offer teacher ratings of students as substantiation of the student perceptions. The assumption here seems to be: if teachers rate boys systematically lower than girls in terms of attention, persistence, and question relevance, additional support is presented for children's perceptions of differential treatment. Such an assumption is certainly open to question.

The analysis of these taped data leaves some concern. Although significant chi-square computations were presented, no indication was made as to the general distribution of the negative teacher-student interaction among the classes. With a 1×2 matrix, it would be possible to obtain this result with the majority of the negative comments coming from students in one or two of the seven classrooms. The distribution of the negative comments among the seven classes should be presented.

At first glance the data on achievement in reading seems straightforward enough to be easily obtained. Typically, we would administer a valid and reliable achievement test and report the results. Finding girls better readers than boys through such a procedure allows the application of several rival hypotheses:

1. Girls mature intellectually faster than boys.
2. School work in general and reading in particular are feminine activities and thus more difficult for boys.
3. Boys react more negatively to schooling than do girls.

McNeil's attempt to eliminate these rival hypotheses through a sexless learning situation (auto-instruction) is a major strength of the study. By establishing a learning situation in which the similarity or difference in teacher-learner sex could not affect the "teacher's" response to the child, he provides crucial baseline data for the test of the hypothesis.

Although he is to be commended for this approach, certain weaknesses are apparent also. McNeil's article does not provide one piece of information crucial to the rejection of maturation differences as the cause of differences between the sexes in reading achievement. He states that auto-instruction required approximately three weeks and that it occurred during kindergarten. But, he neglects to state when. A minimum of three months' time elapsed between this component and the traditional instruction. The article implies that more time than this did occur in the statement that children wished to continue this auto-instruction activity. If this phase of the research was conducted near the beginning of the kindergarten year, maturation differences between boys and girls cannot be dismissed as a rival hypothesis for explaining sex differences in reading achievement.

Another justifiable criticism of the evidence regarding achievement focuses on the instruments used for data collection. Nowhere in the report is evidence regarding their validity and reliability. It is assumed here that the word-recognition tests following the auto-instruction and teacher instruction were constructed for this project. In the absence of validity and reliability data, a question remains about these tests.

The Inference Pattern

A pattern of plausible inference (Raths, 1964) that might be considered as the skeleton of this study may be outlined as follows:

Major Premise:	If A; then B.
Minor Premise I:	B without A is hardly credible.
Minor Premise II:	B is or is not true.
Conclusion:	A is credible; or, no conclusion can be drawn.

Applying this outline to McNeil's study yields the following:

Major Premise: If the hypothesis is a true statement, (i.e., classroom teachers treat boys and girls differently and this difference in treatment is associated with differences in early reading achievement): then (1) systematic differences in treatment will be observed and (2) systematic differences in reading achievement will associate with the treatment differences.

Minor Premise I: These differences in achievement could hardly occur without the hypothesis being true if it can be shown: (1) that boys can achieve as well as girls; and (2) that this study involved a normal population.

Minor Premise II: (1) Group mean word recognition test scores, after four months of instruction, show a difference significant at the .01 level; (2) the sex with the lower achievement is perceived as involved significantly more often in negative teacher-pupil interaction.

Conclusion: It is credible that the hypothesis is a true statement.

Minor Premise I is a significant component of this, or any other, experimental research effort. Without it, the argument that systematic differences in learning could have occurred regardless of the truth of the hypothesis must be accepted (Campbell and Stanley, 1963). As stated earlier, the lack of information regarding dates of the auto-instruction makes it difficult to dismiss maturation as a rival hypothesis. The same must be said about instrumentation.

The credibility of the hypothesis is to some degree supported by McNeil's data in the groups studied. However, two points must be made regarding its generalizability. First, it must be assumed that the age and intelligence distributions for the children who served as S's were not skewed for either sex. Since the article gives only total-group data for these variables, some caution is indicated. Second, and possibly the greatest weakness of the study, no data are presented on a very crucial sample, the seven first-grade teachers. Are these persons college graduates or non-degree holders? Young or old? Single or married? Warm and emphatic or aloof? Secure or insecure? And so on. Until such data are available, the reader of the *American Educational*

Research Journal cannot generalize McNeil's results to another sample of *n* first-grade teachers.

Summary

This discussion of the hypothesis, evidence, and inference presented in an *American Educational Research Journal* article has attempted to highlight the strengths and weaknesses of the material presented. The purpose here is not to question the competency of the principal investigator, for undoubtedly many of the questions raised herein could be answered by referring to the detailed report of the study that was submitted to the U.S. Office of Education. This discussion is presented to call the attention of the readers to strengths and weaknesses of the study, to encourage their consideration of them in reaching conclusions, and to encourage others to engage in the process of critical evaluation of published research articles.

references _____

Campbell, Donald T., and Stanley, Julian. "Experimental and Quasi-Experimental Designs for Research on Teaching." *Handbook of Research on Teaching.* (Edited by N. L. Gage.) Skokie, Ill.: Rand McNally, 1963. p. 175.

Gephart, William J. *Development of an Instrument for Evaluating Reports of Educational Research.* U.S. Department of Health Education, and Welfare, Office of Education, Cooperative Research Project No. S-014. The University of Wisconsin-Milwaukee, 1964. 209 pp.

McNeil, John D. "Programed Instruction Versus Usual Classroom Procedures in Teaching Boys to Read." *American Educational Research Journal* 1: 113–19; March 1964.

Raths, James D. "The Uses of Plausible Logic in Educational Research." Paper presented to the American Educational Research Association, Chicago, February 1964. 10 pp.

comments and questions _____

1. The original "sample" for the auto-instructional program was 132 pupils. McNeil describes some of the characteristics of this "sample." In the second phase of this study only 93 of these pupils were used. The mortality was 39. McNeil gives us no information on whether the 93 differ from the 39. Shouldn't he have?
2. McNeil reports a correlation of 0.512 between the pretest and post-test. Shouldn't he have computed two correlations: one for boys and one for girls?

3. Given McNeil's hypothesis, was a two-tailed test the appropriate statistical technique for both tests presented in Table 1?
4. Ingle and Gephart criticize McNeil for not presenting data on teacher characteristics. This criticism implies that these teacher characteristics would conceivably affect the results. Is there any method of analysis that McNeil could have used in his study to identify results related to teacher differences?

AN EXTENDED VISIT WITH DR. FOX:
Validity of Student Satisfaction with Instruction Ratings after Repeated Exposures to a Lecturer*

REED G. WILLIAMS and JOHN E. WARE, JR.

Equivalent groups viewed two lectures varying in substantive teaching points covered (high, medium, low) and expressiveness of the presentation (high, low). Students rated lecture effectiveness after each lecture and completed an achievement test after the two lectures. Higher achievement was associated with high content coverage and high expressiveness. Students gave higher ratings to expressive lectures. Student satisfaction ratings reflected real differences in content coverage and student achievement with low expressive presentations. Ratings were not sensitive to content coverage and student achievement when lectures were high expressive. Sensitivity of ratings to content coverage and student achievement did not improve for the second lecture.

In a study designed to investigate the degree of correspondence between student ratings of instruction and test performance (achievement) under selected instructional conditions, Ware and Williams (1975) programmed a Hollywood actor so as to achieve six lecturer types. Three lectures differing only in content coverage (high, medium and low) were each delivered in both high and low expressive manners. In the high expressive condition, the actor made free use of humor, movement, enthusiasm and vocal inflection to embellish each lecture. In the low expressive condition, these embellishments were omitted from the three lectures.

Consistent with the observations of Coats and Smidchens (1966), it was observed that students who viewed high expressive lectures without an external incentive to learn performed better on the achievement tests than did students who viewed low expressive lectures (Ware & Williams, 1975). Likewise, students who viewed lectures high in content tended to perform better on the cognitive test than did students who viewed lectures lower in content.

*Reprinted from *American Educational Research Journal*, 14:4 (1977), pp. 449–457. Copyright 1977, American Educational Research Association, Washington, D.C.

The research reported in this article was supported by the Office of Research and Projects, Southern Illinois University at Carbondale. Students were scheduled with the cooperation of Larry Busch.

Student ratings of lectures high in expressiveness exceeded ratings of low expressive lectures and in that respect corresponded with achievement results. However, ratings reflected differences in content coverage *only* under low expressive conditions. Mean student ratings were *not* sensitive to either variations in content coverage or group achievement when lectures were highly expressive. This lack of correspondence between ratings and substance of instruction under high expressive conditions was referred to as the "Dr. Fox effect" (Ware & Williams, 1975).

It is possible that the results reported by Ware and Williams (1975) are not representative of results to be expected when student ratings are collected at the end of a course. Student ratings of a highly expressive, low substance lecturer might more accurately reflect the degree of content coverage after exposure to the lecturer for an entire academic term. Perhaps the student who is seduced by a single dramatic, humorous presentation would see through the cloak of expressiveness after additional presentations. Alternately the student might withhold public judgment until after having experienced additional presentations by that lecturer. In either case, the results would be the same. Whereas student ratings of early lectures would not be sensitive to differences in content coverage, ratings of later lectures would accurately reflect the amount of content covered.

While it was impractical to teach an entire course under these experimental controls, students in the Ware and Williams (1975) study were exposed to the same version (e.g., high expressive-low content) of two lectures on different but related topics. The second lecture was viewed immediately following student evaluation of the first. A comparison of the results for lecture one with those for lecture two should provide some indication of changes in student responses if any after exposure to the second lecture. An incidental advantage of this design is the opportunity to investigate whether the results observed with lecture one might be specific to the topic or other features employed in that lecture. This manuscript describes a comparison of the results observed for the second lecture with those observed for the initial lecture and, in so doing, furthers understanding of the Dr. Fox effect and the conditions under which it obtains.

Participants

The participants were 203 students enrolled in three sections of an undergraduate general studies course. These were the 203 of 207 students from the original Ware and Williams study (1975) who attended the three sections on the day the study was conducted and for whom complete data were available for both lectures.

An experimental design was used in which six lecturer types were studied. Student groups were formed by dividing each of three class sections using a table of random numbers. Lecture conditions were randomly assigned to the six groups.

Videotaped Lectures

Six videotaped lectures on each of two topics, the biochemistry of learning and effects of environmental stimulation on the brain, were produced so as to systematically vary along the two dimensions of interest, namely, number of substantive teaching points covered (content coverage) and degree of expressiveness in the presentation. Twelve tapes were produced in total. Details regarding production and the controls employed are documented elsewhere (Williams & Ware, 1976).

Verbatim scripts were used to ensure control of content coverage. The high content scripts were developed first. The medium content script was prepared by excluding approximately 50 percent of the teaching points through use of a modified random procedure. The same procedure was used to prepare each low content script containing approximately 15 percent of the teaching points covered in each high content script. The video tapes were equated for length by adding filler. The final video tapes for lecture one averaged 20.7 minutes in length with a range from 19.1 to 21.8 minutes. Lecture two videotapes averaged 20.6 minutes in length with a range from 19.2 to 22.4 minutes.

Presentation manner was manipulated by programming an actor to give each lecture (high, medium and low content coverage) in either a high or low expressive manner. Levels of expressiveness were associated with differences in vocal inflection, friendliness, charisma, humor, and "personality." The high expressive scripts for lecture one required an average of 21.1 minutes to deliver while the low expressive scripts averaged 20.3 minutes in length. High expressive lecture two scripts averaged 20.1 minutes in length while low expressive scripts averaged 21.0 minutes in length.

Achievement Test

A 46-item multiple-choice test was constructed to cover the contents of the two lectures. Each teaching point in the high content lecture was tested by a test item. The test was composed of knowledge and comprehension level items (Bloom, 1956). The comprehension items were paraphrase and transformed paraphrase items (Anderson, 1972). The cognitive test covering lecture one had an internal consistency index of .62 and that for lecture two was .70 using Kuder-Richardson formula 20 (Helmstadter, 1964).

Student Evaluation of Instruction Questionnaire

The student evaluation of instruction questionnaire is described in Ware and Williams (1975). Items pertained to a variety of lecturer behaviors and student outcomes including lecturer knowledge, presentation manner, humor and enthusiasm as well as student self-ratings of interest, and learning gain. A total rating score was computed from the sum of the 18 scale items. The internal consistency of the total ratings score was .96 using Kuder-Richardson formula 20 (Helmstadter, 1964).

Procedure

After being divided into their respective treatment groups students viewed the first lecture then completed an evaluation of instruction questionnaire for that lecture. Students then viewed the second lecture and completed an evaluation of instruction questionnaire identical to that used after the first lecture. Finally students took the 46-item multiple-choice test designed to cover the content of the two lectures.

Design

For purposes of analysis, this study constitutes a $3 \times 2 \times 2$ analysis of variance design with repeated measures on the third factor. The factors are content coverage (high, medium or low), expressiveness (high or low), and lecture (first lecture or second lecture) respectively. An unweighted means analysis of variance procedure was used as the sizes of classes and the capacities of rooms available for research varied resulting in unequal cell frequencies. The unweighted means ANOVA procedure is recommended for use where differences in cell size are not related to experimental variables (Winer, 1971, pp. 402, 599–603).

Results

Mean cognitive test and satisfaction rating scores for the twelve treatment groups are reported in Table 1. Analysis of variance results for these two dependent measures are reported in Table 2.

367

Da̶t̶a̶ collection report

table 1

SCORE	HIGH EXPRESSIVE LECTURES			LOW EXPRESSIVE LECTURES		
	High Content $N = 26$	Medium Content $N = 21$	Low Content $N = 30$	High Content $N = 39$	Medium Content $N = 68$	Low Content $N = 19$
Cognitive Test						
Mean-Lecture 1	12.46	10.86	9.53	9.54	7.81	8.42
Standard Deviation-Lecture 1	5.21	3.31	2.67	3.86	2.47	2.16
Mean-Lecture 2	7.35	7.10	5.17	5.56	4.38	5.26
Standard Deviation-Lecture 2	4.72	3.80	2.18	3.55	1.96	2.63
Satisfaction Rating						
Mean-Lecture 1	61.58	62.29	57.60	52.31	39.62	38.53
Standard Deviation-Lecture 1	13.23	14.10	13.18	14.86	11.12	11.29
Mean-Lecture 2	55.65	62.57	55.33	51.00	44.07	37.37
Standard Deviation-Lecture 2	14.25	13.01	12.22	15.25	14.06	11.47

Cognitive test results for the two lectures combined are similar to results observed for lecture one alone (Ware & Williams, 1975). Both expressiveness and content coverage influenced student achievement. Students who viewed high expressive presentations achieved higher scores on the cognitive test than did their counterparts who viewed low expressive presentations. Likewise, Scheffé comparisons revealed that students who viewed high content lectures performed better than did those who viewed the medium content lectures, $F(2,197) = 3.48$, $p < .05$. Students who viewed high content lectures also outperformed those who viewed the low content lecture but the differences are not statistically reliable at the 5 percent level of significance using the conservative Scheffé method, $F(2,197) = 2.35$, $p < .10$. Differences in performance for medium and low content groups are negligible. Expressiveness and content coverage did not interact to influence cognitive test performance. The primary purpose for the achievement dependent variable was to confirm that differences in content coverage are reflected in student learning. The results support this conclusion.

As with cognitive test results, student satisfaction with instruction ratings for the combined lectures closely approximated those found in the Ware and Williams (1975) study based on student ratings after viewing only the first lecture. Expressiveness of the presentations again interacted with content coverage indicating that the three content conditions affected satisfaction ratings differently under the two expressiveness conditions. Figure 1 shows the nature of the interaction for lectures one and two separately.

Statistical ⟋ *for purposes of statistical significance*

ANALYSES OF VARIANCE RESULTS FOR COGNITIVE TEST SCORES AND FOR STUDENT SATISFACTION RATING SCORES

table 2

		COGNITIVE TEST		*STUDENT SATISFACTION RATING*	
SOURCE	*df*	*Sum of Squares*	*F*	*Sum of Squares*	*F*
Expressiveness (B)	1	310.37	20.40*	19980.71	69.36*
Content (C)	2	161.04	5.29*	3621.13	6.29*
B × C interaction	2	87.68	2.88	3045.16	5.29*
Error	197	1837.55		56747.83	
Lecture (A)	1	1333.78	228.53*	82.33	1.08
A × B interaction	1	16.97	2.91	230.46	3.04
A × C interaction	2	14.54	1.25	528.53	3.48*
A × B × C interaction	2	3.33	.29	51.48	.34
Interaction	197	1149.78		14955.85	

*$p < .05$.

Since the interaction between expressiveness and content coverage was significant, Scheffé comparisons were performed in order to determine differences in effects among the six lecture conditions.

None of the three contrasts among pairs of group satisfaction ratings for participants who viewed lectures differing in content coverage but delivered in a high expressive manner were significant. In other words the ratings of students viewing high expressive presentations did not reflect real differences in the amount of content covered in the lectures. This finding stands in contrast to the cognitive test results reported earlier.

Under low expressive presentation conditions, two of the three comparisons among pairs of group means were statistically significant. The high content-low expressive group assigned significantly higher satisfaction ratings than the medium content-low expressive group, $F(2,197) = 2.85$, $p < .05$ or the low content-low expressive group, $F(2,197) = 2.87$, $p < .05$. These findings indicate that under these conditions, student ratings did tend to reflect real differences in amount of content covered by the lecturer. In all of these cases the higher content presentation received the more favorable rating.

Most importantly for this study, the lack of a significant content × expressiveness × lecture interaction suggests that the influence of expressiveness and content coverage on student ratings is the same for lectures one and two. Put another way, student ratings of a second lecture delivered in a high expressive manner did not reflect content coverage any better than did ratings of the

figure 1

Mean student satisfaction ratings for the six lecturer types reported separately for the first and second lecture.

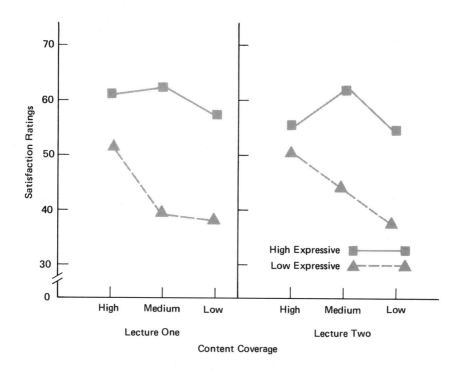

initial lecture. Figure 1 illustrates the similarity of group rating patterns for the two lectures.

Discussion

Ware and Williams (1975) reported findings which suggested that student ratings of instruction generally were not sensitive to either differences in content coverage or to students' actual test performance when the lecturer's presentations were highly expressive. Ware and Williams called this lack of sensitivity to substance of highly expressive presentations the "Dr. Fox effect."

However, Ware and Williams' results could have been transitory. Goffman (1959) suggests that expressive behavior may influence an audience as much as or more than substance when there is little time or reason for the audience to evaluate the presentation. Participants in the original Ware and

Williams (1975) study actually viewed and rated two lectures in close succession. The present manuscript focused on student ratings of the second 20 minute lecture covering a related but different topic. The major purpose was to determine whether the Dr. Fox effect showed signs of washing out when students were exposed to more than one lecture delivered under the same experimental conditions. In Goffman's terms, the students were given added time and additional evidence for purposes of evaluating the lecturer. Thus satisfaction ratings for the second lecture might reflect content coverage and student achievement more accurately than did ratings for the first lecture.

Contrary to what might be predicted based on Goffman's (1959) hypothesis, results of the present study suggest that the correspondence between student ratings of high expressive lectures, and both content coverage and student achievement does *not* improve after viewing a lecturer's second presentation. Inspection of Figure 1 indicates that, as was the case for the first exposure to a high expressive lecture (Ware & Williams, 1975), student ratings of a second high expressive lecture do not correspond to real differences in content coverage and achievement. Ratings of *low* expressive lectures do correspond to content coverage in both lectures one and two.

Even though we have demonstrated that ratings of instruction do not accurately reflect content coverage and student achievement after two lectures when the lectures are presented in a highly expressive manner, Goffman's hypothesis may still be correct. It may take exposure to more than two lectures before students can see through the cloak of expressiveness and provide evaluations of instruction which reflect real differences in content coverage and student achievement. On the other hand an alternate hypothesis remains. Expressiveness may be such a potent variable that currently used evaluation of instruction instruments do not adequately assist the student in differentiating ratings of content coverage and expressiveness.

A number of studies have been completed to increase understanding of the conditions under which the Dr. Fox effect operates. Sensitizing students to focus on the content of a lecture does not control it (Williams & Ware, 1976). Differential weighting of items on teacher rating forms with the purpose of increasing sensitivity to content coverage has been ineffective (Ware & Williams, in press). Finally, this study suggests that the Dr. Fox effect operates through student exposure to at least two lectures.

More research is needed on the longevity of the Dr. Fox effect and on its generalizability to other modes of instruction, to other instructors, to other student populations and to other content domains. However, the results observed to date suggest that student ratings of high expressive instructors may not reflect two important dimensions of teaching effectiveness, namely, substantiveness of instruction and degree of student achievement. The findings highlight the problem of basing decisions about teaching effectiveness on any single indicator.

references ───

Anderson, R. C. How to construct achievement tests to assess comprehension. *Review of Educational Research*, 1972, *42*, 145–170.

Bloom, B. S. (Ed.). *Taxonomy of educational objectives. The classification of educational goals: Handbook I: Cognitive domain*. New York: David McKay Co., 1956.

Coats, W. D., & Smidchens, U. Audience recall as a function of speaker dynamism. *Journal of Educational Psychology*, 1966, *57*, 189–191.

Goffman, E. *The presentation of self in everyday life*. New York: Doubleday, 1959.

Helmstadter, G. C. *Principles of psychological measurement*. New York: Appleton-Century-Crofts, 1964.

Ware, J. E., & Williams, R. G. The Dr. Fox effect: A study of lecturer effectiveness and ratings of instruction. *Journal of Medical Education*, 1975, *50*, 149–156.

Ware, J. E., & Williams, R. G. Discriminant analysis of student ratings as a means for identifying lecturers who differ in enthusiasm or information-giving. *Educational and Psychological Measurement*. In press.

Williams, R. G., & Ware, J. E. Validity of student ratings of instruction under different incentive conditions: A further study of the Dr. Fox effect. *Journal of Educational Psychology*, 1976, *68*, 48–56.

Winer, B. J. *Statistical principles in experimental design* (2nd ed.). New York: McGraw-Hill, 1971.

comments and questions ──────────────────────────────────

1. Were the Findings presented in this study based on new data or were they only a further analysis of the authors' 1976 study? If the latter, why do you suppose they were not reported earlier?

2. At one point the authors talk about a 40-item test. At another time they discuss the internal consistency reliabilities of the tests for lecture 1 and lecture 2. Were there two tests of 46 items each or 40 items total? If the latter, should we not have been told the number of items in each test? Why?

3. The authors state that each teaching point in the high content lecture was measured by a test item. While this was attempted do we have any evidence (e.g., consensual validation of judges) concerning the "match" between test items and content?

4. Were all the subjects of the same sex? If not, would it not have been informative to have had sex as a fourth factor in the research design?

5. Is there any independent verification that the "high expressive" scripts differed significantly from the "low" ones?

6. Would you use the results of this study to support the use of student ratings to judge teacher effectiveness? Why?

7. Rumor has it that the students of a famous (now deceased) statistics professor learned statistics very well because the professor was such a poor lecturer that the students were forced to study a lot outside of class. In the research reported here, the students could *not* compensate for a low content lecture through independent study. Can one generalize about the relationship found in this research between achievement and amount of lecture content to the regular college-type course?

PROPORTION AND DIRECTION OF TEACHER RATING CHANGES OF PUPILS' PROGRESS ATTRIBUTABLE TO STANDARDIZED TEST INFORMATION*

PETER W. AIRASIAN, THOMAS KELLAGHAN,
GEORGE F. MADAUS, and JOSEPH J. PEDULLA

This experiment investigated the magnitude and direction of the effect of standardized test information on teachers' ratings of 1,566 pupils. Forty-seven second-grade Irish teachers were randomly divided into three groups: no testing, testing with no return of test results, and testing with return of pupil test performance. Teachers rated their pupils' class position in mathematics and English reading early in the school year. The Drumcondra Achievement Test Series was administered subsequently and results returned to teachers in January-February. Teachers rerated all pupils in May. Teachers receiving test results shifted more student ratings than teachers not receiving test results. Shifts tended to be positive and for fewer than 10 percent of the students.

Studies of the effects of standardized test information on teachers' perceptions of their pupils have left two important questions unanswered: (a) For what proportion of pupils is test information likely to alter teacher perceptions? and (b) Is there a preponderant direction in which teachers' ratings are revised? It is necessary that these questions be examined to provide a context within which to consider the potential impact of test information on teacher judgments of pupils.

Standardized test information is rarely introduced into a vacuum. Long before the formal introduction of test results, teachers generally have a large store of anecdotes, experiences, and observations to draw upon in forming perceptions of their pupils (Brophy & Good, 1974; Good & Brophy, 1972; Rist, 1970; Silberman, 1971). Moreover, teacher estimates of their pupils' ability tend to correlate highly with the pupils' actual test performance (Brophy &

*From *Journal of Educational Psychology*, 69:6 (1977), pp. 702–709. Copyright 1977 by the American Psychological Association. Reprinted by permission.

Work on this study was supported by funds from the Carnegie Corporation of New York, the Russell Sage Foundation, the Spencer Foundation, and the National Institute of Education.

Requests for reprints should be sent to George F. Madaus, School of Education, Boston College, Chestnut Hill, Massachusetts 02167.

Good, 1970; Willis, 1972; Evertson, Brophy, & Good[1]). It is likely, therefore, that test information gives no cause for teachers to revise their initial perceptions of many pupils, for the simple reason that those perceptions coincide with test results.

Even if perceptions change after the introduction of standardized test results, it often is difficult to determine whether the test results themselves are the causal agent or whether continued observation of and experience with certain pupils—independent of test results—lead naturally to revised perceptions. What is clear, however, is that test information does not lead to revised teacher perceptions for all pupils in a class. Rosenthal (Rosenthal, 1971; Rosenthal & Jacobson, 1968; Rosenthal & Rubin, 1971) and others (Beez, 1968; Palardy, 1969) who have argued that test information can exert a powerful influence on teachers' perceptions of their pupils do not claim that perceptions of *all* pupils are affected by test information. Neither do dissenters from the Rosenthal position (Fleming & Anttonen, 1971; Jose & Cody, 1971; Mendels & Flanders, 1973; Wilkins & Glock, 1973) suggest that test information has *no* effect on teacher perceptions.

To put future research into a more useful perspective, it is important to obtain an estimate of the proportion of students for whom test information can lead to revised teacher perceptions. Further, it is of interest to determine the direction of these changed perceptions—predominantly raised, predominantly lowered, or equally raised and lowered.

Prior research has been limited in seeking answers to these questions. Studies such as Rosenthal and Jacobson (1968), which have endeavored to induce changes in teacher perceptions by providing false information about pupils' test performance, are limited in three regards. First, their very artificiality makes them suspect (Fleming & Anttonen, 1971). Second, they have no comparable control group of nontested subjects to act as a baseline for comparison. Third, ethical considerations have forced them to examine only positive changes in teachers' perceptions. On the other hand, naturalistic descriptive studies of changes in teacher perceptions generally lack suitable control or no-test information groups. In light of these limitations, unequivocal evidence about the proportion of pupils whose teacher's perceptions are actually affected by test information, as well as the direction of this effect, has not been found.

The purpose of this study was to examine experimentally both the proportion of students whose teachers' perceptions were altered by test information and the preponderant directionality of these revised perceptions. The present experiment eliminated many of the problems which have prevented prior studies from addressing these questions. Students' actual test scores (not artificial ones) were reported to teachers, so that the effect of test results on lowered as well as raised perceptions could be determined. Control groups

---

[1]Evertson, C., Brophy, J., & Good, T. *Communication of teacher expectations: First grade* (Report No. 91). Austin: University of Texas, Research and Development Center, 1972.

consisting of no testing and testing with no return of information to teachers were included with the treatment group for baseline comparison. Finally, the confounding of teachers' previous experiences with and attitudes toward standardized tests was minimized by conducting the experiment in a setting in which teachers and students had virtually no prior exposure to standardized testing.

Method

SUBJECTS

A sample of 47 second-grade teachers, teaching 1,566 students, was selected from a larger sample of second-grade teachers and students participating in a societal experiment designed to investigate a wide range of issues associated with the effects of standardized testing (Airasian, Kellaghan, & Madaus).[2] The larger societal experiment is being conducted in the Republic of Ireland with a nationwide random sample of 230 Irish schools, over 1,500 teachers, and over 40,000 pupils at all grade levels. Since teachers and students in the Republic of Ireland had virtually no experience with standardized testing prior to the controlled introduction of such tests in this societal experiment, it was possible to examine the effects of tests on teachers with few confounding conditions.

The second grade was selected for study because most previous studies have concentrated on the lower grades. It was at the lower grades that Rosenthal and Jacobson (1968) found their strongest effects. Further, it can be argued convincingly that it is at the lower grades that teachers' perceptions of pupils are most malleable. By the time a pupil is in the higher grades, the information communication network operating in most schools, in conjunction with the pupil's history of academic performance, may have pegged the pupil with a fairly rigid reputation. The effect of standardized test results on these teachers' perceptions in light of such reputations would, therefore, probably be slight. Since Grade 2 is the lowest grade sampled in the larger study, it was selected for investigation.

PROCEDURE

The study utilized a classical pretest–posttest experimental design with the manipulated variable being whether teachers received norm-referenced standardized achievement test results for the students in their class. The stan-

[2]Airasian, P. W., Kellaghan, T., & Madaus, G. F. *The consequences of introducing standardized testing: A societal experiment.* Proposal funded by the Carnegie Corporation of New York, the National Institute of Education, the Russell Sage Foundation, and the Spencer Foundation, July, 1971.

dardized norm-referenced tests used were the mathematics computation and English reading subtests of the Drumcondra Test Series (Educational Research Centre, 1973). These tests were built specifically for Grade 2 Irish children and normed using a national random sample of second-grade Irish students. In most respects, the Drumcondra tests were very similar to their American counterparts.

In the larger, societal experiment, schools were randomly assigned to treatment groups. One treatment group did not administer any standardized tests. A second treatment group administered the standardized tests but did not receive the results from these tests. A third treatment group administered and received the results from the standardized tests in the form of raw scores and percentile and scale scores based on the national norm group. The three treatments represented a graduated sequence of test experience, from no testing, to testing with no results, to testing with results. One reason for including the second, or intermediate, treatment was to distinguish the effect of simply observing pupils taking tests from the effect of actually receiving information on test performance. It was not clear how teachers' perceptions might be influenced by their observation of pupils' test-taking behavior as distinct from pupils' test performance. There were 11 teachers and 411 students in the no-testing group, 8 teachers and 269 students in the testing but no-results group, and 27 teachers and 878 students in the testing with results group.

The standardized tests of English and mathematics were administered in October and November. At about the same time as the test administration, teachers in all three treatment groups provided ratings of each student's position relative to the other pupils in the class in English reading and mathematics computation. Ratings were on a 5-point scale with "1" signifying that the student was in the bottom fifth of the class and "5" signifying that the student was in the top fifth of the class. In late January to early February, test results, in the form of raw scores, percentiles, and scale scores, were reported back to those teachers who received results. In late May, all teachers rerated each of their students in mathematics and English.

The study sought to examine the proportion of revised ratings which could be associated with the availability of test results. Changes in pupil ratings were examined for the three treatment groups to determine whether the availability of test information resulted in a greater proportion of pupil rating changes. The direction of the rating changes were also examined to determine whether the revised ratings were predominantly higher or lower.

To this end, for each student, three indices were calculated in each of the two rating areas. The first index measured the magnitude of the change in a pupil's rating pair, that is, the absolute value of the difference in that pair. For example, if the teacher rated a student to be in the top fifth of the class in mathematics in the fall (a rating of "5") and the middle fifth of the class in the spring (a rating of "3"), the value of the magnitude measure for mathematics for that student would be 2.

The remaining indices dealt with the direction of rating shifts; one index indicated positive rating shifts. If the pupil's final rating was higher than his initial rating, this index was coded "1"; otherwise this index was coded "0." An index which indicated negative ratings shifts was computed in a similar fashion, that is, if a pupil's final rating was lower than his initial rating, this index was coded "1"; it was coded "0" otherwise. It should be noted that the means for the variables measuring direction of rating shifts are directly interpretable as the proportion of ratings shifting in that direction.

In sum, each student had a total of six indices, three for mathematics and an analogous three for reading: (a) the magnitude of the change from initial to final rating; (b) whether the final rating was higher than the initial rating; and (c) whether the final rating was lower than the initial rating. Each of these six indices was used as a dependent variable in a univariate, one-factor analysis of variance. In each analysis, the independent variable was treatment group membership, that is, no testing, testing but no results, or testing with results. Post hoc comparisons of means were conducted when statistically significant differences were found.

Results

Table 1 presents the correlations among initial and final pupil ratings in English reading and mathematics computation and the corresponding pupil test scores. The correlations between initial ratings and test scores corroborate that teachers have fairly accurate perceptions of their pupils' capabilities prior to the advent of test information. The correlations between final ratings and test scores viewed in conjunction with the correlations between initial and final ratings suggest that test information is not a powerful spur to altering pupil ratings generally. The correlations between initial and final ratings are considerably higher in both subject areas than the correlations between test scores and final ratings. There are slight increases over time in the correlations of ratings with test scores for the group which tested and received test information. The group which tested and did not receive test results evidenced slight decreases in the correlation of ratings with test scores over time. Finally, the consistency of initial and final ratings are somewhat lower for the test information group than for the other groups. Table 1 suggests, therefore, that test information may have an effect on teacher ratings of pupils but that this effect is on a relatively small proportion of students. Succeeding analyses were directed toward documenting this effect in more detail by examining the magnitude and direction of rating changes using the change indices described above.

Table 2 shows that similar results were obtained for the rating-change measures in English and mathematics. This similarity was partially a function of the high correlations between the rating measures in mathematics and English.

CORRELATIONS AMONG INITIAL AND FINAL TEACHER RATINGS
OF PUPIL'S CLASS POSITION AND STANDARDIZED TEST SCORES
IN ENGLISH AND MATHEMATICS BY TREATMENT GROUP

table 1

| | TREATMENT | | |
VARIABLES CORRELATED	No Testing	Testing with No Results	Testing with Results
English reading test score with initial English reading rating	a	.64	.66
English reading test score with final English reading rating	a	.59	.69
Mathematics computation test score with initial mathematics computation rating	a	.62	.53
Mathematics computation test score with final mathematics computation rating	a	.60	.62
Initial and final English reading ratings	.89	.88	.84
Initial and final mathematics computation ratings	.86	.87	.78

[a]Correlations of test scores with ratings could not be computed, since test score data were unavailable.

The correlation matrix is presented in Table 2 and shows that these correlations were approximately .60.

The positive correlations between the magnitude of rating change and the direction of rating change in the same subject area are partially a function of the manner in which these variables were constructed. Non-zero change, in terms of magnitude must, by definition, be related to positive and negative rating shifts. Similarly, the negative correlations between variables measuring positive rating shifts and variables measuring negative rating shifts in the same subject area are a function of the manner in which the variables were constructed, since ratings can shift in only one direction. The correlations are of a high enough magnitude to indicate that the analysis of variance results are dependent and must be interpreted in light of this dependency.

The means and standard deviations for all six dependent variables are presented in Table 3 with the analysis of variance results for these measures presented in Table 4. The analysis of variance results for both the English and mathematics magnitude of rating shift variables were statistically significant ($p < .05$). Pairwise post hoc comparisons of means, using the Scheffé test (Winer, 1971), showed that the group which received test results exhibited significantly greater magnitude of rating change than (a) either of the other two groups for the English ratings and (b) the no-testing group for the mathematics ratings.

CORRELATIONS AMONG THE DEPENDENT VARIABLES

table 2

VARIABLE	1	2	3	4	5	6
1. Magnitude of change in English ratings	—	55	60	33	55	31
2. Magnitude of change in mathematics ratings		—	32	55	30	55
3. Positive shifts in English ratings			—	60	−25	−21
4. Positive shifts in mathematics ratings				—	−20	−27
5. Negative shifts in English ratings					—	62
6. Negative shifts in mathematics ratings						—

Statistically significant differences were also found for both the English and mathematics variables measuring positive rating shifts (cf. Table 4). That is, for both English and mathematics, there was a difference among the three treatment groups in the proportion of initial to final rating pairs which were raised. Post hoc comparisons of means showed that the group which received test results raised more of its ratings in English than the group which tested but received no results. In mathematics, the group which received test results raised more of its ratings than the group which did not test. It is not apparent why these particular patterns of significance on the Scheffé post hoc comparisons were evidenced and the most that can reasonably be inferred is that, on the average, the availability of test information tends to lead to greater magnitudes of rating changes, generally in a positive direction.

The means for the positive rating change measures are directly interpretable as the proportion of rating shifts upward. Keeping this interpretation in mind, one can see from Table 3 that between 13 percent and 23 percent of all ratings shifted upward. An estimate of positive rating shifts which are attributable to teachers' receiving test information can be obtained by finding the difference between the percentage of positive rating shifts in the testing with results treatment and a baseline percentage provided by one of the other two treatments. Given the post hoc patterns of statistical significance, however, there is a problem in picking a single treatment to act as a baseline estimate. Positive shifts in the English reading rating for the testing with results group were significantly different from the testing with no-results group but not from the no-testing group.

In mathematics computation, a different pattern of significance was found; positive shifts for the testing with results group were significantly differ-

MEANS AND STANDARD DEVIATIONS BY TREATMENT GROUP
FOR ALL DEPENDENT MEASURES

table 3

		TREATMENT	
VARIABLE	*No Testing*	*Testing with No Results*	*Testing and Results*
Magnitude of change in English ratings			
M	.39	.39	.49
SD	.52	.54	.61
Magnitude of change in mathematics ratings			
M	.38	.46	.55
SD	.54	.55	.66
Positive shifts in English ratings			
M	.20	.16	.23
SD	.40	.37	.42
Positive shifts in mathematics ratings			
M	.13	.18	.23
SD	.34	.39	.42
Negative shifts in English ratings			
M	.16	.19	.20
SD	.37	.40	.40
Negative shifts in mathematics ratings			
M	.22	.22	.23
SD	.42	.42	.42

ent from the no-testing group but not the testing with no-results group. In selecting a baseline for estimating the effect of test information on positive rating shifts, we elected to follow the pattern of statistical significance. Thus, the baseline group selected for English reading was the testing with no-results group and the baseline group selected for mathematics computation was the no-testing group. The selection of these baseline groups provides an estimate of the maximum effect on pupil ratings due to teachers having test information. Using the appropriate baseline mean, one finds that 7 percent of the English ratings and 10 percent of the mathematics ratings shifted upward as a consequence of teachers being in the test information group.

No significant differences among treatment groups were found for the negative rating shift measures. Thus, receiving standardized test results did not lead directly to a greater proportion of lowered pupil ratings. The means in Table 3 do show roughly 20 percent of the ratings in all groups shifted downward. Since roughly 20 percent of the ratings also shifted upward, approximately 60 percent of all ratings did not change at all.

Thus, the results of this study show that across treatments less than half of the teachers' ratings of pupils changed at all over the course of the school year. Of those 40 percent or so of the ratings which did change, only a small

ANALYSIS OF VARIANCE RESULTS FOR ALL DEPENDENT MEASURES

table 4

SOURCE	df	SS	MS	F	p
		Magnitude of changes in English ratings			
Between groups	2	4.74	2.37	7.04	.001
Within groups	1,515	510.44	.34		
		Magnitude of change in mathematics ratings			
Between groups	2	7.29	3.64	9.33	0.001
Within groups	1,463	571.12	.39		
		Positive shifts in English ratings			
Between groups	2	1.10	.55	3.30	.04
Within groups	1,515	252.60	.17		
		Positive shifts in mathematics ratings			
Between groups	2	2.29	1.15	7.33	.001
Within groups	1,463	228.52	.16		
		Negative shifts in English ratings			
Between groups	2	.34	.17	1.12	.33
Within groups	1,515	233.02	.15		
		Negative shifts in mathematics ratings			
Between groups	2	.02	.01	.07	.43
Within groups	1,463	258.42	.18		

percentage of the changes (7 percent–10 percent) could be attributed directly to being in the group which received test results. Finally, the results from this study indicate that receiving standardized test results tended to raise, but not lower, teachers' ratings of their students.

Discussion

The results from this study indicate that standardized test results do alter Grade 2 teachers' perceptions of their students in a small percentage of cases, 10 percent or less. However, contrary to the supposedly detrimental effect of lowering expectations that some critics of standardized testing have claimed, this study indicates that teachers tend to raise, but *not* lower, their ratings of students' performance as a result of receiving standardized test results. However, it must be emphasized that in the vast majority of cases, standardized test results had no influence on teachers' ratings. Thus, the new piece of information which standardized test results provide to teachers seems to either corroborate their existing expectations or be too weak to alter existing expectations for at least 90 percent of the cases.

Since this study took place in the Republic of Ireland, the relevance of the findings for the United States must be addressed. One comparison that can be made is between American and Irish teachers' attitudes and opinions toward standardized tests. The items for this comparison were employed in a study conducted in the United States (Brim, Goslin, Glass, & Goldberg)[3] and again with Irish teachers (Airasian, Kellaghan, & Madaus).[4] A comparison of the results from the Brim et al. study to the Irish replication found that Irish teachers had more favorable attitudes toward standardized tests than their American counterparts (Airasian et al).[4]

From this finding it can be argued that standardized tests would tend to have more influence on Irish teachers' perceptions of pupils than on American teachers' perceptions. If this is the case, the influence of standardized test results on American teachers' perceptions of their pupils would be slight indeed. This small influence may account for the inability of many American studies to find effects.

This study examined teacher perceptions in the grossest of ways, that is, at the global treatment level, to provide an estimate of the proportion of students likely to have initial teacher perceptions changed as a result of test information. As has been suggested (Brophy & Good, 1974), a clearer understanding of teachers' perceptions can be obtained by examining smaller, selected subgroups, such as teachers within treatment or students within teachers within treatment. Although initial attempts at this approach with the data for this study failed to produce much by way of identifying particular types of teachers or students for whom standardized test results were most influential (Pedulla, 1976), further research in this vein seems necessary. While it was not the purpose of this study to examine the ultimate effect of changed teacher perceptions on pupil performance (the "expectancy effect"), it can be predicted that overall this effect is slight, given the relative stability of teacher ratings over time.

In sum, the results from this study indicate that standardized test results can affect teachers' ratings for only a small number of students and that the influence of the results is to raise, but not lower, ratings. Thus, future studies of the impact of test information on teacher perceptions will require more sensitive pupil stratification and examination to separate that small proportion of pupils for whom test information has an influence on teacher percep-

[3]Brim, O. G., Jr., Goslin, D. A., Glass, D. C., & Goldberg, I. *The use of standardized ability tests in American secondary schools and their impact on students, teachers, and administrators* (Technical Report No. 3). New York: Russell Sage Foundation, 1965.

[4]Airasian, P. W., Kellaghan, T., & Madaus, G. F. *The consequences of introducing educational testing: A societal experiment.* Unpublished manuscript, Boston College, 1975.

tions from the larger mass of pupils unaffected by their test performance. Future studies also will need to identify the characteristics which differentiate those pupils whose teacher ratings are affected by test information from those pupils whose ratings are unaffected.

references

Beez, W. V. Influence of biased psychological reports on teacher behavior and pupil performance. *Proceedings of the 76th Annual Convention of the American Psychological Association*, 1968, *3*, 605–606. (Summary)

Brophy, J. E., & Good, T. L. Teachers' communication of differential expectations for children's classroom performance: Some behavioral data. *Journal of Educational Psychology*, 1970, *61*, 365–374.

Brophy, J. E., & Good, T. L. *Teacher-student relationships: Causes and consequences.* New York: Holt, Rinehart & Winston, 1974.

Educational Research Centre, *Drumcondra Test Series.* Dublin, Ireland: St. Patrick's College, 1973.

Fleming, E. S., & Anttonen, R. G. Teacher expectancy or My Fair Lady. *American Educational Research Journal*, 1971, *8*, 241–252.

Good, T., & Brophy, J. E. Behavioral expression of teacher attitudes. *Journal of Educational Psychology*, 1972, *63*, 617–624.

Jose, J., & Cody, J. J. Teacher-pupil interaction as it relates to attempted changes in teacher expectancy of academic ability and achievement. *American Educational Research Journal*, 1971, *8*, 34–49.

Mendels, G. E., & Flanders, J. P. Teachers' expectations and pupil performance. *American Educational Research Journal*, 1973, *10*, 203–211.

Palardy, J. What teachers believe — what children achieve. *Elementary School Journal*, 1969, *69*, 370–374.

Pedulla, J. J. *The influence of standardized test information on teachers' ratings of their students.* Unpublished doctoral dissertation. Boston College, 1976.

Rist, R. C. Student social class and teacher expectations: The self-fulfilling prophecy in ghetto education. *Harvard Educational Review*, 1970, *40*, 411–451.

Rosenthal, R. Teacher expectation and pupil learning. In R. D. Strom (Ed.), *Teachers and the learning process.* Englewood Cliffs, N.J.: Prentice-Hall, 1971.

Rosenthal, R., & Jacobson, L. *Pygmalion in the classroom: Teacher expectation and pupils' intellectual development.* New York: Holt, Rinehart & Winston, 1968.

Rosenthal, R., & Rubin, D. Appendix C: Pygmalion reaffirmed. In J. Elashoff & R. Snow (Ed.), *Pygmalion reconsidered.* Belmont, Calif.: Wadsworth, 1971.

Silberman, M. Teachers' attitudes and actions toward their students. In M. Silberman (Ed.), *The experience of schooling.* New York: Holt, Rinehart & Winston, 1971.

Wilkins, W. E., & Glock, M. D. *Teacher expectations and student achievement: A replication and extension.* Ithaca, N.Y.: Cornell University, 1973. (ERIC Document Reproduction Service No. 080-567)

Willis, S. *Formation of teachers' expectations of students' academic performance.* Unpublished doctoral dissertation. University of Texas at Austin, 1972.

Winer, B. J. *Statistical principles in experimental design* (2nd ed.). New York: McGraw-Hill, 1971.

comments and questions _____

1. Should the researchers have provided more descriptive information regarding the prior knowledge of measurement terminology among the teachers? If, for example, these teachers had little familiarity and/or specific training in interpreting test scores, is it not conceivable that reporting percentiles and scale scores would be relatively meaningless? Should we have been given more information on *how* the information was presented to the teachers?

2. Each time the teacher rated a student he/she received a rating of 1 to 5 depending upon which fifth of the class he/she was in. (Are these ratings or rankings?) Given this, how could more ratings go up than down? Given a class of 25 students, can you produce some hypothetical data where 15 students' ratings go up, 10 go down, and still have 5 students in each fifth on each rating? If so, you can correctly say that more students' ratings went up than down—but what else is true?

3. Do you suppose that teachers actually gave one-fifth of their students each rating? Should the authors have addressed this point?

4. Do you think it would have been preferable for the teachers to have rated each student on some criterion-reference procedure rather than relative to the other pupils in the class? Defend your answer.

5. Irish teachers hold more favorable attitudes than American teachers toward standardized tests. Given this, is it reasonable to infer that standardized tests would tend to have more influence on Irish teachers' perceptions than on American teachers' perceptions?

6. In what way(s) does this study shed light on the experimenter bias effect discussed on pages 395–421?

COUNSELOR DISCRIMINATION AGAINST YOUNG WOMEN IN CAREER SELECTION*

THOMAS J. DONAHUE and JAMES W. COSTAR

To document counselor bias toward females and identify some of its correlates, six short case studies were devised that could describe either a male or a female. Three hundred randomly selected senior high school counselors in Michigan were asked to select an appropriate occupation for each case study subject. When the case study described a female, the counselors chose occupations that paid less, required less prerequisite education, and were more closely supervised than when the same case study described a male. Female counselors over 40 years of age exhibited the strongest tendency to do this. Counselors who worked in schools located in cities with a population greater than 25,000 tended to discriminate less than other counselors. Counselors whose mothers possessed an average amount of formal education had a stronger tendency to discriminate against females than other counselors.

Women in the United States are faced with many institutional and social obstacles to self-actualization. For instance, women are concentrated in the less rewarding, lower paying occupations that provide few chances for advancement (U.S. Department of Labor, 1973). Counselors become concerned when such barriers are placed in the developmental paths of their clients. Yet they themselves may be detrimental to the self-actualization of their female clients.

Goldberg (1972) performed an extensive series of empirical studies dealing with prejudice toward women and concluded that bias against females is a cultural trait. According to Schlossberg and Pietrofesa (1973), counselors in training exhibit the norms of society and appear to be neither better nor worse than other people with respect to bias against females. Many women have

*From *Journal of Counseling Psychologists*, 23:3 (1976), pp. 221–233. Copyright 1976 by the American Psychological Association. Reprinted by permission.

This study is based on a doctoral dissertation by the first author under the direction of the second author. The authors express their thanks to Mildred Erickson, Raymond Hatch, and Ruth Useem for serving on the dissertation committee, and to John Schweitzer for assisting in the statistical analysis.

Thomas J. Donahue is now principal of the Taipei American School in Taipei, Taiwan.

Requests for reprints should be sent to James W. Costar, Room 438, Erickson Hall, Michigan State University, East Lansing, Michigan 48824.

internal psychological conflicts related to their position in the world of work. Horner (1972) has shown that women, like men, worry about failure; but in addition, most women are anxious about success because success is considered unfeminine. Some women are also upset by a conflict between their roles as mother and worker. Such conflicts occasionally lead women to seek help from professional counselors.

The small amount of available literature related to vocational counseling with women reveals that counselors in general, like other members of their society, are biased against women, and this bias is apparent in their counseling behavior and in their theories. Pringle (1973) found that male counselors were generally more supportive of high achievement in female clients than were female counselors, but male counselors were also supportive of dependence.

Broverman, Broverman, Clarkson, Rosenkrantz, and Vogel (1970) found that actively functioning clinicians held a different standard of mental health for males and for females. Broverman, Vogen, Broverman, Clarkston, and Rosenkrantz, (1972) later replicated the study using a different population and found that "consensus about the differing characteristics of men and women exists across groups differing in sex, age, marital status and education" (p. 59). Maslin and Davis (1975) replicated the study using counselors in training as subjects, but they did not confirm all of Broverman's findings.

The purpose of this study was to determine if high school counselors, when considering careers for female students, have a predisposition toward suggesting occupations that pay less, require less education, and need more supervision than careers considered for male students. In addition, an attempt was made to ascertain if certain personal characteristics of school counselors and selected environmental variables are also correlated with such a predisposition.

Three main hypotheses were related to the central question: Would high school counselors choose jobs that were (a) lower paying, (b) required less education, and (c) required more supervision for female case study subjects than for identically described male case study subjects?

The seven variables of interest were also examined: sex, marital status, age, education, professionalism, socioeconomic background (including parent educational level), and idealism of high school counselors. These counselor variables may be related to differences in the level of remuneration, education, or supervision of the occupations counselors chose for male case study subjects and identically described female subjects.

Method

SUBJECTS

The sample consisted of 300 randomly selected senior high school counselors in Michigan chosen from a population of approximately 2,000. Nearly half were female, 96 percent held master's degrees, and 45 percent had training beyond the master's degree level. There was a near normal age dis-tribution, with 66 percent between the ages of 30 and 50 years. Seventy-five percent had fewer than 11 years of counseling experience. More than one half were affiliated with local and state professional organizations, but only 25 per-cent held membership in a national professional association.

DESIGN

Six case studies were prepared so that the personal characteristics of the student described in each case study could describe either a male or female. Two forms of the case study questionnaire were developed with six identical case studies on both forms. However, in Form A, Case Study Subjects 1, 4, and 6 were designated as males and Case Studies 2, 3, and 5 were designated as females. Form B case study subjects were assigned the opposite-sex designa-tions; that is, Subjects 1, 4, and 6 were presented as females and Cases 2, 3, and 5 were presented as males. A detailed explanation of the instrument, research design, and statistical procedure can be found elsewhere (Donahue, 1976).

Participants were asked to choose the most appropriate occupation, for the person described in each case study, from a list of 28 occupations. The subjects did not know that each occupation possessed weighted coefficients on a 7-point scale for salary range, for level of prerequisite education, and for level of supervision. Using information from the *Occupational Outlook Handbook* (U.S. Department of Labor, 1974), the author determined the remuneration coefficient and education coefficient. The coefficient of remuneration ranged from 1 (below $5,000) to 7 ($20,000 and above), with increments of $3,000 per integer. The coefficient of education ranged from 1 (no education required) through 4 (high school diploma or significant on-the-job or vocational training required) to 7 (graduate degree required). The coefficient of supervision was determined by the mean rating of six experts in the fields of vocational guidance and vocational education. The experts, two professors, two school coop ad-visors, and two employment counselors from the Michigan Employment Se-curity Commission, showed a high degree of agreement in their judgments. The six experts rated each of the 28 occupations. All but 6 of the 168 individual ratings were within 1 point of the mean score for that occupation.

On a short personal data sheet, printed on the back of the case study questionnaire, respondents were asked to provide information regarding their sex, marital status, age, professional training and experience, and socio-economic background.

A respondent's score on each of the three dependent variables of sal-ary, education, and supervision was determined by computing the sum of the coefficients of the occupations chosen for the three female case study subjects and subtracting it from the sum of the coefficients of the occupations chosen for the three male case study subjects. Positive scores indicated a tendency to choose higher status jobs for male case study subjects than for female case study subjects. A score of zero indicated no bias. A negative score indicated a tendency to choose higher status jobs for female case study subjects than for male case study subjects.

Because the tasks posed by the instrument were similar to tasks performed by school counselors and because the questions did not seem directly related to the gender of the case study subjects, the instrument appeared to possess a high degree of face validity. No valid standardized test now exists that could be used to determine concurrent validity satisfactorily, and because the instrument was not desig.ied to predict individual behavior, predictive validity was only considered for counselors in general rather than for individuals.

The data were collected over a 4-month period. Seventy-six percent of the subjects completed usable questionnaires and data sheets. Another 10 percent of the questionnaires were returned in an incomplete or unusable form. The data were analyzed using a variety of statistical tests, including multivariate analysis of variance, univariate analysis of variance, and dependent *t* tests.

Results

A summary of the significant findings can be found in Table 1. The results clearly demonstrated that the counselors in the study tended to choose lower paying occupations that are more highly supervised and require less prerequisite education for female case study subjects than for male subjects. The differences were statistically significant for all three variables.

It was also shown that the educational level of the counselor's mother (a component of the counselor's socioeconomic background) had a significant effect on the kinds of careers that both male and female counselors chose for female case study subjects when compared to male case study subjects. A counselor, whether male or female, whose mother had an average amount of formal education, tended to choose careers for female case study subjects that paid less and required less education and more supervision than counselors whose mothers had either more or less than average formal education.

Differences in the kinds of careers counselors chose for male and female subjects were also related to the demographic location. Counselors who worked in schools located in cities with a population greater than 25,000 tended to choose careers for female subjects that paid less and required less education than those chosen for male subjects. However, counselors from smaller cities and rural areas showed an even greater tendency to discriminate between male and female case study subjects on salary and education than the counselors who worked in the city schools.

When analyzed separately, neither the sex nor the age of the counselor alone appeared to have a statistically significant effect on the kinds of occupations chosen for females. However, there was a statistically significant interaction between them. The results indicated that male counselors over 40 years of

UNIVARIATE ANALYSIS OF VARIANCE TABLE FOR SIGNIFICANT FINDINGS

table 1

HYPOTHESES	REMUNERATION				EDUCATION				SUPERVISION			
	M^a	SD	F	p	M^a	SD	F	p	M^a	SD	F	p
1–3												
All counselors	2.29	3.94	77.09	.0001	.84	3.94	10.43	.0015	2.01	3.32	82.99	.0001
Demographic location												
Metropolitan	2.15	3.83			.82	3.74			2.05	3.13		
Cities 25,000+	1.13	3.96	2.89	.0576	-.52	3.57	3.33	.0377	1.11	3.44	2.04	.1332
Rural	2.86	3.87			1.39	4.15			2.36	3.35		
Mother's education												
Below average	1.27	2.83			.12	2.87			1.15	3.03		
Average	2.83	4.50	3.03	.0469	1.31	4.34	1.83	.1205	2.64	3.59	4.42	.0127
Above average	2.25	3.52			.65	3.99			1.63	2.82		
Interaction analysis												
Sex × Age	2.29	3.94	5.24	.0230	.84	3.94	17.04	.0001	2.01	3.32	.77	.3810
Age × Father's Education	2.29	3.94	4.25	.0156	.84	3.94	1.32	.2688	2.01	3.32	1.73	.1806

[a]Mean differences between scores of male and female case study subjects on a 7-point scale.

age discriminated least against female case study subjects, followed by female counselors under 40 and male counselors under 40. Females over 40 years old exhibited the greatest discrepancy between the careers chosen for female and those chosen for male case study subjects. This finding partially supports a similar conclusion suggested by Thomas and Stewart (1971), who found that counselors with more than 5 years of counseling experience demonstrated less bias than counselors with fewer years of experience.

The only other significant two-way interaction was found between the counselor's age and the level of his or her father's education. A male or female counselor under 40 years of age whose father had an average educational background was least likely to choose lower paying occupations for females, whereas the counselor who is over 40 and whose father had less formal education than most people was most likely to choose lower paying occupations for female case study subjects.

Discussion

Vocational counseling of female clients is performed as well by male counselors as by female counselors. When analyzed by sex, no statistically significant differences occurred in the kinds of occupations chosen for female and male case study subjects by male and female counselors. Although many older male counselors apparently are more likely to consider higher paying, supervisory, professional, and technical occupations for girls, and older female counselors are less willing to consider nontraditional careers for girls, the sex of the counselor does not in itself predispose a counselor to be an open, supportive guide to the world of work, or a restrictive guide who views the various roles in the labor market in stereotypic terms. Even though Hill (1975) found that same-sex pairings had more discussion of feelings by both counselor and client, this research does not support the assertion made by Bingham and House (1973), and referred to McEwen (1975) and Brodsky and Holroyd (1975), that female counselors should counsel girls. A thorough review of research regarding the influence of counselor sex on the counseling process is presented by Tanney and Birk (1976).

Neither counselor education programs nor membership in professional organizations effectively changes biases of high school counselors against females. Membership in professional organizations and the amount of training a counselor received had no statistically significant effect on the intensity of occupational bias shown toward female case study subjects. Even when these two hallmarks of the professional counselor were combined with counseling experience, no statistically significant relationship with the intensity of the bias could be found. Occupational bias toward females seems to be relatively immune to change under present methods of counselor training.

In order to improve counselor education programs, intervention strategies need to be developed that will eliminate or decrease sex bias in counselors. These strategies should focus both on the cognitive and affective aspects of bias. Counselor education programs should incorporate conscious-ness-raising activities as well as other intervention strategies. Schlossberg and Pietrofesa (1973) and Maslin and Davis (1975) recommended intervention strategies for helping counselor trainees understand and deal with their own biases toward women. Verheyden-Hilliard (1976) recently published a hand-book for workshops on sex equality in education.

One of the curious findings of this study was that counselors whose mothers fell at opposite ends of the educational continuum chose less dis-criminatory occupations for girls. Perhaps this pattern was related to whether a counselor's mother had worked. Statistically, we know that the more formal education a woman has, the more likely she is to work outside of the home. It seems probable then that women with an average educational background are the least likely to have work experience outside of the home.

It is clear that the high school counselors in this study tended to perceive occupations suitable for women mainly in terms of low pay, little prerequisite education, and much supervision. The data indicated that even though counselors sometimes chose occupations for females that required for-mal education, they seldom chose a career that paid a high salary or was supervisory in nature. This suggests that it was viewed as socially acceptable for women to have an education, as long as they stayed in a dependent, supervised role.

We are not suggesting that practicing counselors either espouse or reject feminist views in counseling, but that they must understand themselves, as well as their attitudes, beliefs, and values, in order to counsel effectively without subtly imposing their own values on the client. The unconscious accep-tance of social norms that limit client growth and development is not compati-ble with counseling theory or practice, yet it does occur and must be pointed out both to the counselors in training and practicing counselors.

A counselor profile should be developed to help counselor educators and employers ascertain whether or not a candidate aspiring to be a counselor is likely to be discriminatory against females. This study has shown that a coun-selor's family background, personality, sex and age, and work environment are all related to the relative strength of the bias. Other characteristics should also be examined to determine whether they too are correlated with this bias. Some factors might include the number, sex, and constellation of siblings, race, re-ligion, authoritarianism, type of counselor training, risk-taking tendency, theoretical and philosophical orientation, and self-concept. Using actuarial and theoretical research methods, it should be possible to build a profile of the biased counselor. A similar self-test or survey should also be developed so that counselors may examine themselves to see if they are inclined to be biased against females.

Finally, further research is needed to determine how age affects the development of bias toward women. Although age, in itself, did not make a statistically significant difference in the amount of bias counselors displayed in this study, it did interact with other variables such as sex and parental educational level. It would be advantageous to understand the relation between age and bias.

references

Bingham, W. C., & House, E. W. Counselors' attitudes toward women and work. *Vocational Guidance Quarterly*, 1973, *22*, 16–23.

Brodsky, A., & Holroyd, J. *Report of the Task Force on Sex Bias and Sex-Role Stereotyping in Psychotherapeutic Practice.* Washington, D.C.: American Psychological Association, 1975.

Broverman, I. K., Broverman, D.M., Clarkston, F. E., Rosenkrantz, P. S., & Vogel, S. R. Sex-role stereotypes and clinical judgments of mental health. *Journal of Consulting and Clinical Psychology*, 1970, *34*, 1–7.

Broverman, I., Vogel, S., Broverman, D., Clarkston, F., & Rosenkrantz, P. Sex-role stereotypes: A current appraisal. *Journal of Social Issues*, 1972, *28*, 59–77.

Donahue, T. J. Discrimination against young women in career selection by high school counselors (Doctoral dissertation, Michigan State University, 1976). *Dissertation Abstracts* International, 1976. (University Microfilms No. 76-18612)

Goldberg, P. A. Prejudice toward women: Some personality correlates. Paper presented at the meeting of the American Psychological Association. Honolulu, Hawaii, September, 1972. (ERIC Document Reproduction Service No. ED 72 386)

Hill C. E. Sex of client and sex and experience level of counselor. *Journal of Counseling Psychology*, 1975, *22*, 6–11.

Horner, M. S. Toward an understanding of achievement-related conflicts. *Journal of Social Issues*. 1972, *28*, 157–176.

Maslin, A., & David, J. L. Sex-role stereotyping as a factor in mental health standards among counselors in training. *Journal of Counseling Psychology*, 1975, *22*, 87–91.

McEwen, M. K. Counseling women: A review of research. *Journal of College Student Personnel*, 1975, *1*, 382–386.

Pringle, M. B. The responses of counselors to behaviors associated with independence and achievement in male and female clients (Doctoral dissertation, University of Michigan, 1973), (ERIC Document Reproduction Service No. 071 008)

Schlossberg, N. K., & Pietrofesa, J. J. Counselor bias and the female occupational role. *The Counseling Psychologist*, 1973, *4*, 44–54.

Tanney, M. F., & Birk, J. M. Women counselors for women clients? A review of the research. *The Counseling Psychologist*, 1976, *6*, 28–32.

Thomas, A. H., & Stewart, N. R. Counselor response to female clients with deviate and conforming career goals. *Journal of Counseling Psychology*, 1971, *18*, 352–357.

U.S. Department of Labor, Employment Standards Division, Woman's Bureau, *Careers for women in the 70's.* Washington, D.C.: Superintendent of Documents, 1973.

U.S. Department of Labor, Bureau of Labor Statistics, *Occupational outlook handbook 1974–75 edition.* Washington, D.C.: U.S. Government Printing Office, 1974.

Verheyden-Hilliard, M. F. *A handbook for workshops on sex equality in education.* Washington, D.C.: American Personnel and Guidance Association, 1976.

comments and questions _____

1. The purpose, hypotheses, and method are well described, the former two more so than the latter.
2. Should there have been a more thorough discussion about the distribution of forms to subjects? If forms were not randomly distributed would this have affected the study?
3. Is there a contradiction between the text and data presented in Table 1 with respect to educational level in cities greater than 25,000?
4. How are the authors defining "metropolitan"?
5. The text contains a discussion of interaction data. Are these data presented in the table? If not, should they be?
6. The authors "are not suggesting that practicing counselors either espouse or reject feminist views in counseling" but that they should not impose their own values on the client. Could a profile be constructed that would differentiate between one who holds sexist views but would not impose them from one who held sexist views but would impose them?
7. Given that a counselor profile could be developed would it be ethical and legal to use it to screen out people from counselor education programs or employment?

FIVE ATTEMPTS TO REPLICATE THE EXPERIMENTER BIAS EFFECT[*][1]

THEODOR XENOPHON BARBER,[2] DAVID S. CALVERLY,
ALBERT FORGIONE, JOHN D. MCPEAKE,
JOHN F. CHAVEZ, and BARBARA BOWEN

Five investigations, involving 501 Ss and 51 Es, were conducted to cross-validate an earlier study (Rosenthal & Fode, 1963, Exp. 1) that had clearly demonstrated the Experimenter Bias Effect. Each of the five investigations failed to demonstrate that Es' expectancy-biases influence their results (overall $F < 1.0$). The five investigations are related to other studies in this area, the majority of which also failed to demonstrate the Experimenter Bias Effect. It is concluded that the effect is more difficult to demonstrate than was implied in several recent reviews and that, at the present time, it is not known what preconditions are necessary to obtain it.

A recent test (Rosenthal, 1966) delineated several ways that an experimenter might inadvertently influence the results of his research. These "experimenter effects" include an Experimenter Personal-Attributes Effect in which the characteristics or personality traits of the experimenter—for example, his sex, age, race, anxiety, need for approval, hostility, and dominance—influence his Ss' performance. They also include an Experimenter Bias Effect in which E's expectancies, hypotheses, desires, or biases affect the results. For instance, an Experimenter Bias Effect would be present if Es obtain significantly higher scores from Ss on a standard test when they expect high rather than low scores.

This paper is concerned only with the Experimenter Bias Effect. There is little doubt that Es generally expect or desire to obtain different results from Ss assigned to different experimental treatments and that they rarely exclude

*Reprinted from the *Journal of Consulting and Clinical Psychology*, 33 (1969), 1–6. Copyright 1969 by the American Psychological Association and reproduced by permission of the publisher and authors.

[1]These investigations were supported by research grants (MH-07003 and MH-11521) from the National Institute of Mental Health, United States Public Health Service, to T. X. Barber.

[2]The authors are grateful to Robert Rosenthal for supplying the photographs for the person-perception task and to the following for criticizing the manuscript: Robert Rosenthal, Maurice J. Silver, Ralph L. Rosnow, Herbert J. Greenwald, Nicholas Spanos, and Dick Murray. Requests for reprints should be sent to Theodore X. Barber, Medfield State Hospital, Medfield, Massachusetts 02042.

the possibility that their Ss' responses are influenced by these expectancies and desires. If the Experimenter Bias Effect is pervasive—if Es inadvertently influence their Ss to respond in such a way as to confirm their expectancies or desires—a substantial proportion of the "facts" of present-day psychology would be open to question and many if not most earlier psychological investigations would need to be rerun to determine if the results were due to Es' biases. Furthermore, as Rosenthal (1966, pp. 331–400) has emphasized, if the Experimenter Bias Effect has general validity, it would be necessary in further research either (a) to institute complex procedures to obviate the effects of the experimenters' expectancies and desires or (b) to remove human beings from the conduct of experiments—replacing them by automated procedures.

In all of the formal experimental studies that aimed to demonstrate the Experimenter Bias Effect, the Es were college students (Rosenthal, 1966). The criterion instruments in most of these investigations was a person-perception task in which S was shown a series of photographed faces by the student-E and was asked to rate on a scale whether he judged that the persons depicted had been "experiencing failure" or had been "experiencing success." The rating scale employed ran from −10 (extreme failure) to +10 (extreme success) with intermediate labeled points. In investigations which clearly showed the Experimenter Bias Effect (e.g., Rosenthal & Fode, 1963, Exp. 1), one group of student-Es was told, prior to the experiment, that their Ss were expected to give high ratings (averaging +5) on the person-perception task and another group of student-Es was told that their Ss would give low ratings (averaging −5). In addition, all student-Es were told that (a) the expected results had been "well established" in previous investigations, (b) they would conduct the experiment to obtain practice in "duplicating" the previously established findings, (c) if their results came out "properly—as expected" they would be paid $2.00 per hour, and (d) if their results did not come out "properly" they would be paid $1.00 per hour (Rosenthal & Fode, 1963, p. 507). An important consideration is relevant here: The possibility was not excluded in these investigations that, in order to obtain more money or to make the results come out "properly—as expected," some or many of the student-Es may have intentionally failed to conduct the experiment in the way they were told to carry it out. For instance, the student-Es may have (a) verbally reinforced their Ss ("good," "fine," "that's excellent") when they gave the "proper" ratings or (b) misreported their Ss' ratings.

Our first investigation was conducted with the above considerations in mind. When planning the first investigation, the project-coordinator (TXB) hypothesized that the student-Es would obtain high or low ratings from their Ss in line with their expectancies. The main purpose of the first investigation, however, was not simply to demonstrate the Experimenter Bias Effect but to determine whether the effect was due to the student-Es verbally reinforcing their Ss for "proper" ratings or misreporting their Ss' ratings. To ascertain how the student-Es tested their Ss, we carefully concealed a tape recorder in the experimental room and we did not inform either the Es or the Ss that the recorder was present. However, when we (TXB and DSC) analyzed the results of the first investigation, we were surprised to find that the Experimenter Bias Effect was not manifested; student-Es given an expectancy for high (+5) ratings, those given an expectancy for low (−5) ratings, and a control group of student-Es not given expectancies did not differ in the ratings they obtained ($F < 1.0$).

Even though the Experimenter Bias Effect was not demonstrated in our first investigation, we proceeded to listen to the tapes to determine how the student-Es had conducted the experiment. Unfortunately, the tape recorder had been placed at too great a distance from the Es and Ss and, since, the tapes were barely audible, we were unable to analyze them. However, our inability to analyze the verbal interactions between the student-Es and the Ss did not alter the major findings of the first investigation, namely, that the Experimenter Bias Effect was not noticeably present.

Having failed to demonstrate the Experimenter Bias Effect in our first investigation, we (TXB and DSC) then asked: Is this effect replicable? To answer this question, we set up four additional investigations. The principal-investigators who were asked to supervise the second, third, fourth, and fifth investigations (AF, JDM, JFC, and BB) were not informed of our previous negative results. Investigations 2–5 were conducted in the same way as Investigation 1 with the exception that tape recorders were not concealed in the experimental rooms.

We attempted to design each of the five investigations so as to replicate, as closely as possible, the design of a previous study (Rosenthal & Fode, 1963, Exp. 1) that had clearly demonstrated the Experimenter Bias Effect. Our investigations, however, extended the Rosenthal and Fode study in that they included an additional (control) group of experimenters who were not given expectancies. The method and procedures in each of our investigations were as follows.

Method

A total of 558 individuals participated in the five investigations: 1 project coordinator (TXB), 5 principal investigators, 51 student-Es, and 501 Ss.

PRINCIPAL INVESTIGATORS

Four of the five principal investigators (DSC, AF, JDM, and JFC) were teaching classes in introductory psychology at four colleges in Massachusetts. The fifth principal investigator (BB) was a third-year honors student majoring in sociology at a fifth college.

After each principal investigator agreed to supervise an investigation at his college he was told by the project coordinator that he was to *(a)* use a table of random numbers to select about nine experimenters and about 90 Ss from the students available to him, *(b)* randomly administer one of three sets of expectancy instructions (+5, −5, or control expectancy instructions) to each of his student-Es, *(c)* administer the person-perception task to each student-E as a "warm-up," and *(d)* arrange for each student-E to test about 10 randomly selected Ss on the person-perception task. Finally, each principal investigator was asked to state his own expectancies concerning the outcome of his investigation.[3]

EXPERIMENTERS

Four of the five principal investigators randomly selected the Es from the students in their introductory psychology classes; the fifth principal investigator (BB) selected the Es at random from the list of freshmen and sophomores at her college. Investigation 4 included 15 student experimenters and the remaining four investigations each included nine student-Es.

SUBJECTS

The Ss were freshmen and sophomores at the five colleges enrolled in introductory psychology courses. The number of Ss participating in Investigations 1 to 5, respectively, were 81, 90, 90, 150, and 90.

PROCEDURE

There were two parts to the procedure. In Part 1 the principal investigators instructed the student-Es and in Part 2 the student-Es tested the Ss.

Part 1. Each principal investigator read the instructions that are presented verbatim by Rosenthal and Fode (1963, Appendix C) to those student-Es who had been randomly assigned to the high (+5) expectancy condition and to the low (−5) expectancy condition. The instructions read to the student-Es who were randomly assigned to the control expectancy condition differed in that nothing was said concerning "expected" or "proper" results. After the principal

[3]One of the five principal-investigators (BB) apparently had not heard about previous research concerned with the Experimenter Bias Effect and did not proffer any expectancies concerning the outcome of the investigation. The other four principal investigators, who were teaching courses in psychology, had previously heard about the research in experimenter bias. Three of these (DSC, JDM, and JFC) predicted that the ratings would be highest under the +5 expectancy condition, and lowest under the −5 expectancy condition. The remaining principal investigator (AF) predicted that the student Es "would lean over backwards not to bias their subjects" and, consequently, student-Es expecting high ratings would obtain significantly lower ratings than those expecting low ratings. As will be seen when we present the results, in no case were the expectancies of the principal investigators confirmed.

investigator read the (high, low, or control expectancy) instructions to each student-*E*, he asked each student-*E* to read the instructions to himself.

In accordance with the procedures used by Rosenthal and Fode (1963, Exp. 1), each student-*E* was next asked, as a "warm-up," to rate the standardized set of photographs himself.

Part 2. The heart of the experiment came next, when each student-*E* administered the person-perception task to his Ss. The procedures for administering the task were identical with those of the earlier study (Rosenthal & Fode, 1963, Appendix B).[4]

Results

Table 1 presents, separately for each of the five investigations, the mean ratings per photograph obtained by each student-*E* from his Ss, the mean ratings obtained by student-*E*s assigned to the high (+5), control, and low (−5) expectancy conditions, and the *F* ratios yielded by one-way analyses of variance applied to the latter means. The final row of Table 1 presents the overall mean ratings obtained under the high, control, and low expectancy conditions in the five investigations combined. These results can be briefly summarized as follows:

1. One-way analyses of variance performed separately on the results of each of the five investigations yielded *F* ratios for expectancy conditions which were in each instance either less than 1.0 or close to 1.0. These *F*s, of course, are far from significant. A two-way analysis of variance (Expectancy Conditions × Replications) was performed upon the overall results of the five investigations (Winer, 1962, pp. 241–244). This analysis (summarized in part in the final note of Table 1) showed a far from significant effect for expectancy conditions (*F* < 1.0), a nonsignificant effect for replications (*p* = .18), and a far from significant interaction (*F* < 1.0). In brief, analyses of variance performed separately for each of the five investigations and for all five investigations taken in combination consistently failed to show that *E*s with different expectancy-biases obtained different ratings from their Ss. Nonparametric Kruskal-Wallis tests yielded the same null results.

2. None of the five investigations showed a trend in line with the Experimenter Bias Effect; that is, no tendency was noticeable in any one of the five investigations for the mean ratings to be slightly higher under the +5 expectancy condition, next highest under the control expectancy condition, and

---

[4]In these investigations *E*s and Ss were undergraduates taking their first college course in psychology. Their texts and lectures in psychology had not referred to the Experimenter Bias Effect. In none of the five investigations was there any indication that the student-*E*s were aware that they themselves were the objects of investigation or that prior awareness of the experimenter bias phenomenon on the part of the student-*E*s or Ss influenced the results.

MEAN RATINGS ON PERSON PERCEPTION TASK
UNDER HIGH, CONTROL, AND
LOW EXPECTANCY CONDITIONS

table 1			
INVESTIGATION[a]	HIGH EXPECTANCY	CONTROL EXPECTANCY	LOW EXPECTANCY
1. Worcester Junior College[b]	−.63	+.14	+.17
	+.16	−.03	+.17
	+.99	−.39	+.87
M	+.17	−.09	+.29
2. Boston University[c]	+.12	+.79	−.29
	−.26	+.70	+.12
	+.34	−.29	−.10
M	+.07	+.40	−.09
3. Fisher Junior College[b]	+.67	+.66	+.34
	+.27	+.52	+.80
	+.72	−.02	+.73
M	+.55	+.39	+.62
4. Massachusetts Bay Community College[d]	+.66	.00	−.02
	−.24	−.28	+.72
	+.87	+.14	−.37
	−.64	.00	−.61
	−.10	−.33	+.22
M	+.11	−.09	−.01
5. Regis College[e]	+.24	−.18	+1.20
	+.28	−.25	+.10
	+1.22	−.02	−.06
M	+.58	−.15	+.41
Overall mean of five investigations[f]	+.27	+.07	+.21

[a] In Investigation 1 each cell mean is based on nine Ss. In Investigations 2–5 each cell mean is based on 10 Ss.
[b] $F < 1.0$; $df = 2/6$.
[c] $F < 1.14$; $df = 2/6$.
[d] $F < 1.0$; $df = 2/12$.
[e] $F < 1.66$; $df = 2/6$; $p > .25$.
[f] $F < 1.0$; $df = 2/36$ for expectancy conditions.

lowest under the −5 expectancy condition. In Investigations 1 and 3 the highest mean rating (in absolute terms) was obtained under the low (−5) expectancy condition. In Investigation 2 the highest mean rating was obtained under the control expectancy condition rather than under the high (+5) expectancy condition. In Investigations 4 and 5 the lowest mean rating was obtained under the control expectancy condition rather than under the low expectancy condition. Taking all five investigations in combination, the overall mean ratings (.27, .07, and .21 under the high, control, and low expectancy conditions, respectively) were not consistently in the expected direction—the mean under the control condition is lower than the mean under the low expectancy condition.

In brief, these five investigations, taken separately and also in combination, failed to demonstrate the Experimenter Bias Effect.[5]

Discussion

Each of our five investigations attempted to replicate the procedures used in an earlier experiment (Rosenthal & Fode, 1963, Exp. 1) that had clearly demonstrated the Experimenter Bias Effect. Although we attempted to follow the procedures of the earlier study, we failed to demonstrate the effect. The results of our investigations appear to indicate that the Experimenter Bias Effect may be more difficult to demonstrate than was implied in recent reviews (Klintz, Delprato, Mettee, Persons, & Schappe, 1965; Rosenthal, 1963, 1964, 1966, 1967a). This conclusion is supported by the following considerations.

When we (TXB and DSC) began the five investigations, we had received the impression from reading the review papers in this area that the Experimenter Bias Effect had been demonstrated in practically all studies that had been designed to show it. In fact, we *assumed* that the effect would be demonstrated in the first investigation and we aimed to ascertain how the effect would be mediated. After failing to show the effect in five investigations, we (Barber & Silver, 1968a) looked very closely at all of the extant investigations that had attempted to demonstrate that the expectancy-biases of student-*E*s influence their *S*s' responses. Contrary to our original assumption, we found that the majority of studies in this area had *failed* to show the Experimenter Bias Effect (Barber & Silver, 1968a). After considering the matter further, we were able to delineate several interrelated reasons why we and other investigators had failed to demonstrate the effect. To show that expectancies of student-*E*s significantly bias their *S*s' responses, it is necessary for expectancies to be transmitted from the principal investigator to the student-*E* and from the

[5]We gave the raw data of these investigations to Robert Rosenthal for further analyses. He (Rosenthal, 1967b) informed us that if the data are partitioned in various ways and chi-square tests are performed, some of the chi-squares yield ps ranging from .16 to .10. However, even if we accept ps of .16 and .10 as significant and even if we accept the results of the chi-square tests and disregard the results of the Kruskal-Wallis tests and of the analyses of variance (which yielded an overall F smaller than 1.0 with an associated p that was very far from significant), we still cannot conclude that our data support the experimenter bias hypothesis because the means and the medians were not in the direction predicted by this hypothesis—the control (no-expectancy) Es obtained lower mean and median ratings than the Es who expected low ratings.

Rosenthal (1967b) also informed us that significant results were obtained in five statistical tests (chi-squares and a binomial test) which were performed on the data obtained from those S who gave ratings of 2.0 or higher on the person-perception task. We cannot accept these tests as showing the Experimenter Bias Effect because only a very small percentage of Ss (7 percent to 11 percent), who scored 2.0 or above, were arbitrarily selected for these analyses; if equally arbitrary statistical tests had been performed on the data of Ss scoring 3.0 or higher, or below 2.0, the results would have been far from significant. The issue here, pertaining to the misleading conclusions that derive from arbitrary selection of data for postmortem analysis, are discussed in detail elsewhere (Barber & Silver, 1968b).

student-*E* to *S*. In fact, it appears that a complex eight-step transmission process is involved (cf. McGuire, 1967):

1. The student-*E* must attend to the expectancy communication from the principal investigator.
2. The student-*E* must comprehend the expectancy communication.
3. The student-*E* must retain the communication.
4. The student-*E* (intentionally or unintentionally) must attempt to transmit the expectancy to *S*.
5. The *S* ("consciously" or "unconsciously") must attend to the expectancy communication from *E*.
6. The *S* ("consciously" or "unconsciously") must comprehend *E*'s expectancy.
7. The *S* ("consciously" or "unconsciously") must retain *E*'s expectancy.
8. The *S* (wittingly or unwittingly) must act upon (give responses in harmony with) *E*'s expectancy.

In investigations that failed to demonstrate an Experimenter Bias Effect, the transmission process could have broken down at any of these eight links in the chain. There are many possibilities here: the student-*E* may have failed to comprehend or to retain the expectancy communication from the principal investigator; the student-*E* may have comprehended and retained the expectancy communication but may have failed to transmit it to *S*; *S* may have comprehended *E*'s expectancy but may have failed to respond in the way expected; etc. It is apparent that systematic research is needed to determine under what circumstances the transmission of expectancies is most likely and also least likely to break down at each of the eight steps in the chain.

Although we and other investigators have failed to demonstrate the Experimenter Bias Effect, it must be emphasized that the effect has been demonstrated in a number of studies (Barber & Silver, 1968a). At present it is unclear why some studies succeeded and other failed in this demonstration. However, Rosenthal (1967b) has pointed out to us that the contradictory results obtained in our investigations and in the Rosenthal and Fode (1963, Exp. 1) study may be due to subtle differences such as the following: in our investigations *E*s and *S*s were enrolled in the same introductory psychology course; in contrast, in the Rosenthal and Fode study *E*s were enrolled in an undergraduate experimental psychology laboratory whereas *S*s were enrolled in an introductory psychology course and three of the 10 *E*s were first-year graduate students. These subtle factors are related to the following differences between the two sets of studies that may have produced the contradictory results: *(a)* in our investigations, but not in the Rosenthal and Fode study, *E*s were previously acquainted with almost all of their *S*s; *(b)* in our investigations *E*s and *S*s were of equal status whereas in the Rosenthal and Fode study *E*s were of slightly higher status, and *(c)* in the Rosenthal and Fode study *E*s were in a situation (an undergraduate experimental psychology laboratory) in which "widespread data fabrication" is common (Rosenthal, 1966, p. 35). Whether or not these factors are sufficient to account for the contradictory results of our investigations and of the Rosenthal and Fode study is not clear at the present time. Rosenthal (1966, pp. 239–241) has presented data which suggest the hypothesis that the Experimenter Bias Effect is more readily obtained when male *E*s are acquainted with their *S*s and when female *E*s are unacquainted with their *S*s. With respect to the status of *E*s vis-à-vis *S*s, the data are also contradictory (Rosenthal, 1966, pp. 241–245): One study (Vikan-Kline, 1962) indicated that high-status rather than low-status *E*s are more likely to bias their results whereas another study (Laszlo & Rosenthal, 1967) indicated that low-status rather than high-status *E*s are more likely to bias. Finally, although student-*E*s who are enrolled in an undergraduate experimental psychology laboratory may be prone to fudge their data, we have no direct evidence that the presence of this factor accounted for the positive results in the Rosenthal and Fode study or that its absence accounted for the negative results in our investigations.

In conclusion, it appears that the Experimenter Bias Effect is more difficult to demonstrate than was implied in several recent reviews (Rosenthal, 1963, 1964, 1966, 1967a) and further research is needed to determine exactly what preconditions are necessary to obtain the effect.

references _____

Barber, T. X., and Silver, M. J. Fact, fiction, and the Experimenter Bias Effect. *Psychological Bulletin*, 1968, *70*, (6, Pt. 2), 1–29. (a)

Barber, T. X., and Silver, M. J. Pitfalls in data analysis and interpretation: A reply to Rosenthal. *Psychological Bulletin*, 1968, *70*, (6, Pt. 2), 48–62. (b)

Klintz, B. L., Delprato, D. J., Mettee, D. R., Persons, C. E., and Schappe, R. H. The experimenter effect. *Psychological Bulletin*, 1965, *63*, 223–232.

Laszlo, J. P., and Rosenthal, R. Subject dogmatism, experimenter status and experimenter expectancy effects. Department of Social Relations, Harvard University, 1967. (Mimeo)

McGuire, W. J. Personality and susceptibility to social influence. In E. F. Borgatta and W. W. Lambert (Eds.), *Handbook of personality theory and research*. Skokie, Ill.: Rand McNally, 1967.

Rosenthal, R. On the social psychology of the psychological experiment: The experimenter's hypothesis as unintended determinant of experimental results. *American Scientist*, 1963, *51*, 268–283.

Rosenthal, R. The effect of the experimenter on the results of psychological research. In B. A. Maher (Ed.), *Progress in experimental personality research*. Vol. 1. New York: Academic, 1964.

Rosenthal, R. *Experimenter effects in behavioral research*. New York: Appleton-Century-Crofts, 1966.

Rosenthal, R. Covert communication in the psychological experiment. *Psychological Bulletin*, 1967, *67*, 356–367. (a)

Rosenthal, R. The eternal triangle: Investigators, data and the hypothesis called null. Unpublished manuscript, Harvard University, 1967. (b)

Rosenthal, R., and Fode, K. Three experiments in experimenter bias. *Psychological Reports*, 1963, *12*, 491–511.

Vikan-Kline, L. L. The effect of an experimenter's perceived status on the mediation of experimenter bias. Unpublished master's thesis, University of North Dakota, 1962.

Winer, B. J. *Statistical principles in experimental design.* New York: McGraw-Hill, 1962.

ON NOT SO REPLICATED EXPERIMENTS AND NOT SO NULL RESULTS*,[1]

25a

ROBERT ROSENTHAL

Recent research by Barber, Calverley, Forgione, McPeake, Chaves, and Bowen (1969) has been interpreted as a failure to replicate an experiment (Rosenthal & Fode, 1963) showing significant effects on Ss' responses of Es' expectancies. The purpose of this paper is to show *(a)* that the above research, while helpful in its own right, can in no sense be regarded a serious effort to replicate, *(b)* that, in any case, the integrity of the null hypothesis cannot be staunchly defended by an overall low F $(N \times 51\ E$s$)$ in the face of an overall $\chi^2(N = 501\ S$s$)$ with an associated p value of .007 and *(c)* that science is not often served best by employing the null-hypothesis decision procedure in such a way as to avoid looking closely at data.

This paper constitutes a comment on and an addendum to the research by Barber, Calverley, Forgione, McPeake, Chaves, and Bowen (1969). It was the intent of these investigators to replicate the first of a long series of studies of the effects of the expectancy of E on his Ss' responses. In a series of five samples, one-third of the Es were led to expect from their Ss positive ratings of the success of persons pictured in photographs. Another third of the Es were led to expect negative ratings, and one-third of the Es were given no expectation. This last group was a very instructive addition and, as we shall see when we look more closely at the data, provides us with important new evidence. First, however, we must consider the proposition that useful though it was, the

*Reprinted from *Journal of Consulting and Clinical Psychology*, 33 (1969), 7–10. Copyright 1969 by the American Psychological Association and reproduced by permission of the publisher and author.

[1]Preparation of this paper was facilitated by Grant GS-1741 from the Division of Social Sciences of the National Science Foundation.

research described by Barber et al. can by no stretch of the imagination be regarded as a serious effort at replication in the usual sense.

Procedural Differences

Some more general issues surrounding the problem of replication in the behavioral sciences have been raised elsewhere (Rosenthal, 1966) and need not be repeated here. It is enough to say that psychological research is characterized not only by too few efforts to replicate but also by a very high proportion of failures to replicate. In most replication efforts *S*s are different, often *E* is different, the time of year, the locale, and the physical scene are different. With all these built-in differences, careful replication requires at least that the procedures of the original research be followed closely. In the following ways that was not done in the research by Barber et al.

TYPE OF SUBJECT

The original experiment employed, as *S*s, students enrolled in a coeducational state university. Only 18 percent of the *S*s of the "replication" were from a similar population. Another 18 percent were from a 4-year Catholic college for girls and the remaining 64 percent were from junior colleges. Ordinarily such sampling differences might be regarded as trivial. However, because of the casual method of sampling *E*s, to be discussed presently, these differences become quite critical.

SUBJECTS PER EXPERIMENTER

In the original experiment each *E* contacted an average of over 20 *S*s. In the "replication" each *E* contacted an average of less than 10. Such a difference ought not to affect the magnitude of the grand means but it should affect the reliability of the mean response obtained by each *E* and it was these mean responses that were used as the basic data by Barber et al.

SEX OF EXPERIMENTER

In the original experiment most (80 percent) of the *E*s were males while in the "replicate" most (59 percent) of the experimenters were females. For some studies this difference might not be important but evidence has been presented (Rosenthal, 1966) that female *E*s, especially when contacting male *S*s, are less likely to show expectancy effects. Indeed, they have been shown sometimes to obtain data significantly opposite to that expected.

In the original study Es were at least advanced undergraduate majors in psychology, 30 percent were graduate students and all had laboratory course experience. The Ss in the original, as in the "replicate," were beginning students. In all our research involving several hundred Es and thousands of Ss we have always been careful to preserve the differential in status and educational background between Es and Ss, and that fact has been explicitly emphasized (Rosenthal, 1966, p. 306). Not only the evidence from our own research program but the weight of the evidence from the general literature on social influence suggests that higher status influences are more likely to be successful (Rosenthal, 1966).

In the present study Es were selected at random from the subject population. These Es, then, were classmates of their Ss, with not even the slight advantage of knowing something more about laboratories, psychology, research, or science than their Ss. Perhaps most important of all is the fact that their Ss knew this. It is possible that when an E is of very high status he can influence unintentionally an S of equally high status. There are no data on this point but high absolute status may be sufficient without a status differential. In the case of Es employed by Barber et al., not only was there no status differential between E and S but the absolute status of E was about as low as it could get for a collegiate population. Most of the Es were beginning junior-college students.

If the research by Barber et al. had shown no effects of E expectancy (a conclusion drawn by the authors but as we shall see, one that is not all so clearly warranted by the data) an earlier hypothesis (Rosenthal, 1966) might have been given further indirect support. That hypothesis, and there are data to support it, is that more competent, more professional, more experienced Es of higher status are more likely unintentionally to affect their Ss' responses by virtue of their expectancy.

Two Types of Replication

It may be useful at this point to introduce a terminological and conceptual distinction between two types of replication.

REPLICATIONS OF TENABILITY

Replication of the first kind, or replication of an experiment, is characterized by an attempt to reproduce as closely as possible all of the conditions and procedures of an earlier experiment. It is a type of replication addressed to the specific tenability of a specific outcome of a specific experiment. Such replications help us to rule out the operation of unsuspected idiosyncrasies in the original experiment, idiosyncrasies that made the original result unlikely to recur. Such idiosyncrasies include such human factors as errors of observation, recording, computation, and report. They include also such nonhuman factors as undetected equipment failures and differences in the physical arrangements of the laboratory. Finally, they include also such individual difference variables as the particular E's characteristics, the particular sample of Ss standing in a given relationship to some important national or local event, etc.

Quite clearly, it was this type of replication that Barber et al. intended to conduct. Thus, they wrote of their attempt " . . . to replicate, as closely as possible. . . ." It is only in the sense in which they intended it, the sense of a replication of tenability, that their "replication" cannot be considered even a close approximation. That is not to say that their research is addressed to the wrong question by virtue of their altered procedures, but only that it is addressed to a different one.

REPLICATIONS OF GENERALITY

Replication of the second kind, or replication of a relationship, is characterized by a purposeful effort to change some potentially important aspect of a previously conducted experiment. It is a type of replication that usually occurs after some replication of tenability has been conducted and it is addressed to a testing of the limits of the domain over which the earlier found relationship obtains. It would seem quite reasonable to view the research by Barber et al. as a replication of this second type.

Similarly, recent summaries of experiments showing the effects of one person's expectations about the behavior of another person are essentially summaries of replications of generality. One of these summaries is a reconsideration of over 30 studies considered by Barber and Silver (1968)[2] in which the relevant interpersonal expectation is held by an E and is about his Ss' behavior (Rosenthal, in press). Another summary is of studies in which the relevant interpersonal expectation is held by a teacher and is about her pupils' intellectual growth (Rosenthal & Jacobson, 1968). Different as these two types of studies are, they can nevertheless be regarded as replications of a relationship though not, of course, as replications of specific laboratory experiments.

On Looking More Closely at Data

On the basis of their analysis of the data, Barber et al. concluded that they had failed to demonstrate the effect of Es' expectancies. If that were clearly the case

---

[2]Barber et al. cite the conclusion by Barber and Silver (1968) that the majority of the studies they selected for review failed to show effects of Es' expectancies. It would take us too far afield to discuss that conclusion here, but it has been discussed elsewhere in some detail (Rosenthal, in press).

we should not be unduly surprised. Barber et al. give many good reasons in their paper why such "null" results might have been obtained. Indeed there have been a number of studies which quite clearly showed no effects of E expectancy. It would be an unusual area of behavioral research that turned up only p values of .05 or less. Our purpose here is only to give the reader some additional data to guide his judgment.

There were 51 Es and 501 Ss employed in the research reported by Barber et al. They presented the results based on the 51 Es. Table 1 shows the results based on the 501 Ss. For this single overall analysis of all Ss' photo ratings, intervals of .50 were employed, any smaller interval being such as to reduce the expected frequencies below the rounded value of 5. The χ^2 based on Table 1 showed an associated two-tailed p less than .007, but a χ^2 based on 13 intervals in three conditions is not so directly informative even when it seems clear that the entries are not randomly arrayed. We shall first want to see which of the three groups show large differences from one another.[3]

The two groups in which we are most interested, since they were most like the groups employed in other such studies, are those in which Es were given positive $(+5)$ and negative (-5) expectations. That χ^2 was 25.59, $df = 12$, $p < .02$, two-tailed. Inspection of Table 1 suggests that this result was due to the Es' expecting positive photo ratings obtaining too many of the very high ratings but too few of the slightly high ratings. When we compare the ratings made by Ss contacted by Es expecting negative photo ratings with the ratings made by Ss contacted by the Es given no expectancy we find a χ^2 of 29.72, $df = 12$, $p < .004$, two-tailed. Relative to Es given no expectations, Es led to expect low photo ratings obtained too few very high, too many slightly high, and too few negative ratings. The comparison of photo ratings given by Ss whose Es had been led to expect high photo ratings with responses of Ss of the control condition showed only a much smaller difference ($\chi^2 = 16.05$, $df = 12$, $p < .20$, two-tailed). The direction of differences was such that Es expecting high photo ratings, relative to the controls, obtained too many very high ratings and too few slightly high ratings.

The overall pattern of results described, while surprising and certainly quite unpredicted, nevertheless does not make for a strong defense of the null hypothesis that Es' expectations have no effect on their Ss' ratings of photographs. The curvilinear nature of the effect obtained does help us to understand, however, why the analysis of variance, with its insensitivity to such curvilinearity, would show no significant effect of E expectations.

How might we account for the effects obtained? If sheer speculation

---

[3]I want to thank T. X. Barber for making these data available. In an earlier communication to Barber et al. and cited by them, the overall χ^2 was less significant because coarser grouping had been employed (below -2.00 to above $+2.00$ advancing in intervals of 1.00). In that communication, a number of additional subanalyses were reported which were interpreted by Barber et al. as alternative analyses rather than simply as an attempt to check the consistency from sample to sample of the overall effect obtained.

MEAN RATINGS OF PHOTOGRAPHS BY 501 SUBJECTS

table 1

| PHOTO RATINGS | EXPECTANCY OF EXPERIMENTER | | | |
	+5	None	−5	Σ
+3.00 and above	9	5	6	20
+2.50 to +2.99	9	6	0	15
+2.00 to +2.49	8	2	5	15
+1.50 to +1.99	11	19	10	40
+1.00 to +1.49	14	15	25	54
+0.50 to +0.99	14	17	28	59
0.00 to +0.49	30	20	29	79
−0.50 to −0.01	21	26	21	68
−1.00 to −0.51	18	22	14	54
−1.50 to −1.01	16	11	12	39
−2.00 to −1.51	4	10	8	22
−2.50 to −2.01	5	9	0	14
−2.51 and below	8	5	9	22
Σ	167	167	167	501[a]

[a] $\chi = 44.93$, $df = 24$, $p < .007$, two-tailed test.

were permitted, we might wonder whether our sample was made up of two types of Ss. One type may have behaved as did the Ss of the earlier research in which Ss responded substantially in the direction of their E's expectation. The other type of S may have rebelled slightly, giving E responses in a direction slightly opposite to that expected by E. On this point we must agree with Barber et al.; more research is needed.

Science and Statistical Procedures

Barber et al. conducted a series of studies on E expectancy effects and performed overall analyses of variance which led to Fs too small for them to reject the null hypothesis. In spite of certain fairly apparent trends in the data which were pointed out to the authors, they felt it was statistically unjustifiable to look more closely at their data. But that closer look shows that much was missed by their procedure though theirs appears to be a defensible procedure and, in the eyes of some psychologists, the only "proper" one. The null-hypothesis decision procedure has been discussed in detail elsewhere (Bakan, 1966; Rozeboom, 1960). The view of science that underlies many workers' usage of this procedure seems to have the effect of protecting the investigator from a full view of his data. The null-hypothesis decision procedure is perhaps too often employed as an opaque screen placed over the potential for learning something new.

The position of the present writer is that it is not from data that investigators require protection. Some protection is required from prematurely firm conclusions drawn from a set of data, but the protection of a low alpha is not a very secure safeguard. The only ultimate protection is replication. It is often said that what is found serendipitously in the data requires replication. That seems unquestionably true. The implied corollary, however, that a predicted finding requires less replication does not seem to follow. All findings require replication, those that are clear and predicted no less than those that are less clear and "only" discovered. Even this cannot be interpreted too narrowly, however, If the predictions are based on earlier empirical tests of the same prediction we can have increasing confidence as more supporting evidence is obtained (Rosenthal, in press).

There is a frequently held, and implicitly so, assumption that relationships that are not immediately obvious from the way in which an investigator happens to have arrayed his data are somehow less real. It is as though a close look at the data changed the data and made falsely "true" what was truly "false." The analogy to such an assumption is the case of the lookout in the crow's nest who samples the horizon for a view of land. If, deviating from the visual sweep prescribed by his captain, he should see some unexpected land, shall we doubt the lookout's vision because the captain's orders did not include the view?

references _____

Bakan, D. The test of significance in psychological research. *Psychological Bulletin*, 1966, *66*, 423–437.

Barber, T. X., Calverley, D. S. Forgione, A., McPeake, J. D., Chaves, J. F., and Bowen, B. Five attempts to replicate the experimenter bias effect. *Journal of Consulting and Clinical Psychology*, 1969, *33*, 1–6.

Barber, T. X., and Silver, M. J. Fact, fiction, and the experimenter bias effect. *Psychological Bulletin*, 1968, *70*, (6, pt. 2) 1–29.

Rosenthal, R. *Experimenter effects in behavioral research.* New York: Appleton-Century-Crofts, 1966.

Rosenthal, R. Experimenter expectancy and the reassuring nature of the null hypothesis decision procedure. *Psychological Bulletin*, in press.

Rosenthal, R., and Fode, K. L. Psychology of the scientist: V. Three experiments in experimenter bias. *Psychological Reports*, 1963, *12*, 491–511.

Rosenthal, R., and Jacobson, L. *Pygmalion in the classroom.* New York: Holt, Rinehart and Winston, 1968.

Rozeboom, W. W. The fallacy of the null-hypothesis significance test. *Psychological Bulletin*, 1960, *57*, 416–428.

INVALID ARGUMENTS, POSTMORTEM ANALYSES, AND THE EXPERIMENTER BIAS EFFECT*,[1]

25b

THEODORE XENOPHON BARBER

Rosenthal (1969) presented four arguments aiming to show that the five experiments by Barber, Calverley, Forgione, McPeake, Chaves, and Bowen (1969) cannot be viewed as serious efforts to replicate the Rosenthal-Fode (1963) study. These arguments are shown to be invalid. Rosenthal's critique also presented a postmortem analysis of the Barber et al. data. A further look at Rosenthal's analysis indicates that the Barber et al. experiments cannot be interpreted as confirming the experimenter bias hypothesis that *Es'* obtain results in line with their expectancies. It is concluded that the Experimenter Bias Effect is very *difficult to demonstrate.*

Rosenthal's (1969) critique of the five experiments by Barber, Calverley, Forgione, McPeake, Chaves, and Bowen (1969) makes two points: (*a*) The Barber et al. experiments did not closely replicate the procedures used in the original study by Rosenthal and Fode (1963, Exp. 1). (*b*) Although Barber et al. concluded that their data did not show an Experimenter Bias Effect, a different way of analyzing their data yields a significant chi-square. These two points will be discussed in turn.

Discrepancies in Replicating the Rosenthal-Fode Procedures

Rosenthal's critique lists four discrepancies between the Barber et al. experiments and the original study, by Rosenthal and Fode, that was to be replicated:

TYPE OF SUBJECTS

The Rosenthal-Fode study used *S*s from a coeducational state university whereas the five Barber et al. experiments were conducted in a coeducational

*Reprinted from the *Journal of Consulting and Clinical Psychology*, 33, (1969), 11–14. Copyright 1969 by the American Psychological Association and reproduced by permission of the publisher and author.

[1]Preparation of this paper was aided by Grant MH-11521 from the National Institute of Mental Health, United States Public Health Service.

nonstate university, a Catholic college for girls, and three junior colleges. Rosenthal's critique states that "because of the casual method of sampling Es . . . these differences become quite critical." The present writer fails to see why these differences are "critical." If the Experimenter Bias Effect has any degree of generality it should not be limited to coeducational state universities. If Rosenthal is seriously contending that the Experimenter Bias Effect is more readily obtained in coeducational state universities than in other types of colleges or universities, he should present data to support the contention.

SUBJECTS PER EXPERIMENTER

In the Rosenthal-Fode study, each E contacted an average of 20 Ss whereas in the Barber et al. experiments each E contacted about 10 Ss. The point made in Rosenthal's critique, that these differences would affect "the reliability of the mean response obtained by each E," seems to imply that the Barber et al. experiments were less sensitive than the Rosenthal-Fode study to any E bias effects that were present. The implication is invalid. The overall parametric analysis that was performed in the Barber et al. investigation was based on 51 Es (testing 501 Ss) and was *at least as sensitive* to E bias effects as the parametric analysis performed in the Rosenthal-Fode study which was based on 10 Es (testing 206 Ss).

SEX OF EXPERIMENTER

Most of the Es in the Rosenthal-Fode study were males whereas most of the Es in the Barber et al. investigations were females. Rosenthal's critique stated that this difference is important because "evidence has been presented (Rosenthal, 1966) that female Es, especially when contacting male Ss, are less likely to show expectancy effects. Indeed, they have been shown sometimes to obtain data significantly opposite to that expected." A recent paper (Barber & Silver, 1968) has analyzed this contention pertaining to female Es and has shown that it is misleading. Although there is some evidence indicating that female Es, especially when testing male Ss, show reduced or negative expectancy effects (Rosenthal, Persinger, Mulry, Vikan-Kline, & Grothe, 1964), there is also contradictory evidence. For instance, a study by Silverman (1966) showed that, as compared to other combinations of E's sex with S's sex, female Es testing male Ss obtain results more in line with their expectancies (not less in line or opposite to their expectancies, as Rosenthal's critique contends).

Let us look more closely at Rosenthal's contention that the Barber et al. investigations included too many female Es and that this might have made a difference. Did it actually make a difference? That is, when the data of the Barber et al. studies are analyzed to determine the effects of Es' sex, do we find that female and male Es obtained different ratings from their Ss? Not at all! Under each of the expectancy conditions, female and male Es obtained practically identical ratings (all *F*s pertaining to the effects of *E*s' sex were less than 1.0). Did female *E*s testing male *S*s bias their *S*s less than other *E-S* combinations? Not at all! The relevant interaction (*E*s' Sex × *S*s' Sex × Treatments) yields an *F* much smaller than 1.0, which can be expected to occur by chance around 50 times in 100.

EXPERIMENTER STATUS

In the Rosenthal-Fode study 70 percent of the *E*s were undergraduates whereas in the Barber et al. investigations all of the *E*s were undergraduates. Also, the *E*s in the Rosenthal-Fode study were enrolled in an undergraduate experimental psychology laboratory whereas the *E*s in the Barber et al. studies were enrolled in an introductory psychology course. Rosenthal's critique pointed out, in the same way as the paper by Barber et al. had pointed out, that these differences give rise to a discrepancy in the relative status of the *E*s; that is, the *E*s in the Rosenthal-Fode study tended to be of somewhat higher status than those in the Barber et al. studies. Rosenthal's critique also stated that higher status *E*s are more likely to be successful in biasing their *S*s' responses. The latter statement, however, is not clearly in line with Rosenthal's own data (Rosenthal, 1966, pp. 241–245). Two studies have been conducted in Rosenthal's laboratories to determine whether high-status or low-status *E*s exert more bias. As Rosenthal (1966, pp. 244–245) himself clearly pointed out in his recent text, one of these studies (Laszlo & Rosenthal, 1967) showed unequivocally that *low*- rather than high-status *E*s exert more bias. The other study, a master's thesis supervised by Rosenthal (Vikan-Kline, 1962), appeared to indicate that high-status *E*s are "more successful at influencing their subjects to yield the desired data, but only among subjects contacted later in the experiment [Rosenthal, 1966, p. 242.]" However, as Rosenthal (1966, pp. 242–245) clearly pointed out in his recent text, in the latter study the *E*s' status was confounded with several other variables—e.g., age and self-assurance—and the results could *not* be clearly attributed to differences in status. It appears that further research is needed to pinpoint the effects of *E*s' status on the Experimenter Bias Effect.

Fortunately, the required "further research" that was mentioned in the preceding sentence has been conducted. Very recently, Wessler and Strauss (1968) presented a study which attempted to replicate the standard Rosenthal procedures and which was very similar to the Barber et al. studies. However, the Wessler and Strauss study differed from the studies by Barber et al. in that all *E*s were college seniors and their *S*s were freshmen or sophomores. Although the *E*s in the Wessler and Strauss study were higher in status than their *S*s, the results were practically identical with those obtained by Barber et al. Wessler and Strauss reported that *E*s expecting high (+5.0) ratings obtained mean ratings of −0.52 whereas those expecting low (−5.0) ratings obtained mean ratings of −0.64. These differences are very far from significant ($p > .50$).

In brief, it appears that (*a*) the statement found in Rosenthal's critique, that high- rather than low-status *E*s exert more bias, is unequivocally con- tradicted by one study from Rosenthal's laboratory and is not clearly supported by another, and *(b)* when an attempt is made to replicate the basic Rosenthal procedures using *E*s who are relatively high in status, results are obtained which are essentially the same as those obtained by Barber et al.

Postmortem Data Analyses

The basic data that were analyzed in the Rosenthal-Fode study (and in almost all other studies carried out by Rosenthal and associates with the person-per- ception task) were the *mean ratings* obtained by the *E*s. Rosenthal and Fode performed a *parametric* test on these mean ratings. To adhere as closely as possible to the procedures used in the Rosenthal-Fode study, it was incumbent upon Barber et al. to perform a *parametric* analysis on the *mean ratings* ob- tained by their *E*s. This appropriate statistical analysis, which yielded an overall *F* less than 1.0, showed no evidence that *E*s obtain results in line with their expectancies. (Supplementary nonparametric analyses, which included a Krus- kal-Wallis test and a chi-square test, were also performed on the *mean ratings* obtained by the *E*s. These analyses also failed to shown an Experimenter Bias Effect.)

Instead of accepting the nonsignificant results that are obtained when the data of Barber et al. are analyzed in the same way that Rosenthal and Fode analyzed their data, Rosenthal's critique proposes that the Barber et al. ex- periments should be analyzed by a quite different method, namely, by a *non- parametric* chi-square test which is applied to the individual *S*s' *ratings* and which does not take the individual *E*s into consideration. Although there are several objections we could raise here, let us accept Rosenthal's proposal to perform a chi-square test of the ratings of the 501 *S*s. What is the logical way to partition these ratings for a chi-square test? The most logical cut is at the median. When the ratings are thus logically dichotomized above and below the median, we find that *(a)* more *higher* ratings are obtained when *low* ratings are expected (opposite to the results predicted by the *E* bias hypothesis) but *(b)* these differences are not significant ($\chi^2 = 4.36$, $df = 2$, $p > .10$).

Since the ratings given by the 501 *S*s can be partitioned in many other ways, many additional chi-square tests can be performed. Of course, if we continue to carry out postmortem statistical analyses, we may expect by chance to find some "significant" results (Hays, 1963, Chap. 14). Table 1 in Rosenthal's critique presented one of the many additional chi-square tests that can be performed on the Barber et al. data. Rosenthal's overall chi-square test, which was performed on the *S*s' ratings, partitioned into 13 discrete intervals, yielded a significant *p*, indicating that one or more of the 13 intervals deviated from chance. However, Rosenthal's critique failed to make clear exactly where the deviations from chance expectations were localized in the array of data. To

table 1

PHOTO RATINGS	+5.0	None	−5.0	χ^2	*p*
+3.00 and above	9	5	6	1.30	ns
+2.50 to +2.99	9	6	0	8.40	.02
+2.00 to +2.49	8	2	5	3.60	ns
+1.50 to +1.99	11	19	10	3.65	ns
+1.00 to +1.49	14	15	25	4.11	ns
+ .50 to + .99	14	17	28	5.51	ns
.00 to + .49	30	20	29	2.30	ns
− .50 to − .01	21	26	21	.73	ns
−1.00 to − .51	18	22	14	1.78	ns
−1.50 to −1.01	16	11	12	1.07	ns
−2.00 to −1.51	4	10	8	2.54	ns
−2.50 to −2.01	5	9	0	8.71	.02
−2.51 and below	8	5	9	1.18	ns
Total	167	167	167	44.9	.007

EXPECTANCY OF E (column group header spanning +5.0, None, −5.0)

determine where the ratings deviated from chance, it is necessary to look at the component chi-squares that were computed for each of the 13 rows in Rosenthal's Table 1. These chi-squares and their associated *p* values, which Rosenthal's critique failed to present, are listed in Table 1 in this paper. The table shows the following:

1. *Contrary to the E bias hypothesis*, the *E*s' expectancies did *not* significantly affect 11 of the 13 sets of ratings (ratings of −2.51 and below, −2.00 to −1.51, −1.50 to −1.01, −1.00 to −.51, −.50 to −.01, .00 to 0.49, +.50 to +.99, +1.00 to +1.49, +1.50 to +1.99, +2.00 to +2.49, and +3.00 and above).

2. *Contrary to the E bias hypothesis*, a significantly *smaller* number of Ss tested by *E*s expecting *low* (−5.0) ratings have relatively *low* ratings between −2.50 and −2.01.

3. In comparison with Ss tested by *E*s expecting low (−5.0) ratings, a significantly larger number of Ss tested by *E*s with no expectancies and by *E*s with expectancies for high (+5.0) ratings gave relatively high ratings between +2.50 and +2.99.

It needs to be emphasized there that (*a*) the appropriate analysis of variance applied to the mean scores obtained by the 51 *E*s in the Barber et al. studies yielded nonsignificant results (*F* < 1.0) and (*b*) various supplementary nonparametric tests (Kruskal-Wallis tests and chi-square tests) also yielded nonsignificant results. Consequently, the three sets of "findings" presented immediately above, which are due to an additional postmortem chi-square test performed on an arbitrary partitioning of the Ss' ratings into 13 intervals, can be viewed, at best, as three tentative propositions that require experimental validation. Since these three tentative propositions are very specific and have very little if any general interest, it is doubtful that investigators will bother to test them. However, if anyone wishes to validate these tentative propositions, he might note the following: (*a*) The first two contradict the *E* bias hypothesis which states that *E*s obtain results in line with their expectancies. (*b*) The third tentative proposition is partly inconsistent with the *E* bias hypothesis (in that *E*s expecting high ratings and those with *no* expectancies did not differ significantly in influencing the relatively high ratings between +2.50 and +2.99).

references

Barber, T. X., Calverley, D. S. Forgione, A., McPeake, J. D., Chaves, J. F., and Bowen, B. Five attempts to replicate the Experimenter Bias Effect. *Journal of Consulting and Clinical Psychology,* 1969, *33,* 1–6.

Barber, T. X., and Silver, M. J. Pitfalls in data analysis and interpretation: A reply to Rosenthal. *Psychological Bulletin,* 1968, *70,* (6, Pt. 2) 48–62.

Hays, W. L. *Statistics for psychologists.* New York: Holt, Rinehart and Winston, 1963.

Laszlo, J. P., and Rosenthal, R. Subject dogmatism, experimenter status, and experimenter expectancy effects. Department of Social Relations, Harvard University, 1967. (Mimeo)

Rosenthal, R. *Experimenter effects in behavioral research.* New York: Appleton-Century-Crofts, 1966.

Rosenthal, R. On not so replicated experiments and not so null results. *Journal of Consulting and Clinical Psychology,* 1969, *33,* 7–10.

Rosenthal, R., and Fode, K. L. Three experiments in experimenter bias. *Psychological Reports,* 1963, *12,* 491–511.

Rosenthal, R., Persinger, G. W., Mulry, R. C., Vikan-Kline, L., and Grothe, M. Changes in experimental hypotheses as determinants of experimental results. *Journal of Projective Techniques,* 1964, *28,* 465–469.

Silverman, I. The effects of experimenter outcome expectancy on latency of word association. Paper presented at the meeting of the Eastern Psychological Association. New York, April 1966.

Vikan-Kline, L. The effect of an experimenter's perceived status on the mediation of experimenter bias. Unpublished master's thesis, University of North Dakota, 1962.

Wessler, R. L., and Strauss, M. E. Experimenter expectancy: A failure to replicate. *Psychological Reports,* 1968, *22,* 687–688.

REFLECTIONS ON REPLICATIONS
AND THE EXPERIMENTER BIAS EFFECT*

LEON H. LEVY

The value of replications in psychology, the need to distinguish between the probability of data and of hypotheses, and the implications of alternative conceptualizations of the Experimenter Bias Effect *(EBE)*, were each discussed in the light of the failure reported by Barber, Calverly, Forgione, McPeake, Chaves, and Bowen (1969) to replicate earlier findings by Rosenthal and Fode (1963). The position was taken that the value of further research on the *EBE* will depend upon the prior development of a situational taxonomy and a theoretical formulation in which the effect may be conceptualized in terms of a broader class of phenomena.

It is axiomatic among novelists, particularly of the existentialist persuasion, that character is revealed in conflict and crises, and this seems no less true when we turn to questions of the nature of scientific inquiry and thought (Kugn, 1964). Thus, it would be unfortunate were we to focus only on questions of whether the study by Barber, Calverley, Forgione, McPeake, Chaves, and Bowen (1969) should be counted as a serious and legitimate failure to replicate the results of the Rosenthal and Fode (1963) experiment demonstrating an Experimenter Bias Effect *EBE)*, or whether this effect might be revealed by a more fine-grained, post hoc analysis of their data, and failed to take advantage of the opportunity afforded by their study to reflect upon some of the broader and more fundamental issues which are raised by it.

These issues are joined once the question is asked: What are the implications of the failure of Barber et al. to demonstrate an *EBE* in their several replications? The first concerns the value of replications; the second concerns the relationship between data and hypotheses; and the third concerns the implications of the alternative stances which might be taken toward the *EBE*. These are certainly not independent of each other, nor are they specific to the *EBE*, but they are especially relevant at this time since it is apparent that the *EBE* has become an increasingly popular topic and bids fair to rival anxiety as a vehicle for the production of theses and journal articles. And in psychology, as

*Reprinted from the *Journal of Consulting and Clinical Psychology*, 33 (1969), 15–17. Copyright 1969 by the American Psychological Association and reproduced by permission of the publisher and author.

417

elsewhere, there seems to be an inverse relationship between the popularity of activity and the amount of thought given to its meaning or value.

The Value of Replications

The perfect replication is a fiction, and I shall take the heretical position that this is just as well. Therefore, let us stipulate that the Barber et al. experiment differs from Rosenthal and Fode's in several details. Some of these are listed by Barber et al. But does this necessarily disqualify their findings as evidence vis-à-vis those of Rosenthal and Fode concerning the *EBE*? For obvious reasons, no experiment can ever duplicate another in every detail, and so this question turns on whether the variations between them were trivial or important. Thus, we have the choice of either of two conclusions: (*a*) Barber et al. failed to establish one or more of the conditions necessary for the demonstration of the *EBE*; or (*b*) their procedural variations were trivial and the *EBE* is unreliable and/or not very pervasive.

But this choice is an impossible one, for it requires either a theory which states the parameters involved in the *EBE* or a body of systematic research from which these parameters might be induced. While it seems clear that the former condition does not exist in the case of the *EBE*, for reasons which we cannot go into in the space available, it might also be argued that the extensive research which has been performed in the name of the *EBE* cannot be considered systematic. Thus, whether the findings of Barber et al. can be taken as contradictory to those of Rosenthal and Fode is a moot question, and this, I would suggest, will be found true wherever replications are attempted of experiments dealing with phenomena which are not embedded either within some theoretical framework or extensive body of systematic research. Conversely, it might be argued that any dispute over whether an experiment qualifies as a replication of another may be taken as prima facie evidence of the weakness of the conceptual and empirical underpinnings of the phenomenon in question. And so long as this is the case, it would seem that unless we are interested only in the existence of a phenomenon in a particular situation (which is rarely, if ever, the case in science, and certainly not so in the case of the *EBE*) we must ask whether replications are worth the effort. Can we not employ our resources more profitably?

These questions also merit consideration in instances where phenomena are better endowed conceptually and empirically than the *EBE*. For, unless there are serious reasons to doubt the validity of the data reported by an investigator, it would seem wiser to invest our time in exploring the generalizability of the theory concerning the phenomenon through the systematic variation of its parameters and experimental procedures in a manner analogous to that represented by the multitrait-multimethod matrix proposed by Campbell and Fiske (1959) for the study of construct validity. Such experiments would permit an evaluation of the reliability and pervasiveness of the phenomenon in question while at the same time extending our theoretical understanding of it. Since variation from one experiment is inevitable, why not make the most of it? Surely when practice departs from precept as radically as it does in the matter of replications, so that an investigation such as that of Barber et al. is the exception rather than the rule, it may be time to examine the wisdom of the precept rather than lament its neglect. And as a start I would suggest that we consider how much more information was gained by Barber et al. through their second replication, or their third, fourth, or fifth. Measured against information gained, it would seem that these five replications were at least four too many; concerning the relationship between replications and the acquisition of knowledge, they suggest the aptness of the aesthetic dictum: *less is more.*

The Relationship between Data and Hypotheses

The demonstration of the *EBE* in the Rosenthal and Fode experiment and others might be likened to a wife's discovery of a strange shade of lipstick on her husband's shirt collar. Whether or not she had suspected him of infidelity in the past, it seems unlikely that any number of unblemished shirt collars in the future will completely remove her concerns about his conjugal constancy. Thus it seems unlikely that the five failures to reject the null hypothesis by Barber et al. will in itself convince many of the rarity of the *EBE* or that it need not be taken into account in the design and interpretation of experiments. Nor should it. Why this should be so becomes apparent when we recognize the distinction, which is often ignored, between the probability of data and of hypotheses, and the difficulties entailed in drawing inferences from significance tests and null hypotheses. Since there are several excellent discussions of these issues in the recent literature (Bakan, 1966; Edwards, Lindman, & Savage, 1963; Rozeboom, 1960), I shall do no more than point out that they are made most timely by the Barber et al. paper.

The Implications of Alternative Views of the EBE

The *EBE* might be regarded either as a methodological problem or as a member of a class of phenomena of intrinsic interest to psychology. In the former case, it takes its place along with response biases and demand characteristics as, what we might call a "spoiler variable," in that it spoils the image of the rigor and purity of psychology's data collection procedures and complicates the design and interpretation of research by requiring that an "irrelevant" dimension—the *E*—be taken into consideration. Regarded as an exemplar of a class of phenomena such as interpersonal influence or the effects of expectancies and values on perception and behavior, the *EBE* might be considered a convenient vehicle for the investigation of the processes involved in these phenomena and as a medium for testing hypotheses and theories about them. Each of these stances, however, entails a different set of considerations and different order of priorities so far as research and development are concerned.

Regarding the *EBE* as a methodological problem leads to considerations of its pervasiveness, how much of the variance in experiments might be attributed to it, and how it might be controlled or eliminated. Although Rosenthal (1966) has suggested a number of means by which this last concern might be met, the decision to incur the additional costs involved in adopting them cannot be made independently of the first two considerations. However, the information which would be relevant to these prior considerations is dependent, in turn, upon the existence of a taxonomy of situations (tasks or experiments). For without such a taxonomy and the sampling of situations it would permit, it is impossible to make any generalizations about the seriousness of the *EBE* as an epistemological threat to psychology on the basis of successes or failures in demonstrating it in particular instances. But although the value of such a taxonomy has long been recognized, and extends far beyond the problem of *EBE*s (Rotter, 1960), one does not presently exist. Thus we must ask whether it would not be wiser to give precedence to the long overdue development of this taxonomy rather than to additional demonstrations of the *EBE*, however startling and impressive these might be. Certainly, as matters stand at present, it should be obvious that there is no way of assessing the validity of any assertions about the generality or seriousness of the *EBE* as a methodological problem.

While the perverse gratifications which might derive from demonstrations of the *EBE* in its role as spoiler variable are not to be minimized, and regardless of its importance in this role, by far the more rewarding scientific stance toward the *EBE* is likely to be as an exemplar of some theoretically important class of psychological phenomena. The low epistemic yield of the five experiments reported by Barber et al. clearly reveals the wastefulness of research conducted on phenomena which are devoid of any theoretical conceptualization. For had the *EBE* been placed in some theoretical context, these five failures to demonstrate it might have been turned to good account in evaluating one or more theoretical propositions concerning its nature and the processes involved in it, or in deciding on directions for future research. It should be noted also, that if the *EBE* is conceived of as an exemplar of some class of phenomena, it becomes irrelevant whether it is pervasive or rare; the *EBE* could be exotic and still of importance *if* the class of phenomena were important and *if* it was of value in furthering our understanding of these phenomena.

These *ifs* point to the kinds of questions which must be asked if the *EBE* is to be taken seriously from a theoretical standpoint. They require, again, a better conceptualization of the situations in which the *EBE* is manifested than presently exists. And, paradoxically, they also require a high degree of development in the theory and knowledge concerning the phenomena allegedly exemplified by the *EBE* and which the *EBE* is intended to further illuminate. For, as Bordin (1965) has pointed out in a different context, it is only as a phenomenon is more fully understood that it can safely be studied in the laboratory by means of simplifications and analogues without the fear that these may be irrelevant to it. This means, at a minimum, that if the *EBE* is to be regarded as a vehicle for the study of theoretically important processes and phenomena, such as unintended covert communication, as Rosenthal (1967a) has recently proposed, it cannot be the sole means of doing so. It also means that hypotheses based upon *EBE*-type experiments must be tested for their generality in other experiments involving the phenomena in question, and vice versa.

Rosenthal (1967b) has observed that as response variance diminishes so does variance in the *EBE* (p. 621). If this is the case, since two of the most effective ways of reducing (unwanted) response variance are through better experimental controls and more valid and comprehensive theories, it is appropriate to ask whether these should not be our first order of business, regardless of the stance taken toward the *EBE*. For it our reasoning is correct, this shift of emphasis away from the *EBE* to more fundamental methodological and substantive concerns should have the interesting consequences of reducing the *EBE* as a methodological threat while at the same time helping us to understand and use it more wisely in the furtherance of psychological knowledge.

references

Bakan, D. The test of significance in psychological research. *Psychological Bulletin*, 1966, *66*, 423–437.

Barber, T. X., Calverly, D. S., Forgione, A., McPeake, J. D., Chaves, J. F., and Bowen, B. Five attempts to replicate the experimenter bias effect. *Journal of Consulting and Clinical Psychology*, 1969, *33*, 1–10.

Bordin, E. S. Simplification as a strategy for research in psychotherapy. *Journal of Consulting Psychology*, 1965, *29*, 493–503.

Campbell, D. T., and Fiske, D. W. Convergent and discriminant validation by the multitrait-multimethod matrix. *Psychological Bulletin*. 1959, *56*, 81–105.

Edwards W., Lindman, H., and Savage, L. J. Bayesian statistical inference for psychological research. *Psychological Review*, 1963, *70*, 193–242.

Kuhn, T. S. *The structure of scientific revolutions*. Chicago: University of Chicago Press, 1964.

Rosenthal, R. *Experimenter effects in behavioral research.* New York: Appleton-Century-Crofts, 1966.

Rosenthal, R. Covert communication in the psychological experiment. *Psychological Bulletin*, 1967, *67*, 356–367. (a)

Rosenthal, R. Psychology of the scientist: XXIII. Experimenter expectancy, experimenter experience, and Pascal's wager. *Psychological Reports*, 1967, *20*, 619–622. (b)

Rosenthal, R., and Fode, K. L. Psychology of the scientist: V. Three experiments in experimenter bias. *Psychological Reports*, 1963, *12*, 491–511.

Rotter, J. B. Some implications of a social learning theory for the prediction of goal directed behavior from testing procedures. *Psychological Review*, 1960, *67*, 301–316.

Rozeboom, W. W. The fallacy of the null-hypothesis significance test. *Psychological Bulletin*, 1960, *57*, 416–428.

comments and questions _____

1. Levy states, "It might be argued that any dispute over whether an experiment qualifies as a replication of another may be taken as prima-facie evidence of the weakness of the conceptual and empirical underpinnings of the phenomenon in question." Do you agree with this? Is Barber's statement that, "If the Experimenter Bias Effect has any degree of generality it should not be limited to coeducational state universities" related to Levy's comment? If Rosenthal's findings are so situation-specific, doesn't this limit the implications that may be drawn?

2. There is a saying, "There are liars, damned liars, and statisticians." When Barber et al. and Rosenthal analyzed the same data, they obtained different statistical findings and arrived at different conclusions. Who is the statistician?

3. Levy discusses at length the value of replications. Do you understand his position and do you agree with it?

4. Levy states that "The *EBE* might be regarded either as a methodological problem or as a member of a class of phenomenon of intrinsic interest to psychology." From what you have heard (if anything) about *EBE* (or teacher expectancies) which way are educators regarding the phenomenon?

5. One of the current emphases in education is to always make the student feel he has done adequate work. (Occasionally this would mean that we reinforce error.) Would the implications of Rosenthal's findings be consonant with this emphasis?

EPILOGUE

Educators have been accused of manifesting two opposing behavioral syndromes: (1) being slow in changing existing practices when educational research findings strongly suggest the advantages of change *or* (2) being too prone to accept "fads."

We would like you to pay particular attention to the brief report to follow. Sipay has addressed himself to a most relevant topic. He has paid attention to those characteristics that we have attempted to illustrate throughout this text. Considering the nature of his findings, and the fact that his article was published in 1965, do you feel that educators have tended to be too slow or too hasty in incorporating Sipay's main conclusion in the reading instructional program?

THE EFFECT OF PRENATAL
INSTRUCTION ON READING ACHIEVEMENT*

EDWARD R. SIPAY

During the past few years the controversy regarding *how* to teach reading has abated somewhat, only to give rise to a new topic for debate—*when* to initiate reading instruction. In the past, some experts have claimed that a child should have a mental age of 6.6 before reading instruction is inaugurated; others, that children should be taught to read when they reach five years of age. The trend, however, has been towards attempts to teach reading to even younger children. For example, a *Ladies Home Journal* article (May 1963) informed mothers how to teach their two-year-olds to read. Yet no one has suggested that reading instruction might begin even before birth. Such a hypothesis was postulated twelve years ago and a longitudinal study was undertaken to determine the effect of prenatal instruction on reading achievement in the elementary school. The study has been completed and is summarized in this article.

Sample and Procedure

In cooperation with local obstetricians, 112 women in their fourth month of pregnancy were obtained as subjects. California Tests of Mental Maturity and Nelson-Denny Reading Tests were then administered to each set of parents. Based on the assumption that the offspring would tend to approximate their parents in these factors, the average total scores of each set of parents were used to establish three groups which were matched as to intelligence and reading ability. The average CTMM score for each parent group of twenty-five equaled 104.6, and the average reading score 10.8. Next, the expectant mothers were assigned to either the Basal Reader Group, the Phonics Group, or the Control Group.

The instructional programs for the Basal Reader and Phonics groups

*Reprinted from *Elementary English*, 1965, 431–432, with the permission of the National Council of Teachers of English and Edward R. Sipay.

METROPOLITAN READING ACHIEVEMENT TEST:
GRADE PLACEMENT SCORES

table 1

Actual Grade Placement	GROUP		
	Basal Reader n = 25	Phonic n = 25	Control n = 25
1.9	2.7	2.1	1.8
2.9	3.9	3.2	2.9
3.9	5.0	4.1	3.7
4.9	6.2	5.2	4.9
5.9	7.1	6.4	5.9
6.9	8.1	7.3	6.8

consisted of the elements described in the manuals which accompanied these materials; and, what amounted to a placebo, repetition of nonsense syllables, was given to the Control Group. The instructional portion of each lesson was placed on tape and played for each mother individually. These instructions were transmitted concurrently to the unborn child by means of a specially designed fetoscope which was placed against the mother's abdomen. Later as the mother did the workbook or mimeographed assignments, she recited her responses into the fetoscopic device in order to transmit this part of the lesson to the fetus. After eighty-five such lessons, this phase of the experiment was terminated. No further attempts were made to teach the children to read until they entered the first grade.

In kindergarten, the children were tested to ascertain if any significant differences existed among them when they were grouped according to the methods used during the initial stages of the study. No statistically significant differences were found among the children's groups either as to intelligence or reading readiness. Average CTMM scores ranged from 109.2 to 113.4 and Lee-Clark Reading Readiness average scores ranged from 1.1 to 1.3.

Findings

As indicated in Table 1, the levels of reading achievement attained by both experimental groups surpassed those of the control group at every grade level. Moreover, the group which has been exposed to the Basal Reader approach exhibited superiority to the Phonics Group. In every instance the differences between means were significant at the .01 level.

Summary

The results of this study suggest that prenatal instruction does have a positive effect on reading achievement in the elementary school. Furthermore, the use of a Basal Reader approach proved to be the most effective of the methods utilized. The main conclusion to be drawn from this article, however, was best stated by the Roman orator who proclaimed, *"Nimium celeriter ne credas omnia quae legas."*[1]

comments and questions _____

If you do not understand the implications of this article, please refer to our comments on page 9.

[1] Don't be too quick to believe everything you read.

INDEX

429